ADVANCE PRAISE

"*Innovation, Product Development and Commercialization* is a practical book to assist every manager and executive to succeed in today's competitive environment. This book is highly recommended for every high technology executive and product development manager, especially those in embedded software and hardware development. In this unique book, Dr. Dariush Rafinejad not only presents theory and ideas of developing new products, but also true hands-on experience with tremendous lessons learned. He discusses proven strategies to deal with management challenges for high-technology knowledge creation, retention, and protection. Rafinejad covers the entire product development cycle, including the pitfalls to avoid. He presents product development as a customer value-centered engineering endeavor. His writing style is clear and refreshing.

"The book is nicely illustrated with charts and tables and includes a rich menu of pragmatic examples. It provides enough analytical tools to support insightful and intuitive explanations. The compelling real-world case studies are extremely valuable."

> — **Gerald Z. Yin, Ph.D.**
> *Chairman and CEO of AMCE*
> *(Advanced Micro-fabrication Equipment Inc.)*
> *Shanghai, China*

"*Innovation, Product Development and Commercialization* is a rare find in a 'how-to' book that covers technology innovation with real-world constraints in mind-absorbing material constructed in a logical way. Rafinejad makes the process of innovation come alive, with real examples, step-by-step guidance and bottom-line metrics."

> — **John Osborne**, *Strategic Advisory Board*
> *DuPont Electronic Materials Division*
> *Former Executive with Philips Electronics*
> *and Lam Research Corporation*

INNOVATION, PRODUCT DEVELOPMENT AND COMMERCIALIZATION

Case Studies and Key Practices for Market Leadership

Dariush Rafinejad, Ph.D.

ISBN 13: 978-1-932159-70-7
ISBN 10: 1-932159-70-3

Printed and bound in the U.S.A. Printed on acid-free paper
10 9 8 7 6 5 4 3 2 1

Library of Congress Cataloging-in-Publication Data

Rafinejad, Dariush, 1943-
    Innovation, product development and commercialization : case studies and
key practices for market leadership / by Dariush Rafinejad.
        p. cm.
    Includes index.
    ISBN 978-1-932159-70-7 (hardcover : alk. paper)
    1. Product management. 2. New products--Marketing. I. Title.
    HF5415.15.R32 2007
    658.5′03--dc2   2007006360

Phone: (954) 727-9333
Fax: (561) 892-0700
Web: www.jrosspub.com

*To Shanaz, my partner in life, and to
Danny, for enriching my life beyond words*

TABLE OF CONTENTS

FOREWORD

This is a masterful book that should be read by everyone in high-technology industries. In this unique work, an experienced practitioner in the high-technology field tells us how to innovate, develop, and commercialize new products for sustained profitability. The author, Dr. Dariush Rafinejad, presents insight developed over 25 years in Silicon Valley's top high-technology companies to help us develop new products while meeting the demands of global competition and rapid technological changes.

Dr. Rafinejad provides an exceptional perspective on the art and science of high-technology product innovation, development, and management. Commercialization of high-technology products is a key aspect of the book. In an impressive treatment, he translates management and organizational theory into useful everyday practice. He presents state-of-the-art best practices in executing new product development projects and covers the product development cycle, including marketing, R&D, product and process engineering, and commercialization. He also discusses proven strategies to deal with management challenges for high-technology knowledge creation, retention, and protection. Rafinejad shares with us what really works and provides a path to how to be effective.

Innovation, Product Development and Commercialization is highly readable and full of wisdom and conceptual and practical insights into managing new product development. The real-world case studies are extremely valuable and provide specific insight into "lessons learned" from business practices. It overflows with practical insights. Also included are analytical tools to support insightful and intuitive explanations. This accessible book is nicely illustrated with charts and tables and is rich with clear practical examples throughout. Numerous references are provided for further reading. *Innovation, Product Development and Commercialization* is well suited for training or course instruction and as a practical guide for every manager and executive to employ best practices to remain successful in a highly competitive global marketplace.

— **Abbas Emami-Naeini,** Ph.D.
Director, SC Solutions, Inc. and
Consulting Professor of Electrical Engineering
Stanford University

INTRODUCTION

No letup in the rapid accumulation of historical events in the technological innovation and commercialization of the 1990s and early 2000s has occurred in this first decade of the twenty-first century. The role of technology in product leadership is increasing, markets and competitors are becoming more ubiquitous, and the pace of product introduction and demise has quickened. More than ever, products are complex systems that constitute disparate technologies and require multidisciplinary integration. The cost of technology and product development is escalating as well.

The imperative of product development in this first decade of the twenty-first century is to have an integrative systems approach. To succeed, a firm must integrate business, market, technology, and resource strategies into a holistic product strategy and roadmap—and execution must be flawless.

It is within the context of a firm's leadership and management that both the creation of an excellent product strategy and flawless execution are enabled. A company engaged in product development must have the necessary competencies, organizational structure, business processes, and culture to develop winning strategies and to create competitive products that result in sustainable profitability and global leadership.

Too often books about product development have a limited scope—a scope of either the process of product development or the engineering methodologies of a new product (see Chapter 1, References 1 through 15). No matter how good an adopted business process is, if it is not implemented effectively, the process will bear no fruit—and no matter how skillful an engineering team is, a cleverly designed device will not deliver an acceptable shareholder value unless the device is timely and differentiated.

This book offers a *holistic framework* for new product development and commercialization in response to today's need for doing the "*whole* job." It provides a systematic view of the product development environment and addresses the pertinent factors of strategy, marketing, the development process, and the organizational leadership that contribute to product leadership and sustained profitability. Holistic treatment of product development is not examined by most existing product development books, which is what makes this book unique.

Also included are a flexible product development process and guidelines for a customer value-centered engineering practice. Managerial best practices and tools that maximize the effectiveness of a firm's people, technology, and knowledge assets in product development are also discussed. (*Note*: A companion book, *Management and Leadership in Product Development Environment*, offers concepts and methodologies that the author has found to be critical in the leadership of innovation and the commercialization of new products.)

The focus of the book is on business-to-business high-tech products and markets. Development of new software products or products with embedded software is emphasized. The management challenges of high-tech knowledge creation, retention, and protection are also covered. Details and nuances of an effective product development process, including marketing, research and development (R&D), product and process engineering, and commercialization, are presented. The roles and contributions of diverse players, including marketing, R&D, engineering, manufacturing, suppliers, and customers, are discussed. Also covered is business and product portfolio planning, a topic which is critical to proper prioritization of opportunities and sound investment strategies.

Numerous case studies clarify and expound upon the concepts and methods presented. Although the names of the companies and individuals have been altered, the case studies are based on realistic situations in high-tech industries. Some of the case studies encapsulate challenging situations in large companies while others concern situations that are more prevalent in small companies.

The theoretical frameworks and practical tools and methods that are presented are based on the work of numerous researchers and practitioners at many universities and industries and on the hands-on experience of the author (a result of over 25 years of experience in leading development and life cycle management of products in the high-tech environment of the Silicon Valley of California, particularly the development of semiconductor process equipment). Numerous important works are referenced. The reader is encouraged to consult these works for additional or more in-depth information.

The content of this book is applicable to both large and small companies, including start-ups. It is intended as a guide for executives and general managers, who desire to establish product leadership, and for marketing managers, R&D engineering managers, and project managers, who are in companies that engage in new product development and commercialization. In addition, the book may be used as a text by university students in master of business administration (MBA) or management of technology programs and by consultants who teach product development and commercialization courses at corporate universities.

THE CHAPTERS—AN OVERVIEW

Chapter 1 is a discussion of the high-tech context, which is the focus of new product innovation and commercialization in this book. The discussion covers the nature of high-tech products and markets and the challenges and opportunities they offer. Because a product is an application of technology to a targeted context, the product development process is driven by the rapid pace of technological change on one hand and is constrained by the rate of absorption of the new technology by customers on the other. Furthermore, the advent of information technology (IT) has created an unprecedented opportunity in all aspects of product development and commercialization including marketing, product design, supply chain management, and customer outreach and support. The IT, Internet, and networked-market opportunities of today must be understood—isolated from the frenzy of excitement (often at the "headline news" level that dominated the dot.com era of the late 1990s)—and integrated into the business, technology, and market strategies at a firm.

The purpose of Chapter 1 is to present a brief perspective of the high-tech context, how it drives a new product development process, and how the creation of a new product/service concept and development/commercialization process can actively take advantage of it.

Chapter 2 covers business, technology, and market strategies and their integration into a product plan and product development roadmap. The sources of competitive advantage and how they change during technology adoption and product life cycles and during the maturing of an industry are also discussed. Value chain positioning is examined by an enumeration of the factors that impact the position of a firm in the value chain and a discussion of defining the desired position and then devising a strategy to achieve it. Technology strategy and technology portfolio development are discussed in relation to business strategy. Protection of technology and intellectual property (IP) is also discussed.

At many high-tech firms, the roles of marketing and product management functions are often sources of confusion or even disagreement among engineering, marketing, and management, generally resulting in suboptimal performance by product marketing managers. Therefore, a framework for the tasks of marketing and product management in product development is presented in Chapter 3.

Chapter 3 also covers the definition of a product and the *whole* product concept. Understanding what the intended product is—i.e., what customers will receive, experience, and pay for—greatly impacts the development process as well as the business model, supply chain sourcing, and channel management strategies. Product positioning and differentiation and why they are paramount to product commercialization success are discussed. Product pricing theory to underscore the importance of pricing and value capture considerations in product development is briefly introduced.

Chapter 3 presents a product marketing plan and a business plan that can be adopted as a model by practitioners. The content of business plans is also discussed in some detail. Many practical tools and templates for analysis, development, and reporting plans and strategies are offered, including a product roadmap process and templates for market segmentation analysis, fingerprinting the market, product positioning, and product competitiveness assessment. Case studies covering the frameworks and methodologies that are discussed throughout the chapter are included. These cases include the development and integration of business and product strategies, product definition, product marketing, value chain positioning, and customer expectations management.

Product platform strategy and design modularity have profound implications in commercialization success and are discussed in Chapter 4. The chapter begins with a discussion of the purpose of the product development and commercialization process. Insightful platform design is imperative to achieving these goals and maximizes the opportunity for life cycle extension, operational efficiency, and value capture. Chapter 4 also contains a discussion of the nature of technological innovation and continuous, discontinuous, and disruptive technologies. Different types of products that ensue from the characteristics of product/process technologies and newness to the market are also reviewed.

Chapter 5 is devoted to the process of developing a new product. The product development process should be adapted to the product type. In particular, the challenges that are specific to software product development are discussed. Market requirements specification (MRS) is covered in detail and examples are given. A section is dedicated to providing an in-depth understanding of the process for the development of a new product. A few models practiced by leading high-tech companies or recommended by researchers are examined, including a comprehensive, yet flexible, model that can be applied to both hardware and software products and to different types of products. This process allows the practitioner to change the degree of flexibility or the structure in an implementation by proper scaling (going from an organic to a mechanistic process), by insertion or removal of control points and gates, and by overlapping or staggering phases of the process.

Every phase of the product development process is reviewed in depth by stating the purpose, scope, and expected output of each phase. It is through an in-depth understanding of the purpose of each phase that a practitioner can adapt the process to the project at hand because no product, market, or context of development is identical to another. The pressure for short time to market causes (or tempts) many development teams to bypass or overlook essential elements of the product development process—without properly understanding the associated risks of doing so—and to consequently achieve less than desired results. The phases of the product development process are:

- Phase 0—product development proposal
- Phase 1—exploration and feasibility (E&F)
- Phase 2—planning that includes development of a project plan and the engineering requirements specification (ERS)
- Phase 3—development and engineering evaluation
- Phase 4—customer and manufacturing qualification
- Phase 5—market introduction and production ramp

Although the above process is generic and its construct is adaptable, a section is dedicated to the unique features of software development and the specific process elements that must be included.

The next section of Chapter 5 examines a structured approach to the implementation of the product development process. (*Note*: Although Chapters 7 and 8 cover the execution of a development project and the necessary tools, Chapter 5 assists in gaining an understanding of the tasks, organizational responsibility, and expected output of different team members and organization units/departments.) Also provided is a checklist for each phase of development that can be used to monitor progress or to scale a process to a specific product situation.

Several implementation models and tradeoffs that the development team faces are reviewed, including the risk of overlapping phases and the impact of adopting a flexible (organic) or structured (mechanistic) process. Also examined are the resource issues and the challenges of new markets and new technologies in the implementation stage.

Effective product development requires measurable success indicators or metrics of progress during implementation. Therefore a list of indicators for development of hardware and software products and for tracking progress is provided in Chapter 5.

A subsequent section in Chapter 5 discusses the concept of product release for market introduction and unrestricted sales. This section reviews the release concept and presents a framework for analysis and tradeoff between the competing factors of time to market, design completion, and operational readiness of a new product. Product change management (e.g., after a new product has been introduced into the market) and a review of the process of customer change notification are also discussed.

Chapter 5 includes several case studies that apply to the numerous models and frameworks presented in the chapter. These cases demonstrate some of the challenges that practitioners face in implementing the product development process.

Because the product design phase plays a critical role in the ultimate success of the product, Chapter 6 is devoted to this phase. Guidelines are provided for a good design, to define product reliability and robustness, and to discuss the impact of predictability in product performance on a customer's operation. Also reviewed are reliability models and tools that a design team can use. Several references are provided that can be consulted by the reader to gain a more in-depth understanding of the subject and the tools.

The first part of Chapter 6 is devoted to gaining an understanding of the common terminologies that are used in product development—such as conceptual, preliminary, and detail design and the various types of prototypes and the stages of testing and design qualification. The purpose of this section is not to offer a universal or rigid definition for such terms, because there are none, but to create a framework that can be tailored to the needs of the product at hand and the context in which it is developed. Furthermore, the definitions help in the adoption of a common language for team members that can improve communication and augment efficiency of execution.

Chapter 6 concludes with a brief section about quality. The importance of quality in every aspect of a product development process cannot be overemphasized. The overall process output embodied in product/process design, manufacturing, and delivery must be flawless, as measured by success criteria. However, quality results cannot be achieved unless quality is embedded in every step of the project management process. The quality management system (QMS) concept is briefly discussed and a few key methodologies are reviewed, such as house of quality, design of experiment (DOE), and root cause analysis. Ample references that further examine the concepts of quality are provided for the reader.

Chapter 7 focuses on the management and execution of the product development process. The frameworks in Chapter 7 are based on a system "thinking" model to achieve operational excellence. The chapter begins by examining the imperatives of today's environment for discipline and nimble execution of the *whole* job. A few cases are analyzed at the onset of the chapter to illustrate the common challenges that most product development teams face. The cases include issues with a software product and the different types of failures faced by a business unit of a large company over a span of several years. Careful review of these cases should raise the sensitivity of the reader to the importance of using the methods that are included in the remainder of the chapter.

The focus in Chapter 7 moves on to resource and interface management issues as being critical tasks of product development efforts. The characteristics of a winning team and how the team adopts a global perspective of resource utilization are examined. Innovation and entrepreneurship are central to success in a high-tech product development environment; however, managing an innovative R&D team and promoting entrepreneurship and out-of-the-box thinking pose unique leadership challenges when a company grows past its start-up phase. Practical methodologies to enhance effectiveness in the management of innovation are provided. The section ends with an examination of a quest for developing the right product, in the right way, and right the first time.

The next section in Chapter 7 is dedicated to systems analysis, systems engineering, and risk management. Several models of systems analysis are reviewed, including a discussion of their applicability to the management of product development projects. A framework for risk analysis is presented, which is useful when the technology is new, the risk is high, and the team has several technology options that cannot be readily ranked. Event-based or parallel-path development methods in decision making and risk mitigation are discussed.

A subsequent section in Chapter 7 is dedicated to creating a global perspective in resources management, including the resources of the firm and the supply chain. Outsourcing, core technology, and other contextual factors that impact a comprehensive workforce strategy for competitive advantage are reviewed. A broad view of outsourcing for the business units of a large company is provided, in which hiring of an "internal supplier" is also considered in the outsourcing strategy. The internal supplier issue is a subject that most large companies encounter in their quest for economy of scale, often with disappointment. A significant amount of discussion is dedicated to this topic because internal supplier management, if done correctly, can be a great source of competitive advantage, particularly if a core technology at the firm is at stake. (*Note*: Review of the definition of core technology and the consideration of core technology in a make-or-buy decision in Chapter 7 is an extension of the discussion of technology strategy in Chapter 2.) Also examined are strategic alliances and integrated teams in product development.

Chapter 8 is dedicated to project management in product development—a subject that is widely recognized as being important, and researched and written about, but poorly practiced by most high-tech companies. The basic concepts of project management are briefly reviewed and many tools and best-known methods are offered. The discussion begins with the planning of a project and a listing of the associated responsibilities and authority of a project manager. Then the main elements of project management are briefly reviewed, including the statement of work (SOW), work breakdown structure (WBS), design structure matrix (DSM), scheduling, cost estimating, cost tracking, and resource management. The important concept of project organization is introduced in Chapter 8. (*Note*: The reader may consult *Management and Leadership in a Product Development Environment* for a more detailed discussion of project organization by the author.) Most firms face the challenge of managing and integrating multiple projects—a challenge which must be tackled by general managers, product managers, and functional managers. Several useful methods and templates for managing multiple projects and aggregate resource planning are provided. Project and design reviews are also discussed in some detail and many practical templates and frameworks are offered.

Chapter 9 is primarily for managers of product development. This chapter discusses common challenges that managers face in decision making, problem solving, and employee empowerment. It presents a critical perspective on these challenges and offers practical means for dealing with them. A section is also dedicated to improving skills in meeting management and making effective presentations because they are (unpopular) necessities of the complex product development environment.

Chapter 10 is dedicated to the development and management of a product portfolio. Strategy- and ROI-based product development must be an integral part of an aggregate product and IP planning process. Therefore the discussion in Chapter 10 concerns a strategic framework of resource allocation for achieving both local and global optimization of the business. Funding and other resource decisions in product development are based on the priority ranking of the products in the portfolio. Therefore prioritization criteria comprise a set of metrics that ensure a long-term profitable growth.

Chapter 10 begins with a case study. The setting is a large company in which several business unit general managers are fighting for corporate resources. The case demonstrates the need for an aggregate product planning and portfolio management. The key financial metrics of shareholder value are then reviewed and followed by a discussion of how investors evaluate a start-up company and its products.

Chapter 10 is largely dedicated to product portfolio analysis methodology and to a discussion of several useful templates. The chapter continues with a discussion of an R&D investment model and a process for developing a product portfolio that is based on integrating the technology, market, and business strategies at a firm. The portfolio analysis is based on an assessment of individual products with respect to their financial and market impact and their strategic alignment and value. Both the positive and negative attributes of a product in quantifying its impact and strategic alignment are examined. The portfolio analysis also considers the aggregate resource availability. Using these tools, managers can compare products and allocate resources to create a balanced portfolio that ensures customer satisfaction, market leadership, competitive insulation, long-term competitive advantage, and ROI.

A section is dedicated to understanding the holistic approach to new product development in which every decision and tradeoff in the design, development, operation, and commercialization are based on maximizing customer and shareholder values. Also reviewed are a process for preparing a proposal in Phase 0 of the product development process (see Chapter 5) and how to continuously assess the viability of the product that is being developed during the development cycle.

Chapter 10 concludes with a section about the methodology of managing the firm's IP portfolio and a discussion of an IP assessment process that is based on product competitive differentiation as the metric of prioritization and decision making.

The Appendix contains a brief description of the semiconductor manufacturing process and the functions of processing equipment at various steps of integrated circuit (IC) fabrication. IC chips are made through a sequence of steps in a production factory (or fab), in which each step is performed by unique process equipment. A typical equipment architecture and subsystem configuration is presented in the Appendix, which is referenced throughout the book. IC process equipment is generally complex in architecture and design. Therefore process equipment development challenges all aspects of a product development process—and hence is a good example for learning about product development. The Appendix also illustrates selected trends in the semiconductor industry that are excellent examples of high-tech products and markets, which are characterized by a rapid rate of change, a short product life cycle, and endless opportunities for innovation.

CLOSING THOUGHTS

Throughout this book many challenges that an organization faces in "doing the *whole* job" of developing and commercializing a new product are enumerated. The purpose is to offer the best-known methodologies for effectively managing these challenges and attaining world-class success.

ABOUT THE AUTHOR

 **Dariush Rafinejad** has over 25 years of executive leadership experience in global high-technology companies in the Silicon Valley of California. Through hands-on innovation and the commercialization of numerous products in the high-tech industry and extensive academic experience, he has gained deep expertise in the management of technology.

Dr. Rafinejad served as Corporate Vice President at multibillion-dollar Applied Materials Corporation and Lam Research Corporation, where he led the development and commercialization of numerous successful products and was General Manager of several large business units. Dr. Rafinejad also has experience with several start-up companies, serving as an investor and a member of their boards of directors. In 2004, he founded Blue Dome Consulting, a business consulting firm. He lists Novellus, SanDisk, Brewer Science, Aviza Tech, MKS, AMEC (China), and SoloPower among his Blue Dome corporate clients.

Dr. Rafinejad holds M.Sc. and Ph.D. degrees in Mechanical Engineering from the University of California, Berkeley and has conducted post-doctoral research at Imperial College in London, England. His professional education at Stanford University includes an Executive Engineering Management Certificate and several continuing education courses.

As an adjunct professor at the Haas Business School of the University of California Berkeley, a lecturer and visiting scholar at Stanford University, and the Dean of Management at Menlo College in Atherton, California, Dr. Rafinejad has acquired extensive academic teaching and research experience. He has taught courses in high-tech marketing, the management of new product development, the management of innovation, and leadership in the global business arena. He has also taught executive development courses at Budapest University of Technology (Hungary), Chinese State Council in Shanghai, and St. Petersburg State University (Russia) and to Executive MBA and CEO Club students at Jiao Tong University (China).

His current research interests include sustainable product development and manufacturing—research which he is conducting at the Stanford University Alliance for Innovative Manufacturing (AIM) as a Visiting Scholar. Dr. Rafinejad has also published several business and technical papers.

He resides in Los Altos Hills, California.

*Free value-added materials available from
the Download Resource Center at **www.jrosspub.com***

At J. Ross Publishing we are committed to providing today's professional with practical, hands-on tools that enhance the learning experience and give readers an opportunity to apply what they have learned. That is why we offer free ancillary materials available for download on this book and all participating Web Added Value™ publications. These online resources may include interactive versions of material that appears in the book or supplemental templates, worksheets, models, plans, case studies, proposals, spreadsheets and assessment tools, among other things. Whenever you see the WAV™ symbol in any of our publications it means bonus materials accompany the book and are available from the Web Added Value™ Download Resource Center at www.jrosspub.com.

Downloads for *Innovation, Product Development and Commercialization: Case Studies and Key Practices for Market Leadership* consist of teaching notes for selected case studies which appear in the book and a model that may used for identifying underperforming areas of your business which are rooted in innovation, product development, and commercialization practices. For more added value, readers are encouraged to identify ten items within the downloadable model that represent the top underperforming areas of their business. Once identified, e-mail a listing of these items and a brief explanation of your business, the market, and the products to the author at drafinejad@blue-dome.org. The author will engage in limited online discussions with readers of this book to help them identify the causes of underperformance and to provide guidance on opportunities for improvement.

HIGH TECHNOLOGY—
STRATEGIC CONTEXT

The engine of an economy is innovation in product development and commercialization through:

- Taking advantage of progress in technology
- Imagining market opportunities from the application of technology

In a broad sense, a product is defined to include a tangible product, a software product, or a service. The characteristics of the manufacturing process and product delivery constitute the significant distinctions between the different types of products. For a new tangible product, the product development process must encompass the product fabrication methodology and the technology it entails and must heed the product manufacturing cost to ensure profitability. Companies that develop and market products may or may not manufacture them—nevertheless they must be concerned with the manufacturing (process) technology and costs of their product.

Key success indicators in the development and commercialization of a new product include:

- Market development and penetration agility (measured by the time to the "first" customer acceptance of the product)
- Market share momentum, with a sustainable competitive advantage
- Profitability (measured by the rate of return factor after product introduction)
- Shareholder value growth

Achieving world-class performance in any and all of these indicators depends on whether (or not) a firm has superior strategies for global business, the technology portfolio, and the market assets, as well as a plan for the integration and execution of these strategies.

In order to commercialize a new product effectively, the product's technology and concept must match the target application context. A commanding market momentum is attained when the product is differentiated against customers' alternate choices along value dimensions that are important to the customers. In order to extract maximum value from the product and to achieve a high return from the development investment, a firm must attain a strong position relative to other economic value players. Such a position in the value chain is

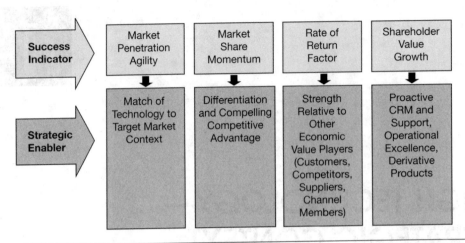

Figure 1.1. Success Indicators and Corresponding Strategic Enablers in New Product Development, Commercialization, and Life Cycle Performance.

attained via a strategic plan that begins with defining the desired position, which is followed by devising the plan and then acting to achieve it. To sustain a winning market and value position throughout the product's life cycle (resulting in an attractive growth in shareholder value), the firm must have an excellent customer relation management (CRM) program and proactive customer support and must operate the enterprise efficiently. Figure 1.1 depicts the success indicators of new product development, commercialization, and life cycle performance and the corresponding strategic enablers.[1–4]

The essential ingredients of flawless execution in product development are the organization's *resource capability* and leadership's/management's *effectiveness* in resource utilization and achievement of results. Product and technology portfolio management and prioritization of funding the development projects (i.e., resource allocation) must be done through an aggregate product planning process.

When a product is selected for development, the development team must apply efficient project management practices to produce the planned results. The R&D and design teams must not only be highly skilled in their functional areas, but they must also have a deep understanding of the business purpose and be cognizant of commercial success in every product decision that they make. Because manufacturing process technology can be and often is a source of competitive advantage, the product design team must also be knowledgeable in manufacturing technology and be well integrated with the manufacturing team.[5–8] (For example, in the semiconductor industry, integrated circuit manufacturing technology, including process equipment, is the key enabler of the digital electronic industry alongside the chip design.)

The above issues will be discussed in detail in the chapters that follow, and operational strategies and practices such as materials sourcing and the supplier management that are important to manufacturing of new products will be reviewed.

Many product development efforts fail, resulting in frustration for the development team in spite of its hard work and disappointment for managers in spite of their desire for success. In most cases, the main reason for failure of product development efforts is falling short of doing the "*whole* job" in product development. Doing the *whole* job means:

- Having a business strategy that is communicated to the development team
- Having an integrated technology/market/value chain strategy that is understood by all development team members

- Having a capable team that understands the market priorities
- Executing the development project with agility and real-time responsiveness to the changing conditions of the marketplace and to the customers

Often a product development team faces resource limitations, time pressures, and technology challenges. Only through a crisp and focused execution, trade-off analyses and timely decisions, and perseverance and hard work can a development effort succeed. [9–15]

Therefore, it is the intent of this book to provide a holistic view of the product development undertaking of *doing the whole job* and to offer winning frameworks and methodologies that should be used by all players in the development process. The roster of players is not limited to only the nominal cross-functional team of marketing, engineering, and manufacturing. It also includes the business unit (BU) managers and corporate managers whose strategies, actions, and decisions profoundly impact the success of the product development effort. Management actions such as resource allocation and prioritization, product and technology portfolio decisions, supply chain and channel strategies, and other actions can help or hinder the product development and commercialization endeavor.

Often top management takes a "snobbish" view toward sharing business strategy with the engineering, R&D, and manufacturing teams, particularly the *why's* of top-level decisions. Management may consider that sharing such information will be distracting to the product development team, or that the information is confidential and the development team does not need to know about it, or that the team is not "mature" enough to handle such knowledge properly. Worse yet, if having information is considered to be having power, some managers may refrain from sharing information to maintain their own sense of power! Nothing is more harmful to doing the *whole* job of developing a commercially successful new product than withholding information.

Throughout this book, in order to elucidate the concepts and demonstrate the methods of developing a high-technology (high-tech) product, the application of the concepts and development methods will be presented for the development of semiconductor manufacturing equipment and the associated processes. Yet the content of this book is equally applicable to the development of any type of new high-tech product. Semiconductor manufacturing equipment has been chosen because it provides an excellent example of a high-tech product that encompasses a wide range of technologies and system design challenges. Additionally, semiconductor process equipment is used in the fabrication of integrated circuit (IC) chips that are in every electronic consumer and industrial product. The design of typical IC manufacturing equipment also includes myriad challenges in mechanical, electrical, controls, and software engineering and material science. Therefore the development of a suitable manufacturing process for semiconductor equipment provides many challenges in the fields of material science, physics, and chemistry. Above all, the systems engineering and integration of equipment function in the IC manufacturing process poses a challenge in all aspects of a product development undertaking.

1.1 HIGH TECHNOLOGY—CHARACTERISTICS

Technology is "the practical application of knowledge, especially in a particular area" and "a manner of accomplishing a task, especially using technical processes, methods, or knowledge."[16] In other words, technology is the application of knowledge in products, services, and

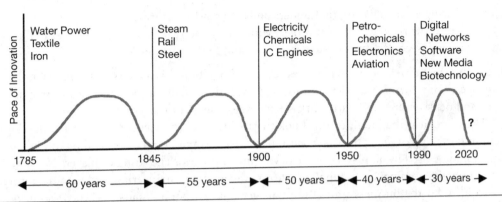

Figure 1.2. Waves of Economic Activities and Business Cycles. (Source: Adapted from *The Economist Magazine*; February 1999.)

processes as well as their production and delivery. Technology is called *high technology* if its rate of change is high and its market context is unstable.[17]

The balance of Chapter 1 will review the characteristics of high-tech markets and products and the opportunities and challenges that high technology offers in product development. Because information technology (IT) and the Internet are linchpins of contemporary high technology, the opportunities they have enabled and the threats they have created in developing and commercializing new products (compared to traditional ways) will be emphasized.

Successful products properly integrate a wide variety of technologies to match the context in which they are applied. The application of technology in product development goes through several stages of knowledge generation and integration (to be discussed in the subsequent chapters), including:

- Market/technology/product strategies
- Feasibility of the technology and product concept
- New design/process knowledge generation
- Verification/integration of the product and process in the context application

Throughout modern history, technology has progressed through many business cycles and has profoundly impacted economic activities. Figure 1.2 shows the cyclic pace of innovation over several economic eras.[18] Each cycle is characterized by the introduction of new materials, new means of productivity improvement, and improved means of transportation and communication (transport of information). In each cycle, technological innovation is made in the factors that impact the economic decisions of what to produce, the means of production, and the distribution of goods. Note in Figure 1.2 how technology has accelerated economic activities and has shortened each cycle. In the early stage of each cycle, new technology has been a "high" technology and it has changed the nature of products, production, and markets. For example, when railroads became the standard, the method of transportation in the United States was revolutionized, which lowered the cost of transportation significantly.[19,20]

1.1.1 Impact on U.S. Economy

Today, as always, technology is the key to future prosperity. In the current cycle of technological innovation, examples of the impact of IT and other high-tech industries on the U.S. economy include:[21,22]

- Between 1992 and 2000, high-tech companies have created twice as many jobs as non-high-tech companies and paid salaries two times higher.
- Between 1996 and 2000, although IT industries represented only 7% of all businesses, they have accounted for roughly 28% of overall real economic growth.
- From 1989 to 2000, inflation in IT-intensive industries has been just 1.3% per year on average, compared with 3% in less IT-intensive industries. IT industries have helped to keep the U.S. inflation rate down by 1%.
- Starting in 1996, the U.S. productivity growth has exploded to 2.5% per year, up from 1.4% per year between 1975 and 1995. IT products and IT industries have contributed roughly two-thirds of this extraordinary growth.
- Agricultural technologies have increased crop yields by up to 25%, while reducing the need to spray herbicides and insecticides on foods and into the environment. The recent mapping of the rice genome could cut world hunger by one-half within a generation according to the United Nations.
- Pharmaceutical and biotechnologies have generated new cures and treatments that help people live longer and healthier lives. Advances in healthcare have increased life expectancies in the United States.
- Technology has improved the environment by increasing energy efficiency—today's automobiles use 60% of the gasoline used in 1972, with new hybrid vehicles having twice the fuel efficiency. Over the same period, auto emissions in the United States have gone down more than 95%. Estimates (in 2000) were that the Internet would reduce worldwide demand for paper by 2.7 million tons a year (in 2003) as companies and organizations moved to paperless offices.

High-tech advances continue at a rapid pace. New innovations such as nanotechnology promise to result in revolutionary advances in computing and medicine. Mapping of the human genome has created new opportunities for breakthroughs in biotechnology. Improvements in hydrogen fuel cells hold the promise of radically different energy and environmental industries.

1.1.2 Impact on Global and Local Markets, Products, and Services

For high-tech businesses, however, IT contributions are not without challenges. Stiff global competition, intellectual property (IP) protection, and regulatory changes are just a few. The Internet presents many traditional distributors and middlemen with significant new challenges—adopt new business models in response or become extinct.

Business success in the twenty-first century depends on the ability to "globalize" and to "be local" at the same time; on developing and commercializing environmentally sustainable products; and on resource-efficient operation, including sustainable manufacturing—all of which are possible from the endless possibilities of technology.

High technology (IT, electronics, and biotechnology) today has changed markets, products, services, and marketing systems. Briefly, some of these changes include:

- Technology, which is characterized by a rapid rate of change—as witnessed in computing, software (new powerful languages, operating systems, and object-oriented programming), controls, communications, and biotechnology and bioengineering. In many areas, standards are nonexistent or in development.

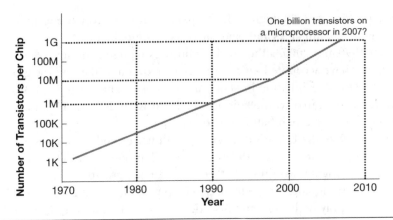

Figure 1.3. Moore's Law of the Semiconductor Industry.

- The life of new products, which is shortened by technology obsolescence. A popular example is the transition in personal computer storage devices—from floppy disk, to zip-drive, to CD/RW, to DVD, to flash-memory cards—all in span of 20 years. New distribution channels are enabled by the Internet, such as in the entertainment, news, and music media, which have gone from LP recording disks, to CD/DVD, to MP3 downloads.
- The pace of technology development and application, which is so fast that catching up is difficult once a company falls behind. High technology has "globalized" communications and transportation and has changed the industrial infrastructure through application software such as enterprise resource planning (ERP). It has created new industrial products and Internet services that have replaced traditional banking services (e.g., ATMs and online capability) and the air travel business (e.g., e-tickets).
- The Internet, which is "metamorphosing" the classic marketing mix concept of a marketplace into a virtual global space (e.g., eBay). (*Note*: e-Business opportunities will be discussed in more detail later in this chapter, e.g., the emergence of *digitizing* the information-intensive steps in a value chain as being the opportunity of our time.)
- The rapidly changing nature of high technology, which provides no relevant historical trend for obtaining guidance for future strategy. The fundamental marketing and product development questions of *what* to sell, *how* to sell, and *where* to sell require significant innovation on the part of business leaders. The differences in the business models of Inktomi, Yahoo!, and Google and the variety of business models in mobile phone service are examples of the possibilities in the high-tech marketing mix.
- High-tech market conditions, which rapidly change, and a market window, which is usually small. Market share and customer value must be captured as quickly as they develop.

Several examples from the semiconductor industry demonstrate the rapid technological change and the small market window. Figure 1.3 shows the impressive increase in the number of transistors on a microprocessor chip, following what is known as Moore's law in the semiconductor industry—the computing power of microprocessors doubles every 18 months.

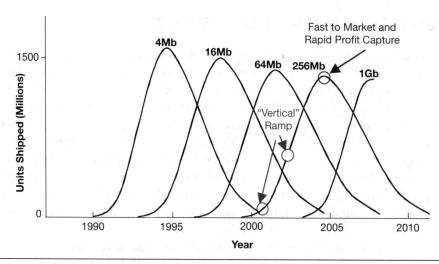

Figure 1.4. DRAM Life Cycle. Gb, billion bit; Mb, million bit. (Source: Data from Integrated Circuits Engineering and SEMATECH.)

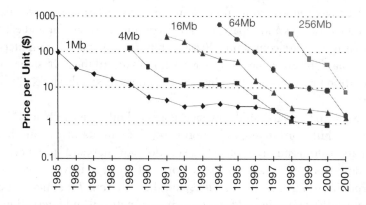

Figure 1.5. DRAM Unit Price by Density, Yearly Averages. (Source: Data from Integrated Circuits Engineering and Applied Materials Corporation.)

Moore's law drives equally impressive progress in dynamic random access memory (DRAM) chips (Figure 1.4) and enables new powerful application software, as the other two major elements of a personal computer. As Figure 1.4 demonstrates, an "endless" stream of powerful new chips flows into the market, making the market window for each generation of design very short. In the semiconductor industry, therefore, the compelling competitive advantage is speed in designing the next-generation microprocessor or memory chips; in developing the next-generation chip fabrication process; and in the required equipment and production ramp agility. As each new generation of chips is introduced, the price of the last generation of chips drops dramatically, eroding the profitability of suppliers. Therefore the market window for high-volume, but high-price DRAM is fairly small (Figures 1.4 and 1.5).

Note from Figure 1.5 that the pace of DRAM price erosion has accelerated over the last 15 years. The price at every generation, irrespective of capacity, rapidly reduces to about $1. Figures 1.4 and 1.5 underscore the need for agility and superb operational efficiency in product development and in the manufacturing ramp in a high-tech business.

1.2 HIGH-TECH MARKETS—CHARACTERISTICS

High-tech customers, competitors, suppliers, and investors are globally located. For example, in the semiconductor industry, two-thirds of the customers of Applied Materials Corporation (AMC), a leading IC process equipment supplier, are located outside of the United States. Tokyo Electron Limited (TEL), a major competitor of AMC, is headquartered in Japan, but competes in all segments of the semiconductor fabrication equipment market, including the United States, Europe, Japan, Korea, Taiwan, China, and other regions. Taiwan Semiconductor Manufacturing Corporation (TSMC), the largest foundry operation for fabrication of IC chips, is located in Taiwan, serves customers on every continent, and is expanding its operation into China. Semiconductor Manufacturing International Corporation (SMIC), a Chinese foundry chip maker founded in 2000, has major U.S. ownership (Goldman Sachs) and is targeting customers worldwide, in competition with TSMC.

Examples of global markets and competition also abound in consumer markets. In the mobile phone business, major players include Nokia in Finland, Motorola in the United States, and Samsung in Korea. The consumer electronics business is a worldwide competitive battleground between the giant participants Sony and Philips.

Because of efficient global communication and transportation that are enabled by high technology, product features and capabilities are becoming more similar and expectations and preferences of customers are converging. Pizza, hamburgers, personal computers, and mobile phones are in demand by everyone in the world who can afford them. In some cases, however, this homogenization process is impeded by a lack of universal standards (e.g., as in the mobile phone industry).

High technology has created fundamental changes in both "high-tech" and "low-tech" marketing systems—a shift from mass-production goods into an era of custom-made consumer products (or mass customization). From a huge portfolio of "standard" products, one can order a custom window from Andersen Windows Corporation or a bicycle the National Bicycle Industrial Corporation. *The Los Angeles Times* and the *New York Times* newspapers have zone editions that report local news in addition to "common" national and international news.

Because of fierce global competition, suppliers have taken advantage of high-tech manufacturing opportunities and have created a greater variety of goods and services for competitive differentiation—creating confusion in consumer markets in which customers have *too many* choices and must sort through *many* options (e.g., the many similar products on a supermarket shelf). IT has somewhat alleviated the situation for both suppliers and customers through mass customization and customers being able to obtain what they want how, where, and when they want it.

1.3 HIGH-TECH PRODUCTS—CHARACTERISTICS

Compared to consumer commodity goods, the emphasis on features and capabilities is greater in high-tech products. However, as high-tech products become more complex, delivering benefits to customers rather than selling technology is important. Often new features and capabilities are introduced for differentiation or for demand creation. Bridging the gap between technological capabilities and customer benefits requires customer education. For example, cell phones today have numerous capabilities and features that most consumers do not understand, do not know how to conveniently use, and do not even need. If a customer has to make too many decisions or if a product is not user friendly, it will not attract the customer's imagination or satisfy his/her needs or wants. This is true of both consumer products and industrial high-tech products (although in the latter case, customers are more rigorous in their evaluation and use of a product).

For high-tech products, definition of the product in terms of the value that is delivered to the customer and in what the customer receives, experiences, and pays for is critical. Because of the instability of technology, market, and competitive conditions, the definition of a high-tech product is also unstable, which creates both a competitive opportunity and a threat and greatly impacts the business model for the product. The examples of selling a mobile phone versus mobile phone service or selling a satellite TV antenna versus digital television service are two of many situations in which the product definition can be vastly altered for competitive differentiation. (*Note:* Product definition will be discussed in detail in Chapter 2.)

1.4 HIGH-TECH ENVIRONMENT—MARKET PENETRATION AND MARKETING MANAGEMENT

Early innovative high-tech products begin as a fad, with a market value or purpose that is recognized by only a limited group of customers such as technology enthusiasts in consumer markets or leading R&D engineers in an industrial high-tech market. The question is whether the product will continue to be a fad or whether it will move up the technology adoption life cycle[23,24] and be adopted as a mainstream product.

The turbulent nature of high-tech markets, rapidly changing high technology, and the characteristically short life of high-tech products create exigency for an endless stream of new products. For example, Hewlett-Packard (HP) Corporation has reported that 77% of its revenue in the early 1990s came from products that had been introduced in the previous 2 years. HP studies also show strong sensitivity of return on investment (ROI) to the development schedule compared to the cost of product development or investment[1]—one reason why development teams are always under significant pressure to introduce new high-tech products to market rapidly. At the same time, because of rapidly changing market conditions, *marketing* is frequently hindered in providing the engineering team with a detailed and stable set of market requirements.

Frequent product introduction can serve as a sampling technique to gather market data.[1] However, short time-to-market acceptance of new products requires *marketing* and *engineering* to work closely and to partner with *suppliers* and *customers* for concurrent development.

In a business-to-business (B-to-B) market for industrial products, such as process equipment for IC manufacturing, the supplier's product must be designed into the customer's product or production process. Because the customer's time to market is often very short, concurrent development (i.e., co-development) with the customer as a partner is often essential—the supplier must invent new technology and new products at the same time that the customer is inventing its own product and fabrication process. Co-development can be frustrating for suppliers because customers' needs are often not well defined or specified at the onset. The supplier must be intimate with the customer and be agile in developing flexible platforms and capable technologies along an aggressive product roadmap, which can be quickly adapted to the customer's unique and changing applications.

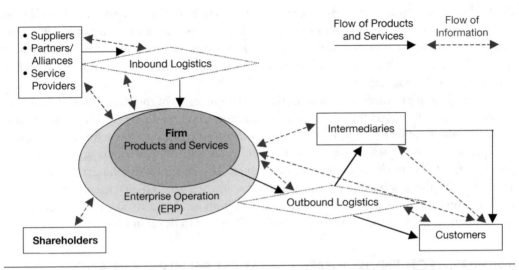

Figure 1.6. Marketing System and Value Chain Network. ERP, enterprise resource planning.

Real-time market data collection and product performance feedback, using the Internet and other high-tech communication means, enable suppliers to add a new dimension to customer support and responsiveness and to ensure that their technology matches the application context. For example, through remote access to information about a product, a supplier can receive real-time performance data directly from the customer's manufacturing floor, perform remote troubleshooting, and take immediate corrective action through local service personnel or customer technicians. Computer-based training (CBT), including virtual reality graphics and video, allows accepting a new product or upgrades to an existing product in the installed base to be easier for customers.

Often opportunities for new applications are identified by customers—opportunities that would not have been envisaged by the supplier. Customer intimacy and real-time data collection are therefore necessary for taking advantage of such opportunities. Furthermore, in high-tech markets, *marketing and the sales force* must be technology-savvy to effectively communicate with customers and to perceive market and business opportunities.

1.5 IT—INTERNET OPPORTUNITIES

IT has created opportunities for improved efficiency and effectiveness in every business aspect that affects development and commercialization of a new product. IT impacts marketing, engineering, materials sourcing, manufacturing, sales, customer support, and the effectiveness of a firm's operational systems, including human resources, finance, and other operational infrastructure. Whether it is attracting customers, investors, or top, talented people or interacting with customers, suppliers, and other stakeholders, IT offers unique opportunities for improvement.

IT enables high efficiency in the generation, retention, and application of knowledge by impacting the information flow in the marketing system. The model in Figure 1.6 illustrates the value network of suppliers in a marketing system. Flow of products and services and the flow of information are shown by solid and dashed arrows, respectively. As Figure 1.6 shows,

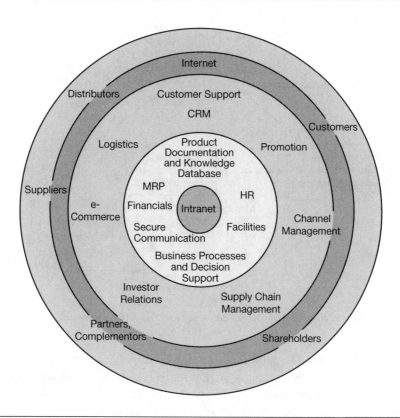

Figure 1.7. Networking Enterprise Operations, Customers, Value Chain Players, and Shareholders.

IT can be applied where information flows, i.e., in all aspects of the marketing system, to perceive, create, and deliver customer value.

IT has also created a new concept of the marketplace and has enabled the communication and operational infrastructure of business enterprises to enhance efficiency and effectiveness. Figure 1.7 illustrates how IT, through integration of a firm's intranet and the resources of the Internet, supports an efficient network of internal and external business operation, information exchange, and e-commerce.

A firm's operational infrastructure—materials resource planning (MRP), the financial system, product documentation, the knowledge (IP) database, the human resource management system, the (secured) global communication system, facilities, and the decision-making process—is enabled by the intranet system. The intranet is also linked to customers, market assets, and investors via the Internet.

An example of an e-business opportunity in customer order fulfillment in a B-to-B market is shown in Figure 1.8. In Figure 1.8, the firm's product is intended for delivery to the customer's factory for either integration into the customer's product as a subsystem or installation as fabrication equipment for production capacity. Figure 1.8 illustrates how the interfaces between the customer, the firm, and its suppliers are linked to the firm's intranet system for order entry, product configuration and design customization, materials resource planning, procurement, inventory management, tracking manufacturing status of the order, source inspection, shipping, installation, spare parts delivery, customer support, and financial transactions.

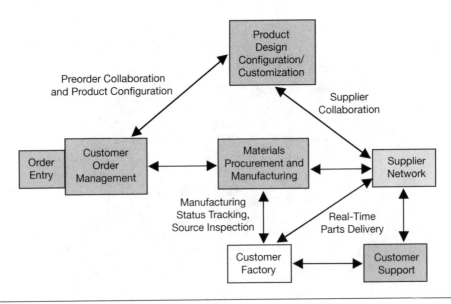

Figure 1.8. e-Business Network for Business-to-Business Customer Order Fulfillment.

According to Bill Gates, IT applications through e-business have improved the operational effectiveness of companies by creating a "digital nervous system."[25,26] In large companies, IT can enhance operational efficiency by improving communication that would otherwise be slowed down by their large size. On the other hand, IT enables smaller companies to extend their customer reach and to make offerings through partnership and alliances that are competitive with larger companies.

In the digital economy of today, in which speed is the determining factor of success, e-business has become prevalent and IT applications have proliferated throughout every aspect of the enterprise operations, some of which are highlighted below:

- Human resources (HR) management—A Web-based HR system is used for employee benefits (salary administration, stock options, and health insurance), recruiting, global workforce management, performance management, and organizational development (through a corporate university, e.g., employee functional competency and leadership development).
- Employee communication system—Company information can be shared to worldwide employees and partners in real time for a multiplicity of purposes, such as awareness of the company strategy, cultural reinforcement and renewal, business and financial reporting, and new product launching.
- Technology and product development—Collaboration through virtual teams is possible among a global workforce and with customers, partners, suppliers, and university researchers. Product development teams in the United States and India, for example, can work around the clock. Retention and sharing of knowledge about product design, best-known methods, a standard parts library, and customer/competitive information are made accessible in real time. Real-time participation in teleseminars at research universities through e-meetings or in the company's internal symposia allows leading-edge technical knowledge to be readily accessible to worldwide scientists and engineers of a firm.

- Procurement of direct or non-direct material—The procurement process is enabled through online demand planning and procurement, forecasting, inventory management, online bidding (reverse auction) for commodity parts, electronic requests for proposal (e-RFP) with automatic pull-up of the latest revisions of drawings, and electronic purchase order (PO) approval systems. Through outsourcing and real-time management of suppliers, a company can set up virtual manufacturing (e.g., similar to what Cisco has done).

- Inbound and outbound logistics—Having access to accurate and real-time information has enabled effective channel inventory management, warehousing, distribution, and delivery (e.g., as Wal-Mart has mastered).

- Operations—Real-time information exchange between sales and manufacturing groups allows for the set up of an efficient forecasting, production planning, and customer order fulfillment system that reduces production cycle time, defects, and costs. Through a networked ERP system, the company can provide real-time input and receive responses from suppliers, distributors, retailers, and the sales force. Inventory management can be improved for better customer service and lower operational costs by tracking parts in the supply chain, the finished goods inventory, and the distribution system. Real-time tracking of where products are and how they are selling in the distribution system is of major importance to operational and marketing efficiency (e.g., Wal-Mart has maintained its low cost leadership through a world-class ERP system that provides real-time knowledge about what customers are buying at which store, worldwide, etc.).

- Marketing and sales—Real-time customer and competitive information, trends in consumer buying behavior, dynamic pricing, product configuration, and push advertising are a just few examples of Internet and IT applications in marketing and sales. Internet e-commerce provides a great opportunity for small companies with limited resources. Web businesses can add new customers with little or no additional cost (e.g., in the size of the sales force). A virtual store is open around the clock and around the world, reaching a much bigger market than is possible otherwise. e-Catalogs and automated configuring and ordering systems by customers can be used by small and large companies alike (e.g., similar to what Cisco, Dell, and many other companies have done).

- After-sales service and support—The quality and speed of customer service have been revolutionized by the use of Internet capabilities. Databases of customer profiles and product information in the installed base can be accessed online by all company employees to support customers. Service personnel can access online customer information and pull up the appropriate troubleshooting guides to service a product remotely or in person in a customer's factory. Engineers can access the database of product problems reported by customers, develop upgrade/retrofit solutions, and deliver the solution online directly to a customer or to local service personnel for implementation at a customer's site. Customer self-service has added benefits in cost savings and customer satisfaction, e.g., online product descriptions, operations-and-maintenance instructions, troubleshooting and technical support, frequently asked questions (FAQs), order status information, downloads of software products and upgrades, etc.

1.6 IT—ENABLEMENT OF NEW PRODUCTS AND INDUSTRIES

IT has been enabled by advances in digital computing and communication industries at an unprecedented rate. In 1980, one page of text per second could be sent over copper wires—20 years later, 90,000 pages of an encyclopedia could be sent per second over optical fibers! In addition to the rapid increase in power and speed, IT prices have also been falling. The price of microprocessor function in millions of instructions per second (MIPS) has fallen by orders of magnitude, from $230 in 1991 to just 10¢ in 2003.

The rapid price erosion of IC chips implies that during each technology node (Moore's law), the profitable market window is small. In other words, there is only a short period of time during which the sales of new semiconductor chips can be profitable. Charles Webber of MIT has modeled the effect of rapid price erosion of IC chips on the economics of chip manufacturing and has concluded that rapid yield learning in production ramp is the crucial and determining factor in the profitability of IC manufacturing.[27]

The dramatic rise in the number of people accessing the Internet has created a network effect that increases the power of the Internet exponentially. According to Robert Metcalf, founder of 3Com Corporation, the "value" or "power" of a network increases in proportion to the square of the number of nodes on the network, i.e., going from 10 to 100 users on the Internet increases the value of the network by 100.[28]

Internet applications, in addition to e-commerce applications, have exploded in the areas of customer support, virtual manufacturing, and e-learning. The corresponding network effect has resulted in a diversity of products and services, customization and personalization, customer empowerment, and increased satisfaction. Furthermore, Internet applications have resulted in significant cost reductions and productivity improvements for suppliers and customers alike. David Moschella illustrates the increasing network effect of IT in several waves of IT development, going from the era of big computer systems in the 1970s–1980s to a content-centered era in the early half of the twenty-first century.[29]

The digital revolution is bound to continue at a strong pace for a long time to come. As the U.S. Department of Commerce reported in 1998, business opportunities abound and will be driven in many areas, including building out the Internet, electronic B-to-B commerce, digital delivery of products and services, retail sale of tangible products, new products enabling wider use of the Internet, and an enterprise "digital nervous system" for enhanced efficiency.[30] Hundreds of new firms are already set up to help businesses to use the Internet effectively—to design Web sites and advertising banners, to design search engines (Inktomi, Google, Yahoo!, Microsoft) and service provider sites, to design tools facilitating trade (maps, weather, news, public libraries, and government publications), to create Web-based catalogs, and to build security tools.

Building the communications infrastructure and developing technology to speed the flow of data and information across the network increase the ease of use, reach, and content of accessible information and accelerate the network effect. A 3.5-minute video takes 46 minutes to download using a 28.8-Kbps (thousand bits per second) modem. New technologies such as the 10-Mbps cable modem can send the same 3.5-minute video in 8 seconds.

Opportunities for building the telecommunications infrastructure are ever-present in developing hardware and software products that enable higher-bandwidth communications across existing telephone lines, including compression and faster electronic switches.

Telecommunication companies around the world are building out fiber optics networks. Optical amplification and photonic switches have been developed.

Over the past few years, there has been an explosion in the delivery of intangible goods to customers in digital form, including software, music and video content, magazine articles, radio and TV broadcasts, library content and databases, stocks trading, banking, airline ticketing, insurance policies, dictionaries, encyclopedias, and virtual trade shows and exhibits (enabling a person to "walk" through the halls of a trade show and examine the products from various suppliers). Important to note is that the supplier base of these services can be in any part of the world. Consumers can listen to classical music on their local or town radio or on the worldwide BBC radio network. Small artists can tap into a wide market. Obscure broadcasters, low-circulation journals, musicians, writers, and artists have an opportunity to make their products available to a global customer base. Global news is now available on a real-time basis from myriad sources worldwide.

Market fragmentation and diversity of products and services have also exploded. These ever-widespread changes have upset the market structure of many industries. Many businesses are disappearing (e.g., physical travel agencies) and many new ones are appearing. The cost of entry into these markets is lower because much smaller amounts of capital investment in bricks and mortar are needed and the costs of distribution and middlemen are eliminated. Marketing imagination is needed to capitalize on the tremendous opportunities that the changing world offers in developing new products and markets, reaching target customers, and capturing customers' attention.

In addition to access and choice benefits to consumers, IT has tremendously lowered costs to suppliers, increasing their profitability and shareholder value. The U.S. Department of Commerce reports that the cost of processing an airline ticket on the Internet is 8 times less than using a travel agent and the cost of retail banking transactions on the Internet is 100 times less than banking at a branch.[30]

In the field of education, including the continuous education of employees in a business organization, the opportunity for new products and services and for improvement in efficiency and reach is tremendous. Students and teachers are the ultimate knowledge workers benefiting from IT. The Internet is used as a source of global information, including great lectures and course syllabuses. Virtual classrooms are held on the Web in which students can interact, receive assignments, and submit homework. The content and pace of learning can be customized to individual student circumstances. Videoconferencing and Web-meetings allow virtual field trips to other parts of the world, tours of museums, and study at other schools. Big cost savings can be realized by not having to buy physical books because CD books can be much cheaper. For example, in 2003 a hard copy set of the *Encyclopedia Britannica* cost $600 (previously the cost was $3000) versus $60 for a CD equivalent from Microsoft. Corporate training and employee development have improved a great deal by offering many courses online, networking with universities in Web seminars, and accessing the huge global database of knowledge on the Internet. At Applied Materials Corporation Global University, 70% of courses are taken online.

For the retail sale of tangible goods, the Internet has played the role of being a huge digital marketplace in which anyone can sell anything to anyone else. Virtual stores with a virtual shopping cart, such as eBay, Amazon, and many others, have become as commonplace and as familiar to the consumer as the local town store to buy books, cars, antiques, computers, flowers, gardening supplies (with gardening tips), and much more. By contrast, businesses with physical stores offer the benefit of consumers being able to return products to the store and get their money refunded. However, even in purely virtual marketplaces, intermediaries are being created with physical stores to sell consigned goods via eBay and to handle returned products.

Web businesses are tracking customer buying patterns, targeting sales promotions, and making future purchases more convenient for customers. For example, depending on the kind of product that a customer has purchased, new models of the product or ancillary products can be offered. Barnes & Noble, Amazon, and online bookstores can present customers with a list of books on a subject that is related to a subject that they are inquiring about or to a book they have recently purchased. Two distribution models have emerged:

- *Funnel distribution*, in which a limited number of sites such as AOL, MSN, and Yahoo! control consumer access to the Internet content—Businesses are required to pay fees to secure "shelf space" on those sites.
- *Agent distribution*, such as Google, in which consumers specify their needs and search for a supplier—Suppliers pay the search engine company for a prominent listing or for a simultaneous advertisement of their products.

As the bandwidths of transmission increase, three-dimensional (3D) images of a product can be sent and "tried on" for looks and fit. For example, a customer can "try" a pair of sunglasses on an image of his/her face or "drag and set" a new piece of furniture inside his/her living room to verify that the fit and style are desirable before purchasing online. The explosion of digital appliances enables a wider use of the Internet, including sending and receiving images, voice, and data over the Internet from remote devices.

Opportunities that are enabled by IT and digital technology stretch into many new fields. Bionanotechnology and nanobiotechnology are just two examples of current fields of research at leading universities which promise new frontiers in innovative products and markets. As Carl Sagan once said, "The prediction I can make with the highest confidence is that the most amazing discoveries will be the ones we are not today wise enough to foresee."

1.7 IT AND DIGITAL TECHNOLOGY—IMPLICATIONS FOR NEW PRODUCT DEVELOPMENT AND COMPETITIVE ADVANTAGE

Rapid and continuing advances in digital technology also have profound implications in product development in many dimensions. Because of rapid change, the threat of substitution is high and a product team is often faced with a dilemma in selecting the appropriate technology. For example, in developing a new generation of a software application, a development team must decide whether to build the new application on a legacy operating system and product architecture or to adopt new ones. Lam Research and Applied Materials faced this challenge when selecting software technology in designing their next-generation 300-mm wafer products in 1998. Knowing that their product, semiconductor processing equipment, had a 10- to 15-year life, the development team had to decide whether to adopt a path of incremental improvement of the legacy and outdated (circa 1988) real-time operating system and software architecture or to adopt a discontinuous innovation path and switch to the latest software technologies in 1998 and beyond. (*Note:* A thorough study of this case will be presented in Chapter 3.)

The temptation to change the technological basis of a design also occurs in the midst of product development as new technologies become available. What should a team do—go back to the conceptual design stage and use newly available technology; ignore the new advances and stay with the original technological framework; or perhaps initiate a parallel competing path and select the "best" solution based on certain schedule/performance/cost criteria?

In the above example for development of a real-time software application, a lesson to be learned for the product development managers might be the necessity of developing a flexible, modular, object-oriented (OO) architecture that can readily migrate (at an evolutionary pace) to new technologies later in the product life cycle.

Another significant enabler in product development, made possible by digital technology, is the availability of increasingly powerful development and design tools (such as 3D solid model design), models, and simulation techniques. Modeling and simulation in product development accelerate time to market by reducing cycles of learning, reducing the need for time-consuming and costly hardware prototyping, and minimizing the risk of too-early beta testing (that can jeopardize the product and the company's credibility in the customer's mind) by simulating the customer application environment in-house and establishing a high confidence in the product's reliability before shipping it to a customer.

Collaboration among product development team members from different parts of the world is another opportunity enabled by IT. A global virtual team increases the talent pool that is available for product development and accelerates the project. For example, an engineer in India can send a new design concept or software code by e-mail at the end of the day to his/her counterpart in California for review and receive a response by time to start his/her work the next day. Currently, a widespread, common practice is to have many Indian or Russian engineers on development teams for companies in the Silicon Valley (California). For example, JPS Corporation, a small California company, manufactures global positioning systems that are developed by the company's Russian division (50 employees) at a substantial talent/cost advantage.

Another opportunity created by IT and communication technologies is the possibility of organizing and disseminating project information to all team members worldwide. Project schedules and milestones, schedule dependencies, market requirements, engineering and cost requirements, design information, test results, risk analyses, action items, and project financials can be communicated on a real-time basis to specific team members, anywhere, at the appropriate time. Project meetings and design reviews can be held as e-meetings on the Internet, circumventing the need for co-locating team members that has traditionally been deemed to be essential for communication efficiency.

The Internet "levels the playing field" in which access to information (or information flow) has been a source of differentiation in any one of Porter's forces of competition.[31] For example, because of the Internet, access to customers and suppliers is easier, the power of channels is reduced, and the cost of entry into a market is reduced (e.g., less need for a sales force, a channel, or physical assets). According to Porter, the basic forces of competition are:

- Competitor rivalry
- Entry barrier (for new competitors)
- Threat of substitute offering
- Bargaining power of suppliers
- Bargaining power of channels (distributors, resellers, etc.) and end users

The Internet does not change the nature or the forces of competition, but it weakens or strengthens the impact of certain parameters in Porter's model by leveling the information accessibility field.

For additional information about the opportunities and concepts discussed in this chapter, readers may consult the resources listed in the *Additional Reading* section.

REFERENCES

1. Patterson, M.L. *Accelerating Innovation: Improving the Process of Product Development.* Hoboken, NJ: Van Nostrand Reinhold; 1993.
2. Wheelwright, S.C., Clark, K.B. *Revolutionizing Product Development, Quantum Leaps in Speed, Efficiency, and Quality.* New York: Free Press; 1992.
3. Wheelwright, S.C., Clark, K.B. *Managing New Product and Process Development*: New York: Free Press; 1993.
4. Ulrich, K.T., Eppinger, S.D. *Product Design and Development.* New York: McGraw-Hill; 1995.
5. McGrath, M.E., Anthony, M.T., Shapiro, A.R. *Product Development: Success through Product and Cycle Time Excellence.* Woburn, MA: Rbhp Trade Group; 1992.
6. Hall, J.A. *Bringing New Products to Market, the Art and Science of Creating Winners.* New York: American Management Association/AMACON; 1991.
7. Kuczmarski, T.D. *Managing New Products.* Upper Saddle River, NJ: Prentice Hall; 1988.
8. Scheuing, E.E. *New Product Management.* Columbus, OH: Merrill Publishing; 1989.
9. Smith, P.G., Reinertsen, D.G. *Developing Products in Half the Time.* New York: Van Nostrand Reinhold; 1991.
10. Bergen, S.A. *R&D Management, Managing Projects and New Products.* Oxford, UK: Basil Blackwell; 1990.
11. Shina, S.G. *Concurrent Engineering and Design for Manufacturing of Electronics Products.* New York: Van Nostrand Reinhold; 1991.
12. Cooper, R.G. *Winning at New Products: Accelerating the Process from Idea to Launch.* New York: Perseus; 2001.
13. Kahn, K.B., Ed. *PDMA Handbook of New Product Development.* New York: John Wiley & Sons; 2005.
14. Belliveau, P., Griffin A., Somermeyer, S., Eds. *The PDMA Toolbook for Product Development, Volume 1.* New York: John Wiley & Sons; 2002.
15. Belliveau, P., Griffin A., Somermeyer, S., Eds. *The PDMA Toolbook for Product Development, Volume 2.* New York: John Wiley & Sons; 2004.
16. Merriam-Webster Online dictionary. Available at: www.m-w.com/.
17. Moriarty, R.T., Jr., Kosnik, T.J. *High-Tech vs. Low-Tech Marketing, Where Is the Beef?* Harvard Business Review Article #588012. Boston: Harvard Business School Publishing; 1987.
18. *The Economist Magazine*; 1999 February.
19. Valerian, H. *New York Times*; 2003.
20. Shapiro, C., Varian, H. *Information Rules, a Strategic Guide to Network Economy.* Boston: Harvard Business School Press; 1999.

21. Ecological Society of America. Remarks: Bruce P. Mehlman, Assistant Secretary for Technology Policy, U.S. Department of Commerce, to European-American Business Council, Digital Economy Workshop, Brussels, Belgium; April 10, 2002.
22. U.S. Department of Commerce. *Digital Economy 2002*. Washington, DC: The Economics and Statistics Administration; 2002.
23. Moore, G.A. *Crossing the Chasm*. New York: HarperCollins; 1991.
24. Moore, G.A. *Inside the Tornado*. New York: Harper Business; 1995.
25. Gates, B. *Business @ the Speed of Thought: Using a Digital Nervous System*. New York: Warner Books; 1999.
26. Gates, B. *Video: The Communication Revolution*. Speech: Stanford Breakfast Series, Stanford, CA; 1996.
27. Weber, C. Yield learning and the sources of profitability in semiconductor manufacturing and process development. In *13th Annual IEEE/SEMI Advanced Semiconductor Manufacturing Conference. Advancing the Science and Technology of Semiconductor Manufacturing* (ASMC); 2002.
28. Gilder, G. Metcalf's law and legacy. *Forbes*; 1993 September 13.
29. Moschella, D.C. *Waves of Power: Dynamics of Global Technology Leadership 1964-2010*. New York: American Management Association/AMACOM; 1997.
30. U.S. Department of Commerce. *Emerging Digital Economy*. Washington, DC; 1998.
31. Porter, M.E. *Strategy and the Internet (OnPoint Enhanced Edition)*. Harvard Business Review Article #6358. Boston: Harvard Business School Publishing; 2001 January 1.

ADDITIONAL READING

Burke, R.R. *Virtual Shopping: Breakthrough in Marketing Research*. Harvard Business Review Article #96204. Boston: Harvard Business School Publishing; 1996.
California Management Review. Special Issue: *Knowledge and the Firm*, 40(3); 1998 Spring.
Cover Story: Beyond the PC. Table: The New Post-PC Products, *Business Week*, 1999 March 8. Available at: http://www.businessweek.com/1999/00_10/63619004.htm.
Kawasaki, G., Moreno, M. *Rules for Revolutionaries*. New York: HarperCollins; 1999.
Mathiesen, M., Yang, J. *Marketing on the Internet: A Proven 12-Step Plan for Promoting, Selling and Delivering Your Products and Services to Millions Over the Information Superhighway*. Gulf Breeze, FL: Maximum Press; 1996.
Rayport, J.F., Sviokla, J.J. *Exploiting the Virtual Value Chain*. Harvard Business Review Article #95610. Boston: Harvard Business School Publishing; 1995.
Silverstein, B. *Business-to-Business Internet Marketing*. Gulf Breeze, FL: Maximum Press; 2000.

PRODUCT DEVELOPMENT STRATEGIES

Most causes of failure for a new product, such as unclear product definition, inability to match technology to an application context, lack of compelling differentiation, poor design, or commercialization mistakes, have their roots in misalignment with business or market strategies. The purpose of Chapter 2 therefore is to present a holistic framework of business, market, and technology strategies in product development. The need for integrating these strategies into a winning product strategy will also be discussed. The focus of the strategies presented will be on high-tech products in business-to-business (B-to-B) markets.

Remember from Chapter 1 that high-tech products and markets are characterized by a global, diverse, and rapidly changing nature in which global competition is stiff and customers are demanding better and cheaper products and services and demanding them faster.

Chapter 2 is divided into three sections that cover aggregate strategy, marketing management, and the product roadmap, with the following scope:

- Aggregate strategy—The principles of establishing a company's business strategy are discussed first. Next the elements of market strategy, including a holistic value chain framework and the way it relates to the changing basis of competition, are examined. Also examined are the principles of an outsourcing strategy and how product architecture and modular design should play a decisive role in an outsourcing strategy within the value chain framework. Then a framework for developing a technology strategy that is integrated with the business and market strategies is presented. Corporate aggregate strategy must be inclusive of a firm's resource strategy, identifying the resource capability gaps and the plan to fill them. (*Note*: Chapter 10 presents an aggregate product planning process that is based on the aggregate strategy discussed in this chapter.)
- Marketing management—The role of marketing in a product development environment is discussed and the job of a product marketing manager is defined. Next the *whole* product concept is discussed because the definition of a product, in the value rendered to customers, impacts the product development process, the product business model, and the product commercialization plan.

- A product roadmap—A framework for developing a product plan and a roadmap that is aligned with the firm's and the business unit's (BU) aggregate strategy is developed. Several tools and examples that are useful in developing a product roadmap and communicating it across the organization are presented.

Chapter 2 will present a model for an aggregate strategy for achieving the desired business objectives by *developing* and *integrating* the business, market, technology, and resource strategies in which the market strategy is inclusive of the firm's competitive strategy. Chapter 2 also includes several case studies in business and value chain strategy and product definition.

2.1 BUSINESS, MARKET, TECHNOLOGY, AND RESOURCE STRATEGIES

Strategy is "a scheme for gaining an end and the art of devising or employing plans toward a goal."[1] A *business strategy* must gain the "end" and the "goal" that are inspired by the corporate vision and mission statements. To be effective, strategies must be concise in vision and long in detail. Strategies should include *objectives* and how to accomplish them. They should define the critical relationships that establish priorities in decision making. Capturing the essence of an enterprise strategy in a simple and concise phrase[2] and articulating the firm's response to the *essence of the challenge* for gaining competitive advantage are important. This is particularly important in large companies in which the enterprise focus can become lost in myriad complexities and local daily priorities.

Tactics are specific actions that must be undertaken for effective implementation of a strategy. Tactics must identify the expected output of the task at hand, the time frame for completing it, and the person responsible for carrying out the action and producing the result.

A single-page "strategy template" is presented at the end of Chapter 2 to facilitate capturing the objectives, strategy, and tactics of a business endeavor.

2.2 BUSINESS STRATEGY

Burgelman et al. (1986, 1996) present various views of strategy: [3,4]

- A *positive* view that is concerned with the firm's actual strategy (stated versus practiced strategies)
- A *normative* view that is concerned with what the firm's strategy should be
- A *market/product* view that is concerned with how the firm competes with its products (*Note*: Factors for competitive advantage are reviewed later in this chapter and covered in depth by Porter.[5,6])
- A *resource-based* view that is concerned with how to secure factors (including resources) to create core competencies and alliances for competitive advantage

Some companies are disenchanted with strategic planning because they feel that the rapid pace of change in high-tech markets makes any strategy obsolete within a short time. However, without a strategy, any success will be short-lived. Without a *clear* strategy, people will become disillusioned and their strength will be fragmented by not knowing where they are headed, what their priorities are, and how they are to proceed. Successful strategies are updated as frequently as necessary to respond to changing market conditions and contextual influences within the company.

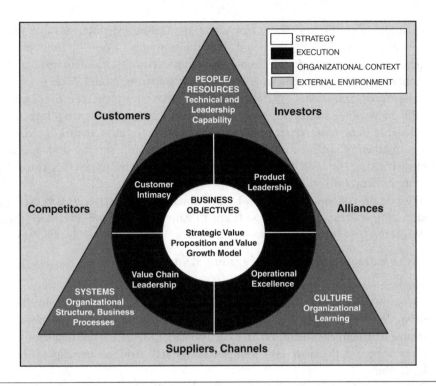

Figure 2.1. Framework—Aggregate Strategy for Sustained Business Leadership.

Figure 2.1 illustrates a holistic framework for an aggregate strategy, relating the core business objectives to the success factors in formulating and executing plans, to the factors of the organizational context, and to the players in the external environment. The remainder of this chapter will apply this framework in examining the strategies that a firm must develop and enact for success in product development and commercialization.

As Figure 2.1 demonstrates, a multitude of factors must be considered in the development of a firm's aggregate strategy in order to achieve sustained business leadership that is characterized by:[7-9]

- Delivering customer benefits that are different from those of competitors
- Managing customer value and profitability
- Extracting customer value in terms of enhanced cash flows and reduced risk and vulnerability, thereby driving shareholder value
- Achieving sustained profitability by setting goals for superior return on investments (ROI) in technology assets and product development and by devising a detailed action plan for flawless execution
- Balancing profitability, growth, and risk across multiple businesses and opportunities
- Establishing value chain leadership by acquiring a commanding power position and by adopting *distinctive* technology-enabled practices, e.g., manufacturing, logistics, service, and human resource management that are different/better than rivals (Merely adopting the best-known methods at best creates competitive parity.)
- Not attempting to be all things to all customers (Robust strategies result from trade-offs that abandon certain products or activities, so the firm can gain focus and acquire uniqueness in other areas.)

- Maintaining continuity of strategic direction (Define a distinctive value proposition and stand up for it, which will allow the company to develop unique capabilities in people skills and technology, to develop assets, and to gain a strong reputation with customers, thereby establishing a strong brand value.)
- Assessing organizational capability gaps in achieving business objectives and establishing a resource strategy that includes people, assets, and systems for operational excellence (The resource strategy must define how all the elements of a company, e.g., marketing, engineering, manufacturing, sales and service, and operational infrastructure, fit together and reinforce each other, which makes competition more difficult for rivals, who can easily excel in one element.)
- Aligning the corporate culture and value system with the strategic context, e.g., by attracting and retaining the best talent to gain a competitive advantage through people

Additionally an enterprise business strategy must identify:

- The business the firm is in, based on its mission and vision statements
- The strategic value proposition for competitive advantage, including products and technologies—State the strategic principle in a simple and concise phrase. The strategic principle is the differentiating essence of the enterprise that should guide every action in the firm. For example, Wal-Mart's strategic principle is low-cost leadership.
- Revenue, profitability, market position, and growth objectives based on the corporate business model in different business cycles (including downturns, steady state, and upturns)
- Operational plan priorities in systems, infrastructure, and the supply chain
- Resource capability in makeup, core competency, and cultural values
- Strategic initiatives for new business and for improvement in organizational effectiveness and efficiency

2.3 MARKET STRATEGY

Market strategy is a careful plan and a method of business that is exercised to meet the competition in the marketplace under advantageous conditions and to gain maximum customer value. The terminology of *market* strategy (not *marketing* strategy) is used purposefully. Traditionally marketing experts and practitioners use the term *marketing strategy* to mean "a strategy that is limited to the marketing mix and establishes a plan of being customer-centered in development and delivery of differentiated value to the customers." While supporting that need, marketing and business leaders must *go further* and develop and implement a *market strategy* that creates loyal customers and maintains competitive advantage, but that also extracts the maximum value in the value chain. Extracting maximum value means having an advantageous bargaining position with respect to other players in the value chain, including customers, suppliers, partners, complementors (suppliers of other products that customers use in conjunction with your product to satisfy their needs), distributors, and retailers. A market strategy must be comprised of three objectives:

- To establish the firm's desired position in the value chain ecosystem

- To assess the industry's structure, market forces, and players and their interactions
- To devise a plan for achieving the desired position

It is important to note that over business cycles, the ecology of the market transforms and shifts the balance of force among the participants. This creates a continuous challenge in achieving the desired value chain position with respect to the customers, competitions, suppliers, complementors, and channels (horizontal and vertical). Forces acting on the value chain ecosystem include:

- The customer's product life cycle and technology roadmap
- Continuous and discontinuous technological innovations
- The customer's acceptance/absorption rate of a new technology and the compatibility of the technology with the customer's operating practices and products (A discussion of the technology innovation adoption life cycle is presented later in this chapter.)
- The customer's operating environment, buying behavior, and business model
- Changing basis of competition from technology and function to reliability, user-centricity, and cost
- Industry maturity and transition from push (new product, application, technology) to pull (mature, known, high dependency) market conditions
- Standardization of platforms and interfaces within the company and across the industry
- Formation and demise of market network relationships and alliances
- Distribution channel transformation by technology and alliances

To formulate an aggressive but realistic market strategy, a firm must understand the sources of sustained business leadership as the overarching goal of the enterprise. The main constituents of business leadership are *product and technology leadership* (through innovation and commercialization); *market leadership* (through competitive differentiation, customer intimacy, and a commanding value chain position); and *operational excellence* (through global resource leadership and flawless execution). In the following sections, these elements are discussed in more detail and illustrated with case studies.

2.3.1 Product and Technology Leadership

Factors that contribute to product leadership are discussed throughout this chapter in more detail. These factors include:

- Innovation in technology and in product and process design
- Commercialization timeliness and effectiveness
- Competitive differentiation in product and service offerings and in customer experience
- Company and product positioning and customer value perception
- Customer intimacy and relationship management
- High switching cost to customers (*Note*: The switching cost is high when customers cannot readily define or verify the desired product performance and when it takes a long time to qualify a new supplier.)
- Control of interdependent product interfaces (See *Bases of Value Capture and Competition in the CMP* in Chapter 3.)

CASE STUDY—INTEL PRODUCT LEADERSHIP IN THE PC MICROPROCESSOR MARKET

A senior executive at Intel Corporation has explained why Intel developed a motherboard for personal computers (PCs). First, Intel developed a motherboard product not only because they wanted to enter the motherboard business, but because they also wanted to demonstrate that Intel microprocessors could be properly integrated onto the motherboard of a PC system. Unless Intel could demonstrate that, the Intel microprocessor was not useful to PC-maker customers such as Compaq or Dell Corporation. Second, Intel developed the motherboard to enhance Intel's power position in the supply chain, particularly with respect to their customers. Intel did not want any of its customers to become too strong. Therefore Intel helped their smaller customers with motherboard design (among other things) to gain strength against larger PC providers. For example, at one time, Intel helped Compaq to compete more effectively against IBM and later helped Gateway to compete against Dell. Third, Intel wanted to control the interface of the microprocessor with the motherboard and hence retain the value of the microprocessor, allowing the motherboard rather than the microprocessor to become a commodity. This strategy gained a commanding position for Intel in the PC market (to be discussed later; also see Figure 2.4).

- Customer interface control
- The opportunity and threat of disruptive technology as the market and technology evolve[10] (See *Bases of Value Capture and Competition in the CMP Supply Chain* in Chapter 3.)
- Strength and defensibility of the intellectual property (IP) portfolio in the differentiators and enablers of customer value parameters
- Tools and practices of design and development
- Product life cycle management capability in extending the product life through successive introduction of upgrades and derivative products, maximizing profitability and in managing the end of life
- Manufacturing technology and manufacturing processes (For example, in semiconductor manufacturing, *process* includes methods of depositing, patterning, and etching thin films using the appropriate process equipment. For equipment manufacturing, *process* includes methods of fabricating specialty materials of construction, e.g., the process of coating high-purity graphite with silicon carbide, or of making polishing pads and slurry for planarizing thin films, e.g., in the chemical mechanical planarization process.)
- Integrating complementary products and services from a network of suppliers and alliances and offering customers a total solution that fulfills their needs and provides a satisfactory experience
- Ease of integration of the product into the customer's product or process

2.3.2 Market Leadership

Market leaders have a commanding market share and attract superior customer value for their products. Commanding market share is achieved through competitive advantage and by delivering differentiated benefits to customers. The value of a product is related to a firm's power position in the supply chain relative to the other players. Figure 2.2 depicts the players in the value chain and a brief analysis of the sources of power that a firm must consider in developing a strategy for value superiority. This analysis is based on Michael Porter, who identifies the

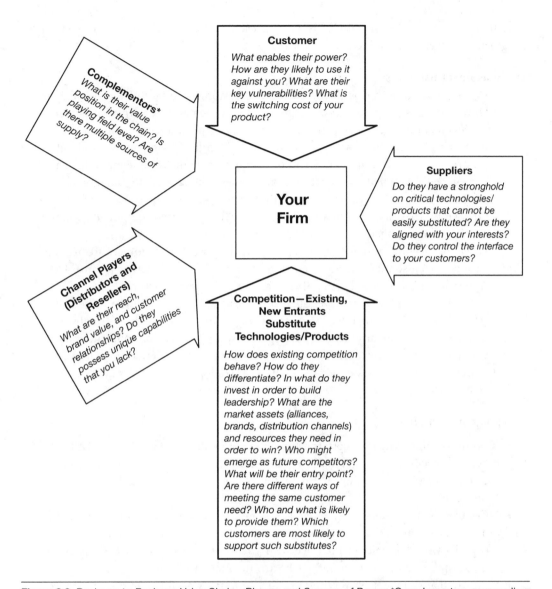

Figure 2.2. Business-to-Business Value Chain—Players and Sources of Power. *Complementors are suppliers of other products that customers use in conjunction with your product to satisfy their needs.

basic forces of competition as being competitor rivalry, the entry barrier for new competitors, the threat of a substitute offering, the bargaining power of suppliers, and the bargaining power of channels and the end users.[11] In addition to the factors listed in Figure 2.2, other value chain power factors include:

- Control of industry standards in products/process architecture and customer interfaces
- The "choke point" in the value chain created by formation of alliances or holding a controlling position on a technology or product
- Strategic asset management and control, including manufacturing facilities, global support infrastructure, installed base, brands, and channels

Actions that a firm can take with respect to each of the players in the value chain to strengthen its power position include:

Actions against Customers:
- Develop a relationship with the customers' customers. Intel did that with their "Intel Inside" strategy to cause PC consumers to demand PCs with Intel microprocessors rather than an AMD microprocessor. Semiconductor equipment manufacturing companies can collaborate with "fab-less" companies to develop proprietary process technologies (on their equipment) that enable manufacturing of new chips designed by the fab-less companies. The fab-less IC (integrated circuit) companies, in turn, will demand that their suppliers (the contract manufacturing foundries) use their new process and buy the associated equipment from the collaborating supplier.
- Level the playing field for customers by helping weaker customers to become stronger against their stronger customers. Intel helped Gateway against Dell. Applied Materials could help SMIC, a young IC manufacturer in China, to become a strong foundry player against the leader, TSMC of Taiwan. When IBM refused to design-in the Intel 386 microprocessor into their PC unless Intel would give IBM a 10-year pricing guarantee plus a second source option, Intel helped Compaq to move ahead of IBM in the PC business. Suppliers can "light a fire" under late-adopting customers by helping early adopters with their new enabling technologies.

Actions against Suppliers:
- Minimize the switching cost to your company—Buy "commodities" with well defined specifications and retain the value in the final product with the firm's proprietary methods. Develop alternate sources of supply and "commodify" their products.
- Control the value-added subsystems or interfaces of your product by keeping the design and manufacturing of subsystems or interfaces in-house. Standardize the supplier's product and its interface with your system. Do not allow suppliers to move up the value chain from their horizontal market space.
- Ensure that suppliers extend their product support (warranty and on-site service) to your customer's site (at no charge) to lower your installation and warranty costs. This should be done without allowing suppliers to become intimate with the end users or to manage the interface with your customers. On the surface, this approach might appear to be in sharp contrast with the strategy of a "win-win partnership with suppliers" as advocated by Dyer.[12] According to Dyer, U.S. car manufacturers "have radically pruned the ranks of their suppliers and given more work to the survivors in return for lower prices. And by getting their remaining suppliers to deliver parts Just in Time (JIT) and to take responsibility for quality, they have managed to slash inventories, reduce defects, and greatly improve efficiency of their own production lines." This strategy of "partnership" works well. It is recommended as long as the above-stated provisions are built into the relationship with suppliers and the balance-of-value vector is in your company's favor.

CASE STUDY—SUPPLIER MANAGEMENT STRATEGY AT HYTEC CORPORATION

Setting. HyTec is a leading semiconductor supplier with a reputation for excellence in operational excellence. The HyTec supplier management manual (internally know as PICOS) outlines a comprehensive strategy of dealing with suppliers that includes contractual, financial, formal/informal communications, and even psychological guidelines. The manual also indicates that supplier management is the job of every employee who interacts with a supplier, from the R&D and Engineering Departments to the Purchasing Department and to executive management. The objective of the manual is for HyTec to have a unified approach toward its suppliers to enhance the company's power position with respect to suppliers and to maximize the value of HyTec's products in the supply chain.

Situation. The following example demonstrates HyTec's PICOS methodology in action in dealing with suppliers. The situation is a typical meeting between the executives of a supplier of process equipment and HyTec executives in charge of managing the suppliers of factory (fab) equipment. The executives represented technical, sales, contract, and business expertise from both sides. The objectives of the meeting were twofold—to inform the supplier of a HyTec request for quotation (RFQ) for new equipment that should enable HyTec to manufacture its next two generations of IC devices and to review the performance of the supplier (as a company) and of its products that are installed at HyTec fabs worldwide.

HyTec demanded that the supplier's response to the RFQ must include a 5-year firm pricing quotation for the next two generations of equipment, irrespective of the fact that neither HyTec's requirements nor the supplier's product design or technology were known 5 years previously. Additionally, the supplier would not know the required investment to develop the next-generation equipment. Although the supplier knew the timing of the HyTec technology roadmap, it did not know the precise timing and the scope of the new product development. Nevertheless, HyTec obtained a firm price commitment for the undefined future product with the expectation that the supplier would "make" the product meet HyTec's requirements (when they are defined) and severe penalties would be levied if the supplier did not!

HyTec also expected that the performance of the supplier's product would be continuously improved over its life cycle, after the product had been delivered and was operating in their fab. Additionally, the supplier had to upgrade the product, at no cost to HyTec, to meet a continuous improvement program (CIP) roadmap that would be committed to by the supplier at the time of the initial product purchase. A typical CIP roadmap included improving product reliability, defect level, process performance, consumable life, unscheduled and scheduled maintenance requirements, and mean time to repair (MTTR).

In regard to the supplier's overall performance, as a company, HyTec executives asserted that the supplier was too slow and was incompetent in the execution of its commitments. Furthermore, the supplier's business processes and decision-making methodology were subpar.

Outcome. At the end of the meeting, a HyTec purchasing executive requested a detailed, written plan in response to the issues discussed at the meeting within a week. The response had to address all HyTec demands without exception.

Comment: It is important to examine the reasons why the supplier in the above case was not able to negotiate more effectively and why it capitulated to every seemingly unreasonable request by the customer. The answer lies in the fact that the power position of the customer (HyTec) and the supplier were vastly different. HyTec was the number one customer of the supplier, representing 20% of its annual bookings. Furthermore, HyTec was the technology leader of the industry. When HyTec decided to buy from a supplier, instant credibility was created for the supplier's equipment and technology in the eyes of other customers. At the same time, HyTec led the supplier to believe that HyTec had other options and that the supplier had no competitive advantage. HyTec's strategy was to make all suppliers believe that they always fell short of meeting requirements and that their business with HyTec was in jeopardy.

Actions against Competitors:

- Market domination, i.e., owning a large market share (>50%), creates a major barrier for competitors. The dominant player sets the "rules of the game" and holds the upper hand in development and commercialization of new products. For example, for many years, Intel has held more than 80% of the PC microprocessor market share against AMD. Intel has kept AMD in a defensive position and a catch-up mode with inadequate resources. (*Note*: This subject will be discussed in more detail in two later sections on competitive strategy and IP protection.)
- Setting industry standards and controlling the supply chain by establishing alliances and long-term partnership with the strong suppliers are also effective methods of establishing competitive advantage. The latter limits competitors' supply routes to only weak suppliers.

Actions against Complementors:

- Positioning your product as the most "valuable" component in an assembly or manufacturing process of an end user product is important. This must be achieved by creating the perception that your product has the most critical technology or function, is the most complex in design, is costly to make, and is the least substitutable among all other components.

The next case study examines Intel's positioning of its microprocessors against the other components of a PC, such as the memory chip, flat panel screen, the motherboard, and the operating system (OS) software. The case illustrates how the value of Intel's product has steadily gone up in comparison with the other components of a PC.

CASE STUDY—DRAMATIC ENHANCEMENT OF THE POSITION OF THE INTEL MICROPROCESSOR IN THE PC VALUE CHAIN

Figure 2.3 shows the hardware and software components of a PC. For Intel, positioning against its complementors is establishing the Intel microprocessor as being the most "valuable" component of a PC and hence extracting the biggest share of the money that an end user pays for a PC.

Figure 2.4 shows how the value of the Intel microprocessor, as a percent of the total cost of the components to a PC manufacturer, has dramatically increased over the first 20-year life of the PC industry. The relative increase in the "value" of the microprocessor has been achieved not at the expense of the end user consumer of a PC, but by redistribution of the product's market value among the value chain players. This superior value extraction by Intel has been accomplished by flawless execution of an effective strategy that utilizes the techniques discussed above.

Rajendra Srivastava notes three sources of gaining a superior supply chain position in delivering value to customers:[7]

- Innovation and new product management (Intel)
- Operational excellence and supply chain management (Dell)
- Market-based asset management, e.g., of alliances, brands, distribution channels (Microsoft)

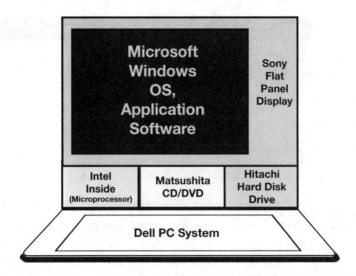

Figure 2.3. Major Components and Suppliers for a PC.

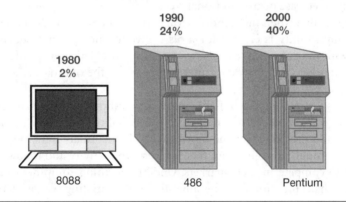

Figure 2.4. Percent of PC System Cost Attributable to the Microprocessor.

2.3.3 Operational Excellence

Operational excellence is another factor in achieving sustained business leadership. To execute flawlessly, a company must maintain value discipline in everything that it undertakes. The company must also deploy technology-enabled business processes in all operations including customer relationship management (CRM), product innovation, and the enterprise resource planning (ERP) functions as discussed in Chapter 1. (*Note*: Chapter 4 will discuss key issues in flawless execution of the product development process.)

2.4 BASIS OF COMPETITION

The differentiating features and capabilities of a product that merit premium prices will evolve as the technology and market mature. With a new technology in an emerging market, the functionality of the product is of prime importance to customers and hence is the basis of competition. According to the disruptive technology model of Clayton Christensen, the initial

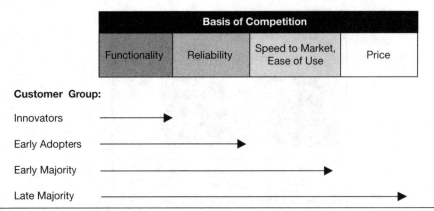

Figure 2.5. Evolving Basis of Competition over Phases of Technology Adoption Life Cycle.

technology drive of high-tech companies and markets will, as the market matures, eventually result in a situation wherein the performance of the offered product overshoots the performance demanded by the market tier participants and hence the basis of competition changes to reliability, time to market, ease of use, and finally cost.[10,13]

Christensen argues that when the technological performance of a product exceeds the customers' needs, an opportunity is created for a disruptive technology that begins with lower functionality, but with much higher ease of use and lower cost. This new product technology often creates a new market and a new customer base, making the old market and technology obsolete.

In the early 1980s, increasing functionality merited premium value for process equipment in the semiconductor IC manufacturing market. As the size of the electronic market grew and many competitors could provide the same functionality, IC manufacturers looked for equipment reliability and throughput to increase their factory productivity and to lower their operating cost in order to compete in their markets. Underperforming equipment reliability and throughput, rather than functionality, became the differentiating value that customers demanded from equipment suppliers.

In addition, as the competition stiffened in end-user electronic markets, time to market for new IC capabilities became the compelling competitive advantage for the IC manufacturers. Therefore, short time to market was also demanded of the equipment suppliers. Although cost has always been a factor in the customer's decision-making process, cost is becoming the prime differentiator of the process equipment in the first decade of the twenty-first century. The semiconductor equipment market is maturing and products are becoming commodities that multiple suppliers can provide with the same functionality, reliability, manufacturing capacity, and time to market.

The basis of competition also changes in the technology innovation adoption life cycle in a similar manner. As the customer base changes from innovators and early adopters to the majority adopters of the technology, the basis of competition shifts from functionality to reliability, speed to market, and finally to price, as illustrated in Figure 2.5.

The market strategy for winning a strong power position in the value chain and for creating compelling competitive advantage has profound implications on product design development, manufacturing, and outsourcing choices. (*Note*: Chapter 3 discusses product design architecture and platform in detail and demonstrates how they greatly impact where value goes and therefore should be carefully considered in formulation of the market, technology, and product strategies.)

2.5 COMPETITIVE STRATEGY

In developing a competitive strategy, the sources of competitive threat, the basis of competition, the customer's buying behavior, and the framework for value chain positioning that have been discussed above must be understood. Competition for a firm's product or service is a customer's alternative means of satisfying his/her needs and wants. Factors shaping a customer's buying behavior include:

- Choices offered by competitors
- Threat of substitution by a disruptive technology
- Mismatch to the customer's context or operating environment

Choices. The choices offered to a customer by the existing, new, or planned products and services of competitors are traditional sources of threat that influence the customer's buying behavior.

Disruptive technology. The threat of substitution by a disruptive technology can make a firm's product or even a market obsolete. For example, the read/write compact disc storage device has replaced the Zip drive that in turn had rendered 3.5-in. floppy drives antiquated. DVD technology is replacing video tape players and is destroying the cellular tape market for home video applications. Copper interconnects have replaced aluminum in the manufacturing of IC logic devices. Digital imaging will replace dental and medical X-ray films (similar to digital photography) and will render the market for X-ray films and processing equipment obsolete. Disruptive technology may be invented internally by a firm's own engineers (in competition with their older technologies), by competitors, or by neutral third parties such as universities and government labs. Disruptive technology might even be imported from another industry. For example, providers of automation technology to the automotive industry are applying their technology to automate semiconductor manufacturing factories (fabs), which is threatening many "old time" players in the semiconductor industry.

Mismatch. Mismatch to a customer's context and operating environment is a barrier for market penetration of a new product or technology. Mismatch manifests itself as a customer's resistance to changing his/her "old" mode of operation. This occurs when the supplier's high-tech product is not simply replacing an older technology and is not equivalent in function and method of use to the existing products (in use by the customer), but requires a change in the customer's behavior or environment.

Customers resist changing their behaviors because the new product lacks a compelling benefit, it is perceived as a high risk, and it is not useful to the customer without a complementary product that is not yet available in the market. For example, in the semiconductor fabrication market, customers may negatively react to an etch-back alternative to their existing and "proven" CMP practice for planarization of thin films because etch-back and CMP are not "identical" methods and because much data is required to demonstrate that the etch-back benefits clearly outweigh its risks. Similarly, dentists and insurance companies have been using X-ray films to record images of patients' teeth and have transmitted information by mailing X-ray and paper copies for a long time. Switching to an all-digital processing system will be resisted unless its benefits versus its perceived risks are demonstrated and until a majority of the players in the dental market (including dentists, insurance companies, transaction processing intermediaries, and lawyers) have adopted the new technology, thereby creating a network effect that renders the digital technology useful. Therefore, to successfully commercialize a new technology product, a supplier must have a deep understanding of the customer's operating environment and enable a total solution (including the complementary products and services) that creates a compelling customer benefit that outweighs the risk and "pain" of switching to the new technology.

The process of developing a competitive strategy is comprised of three steps:
- Analyze the situation within the strategic context.
- Devise a strategy, listing what must be done.
- Create an implementation plan.

Step 1. Analyze the situation within the strategic context. The purpose of this step is to gain an understanding of the market "battlefield," including the customer's mind, relative to your product's positioning, economic situation, and trends—what is your product's position in the market segment and is there a compelling reason to buy your product? Next is to understand the competition—who or what is your competition, what is the basis of competition, what is the competitors' position and strategy in the segment, and what are the competitive threats and market barriers that you are facing? Articulate why you are losing or winning. Assess the factors that shape the customer's buying behavior in the target segment as discussed above. The competitive strategy must be an element of the firm's aggregate strategy to capture not only market share, but also value. Analysis of the strategic context must include an analysis of the distribution of value in the chain and where the money goes. Is your market position being limited by the content of your product offering or by your outsourcing strategy? (*Note*: The CMP case discussed later in this chapter examines some of these issues.)

Step 2. Devise a strategy and list the things that must be done. The strategy must be responsive to the root causes of the gap between the firm's current position and the desired market position. The company may need a new product or it must fix the problems with the current product that are causing a loss of market share. Perhaps a better definition or revision of your *whole product* is needed when that product might lack the necessary ancillary products, development tools, and even documentation that enable a customer to use the product efficiently. In other words, a complete solution to customers' needs/problems might be missing. Educating customers to mitigate their uncertainty, or to improve their productivity and ability to use your products efficiently, may be needed. Another part of the competitive strategy might be a definition or clarification of your positioning statement that not only does not play to competitors' strengths, but also builds on your firm's own strengths. A new promotional and public relations (PR) campaign might be in order. Providing more information and references to customers to mitigate their fears, uncertainties, and doubts (the FUD factor) might be the next action, particularly when the product and technology are new and would change your customers' current modes of operation. The early majority customers in a technology adoption life cycle want to see your competitor's products before they feel comfortable enough to buy. Therefore your company should articulate for customers what solutions and which companies are the competition and what the advantages and disadvantages of the competing solutions are compared to your value proposition. Another important action in competitive strategy is to create barriers to blunt prospective attacks from competitors. Barriers that make entering a market costly for competitors include customer loyalty; protected technology and know-how; sustained first-mover advantage through agility in product introduction; and control of market-based assets (e.g., manufacturing facilities, global support infrastructure, installed base, exclusive alliances and channels, and brands.) A competitive strategy should also include a plan to create competition for your own products and be your own best competition, through discontinuous innovation and continuous improvement of existing products and services.

Step 3. Create an implementation plan. The strategy in Step 2, *Devise*, must accompany a detailed implementation plan, which identifies task ownership, milestones, success indicators, and a schedule for accomplishing the action items.

CASE STUDY—JAPANESE SEMICONDUCTOR MANUFACTURERS— LOSS OF LEADERSHIP DUE TO INADEQUATE RESPONSE TO THE CHANGING BASES OF COMPETITION AND MARKET NEEDS

Setting. In the 1980s, Japanese semiconductor providers focused on DRAM (dynamic random access memory) manufacturing, heavily invested in R&D, developed novel manufacturing expertise, and hence achieved unprecedented excellence in yield enhancement and captured the "high ground" of the global market. The basis of the competitive advantage of DRAM was function, low cost, and high quality. Japanese firms excelled in everything—higher yields enabled aggressive pricing and excellent quality management practices delivered superior product reliability and performance. Companies such as Toshiba and NEC drove most American competitors out of the DRAM market (notably Intel).

Situation. The impressive success in the 1980s and early 1990s made Japanese companies extremely manufacturing oriented and overconfident. One effect of this spectacular success was a gradual and significant reduction in R&D investment. By the year 2003, projections were that the top five Japanese semiconductor companies—Hitachi, NEC, Toshiba, Sony, and Fujitsu—would invest $2.3 billion in semiconductor R&D combined. This amount was about half of the projected investment by Intel alone in that year!

Another effect of this success was becoming "blinded" by the old paradigms and "looking at the rear window mirror" when forming future strategies. As a result, Japanese companies continued to focus on the old paradigm of yield enhancement to maintain competitive advantage.

Outcome. In reality, by the mid-1990s, the major competitors in the United States (Micron) and Korea (Samsung) had already caught up with the Japanese in high-yield manufacturing techniques. Japanese yield levels in the late 1990s were quite high—in the 90% range. Therefore Japanese companies wanting to improve their yield even further (by only a few percentage points) had to add many inspection steps (and tools) to the manufacturing process and use many monitor wafers. These added steps increased the manufacturing cost, cycle time, and time to market, offsetting the productivity benefits of a slightly higher yield. In contrast, U.S. and Korean competitors were reducing manufacturing costs and manufacturing cycle times with new and innovative techniques such as simplifying the manufacturing process, reducing the number of mask layers and process steps, and using fewer inspection tools and fewer monitor wafers. In a 2002 fab design, Micron was using 50% less processing equipment than Toshiba for the same output capability!

Additionally, in the late 1990s and early 2000s, the nature of products, solutions, and markets was changing in the semiconductor and electronics industries. DRAM had become a commodity whose price collapsed to $1 to $2 only a few months after the production ramp, irrespective of its capacity and technological complexity. There was an explosion of software and systems products. The complexity of the surrounding industry (for ancillary products) was increasing and the interdependency in the value chain was increasing. Because the components had become mostly commodities, product differentiation (and value creation) was shifting toward more complex system solutions.

By the dawn of the new millennium, Japanese companies, recognizing these new realities, were aggressively remodeling their strategies, alliances, partnerships, and internal organizations and planning to respond to the emerging digital convergence of consumer, enterprise, entertainment, and data processing segments of the electronics market. There was a need for new and innovative platforms for IC, software, and application designs. The market had shifted from an industrial- and manufacturing-focused economy to an applications-driven and custom solutions-focused market.

2.6 TECHNOLOGY STRATEGY AND ROADMAP

The objective of a technology *strategy* is to guide a firm in acquiring, developing, and applying technology for a competitive advantage and for enabling the aggregate business/market strategy. A technology *roadmap* specifies the technological requirements that a firm needs to enable its aggregate strategy, irrespective of how the firm will access the technology. Technology can be accessed through multiple means, including in-house development, the purchase of technology rights from a third party (e.g., a university), the formation of a network alliance, and access to a suppliers' technology by outsourcing the design or manufacturing of the product, its subsystems, and its components. In addition to the traditional tangible assets, technology knowledge is also recognized as an asset.

Peter Drucker posits the emergence of a "postcapitalist society," in which "the real controlling resource and the absolutely decisive factor of production" is neither capital nor land nor labor. It is knowledge. Instead of capitalists and proletarians, the classes of a postcapitalist society are "knowledge workers and service workers."[15]

The ubiquitous acceptance of the Internet and IT as effective tools of commerce and communication underscores the role of high technology as the enabler of a knowledge-based society. The Internet is transforming information endeavors in the marketing mixes of place and promotion away from traditional means. The Internet is enabling new products and is changing value (pricing) strategies (see Chapter 1).

2.6.1 Technology Strategy—Objectives and Methods

As stated earlier, products are the application of technology to the market context. As such, either technology or application is the driving force for the industrial production of products and services.

When technology is new, imaginative applications in existing or emerging markets are perceived. These perceived future opportunities fuel the investment of resources in development of the technology. In the semiconductor industry, Moore's law, which predicts that the speed of IC devices will double every 18 months, has established a technology roadmap for the semiconductor industry that drives the entire value chain of products and markets. New technologies, products, and markets have emerged for chip design, chip manufacturing, process equipment design/manufacturing, and many supporting businesses. The semiconductor industry roadmap for technology development, or the International Technology Roadmap in Semiconductors (ITRS), became the industry driver as imaginative entrepreneurs envisioned more powerful and lower-cost computing and communication applications and created the digital economy. Today genetics and bioengineering applications are seen, with new innovations such as stem cell research driving an explosive growth in the medical, agriculture, and biotechnology industries. As technology matures, or as the functions of technology surpass customers' needs, an industry will transform from a technology-driven to an application-driven mode in which new applications drive the technology for new and improved functions, higher reliability, improved ease of use, and lower cost. Video games with movie-like resolution, flash memory cards for digital cameras, low-cost computers (<$1000), and video cell phones with Internet connectivity and wireless networked appliances are a few examples of applications that have been driving many technological development in the semiconductor industry. New semiconductor technologies such as system-on-chip (SOC) technology are now being driven by the demand for new market applications. (*Note:* This discussion does not include the early research phase of science and technology development when applications or productizing opportunities are not yet perceived.) Whether an industry is technology driven or application/market driven, the technology strategy and technology roadmap of a company should be based on several types of opportunities, including:

1. The future needs of existing business customers based on their technology and product roadmaps, e.g., process equipment design and process technology in 2004 for 45-nm IC manufacturing in 2007

2. The evolution of derivative technologies that improve the capabilities and competitive differentiation of existing products, e.g., adoption of Java software language and other object-oriented (OO) software technologies in semiconductor process equipment for better reliability, shorter time to market, and a more friendly graphical user interface (GUI)

3. Enabling new applications and emerging market, e.g., voice-over IP and SOC

4. Creating competitive insulation/entry barriers and enhancing competitive advantage through manufacturing process, logistics, or operational efficiency

5. Inventing disruptive products to substitute the existing products and markets, e.g., digital cameras obsolescing cellular camera film

6. Inventing new products to create new markets, e.g., nano-/biotechnologies for energy generation

---

EXAMPLE OF A TECHNOLOGY ROADMAP—DEVELOPMENT OF PROCESS EQUIPMENT FOR DEPOSITION OF VERY LOW DIELECTRIC (VLD) CONSTANT FILM IN THE SEMICONDUCTOR MARKET

The technological bases for this product are the first two opportunities in the above list:

- **Type 1.** Process technology for depositing a thin film that has the required electrical (the dielectric constant), mechanical (structural strength), and other properties—The electrical and mechanical properties were specified by the industry's ITRS for the 45-nm technology node. The other properties were derived from the IC manufacturers' needs for process integration and device yield. A new material and thin film deposition technique was needed. The new material required new technologies in its chemical formulation and production process. The deposition technique of the new material required a new process equipment design, a new deposition process recipe, and a new integration scheme in IC manufacturing. The new material had to be developed in partnership with chemical suppliers; the process equipment and deposition technique were slated for in-house development; and the IC integration technology had to be developed in partnership with the customers. In addition to developing the new process chambers, the company had to develop new sensors and measurement algorithms that enabled advanced process control (APC) and diagnostics that were necessary for the process of depositing the new film.

- **Type 2.** Technologies that were independently planned for development by other divisions of the corporation as a part of their technology roadmap to improve equipment throughput and productivity for competitive advantage—These improvements were deemed necessary in the new VLD product for competitive advantage. They included (1) factory automation (FA) software that incorporated the industry's automation standards to enhance the productivity of the emerging 300-mm fabs and (2) a new vacuum robot in the transport chamber (see Figure 4.10) that would improve the system throughput to the best-of-breed status in the industry.

The above technological advances constituted the technology strategy and technology roadmap of the product BU and were integrated with the division's market strategy, product roadmap, and resource strategy.

2.6.2 Framework for Developing a Technology Strategy

The advent of knowledge-based markets and high-tech products/services has created an unprecedented entrepreneurial opportunity for both large and small companies. Technology has emerged as a primary asset of an enterprise and technological entrepreneurship has become a competitive imperative in promoting innovation within the enterprise. Corporations need more technology-savvy managers who understand the technology, seek and judge relevant advice, and frame strategic questions related to technology. Because of the rapid pace of change in technology and in the high-tech market environment, the integration of technology and business strategies must be a dynamic process.

Figure 2.6 depicts a framework for development of a technology strategy based on a firm's business and market strategies.[16] (*Note*: Development of a technology portfolio will be discussed in more detail in Chapter 10.) Technology strategy is driven by the firm's strategies for achieving the business objectives and the desired position in the value chain according to the basis of competition. Also, in an iterative process, the technology and resource strategies interact based on what is considered to be the firm's core competency and the existing technology portfolio (Figure 2.6). The interdependency of the technology and resource strategies and their purpose in enabling a firm's business and market objectives underscore the need for an aggregate planning process. Technology strategy maps:

- How to build a technology portfolio that creates sustained competitive advantage by means of one or more of the following—product and process differentiation, manufacturing efficiency, infrastructure capabilities for operational excellence, unique distribution system, and differentiated customer service and support (see Chapter 10).
- How to build a technology portfolio for competitive insulation or for defensive purposes
- Whether the technology should be developed in-house or be acquired through cross-licensing, alliance networking, or through the supplier base
- A plan for the existing technologies that should be targeted for divestiture or cross-licensing
- A plan for protecting the firm's existing or new IP through patents and other means (see Chapter 10)

In order to assess the strengths and weaknesses of an existing technology portfolio and to develop an investment strategy for attaining the desired portfolio, the firm must examine its needs for technology in enabling competitive differentiation and superiority. The enabling technological opportunities must be identified along three strategic dimensions of the enterprise:

- Development of products and services
- Strengthening the firm's value chain assets (distribution, customer service, customer relation, market intelligence, and others)
- Improving its operational efficiency (manufacturing and enterprise systems)

The company must also understand its "technology position," i.e., protect the existing IP, develop new technologies, and acquire the needed technology from a third party. Figures 2.7a, 2.7b, 2.8, and 2.9 provide frameworks for a technology assessment.

Figure 2.7a depicts the key technologies and the BU's (or the company's) existing products (or the products that are on its product roadmap) and identifies the firm's relative strength in

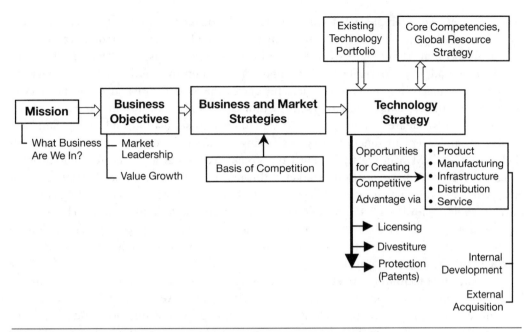

Figure 2.6. Framework—Development of a Technology Strategy.

each technological area vis-à-vis competitive advantage and IP control and protection. Figure 2.7b depicts an example for a semiconductor process equipment supplier. Figure 2.8 helps to identify opportunities for applying technology for competitive advantage in various strategic dimensions of the enterprise, including products, processes, manufacturing, operations, logistics, marketing management, sales, and service and customer support. Figure 2.9 depicts a portfolio analysis by categorizing technologies according to their importance in gaining competitive advantage versus the firm's position in possessing and controlling them. Each circle in Figure 2.9 represents one technology. The size of a circle is proportional to the level of investment in resources that is required to acquire and develop that technology into a commercially successful product.

2.6.3 Technology Asset Management

Management of technology is different from the management of traditional assets. This section will briefly review the nature of technological assets and discuss the major issues in the management of technology assets, including asset utilization, asset valuation, technology acquisition, and protection of technological assets and IP.[17,18] (*Note*: Patent portfolio issues are discussed in Chapter 10.)

Nature of technological assets. Technological assets are intangible assets. They are not listed in the inventory of corporate assets on a balance sheet. Their valuation is difficult due to the lack of a reference asset or because of uncertainty in their utilization and effective commercialization. Technology is potentially reusable in multiple applications simultaneously. Its value appreciates, for a while, as utilization risk goes down. The value of technological assets also appreciates when they are protected and when the product technology is closer to commercialization. The methods of protecting IP are also different from the methods for protecting tangible assets. For example, new technology assets can be more accessible to an entrepreneur with limited resources who can innovate compared to tangible assets that require capital.

Utilization of technology assets. As seen in earlier discussions, technology assets can be used in myriad ways to create market opportunities, improve competitive advantage, or enhance manufacturing and operational efficiencies that lower cost and create barriers to entry. For example, technological assets can be utilized not only in the product and process, but also in the tools that are used for product design, modeling, simulation, and testing. Similarly, marketing management functions (e.g., collecting market information, analyzing customer behavior and CRM) can greatly benefit from potent technological assets. Technology assets might also serve as products to be marketed through licensing.[19] (Also see Reference 19 for marketing and contractual issues of licensing.) Technology can be used as a trading chip in a strategic alliance for joint R&D, co-marketing, cross-licensing, or joint ventures. The technology portfolio can also serve as a defensive or offensive arsenal in support of a firm's actions in removing entry barriers created by competitors and against other value chain players who threaten the firm's market position.

Valuation of technology assets. Valuation of technology is very important in formulating and implementing decisions regarding acquisition, licensing, divestiture, and resource allocation in development and commercialization of a technology. Several questions and issues must be considered in evaluating the worth of a technology. (*Note:* The methods shown in Figures 2.7a, 2.7b, 2.8, and 2.9 should also be employed.)

- What will the market bear? This might be difficult to determine because of the desire not divulge details to a third party or prospect and because of the uncertainty in the cost of commercializing a new technology.
- What is the technology worth as a differentiator and what is the return on the investment of acquiring the technology? In other words, what is the potential value of benefits from the technology asset in market share and profitability less any development cost? (*Note*: The case study about technology acquisition at the end of this section illustrates a few pitfalls and gains.)
- Is the technology protected? Consider protection of the technology in design, process, manufacturing, and complementary products.
- What is the stage of technology in its life cycle? Is the technology commercialized, is it mature, or is it in decline?
- What is the IP position of competitors and is there a threat of substitution by other technologies (competitive threat assessment)?

If the technology is protected by a patent, consider these additional questions:

- What is its synergistic value to other patents and products in the firm's portfolio?
- What is its value in protecting the firm's total product portfolio?
- What is its worth against competitors' patent portfolios in cross-licensing negotiations to gain access to a desired technology or to neutralize the threat of infringement law suits?

2.6.4 Technology Acquisition

The purpose of acquiring technology is to start a new venture or product line, increase competitiveness of existing products, and/or supplement a firm's captive technology portfolio. To

	Product or Process Application A	Product or Process Application B	Product or Process Application C	...	Product or Process Application N
Technology 1	Relative strength of firm vis-à-vis its competitive advantage; IP control; impact; state-of-the-art status				
Technology 2					
...					
Technology K					

Figure 2.7a. Technology/Product Matrix.

	Dielectric Etch Product Line	Dielectric Deposition Product Line	Sputtering (PVD) Product Line	...	Planarization (CMP) Product Line
1. Inductive Plasma Generation and Control	Application-critical; not protected; mature technology	Application-critical; not protected; mature technology	NA		NA
2. 6-Axis High-Speed Vacuum Robot	Not application-critical; creates competitive advantage; protected by company	Not application-critical; creates competitive advantage; protected by company	Not application-critical; creates competitive advantage; protected by company		NA
3. CMP Polishing Pad	NA	NA	NA		Application-critical; owned and protected by suppliers; alternate technology might be developed at high cost and in 2 years; high-value item
4. CMP Endpoint Detection	NA	NA	NA		Application-critical, protected by us; superior to competitive alternative

Figure 2.7b. Technology/Product Matrix—Semiconductor Process Equipment Supplier. NA, not applicable.

Strategic Dimension	Technology 1	Technology 2	Technology 3
Products			
Processes			
Manufacturing			
Operational Infrastructure and Systems			
Logistics			
Marketing/Sales			
Service			

Figure 2.8. Identifying Technology for Competitive Advantage in Strategic Dimensions of the Enterprise.

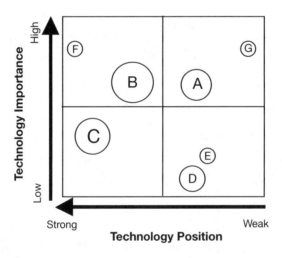

Figure 2.9. Technology Portfolio Analysis. Size of circle denotes required investment in resources for producing technology through development or acquisition.

acquire technology, first identify the desired technology and sources of supply and decide on selection criteria. Next, assess the state of development of the technology, the resources needed to commercialize the technology, the manufacturing complexity, and other relevant issues such as safety and environmental impact on the firm. This evaluation process should result in a ROI analysis (based on technology valuation) and risk assessment for review and approval by the BU general manager or company president.

2.6.5 Protection of Technological and Intellectual Property Assets

The first step is to identify inventions and know-how that create a competitive advantage. The engineering and R&D community as well as marketing and operational personnel must be astute in recognizing valuable IP. Then they must initiate the next step of protecting IP by filing for a patent or copyright and applying confidentiality protection practices. Company management must also instill this discipline of identifying and protecting IP throughout the company. Proper confidentiality practices must be exercised in communications and transactions with any outsider of the firm, including customers, alliance partners, and suppliers. Engineers and technologists who are involved in a joint development project (JDP) with a customer, the co-development of a new product with a partner, and/or the integration of a supplier's technology and product into their own new product must be cognizant of and protect the company's IP.

In a co-development effort with a customer, partner, or supplier, the team must make a distinction between the two types of IP—*background* IP that previously existed and is owned by either party and *development* IP that results from a joint effort. Development IP is comprised of IP developed by the firm, IP developed jointly, or IP developed by the partner. The ownership and rights to development IP should be assigned accordingly. Before a joint development effort is started, having the above provisions agreed upon in writing by all parties is important. In the agreement, the parties should identify background IP and document the process by which all types of development IP are identified and ownership is assigned.

2.6.6 Technology Management Issues

Shortcomings in the management of technology manifest themselves through many symptoms, including an unwillingness to share or license the "crown jewels;" a "not-invented-here" tendency against infusion of technology; turf protection; refusing to license to competitors; developing technology for its own sake; and risk averseness. These practices hinder innovation and limit creative utilization of technology assets. The root cause of these issues usually lies in lack of a technology strategy that is synergistic and integrated with the firm's business strategy.

CASE STUDY—TECHNOLOGY ACQUISITION

Setting. SPEq Corporation, a leading supplier of semiconductor process equipment, acquired free abrasive (FA) CMP technology in 1997 from FAP Inc., a start-up company, for $100 million. The CMP process is an important step in the fabrication of modern IC chips. The CMP process is used after the deposition of dielectric or conductor thin films to achieve the necessary planarity for the subsequent photolithography step to pattern the film (see Chapter 8 for more detail on semiconductor manufacturing sequence).

In this case, the FA technology is related to the method of design and fabrication of a polishing pad that was used in the FAP CMP system for polishing wafers. The FA pad is the heart of the acquired value. It enables a unique capability in the CMP process that had not previously been possible with alternate technologies and processes. Unlike pads commonly used in other CMP tools, the FA technology does not require slurry (a liquid chemical mixture) for polishing wafers. This slurry-free process resulted in production cost reduction, enhanced process performance, and improved fab safety. Additionally, FAP's novel product hardware design and their unique FA technology are also attractive because of company's solid patent protection in the use of the slurry-free process and several hardware design features. FA pads are supplied by MChem, a large chemical manufacturing company, which developed the technology for CMP applications in conjunction with FAP engineers.

CASE STUDY—TECHNOLOGY ACQUISITION (Continued)

Situation. At the time of the SPEq acquisition, FAP and MChem had developed the CMP tool and the FA pad to only an engineering prototype stage. Early prototypes of the product had been evaluated by two key customers and the FA technology had been demonstrated to be superior to the conventional technology. However, the product hardware, process, and most importantly the FA pad design and manufacturing were far from being ready for commercialization and volume production. Significant investment would still be needed to complete the product development. MChem was the sole-source supplier of the FA pad and, in fact, had an "iron" grip on the FA material and manufacturing technologies through several excellent patents and confidential IP.

After the acquisition was completed, SPEq executives discovered many new and unpleasant realities. They were faced with unexpected financial, product development, and marketing challenges. MChem demanded that SPEq pay $10 million upfront to complete the pad R&D up to the commercialization stage and to pay additional amounts (to be negotiated) for volume manufacturing tooling and life cycle performance/cost improvements. Furthermore, MChem would not relinquish technology ownership or manufacturing IP rights.

Meanwhile, SPEq product managers were faced with another major strategy problem. After the acquisition, they embarked on formulating a product marketing strategy for the acquired product in alignment with Mirror, the company's existing product line, which was very successful and had a large market share. At the time of the FAP acquisition, SPEq had 50% of the overall CMP market share and, thanks to the FA technology, had gained a 90% market share in the segment in which FA technology had proven to be most competitive.

The architecture of the FAP platform was substantially different from that of Mirror. In order to avoid having two different product platforms, engineers had to import the unique FA module of the FAP product onto the Mirror platform through a substantial, $5-million, 18-month development effort. The alternative was to offer and support two different product architectures—an approach that was unattractive to customers and costly for SPEq. This approach was not pursued.

Outcome. The FAP acquisition proved to be unfortunate for SPEq. It never produced a positive return on the investment. The market segment in which the FA technology had a compelling superiority over other technologies was small (about 15% of the total CMP market). The product's gross margin was too low to sustain development of the product and to turn a profit. Most of the market value went to the pad supplier.

MChem kept SPEq "hostage" as the installed base of the product grew (although small), asking for more development money on their own terms. Additionally, MChem would not commit to any reasonable production pricing or to a long-term supply of pads. Through the control of FA IP, MChem had a commanding power position in the value chain. The CMP pad business and the semiconductor industry were also not very important to MChem!

By the year 2000, a few key customers of SPEq had become dependent on the FA pad in their R&D labs and were weighing the decision to release the FA technology into volume production. These customers demanded to intervene in the negotiations with MChem to ensure an uninterrupted supply of FA pads should they decide to go to production. MChem cooperated (reluctantly), but at a high cost, arguing that the business opportunity was too small for them.

The only advantage of the acquisition for SPEq was, perhaps, in preventing the FA technology from falling into the hands of a formidable competitor who might have used it as a springboard to enter the CMP market.

This was the selling argument used by the executives of FAP Inc. to convince SPEq executives to acquire their company at a premium price. It worked!

2.7 PRODUCT STRATEGY

Product development and commercialization strategy is an output of the aggregate business and market and technology strategic planning, as shown in the framework of Figure 2.10. Product strategy guides the BUs of a corporation in planning the development and commercialization of a portfolio of products that enables the firm to achieve its business objectives. Product strategy also defines where to invest product development (R&D) resources. For example, should a firm direct its product development effort to serve horizontal or vertical markets, e.g., as WindRiver Systems (WRS) Corporation had to decide in 1999?

In 1999 WRS was a supplier of embedded real-time operating system (OS) software and development tools for microprocessors in a broad range of market applications, including digital imaging, industrial automation, and automotive, military, and consumer electronics and communications products. The company was weighing the decision to continue providing OS in the served market segments (horizontal markets) or to focus only on a few microprocessor-class segments and to provide a complete set of software products that went beyond the OS and included applications and the GUI—a vertical market strategy.

Another market-strategy factor impacting product development is the distribution channel design. A direct sales model differs greatly from sales through a value-added-reseller (VAR) channel in requirements for product packaging, documentation, training, and post-sales support. If multiple channels are used, the impact of product offering on creating channel conflict must also be considered in product planning.

Product strategy should also identify the mix in the *whole* product offering and decide if the company will offer a total solution to customers and assume the system integrator role in the value chain.

The commercial success criteria for a product must also be clarified and used in choosing products for the portfolio and in making investment decisions. "Breakeven time" and "return factor 1 year after commercialization" could be selected as success metrics and monitored against appropriate hurdle rates (see the Return Map in Chapter 10 for more details). As an example, Jack Welch set the success criteria for GE product lines as attaining the number one or number two market position.

The most important output of a product line strategy is the product roadmap that maps the development, commercialization, and life cycle evolution of the product in meeting the market segment needs over time. The product roadmap also provides a general guideline for the product life cycle management strategy and end of life scenario. (*Note*: The product roadmap will be discussed in detail in Chapter 3.)

The integrative nature of the framework in Figure 2.10 and the impact of aggregate strategies on product development decisions are shown in more detail in Figures 2.11 and 2.12. Figure 2.11 illustrates the technology strategy to drive the development and acquisition of necessary technologies in time for design and development of products that capitalize on market opportunities. Also shown is the market strategy to invent new product concepts and create a balanced portfolio that is commercialized to produce the desired business results in revenue and profitability. Note that the innovation and product development process grows the IP portfolio and enables the firm to further leverage its knowledge base. Figure 2.12 illustrates the market strategy (in creating a differentiated customer benefit and extracting maximum value) driving the product development decisions in innovation, commercialization, and global resource scenarios, including outsourcing and formation of partnerships.

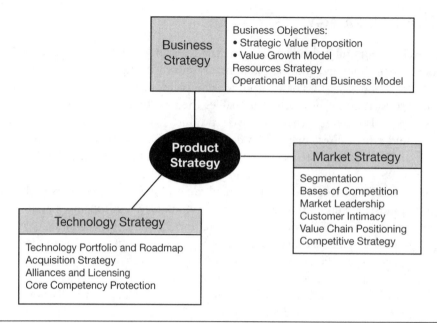

Figure 2.10. Product Strategy Framework.

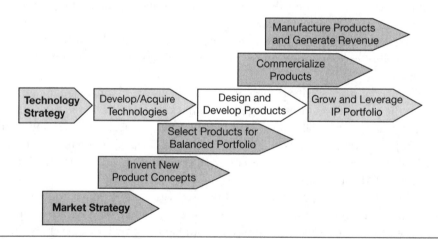

Figure 2.11. Integration of Market and Technology Strategies in Product Development.

2.8 GLOBAL RESOURCE STRATEGY

Global resource strategy considers the entire value chain and identifies the capabilities that are necessary for successful execution of a firm's strategies. Resource strategy creates a workforce scenario (e.g., identifying who, what, and where) and a competency map for the organization as well as its suppliers and complementors. "Who" identifies the competencies, diversities, and the size (how many) of the firm's work force. "What" identifies the "in"-sourced and "out"-sourced functions. "Where" defines the geographic distribution of the in-sourced and out-sourced resources.

The firm's resource strategy must be based on an assessment of the gap between the existing capabilities and the required capabilities within the firm, throughout the supply chain, and

Product Development Decisions

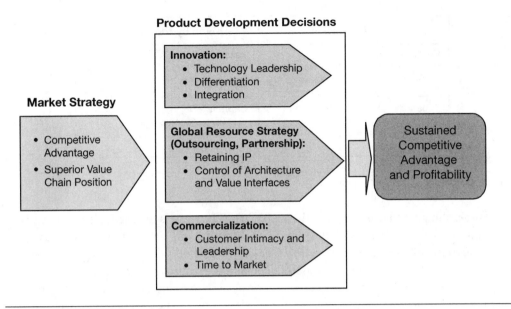

Figure 2.12. Market Strategy Driving Product Development Decisions.

in accordance with the firm's desired position in the value chain. For example, a company may decide to outsource manufacturing of commodity subsystems to contractors and to perform final assembly and testing in-house. The decision must also include where to do the final assembly (within the firm globally) and to which countries to outsource the subassemblies to achieve the lowest costs and highest-quality output. Numerous corporations also outsource many functions of the infrastructure (e.g., IT support, payroll, facilities maintenance, and HR services).

Business needs change rapidly and so do the necessary resource requirements and the optimal strategy for acquiring them. Therefore, a firm's global resource strategy has to be well integrated with the other enterprise strategies. Global resource strategy should also be formulated and reviewed on an annual basis while resource needs, plans, and prioritization decisions pertinent to product development tasks are made daily and in congruence with global resource strategy. For the annual review, the organizational capability gap in meeting the BU objectives should be identified and plans should be formulated to fill these gaps.

2.9 IMPLEMENTING STRATEGY

The challenges of implementing business, market, and technology strategies are numerous in the tough competitive environment of high-tech markets. Some of these challenges are due to environmental and competitive factors and others are related to a company's internal factors. The latter become more daunting as the company grows in size.

The development of a cohesive aggregate corporate strategy is a challenging task, but communicating that strategy, aligning priorities, and creating a linked hierarchy of objectives across organizational units are even more challenging. Often the organizational units of a large company have strategies that are not aligned with the corporate strategy and therefore possess "local" cultures that are counter to cross-peer collaboration. On the other hand, most problems

Driving the Market	Driven by the Market
Reinvent: • GE (pay by the hour at GE Aircraft) • Sony (endless innovation)	**Transform:** • Intel (memory to microprocessor) • IBM (mainframe to service)
Expand: • Cisco (acquisitions) • 3M (divide and grow)	**Capitulate:** • Lucent (weak player) • Compaq (acquired by HP)

Figure 2.13. Strategy Changes Companies.

need "local solutions" that are "close to the action." The challenge is to practice local customization while also maintaining global synergy. An effective implementation of strategy also requires accountability from everyone that is based on a set of well-understood key performance indicators (KPI) as metrics of assessment and a results-based reward system. (*Note*: Chapters 6 through 9 are devoted to *execution* of product development plans. Issues are discussed in detail, including managerial tools for effective implementation of strategies in the product development context.)

The remainder of this section will illustrate the *impact* of strategy on a company's product development and commercialization success using examples from large companies. According to Dan Maydan, president of Applied Materials, a major semiconductor equipment supplier, "Strategy changes the company." Figure 2.13 depicts several major companies whose strategy has changed them profoundly. The companies are grouped into two categories—companies who have driven their markets and companies who have been driven by the markets.

GE and Sony are excellent examples of companies who have driven their markets through continuous reinvention of their businesses, their products, and their services and have sustained their business leadership. Cisco and 3M have driven their markets through a strategy of expansion of their product lines and the market segments they serve. The companies that have been driven by their markets have either transformed themselves to survive and prosper (e.g., Intel[20] and IBM[21]) or they have capitulated to competitive pressure and have emerged as weaker players such as Lucent and Compaq (which was acquired by HP).

2.10 STRATEGY OFFICER

Some large companies create a strategy officer position at both the corporate and the BU levels as the focal point and the coordinator of:

* A strategic planning process
* Alignment of corporate and BU strategies
* Implementation of a strategic roadmap

Even with this setup, BU general managers (GMs) are to assume the "chief strategy officer" responsibilities for their organization. BU GMs, in collaboration with their peers, are responsible for the formulation of fully aligned corporate and BU-level strategies and for implementation of their respective BU-level strategy. A BU strategy officer is an assistant to the BU GM and performs several functions:

CASE STUDY—DEVELOPING AND IMPLEMENTING AN AGGREGATE STRATEGY—E-BUSINESS TRANSFORMATION OF IBM TO A SERVICE-SOLUTION AND CUSTOMER-CENTRIC COMPANY[21, 22]

Situation. Before *the transformation* in late 1980s, IBMers had become internally focused (talking to themselves most of the time) and arrogant — not listening to their customers. IBM's business was spiraling downward, with the very existence of this icon of technology innovation and marketing being in jeopardy. The solution for IBM was to become customer centric. In order to do so, IBM had to change its cultural underpinning and attitude.

The change process led by Lou Gerstner, IBM's new CEO in 1990, resulted in a major overhaul of the IBM management structure and replacement of 40 to 60% of top management. The new management structure consisted of the CEO plus a nine-member management committee, each of whom was in charge of a business or a business process.

The foundation for the change also constituted a new business strategy, a cultural and attitude transformation, and a different set of business processes, with Gerstner stating that IBM did not need technology alone, but that IBM must put customers first. The new order of priorities for IBM was established as customer *first*, company *second*, and BUs *third*.

The new customer-centric culture meant creating customer loyalty and therefore a competitive advantage for the customers. This customer-centric strategy was integrated with a new value chain/outsourcing strategy to do what was best for the customers, which even meant using a competitor's products in an IBM solution offering if a customer so preferred. The order of market priority was defined as customers *facing* the application *first* and customers *behind* the application, such as framework and infrastructure, *second*.

The next step in the change process was to improve effectiveness at the individual level and to establish a culture of "business process simplicity." The company reengineered the market planning and product development processes and integrated them with new processes in the supply chain, procurement, and production organizations. The design of the procurement process was transformed and deployed through the Web. By 2001, most procurement at IBM was Web-based. Adoption of a secure, reliable, scaleable, and extendable e-business infrastructure helped to improve integration and collaboration with customers and suppliers.

Supply chain management was transformed to reduce planning time and to implement pull replenishment and end-to-end inventory management systems. The focus was to shorten the cycle time from order entry to delivery. Inventory management improved dramatically. For example, pre-change, IBM would have 30 days of Intel Pentium chip inventory. When chip prices fell, IBM would absorb the loss. In 2001, IBM maintained a few hours of stock.

Outcome. The focus on customers became the enabler of the new service-based business strategy at IBM. The strategy was to stake out the high ground and dominate this space. IBM's overall execution approach was to centralize vision, strategy, direction, common processes, messaging, and marketing framework and to decentralize implementation. Every employee was empowered to become a change agent in the new strategy. In 2001, the service business amounted to 68% of revenue in the high-tech business segment and 45% of total company revenue.

- Represents the BU in corporate strategy activities, including quarterly reviews and annual planning meetings; resolves cross-organizational issues, develops tools, and creates an information database within a network of strategy officers throughout the company
- Supports the BU GM in setting and meeting key strategic objectives:
  - Coordinates strategic planning process
  - Ensures a strategic focus in decision making for prioritizing tasks

- Monitors strategic roadmaps of major customers and competitors and the trends in the industry; identifies misalignment between the company and customer roadmaps; anticipates competitor moves and identifies value chain and industry-strategic opportunities (This function must be closely integrated with that of the marketing managers.)
- Identifies growth opportunities in white space areas; proposes, champions, and supports creative solutions to key threats
- Adopts and deploys best-known planning and decision-making tools within the BU

2.11 GUIDELINES FOR PREPARATION AND IMPLEMENTATION OF STRATEGIC PLANS

This section provides an outline for a strategic plan document and a template for reviewing the status of progress in implementing the plan. The strategic plan document can be used as a checklist in ensuring that all pertinent issues are attended in the strategic planning process. The template is a tool that captures the key business, product, and market issues on a "single page." Using the template is recommended for regular product/marketing reviews. During these reviews, a presenter might attach additional supporting information on various issues to further an in-depth discussion. (*Note*: Similar single-page formats for reviewing product development and problem-solving projects are presented in Chapter 8.)

2.11.1 Outline—Business Strategy and Operating Plan

1. Corporate Strategy
   - Mission (What is our business?)
   - Vision (What is the future state of the business and organization?)
   - Strategic Value Proposition
   - Industry Trends
   - Opportunities and Threats in the Strategic Context
   - Firm's Response (e.g., to capitalize on opportunities, mitigate threats, create competitive advantage, and maximize value capture)
2. Strategic Plan
   - Strategic Decisions (for business objectives and priorities)
   - Product and Technology Imperatives and Objectives
   - Operational Priorities and Objectives (e.g., systems/ERP, costs, quality, HR)
   - Strategic Initiatives (e.g., new markets, programs)
3. Business and Company Makeup in the Plan Period (e.g., 3 years)
   - Resource Alignment Plan
4. Business Model and Operating Plan Assumptions and Constraints (business cycle dependence)
   - Profitability, Gross Margin as Percent of Revenue
   - Equipment versus Service Revenue Mix
   - Existing versus New Business Mix
   - Cash Flow

5. Resource Distribution and Allocation Model (for R&D, new ventures, marketing, sales, support, market assets, infrastructure, and others)

In planning a strategy, management (and the strategic officers) must ensure that the strategies of organizational units and the corporation are aligned and consistent.

2.11.2 Single-Page Strategy Template

This template for reviewing progress is purposefully designated to be a "single page" to constrain the presentation content to the confines of a single page. In this way, a presenter is forced to focus on what is most important to the successful implementation of the strategy and to highlight critical changes and risks.

1. **Vision**—Future state of the BU in market position, business, product mix, and resource capability
2. **Objective**—Specification of BU strategic objectives in the following areas:
   - Business leadership (1- to 3-year revenue, profitability, and returns targets)
   - Market and value chain leadership (market share)
   - Product and technology leadership
   - Operational excellence
3. **Opportunities (and Threats) in Strategic Context:**
   - Market environment and trends
   - Opportunities (to capitalize on)
   - Threats (competitive landscape, value chain structure, risks, technological challenges, and resource gaps)
4. **Strategy and Action Plan:**
   - List of specific actions to meet the above objectives by taking advantage of the opportunities, defending against the threats, and mitigating the risks (or turning them into opportunities)
   - Identification of key milestones, completion dates, and responsible people

APPENDIX I. OUTLINE—BUSINESS PLAN FOR A NEW PRODUCT

The following table of contents for a business plan is provided as a reference for practitioners. Elements of this plan are discussed throughout the book.

1. Executive Summary
   - Business and Market Opportunity
   - Mission and Strategy
   - Objectives and Success Criteria
   - Key Actions and Milestones
   - Executive Team
   - Funding Requirements and Return Factor
2. Business Scope and Customer Needs
   - Business Purpose, Category, and Scope
   - Value Proposition and Differentiation
   - Impact on Customers

3. Business Strategy
   - Industry Characteristics and Market Trends
   - Segmentation
   - Demand Forecast—Total Available Market (TAM) and Served Available Market (SAM)
   - Competition and Market Barriers
   - Company Strategy in:
     - Technology and IP
     - Market Assets
     - Competitive Insulation
4. Product Strategy
   - Product Development Focus
   - Key Success Factors
   - Market Penetration and Initial Target Customers
5. Business Model
   - Financial Model and Pricing
   - Sales Forecast
   - Cost Structure
   - Key Assumptions
6. Financial Plan
   - Proforma P&L
   - Balance Sheet
   - Cash Flow Statement
   - Funding for Growth
7. Operation Plan and Required Investment
   - R&D, Marketing, Sales, and Support Headcount
   - Critical IP and Protection
   - Manufacturing and Materials Plan (Outsourcing, Capacity)
   - Enterprise infrastructure (IT) and Facilities
   - Logistics
   - Partnerships
   - Investment Dollars Including Capital
   - ROI and Shareholder Value Growth
8. Implementation Plan
   - Management Team
   - Internal Alignment
   - Schedule Milestones and Accountability
   - Risk Analysis and Mitigation Strategy

APPENDIX II. CASE STUDY—AGGREGATE STRATEGY OF AN INTERNAL SUPPLIER

CASE STUDY—AGGREGATE STRATEGY OF TSI—INTERNAL SUPPLIER OF PLATFORMS AND SOFTWARE

Setting. Technology Solutions, Inc. (TSI), a large multiproduct supplier of wafer fabrication equipment in the semiconductor manufacturing industry, was founded by an entrepreneur in 1985. By 2003, TSI had grown to be a multibillion-dollar corporation. The company's growth was the outcome of an aggressive strategy of diversification and superior execution. TSI grew its product portfolio by diversifying into myriad applications of the IC fabrication process, building on its technological strength and a culture of "innovation for commercialization." By 2003, the company had over 10 different product lines that covered over 100 process steps in the IC fabrication sequence. A key contributor to the company's growth was its management philosophy of empowering the product divisions to operate akin to an independent company with P&L responsibility and autonomous product and marketing decision authority.

Although different, the products of the different divisions had much in common. They all needed the same basic wafer-handling platform and very similar control and software capabilities. When the company grew past $1 billion in revenue, the COO created a centralized manufacturing facility to serve all of the product divisions. The objective of forming a central manufacturing organization was to take advantage of economy of scale and to increase efficiencies in asset management, manufacturing overhead, and supply chain management.

Situation. The intended efficiency, however, was not recognized because the products of the different divisions were designed differently and had little in common to create an economy of scale. The obvious answer was for all product lines to use common parts whenever possible, but without jeopardizing their product's competitiveness and profitability. Hence, top TSI executives created a centralized common engineering organization in 2000, with the mission of engineering a common platform of wafer handling, system controls, and software for the products of all divisions. The initiative made a lot of sense and had the potential to minimize duplication of engineering efforts in different divisions and to maximize commonality between the different products, which was what was needed for increasing manufacturing efficiency and the company's overall profitability.

In practice, however, it did not work. The Common Platform Division (CPD) had a turnover of three vice presidents/general managers in 3 years. Two of them were veterans of the company and one was hired from the outside. A key reason for the dysfunction of the new division was that it was competing with engineers in other product divisions. The product business divisions were autonomous, had a substantial engineering capability, and had a strong NIH (not-invented-here) bias. Hence, they developed their own platforms and software and ignored the CPD. The last thing the business divisions wanted was dependence on a centralized corporate group that did not dedicate resources to meet the needs of the business divisions, was not responsive, and reported to corporate management. Another major problem was misalignment of objectives between the centralized engineering group and the business divisions. The central group's objectives were synergy and commonality of solutions across the company while the business divisions were focusing to gain competitive advantage in the market and win customer business, even if their solution was not globally optimal for corporate-wide efficiency and synergy. The lack of alignment in objectives and priorities had not been reconciled by corporate management, who preferred to have competition between the groups to promote innovation and to let the best solution win! The net result was 3 years of political infighting, causing everyone to lose. The company became internally focused and the intended efficiency of commonality and synergy was not realized.

A New Approach. In 2003, top management decided to bring in yet another outsider to lead the platform division. Upon her arrival at the company, this new vice president reviewed the history of the division and analyzed the root causes of the past failures. She knew that if she repeated the strategy of her predecessors she would get the same results. A new approach was needed. After much internal brainstorming, literature searching, and benchmarking of other large corporations (e.g., HP and GM, which had faced similar challenges), the new VP arrived at a new strategy:

CPD Strategy:

1. **Market Strategy**—Identify the market drivers and the required timing based on the customer roadmaps:
   - New applications needing a new platform
   - Need for a smaller and faster modular platforms at new fabs
   - New throughput requirements because of competitive pressure or opportunities due to changing process times
   - Cost reduction to meet business divisions' profit margin targets
   - New capabilities such as wafer preheat
   - Increasing importance of price and delivery as the primary differentiators for platform, software, and automation products

2. **Competitive Strategy**
   - Create and maintain a database of competitors, complementors, and suppliers. Have full knowledge of competitors' current products and technologies, SWOT (strengths, weaknesses, opportunities, and treats), and expected future strategies.
   - Develop the core strategy for establishing and maintaining a competitive advantage in the following factors:
     - Performance
     - Advanced technology differentiators, expandability, longevity
     - Cost
     - Footprint
     - First to market
     - Protected IP

3. **Technology Strategy**—Develop a technology roadmap for leadership in the following areas:
   - Robotics
   - Vacuum systems
   - Valves
   - Controls
   - Software
   - Tools for efficiency (software development, simulation, modeling, throughput analysis)

4. **Product Strategy**—Based on market and competitive strategies, develop a roadmap of products (platforms, subsystems, and components) taking advantage of the technology roadmap. Each product should have a clear competitive advantage in customer benefit and availability (timing). The target customer(s) and applications for each product and the compelling reason to buy the product must be identified. Also:
   - Identify the required product portfolio in platform, robotics, isolation valves, factory interface, software, and controls.
   - Identify new product development and CIP projects.

Note: Because CPD as an internal supplier has no IP protection within the company, CPD is constrained in implementing certain product strategies that external suppliers would be able to do. CPD must differentiate in speed of execution and product cost to win the trust of the business divisions. Having a patented superior technology does not create a barrier for business divisions in developing their own platforms.

5. **Resource Strategy**—Develop core competencies in critical automation, controls, and software technologies; marketing; and product management. (*Note:* Inclusion of marketing as a necessary function for CPD was new to the company, resulting in much skepticism by top management and peers.) An excellent marketing competency is required to penetrate the internal business division market and to perform competitive benchmarking. Marketing capability as a core competency is particularly critical for CPD because it transitions out of an engineering organization into a business operation.

6. **Positioning Strategy**
   - Our objective is to capture a 100% share of the TSI platform product market and be the *supplier of choice* for platform and software in the company. We want our customers (the product divisions) to come to us when they need a platform solution.
   - In positioning CPD, we need to know what value factors (metrics) customers use to evaluate CPD products and services and to assess CPD as an organization. We also need to know the relative importance of these factors to the customers. (For example, value factors might be product performance and technological innovation; timeliness of delivery of solutions; cost; and customer relationship.) In the customer's mind, CPD must have the best platform and software technologists and engineers; the best project management capability (to deliver timely and competitive solutions); and the best marketing capability to understand/anticipate customer needs and to become involved early in a customer's development cycle. We must enable our customer to win.

The Business Model. CPD business will be modeled akin to an external supplier of platform products. CPD, being an internal supplier, however, will reinvest its entire "earned margin" in R&D and marketing. CPD will not be a for-profit organization.

CPD must deliver significant benefit to the product divisions by improving their gross margins and reducing their R&D expenses. CPD must reduce the overall cost of R&D for the corporation. These objectives can be accomplished with the following strategy:
- Reduce R&D costs for the product divisions by offering them timely solutions.
- Improve the gross margins for the product divisions through materials' cost reduction CIPs in conjunction with manufacturing.
- Further improve the gross margin through manufacturing cycle time reduction as a result of increased commonality in platforms and components across product lines.
- Reduce corporate R&D costs through enhanced commonality and synergy among products and through increased efficiency to have a core competency in platform technologies that is on par with (or better than) the best in the industry.

Additionally,
- The CPD business model will allow an internal "sale" of platforms, subsystems, and components to fund its R&D, marketing, and operations.
- CPD pricing will be "cost-based" as the floor plus "value-added" to establish the ceiling. The reference price will be the competitive market price of external platform suppliers.
- The business model must allow a reduction in the sales price as the production volume increases (volume discount) and as the product line matures (less R&D needed).
- The transition of CPD from an allocation-based R&D organization to a product P&L operation must have no adverse impact on the gross margin of product divisions and no adverse impact on the corporate bottom line.

Outcome. A year Later, in the end-of-year report in 2003, CPD demonstrated success and maturation of the initial strategy in becoming an internal supplier of common platform products. The following information was presented to the TSI president as the CPD strategy for the following year.

CPD Vision and Mission: Offer a portfolio of common platform products and components that can be readily adopted by various product divisions to deliver differentiated solutions. Improve market share, gross margin, and profitability of company products. Co-develop new platforms with the product divisions and proliferate common platforms and components to maximize synergistic implementation of the collective capability of the company and enable proliferation of knowledge and innovation.

Objectives:

- Be a supplier of choice for the product divisions and lead customers.
- Achieve product leadership through innovation in systems, software, controls, robotics, and fab automation technologies.
- Achieve organizational excellence in engineering, marketing, operation, and product support. Be the center of excellence in systems engineering.
- Achieve customer intimacy through responsiveness and collaboration.
- Achieve 90% market share of all new products in 1 year. Reduce cost of Product A by 30%. Establish and meet cost targets for Platforms B, C, and D.

Opportunities/Problems:

- Lack of focus for development of common platforms across the company has resulted in duplication of effort and loss of operational efficiency and has precluded synergistic benefits of cross-divisional collaboration.
- A common factory interface and factory automation strategy, across all company products, is required to achieve requirements of factory productivity demanded by IC manufacturers.

Strategy:

- Products:
  - Own the life cycle competitiveness and support of the following common platforms— A, B, C, D. Develop new common platforms.
- Be the supplier of all common components and subsystems for all company products.
- Provide system engineering services, in collaboration with the product divisions, to enable successful integration of platforms in product division systems and to demonstrate system performance against the market requirements specification (MRS).
- Marketing and Business:
  - Position CPD in alignment with its mission.
  - Develop strategies to manage inefficiencies of an "internal market" (e.g., nature of rivalry, customer choice, value equation, IP ownership).
  - Increase power in the value chain through a total solution model, including product life cycle ownership and fixed price for new products through engineering, manufacturing, and outsourcing.
  - Establish the business model and obtain executive approval.
  - Maintain an accurate and timely competitive database, perform gap analysis, and develop a competitive strategy.
- Organization and Resources:
  - Develop the best technology and engineering capabilities. Fill the resource gap created as a result of the expanded product portfolio by consolidating expertise from the product divisions, improving efficiency, and headcount increase.
  - Develop systems engineering, operation, service, and account management functions to achieve organizational objectives.

REFERENCES

1. *Merriam Webster Online Dictionary*. Available at: http://www.m-w.com/.
2. Kaplan, R., Eisenhardt, K., Sull, D., Tufano, P., Gadiesh, O., Gilbert, J., Sawhney, M., Porter, M. *Harvard Business Review on Advances in Strategy*. Boston: Harvard Business School Press; 2002.
3. Burgelman, R.A., Modesto, A.M., Wheelwright, S.C. *Strategic Management of Technology and Innovation, Second Edition*. New York: Irwin/McGraw-Hill; 1996.
4. Burgelman, R.A., Styles, L.R. *Inside Corporate Innovation*. New York: Free Press; 1986.
5. Porter, M.E. *Competitive Strategy*. New York: Free Press; 1980.
6. Porter, M.E. *On Competition*. Boston: Harvard Business School Press; 1998.
7. Srivastava, R.K., Shervani, T.A., Fahey, L. Marketing, business processes and shareholder value: an organizationally embedded view of marketing activities and the discipline of marketing. *Journal of Marketing* 1999; 63(Special Issue): 168–179.
8. Hagel, J., III, Singer, M. *Unbundling the Corporation*. Harvard Business Review Article. Boston: Harvard Business School Publishing; 1999 March–April.
9. Treacy, M., Wiersema, F. *Customer Intimacy and Other Value Disciplines*. Harvard Business Review Article. Boston: Harvard Business School Publishing; 1993 January–February.
10. Christensen, C.M. *Innovator's Dilemmas: When New Technologies Cause Great Firms to Fail*. Boston: Harvard Business School Press; 1997.
11. Porter, M.E. *Struggle for Power*. Boston: Harvard Business School Press; 2000.
12. Dyer, J. H. *How Chrysler Created an American Keiretsu*. Harvard Business Review Article. Boston: Harvard Business School Publishing; 1996 July-August.
13. Christensen, C.M., Raynor, M., Verlinden, M. *Skate to Where the Money Will Be*. Harvard Business Review Article #R0110D. Boston: Harvard Business School Publishing; 2001 November, 72–81.
14. Baldwin, C.Y., Clark, K.B. *Design Rules, Volume 1, The Power of Modularity*. Cambridge, MA: The MIT Press; 2000.
15. Drucker, P.F. *Post Capitalist Society*. New York: HarperBusiness; 1993.
16. Capon, N., Glazer, R. Marketing and technology: a strategic co-alignment. *Journal of Marketing* 1987; 51: 1–14.
17. Tufano, P., Sawhney, M., Gadiesh, O., Eisenhardt, K. *Harvard Business Review on Advances in Strategy*. Boston: Harvard Business School Publishing; 2002.
18. Copeland, T.E., Murrin, J. *Valuation: Measuring and Managing the Value of Companies, Third Edition*. New York: John Wiley & Sons; 2000.
19. Ford, D., Ryan, C. *Taking Technology to Market*. Harvard Business Review Article. Boston: Harvard Business School Publishing; 1981 March/April, 59: 117–126.
20. Grove, A. *Only the Paranoid Survive*. New York: Doubleday; 1996.
21. Gershner, L.V. *Who Says Elephants Can't Dance?* New York: HarperBusiness; 2002.
22. Reed, Rory, IBM Executive. Speech to Silicon Valley executives: *Electronics Hi Tech Industry*. Santa Clara, CA, November 5, 2001.

3

MARKETING MANAGEMENT

The essence of a marketing concept is to fulfill the purpose of a business in creating economic value. A firm does this by:

- Producing and delivering products and services that customers want
- Providing value at a price that is attractive relative to the price offered by competition
- Having a price that is more than the cost (hence making a profit)

In order to achieve all of this, a company must have a clear purpose and a strategic plan that is well communicated and executed by employees. Taking a long-term view of a business for sustained profitability, Theodore Levitt defines the purpose of a business as creating and keeping a customer.[1]

Among the fundamental functions of a company to produce and deliver products and services and to serve a business purpose, the role of marketing is illustrated in Figure 3.1. The fundamental functions of a company—marketing, development, manufacturing, and selling/supporting—are enabled by the company's infrastructure, including human resource services, finance, the enterprise resource planning (ERP) system, and facilities management.

The roles and responsibilities of the marketing function in Figure 3.1 must be defined in relation to the players in the external and internal environments, including customers; industry network members; the enterprise's executive management, engineering staff, and sales force; distribution channels; and other market asset contributors. These relationships are particularly important in high-tech markets in which intimate and real-time interactions are required in order to capitalize on rapidly changing technology and market opportunities.

3.1 MARKETING—DEFINITIONS

Based on the purpose of a business and the fundamental functions of an enterprise (a company), marketing scholars and business leaders offer a multitude of definitions for marketing to underpin the essence of marketing imagination and the output of the marketing process:

- Peter Drucker—"Marketing is viewing the enterprise from the viewpoint of the customer and that is the same as management of the enterprise as a whole."[2]

Market	Develop	Make	Sell/Support	
Marketing	**Technology and Engineering**	**Manufacturing**	**Marketing/Sales**	**Sales/ Support**
• Strategic Marketing (perceive opportunity and set direction) • Define Products • Prepare MRS and Marketing Plan	• RD&E • Innovation • Technology Development • Product Design and Development	• Materials Management • Manufacturing • Supply Chain Management	• Product Marketing • Management of Marketing Mix • Commercialization • Sales Support • CRM • Product Management (including Configuration and Life Cycle Management)	• Personal Selling • Distribution Channel Management • Customer Post-Sales Support
Operating Infrastructure (Human Resources, Finance, ERP, Facilities)				

Figure 3.1. Fundamental Functions of a Company. CRM, customer relation management; MRS, market requirements specification; RD&E, research, development, and engineering.

- Theodore Levitt—"Marketing is, most importantly, a comprehensive view of the business process, a way of doing business that this view entails … Discovery of the simple essence of things is the essence of the marketing imagination."[1]
- William Davidow—"Marketing is a civilized warfare. The essence of good marketing is the commitment to be something. Marketing must invent complete products and drive them to commanding positions in defensible market segments."[3]
- Bob Noyce—"Marketing makes products."[3]
- Geoffrey Moore—"Marketing means taking actions to create, grow, maintain, or defend markets."[4]
- Regis McKenna—"Marketing is a process of educating customers to overcome their fear, uncertainty, and doubt (the FUD factor!)."[5]

Marketing can be conceptualized as a *systems discipline* in which markets are *economic systems* and the *role of marketing* is to facilitate the transfer of money from the market into the company by ensuring that the company is delivering value out to the market. In order to have an effective marketing process, a firm must have the "right" culture and structure, a customer-centric culture in which attracting and keeping customers is the main focus, and an efficient structure that facilitates communication between marketing and engineering and allows flawless execution of the business strategy. The function of marketing in the economic system is to connect the market needs with a firm's capabilities and technology assets by defining:

- Who the "right" customers are
- What they need
- What *whole product* can fulfill that need and deliver value

In high-tech and emerging markets, often it is important to **not** "listen" to customers, but to perceive the possibilities of new technologies in creating products and market demand. In many successful companies, the process of inventing a new technology and exploiting it to address an *unarticulated* need of customers usually takes a path that is not, at least initially, led by marketing.

For example, an engineer imagines something new, everyone in engineering becomes excited about the idea, and a project is initiated, but marketing, which is very customer driven and focused on satisfying existing customers, resists this new idea as a low priority. However, when the technology becomes more mature and there is a clearer definition of how it matches the market context, the quality of marketing input in defining the customer requirements grows along with the *whole* product concept. To perceive future opportunities, therefore, marketing must be technology savvy, have a strong link to technologists, and imagine new possibilities—which can benefit a potential user, solve an existing problem, or provide an "elegant" alternative to an existing solution.

Traditional market research methods (e.g., surveys and focus groups) do not add any value in defining the requirements for novel (technology) products in emerging markets. For example, using traditional market research methods, the Walkman or beepers for high school students would not have been invented—market researchers would merely have received more information from customers on how to improve existing products such as cassette tape players. Traditional market research methods are useful only when the product category has already been established and customers have a fairly clear idea of the circumstances in which they will use the product. Customers do not perceive new product ideas—marketers should. Walkman and beepers are products of marketing imagination in matching new technologies to unarticulated customer benefits.

William Davidow relates a story about the invention of the microprocessor. As Ted Hoff of Intel "was listening to a Japanese customer one day, it occurred to him that the customer was trying to solve his problem the wrong way. The microprocessor was born!"[3]

Invention of TCP (transformer coupled plasma) technology at Lam Research Corporation is another example of a forward-looking technology innovation. For many years, technologists in the IC manufacturing industry thought that it would be *nice* if ion density and ion energy in a plasma reactor could be controlled independently, although no customer had *asked* for that capability. John Ogle, an innovative electrical engineer at Lam, invented that capability with TCP design while tinkering in his lab in 1986. His supervisor and the marketing manager of the BU thought Ogle was "out of control" and tried hard to refocus him on finishing up the documentation of the last design that he had done which was being shipped to beta customers. A high-level executive of a leading customer had even scorned Lam Research for diverting scarce resources to the development of a technology that its customers had not yet required from them rather than solving existing customer problems. Ogle, with encouragement from the vice president of R&D, continued with his passion. Through an under-the-table network in the engineering organization, Ogle built a prototype and demonstrated very encouraging wafer etch results with TCP technology. Nine years later in 1995, TCP technology enabled Lam Research Corporation to capture 40% of poly (silicon) and aluminum etch equipment market share and to sustain its market leadership in poly through 2003! At the 2003 annual shareholders meeting, John Ogle was recognized by the CEO of Lam Research for his contributions to the company.

As the technology matures and the market grows, an industry evolves into a complex network of interdependent and competing suppliers and customers and the task of marketing management and development of a winning market strategy becomes more complex. The following example from the semiconductor industry illustrates the changing characteristics and increasing complexity of a maturing market.

> ## SEMICONDUCTOR PROCESS EQUIPMENT—CHANGING MARKET CHARACTERISTICS
>
> The semiconductor industry began in the late 1960s. By 2003, it was a $150+ billion maturing market with the following characteristics:
>
> - New products rapidly "commodified" and prices declined. In this environment, agile production ramp and short IC manufacturing cycle time were key sources of competitive advantage.
> - The cost and risk of developing new technology and products over ever-shorter cycles exceeded the resources of many IC manufacturers, giving rise to technology licensing by a few strong technology players (e.g., IBM) and consolidation of suppliers.
> - Manufacturers of equipment consolidated, competing fiercely under severe pressure to enhance equipment productivity and lower prices. Equipment maturity cycle time was a key competitive advantage.
> - This environment gave rise to new structures:
>   - Electronics product suppliers and IC manufacturers formed vertically integrated alliances in the supply chain to share the risks and costs of technology development and building new factories, to ensure production capacity, and to "ride out" industry economic cycles.
>   - Process equipment suppliers broadened their horizontal product portfolio and moved up the value chain by offering integrated solutions, including fab equipment services. Although equipment manufacturers were denied an "entry ticket" to customer alliance networks, they collaborated in the concurrent development of new devices, manufacturing process integration, and equipment.
>   - The advent of customer alliance networks increased their leverage over equipment suppliers, but because they were loosely structured, alliances did not offer any economy of scale benefit to equipment suppliers in product development, customization, and marketing. Equipment suppliers were being squeezed.
>   - Subsuppliers of components, subsystems, and consumable products consolidated to grow and survive. They responded to commoditization and price pressures by creating technology synergy (or at least operational efficiency) through economy of size and leverage of infrastructure in down cycles. They offered products in both vertical and horizontal markets.

3.2 THE ROLE OF MARKETING IN HIGH-TECH MARKETS—MISCONCEPTIONS

Many high-tech companies are technology driven, with marketing's role diminished to a sales support and promotional function. Product and competitive strategies are developed reactively and extemporaneously. Among technologists and even the top-level managers of these companies, the perception is that marketing is not very important to fast-changing high-tech markets, particularly in a business-to-business (B-to-B) market. The belief is that marketing is primarily a sales promotion function that is appropriate for consumer markets.

The following statement is from a product marketing director at a semiconductor equipment company in the year 2000: "In our division, marketing is quite neglected and underutilized. Marketers have no influence on product or business strategies. Success of the product marketing function is measured by its effectiveness in sales support, sales collateral preparation, impressing customers by sleek presentations, and supporting customer penetration activities." This marketing director perceived that he and his peers were "loners" who received little notice: "We do technical and sales-driven activities, but very limited strategic planning. Market requirements specification is normally documented after a product development program has started or even after it is nearly completed!"

Marketing managers and companies who practice according to such beliefs will find the growth of their enterprise limited and the profitability of their business short-lived when the initial enthusiasm of their new technology is challenged by potent competitors.

In high-tech industrial markets, the selling process for a new product is often very long and occurs as a result of a lengthy evaluation of the product and the technology by customers. Consequently, the sales team develops an intimate working relationship and a good understanding of the current and near-term requirements of account customers. This situation results in a perception by the sales team and company management that *necessary* "marketing" functions are performed by sales and that additional market research and customer relationship management (CRM) are unnecessary. This short-term focus, although necessary in the selling process, makes the company susceptible to competitive surprises, such as a competitor's new product or substitution by a new technology.

What *marketing* should define is the nature of marketing "warfare" in the future—what product capabilities and communication and customer support tools are required, who the new entrants are, and what the SWOT (strengths, weaknesses, opportunities, and threats) of players in the emerging competitive landscape are. Although the sales force must have a short-term focus and concentrate on generating revenue from existing products and services, marketing must understand the minds and the business of customers and discern future, unfulfilled, and unarticulated needs. The role of strategic marketing is not unlike a warfare strategist who must define the nature of future warfare (the basis of competition and value), new weapon systems (products and technologies), and the size and competencies of the future fighting force (the sales, distribution, and support network).

Although sales teams create strong and intimate relationships with account customers, CRM in a high-tech industrial market takes a much broader scope, requiring a proactive global strategy and actions beyond individual accounts. Effective CRM requires building relationships with all levels at a customer organization. Marketing must be the creator and manager of the hub of a CRM network between the company and the customer's key players. For example, the marketing CRM network in a semiconductor capital equipment company enables technologists, engineers, division general managers, manufacturing executives, and company senior executives (including the CEO) to establish proactive and synergistic relationships with the customer's key players, including the CEO, fab managers, procurement executives, equipment selection committee personnel, the vice president of technology, influential technologists, and fab engineers.

Global markets also demand synergistic order fulfillment across global customer operations, including product configuration (commonality), pricing, and support. This too is the responsibility of marketing.

The high speed of change in high-tech markets underscores the need for a crisp strategic market plan and an agile decision-making process. Lack of strategy causes product marketing managers to be reactive and focused solely on crisis management, which provides an opportunity for competitors to set industry rules and define the basis of competitive advantage. Only with the aid of a clear market leadership strategy can product marketing managers make timely, prioritized decisions about what to do and what not to do.

Product marketing managers are also responsible for planning and managing products throughout their life cycle. Although high-tech consumer products have a very short life, industrial products tend to have a different life cycle characteristic. In high-tech industrial markets, the applications and derivative technologies and products change rapidly, but the product platform can have a long life if it is properly conceived and executed. For example, semiconductor equipment applications, and hence reactors, change rapidly to keep up with the requirements of Moore's law. Yet wafer size has only changed once every 10 years (from 150 mm in 1980s, to 200 mm in 1990s, to 300 mm in 2000s). Cleverly conceived platforms have also lasted as long. It is the role of marketing to create a product roadmap that plans a long product life by designing an extendable platform and by devising continuous improvement programs (CIP) that extend the product life with new applications and enable diversification into new market segments.

Another important job of a product marketing manager is building strong brand equity for the company and its products. Branding is as important in high-tech B-to-B markets as in consumer markets. Psychological factors and customer loyalty to a brand in an industrial market can be even more powerful than in consumer markets because the switching cost of products to a business customer is often very high. In industrial markets, such factors as trust, long-term commitment, ease of working relationships, global presence, perception of supplier's breadth, and depth of technological capability can play an important role in customer loyalty and the perception of value.[6] Some companies have branded industrial products with their customers' customers, e.g., as Intel has successfully done through their "Intel Inside" label in the personal computer (PC) market. In high-tech industrial markets, customer R&D engineers should be developed into champions of the supplier's products and technology so that they will perceive their own career success in terms of the success of the supplier—which creates strong customer loyalty.

A company's marketing managers and engineering technologists must team-up in building and perpetuating brand equity. Lack of such a strategy and lack of proactive action will result in a rapid erosion of market position and the perception of value in the eye of the customer as technology changes. Steve Frankel of Micron Corporation, in discussing his company's success, said, "My organization, Marketing and Development, has the corporate responsibility for all marketing. At Micron, marketing and development groups work together to define new directions and solutions."[7]

3.3 MARKETING MANAGEMENT FUNCTIONS

Job titles and the organizational functions of the various people who are collectively responsible for performing the functions of the marketing process differ significantly between companies. Companies design their organizational structures and define job titles and responsibilities based on company size, the nature of the business, structural design preferences, established business processes, company culture, and complexity of the operation as well as other factors. Therefore titles such as Vice President of Marketing, Marketing Director, Marketing Manager, Product Marketing Manager, Product Line (General) Manager, Product Manager, Product Unit Manager, Global Product Manager, Regional Marketing Manager, Strategic Marketing Manager, Marketing Communications (Marcom) Manager, and other titles are found on the organizational charts of different companies. Some functions of the marketing process are even assigned to account managers in some firms.

This section discusses the marketing management functions that must be performed to develop and implement an effective market strategy. The discussion will focus on what must be done in the marketing process. No attempt is made to give a generic definition for any of the above titles or to assign functional responsibilities to them. Because marketing job titles are somewhat arbitrary and situational, the most important functions and activities that must be undertaken and the collection of responsibilities that must be assumed by the marketing organization will be discussed. The practitioner should group the functions in an organizational structure that is most suitable to his/her company's strategy, business processes, culture, and management preferences. For example, some companies structure their marketing functions according to market segment, e.g., consumer, business, or government markets. Other companies structure their marketing organization according to product technology or application, e.g., a semiconductor equipment company might organize by etch, CVD, and integrated solutions. Another possibility is to structure the marketing organization by regions such as countries or states in the United States. Some companies dedicate marketing organizations (and sales organizations) to large global customers. Larger companies usually find it necessary to adopt a combination of the above structures.

To design an effective organizational structure, you must first understand the marketing process and the functions of marketing management and then you must assign a clear owner with discernable accountability for each function. Numerous sources provide additional discussions of the role of marketing.[8–13] (*Note: Leadership and Management in a Product Development Environment*, a manuscript in preparation by the author, will be completed in 2007. This work will provide an example of a marketing organization.)

Some researchers report a shift from product or geographical marketing structures to customer-focused marketing, resulting in a decline in the influence of product managers and in an increase in the influence of account managers. Other researchers report that marketing is becoming responsible for managing connections in the marketing process, including the customer product development process, customer service delivery, customer relationship management, information use and research process, customer financial accountability, and value/supply chain management. Marketing is *everyone's* business.

Effective marketing management encompasses an assumption of ownership and performance of several tasks:

1. Create and drive market strategy including the value chain and channel strategy. Set marketing objectives.
2. Understand the market, industry, customers, and competition. Quantify trends and SWOT.
3. Establish and drive competitive strategy. Understand competitors' positioning and strategies.
4. Anticipate and perceive opportunities.
5. Invent products—Lead definition and development of new products and services in conjunction with engineers and technologists.
6. Integrate customer and market requirements with the firm's technologies, platforms, and products and create synergistic (total) solutions.
7. Develop a product roadmap based on the market strategy and technology roadmap. Set product direction based on market trends.

8. Develop new markets and businesses (new segments, customers not served in existing segments, etc.).
9. Establish value pricing for products and services.
10. Define sales strategy and market entry points such as OEM (original equipment manufacturer), end users, distributors, and retailers.
11. Manage demand.
12. Establish and manage the product, market, and business unit (BU) positioning strategy. Establish the desired position and implement required actions to achieve it.
13. Understand the dimensions (metrics) that customers use to evaluate the company's products and services and to assess the company as an organization (including brand, trustworthiness, can do business with, technology superiority, and marketing mix capabilities). Understand the relative importance of these dimensions to customers in their purchase decision.
14. Create and manage brand equity. Develop branding and positioning message.
15. Manage a profitable CRM. Customer intimacy is the linchpin of marketing success. CRM is the primary responsibility of marketing. Customer intimacy must be developed, remembering that the customer is "king" and never forgetting that the customer is the only source of revenue and livelihood for the enterprise. Customer partnering strategy, including selection of co-development, alpha, beta, and evaluation customers and priority setting, are responsibilities of marketing.
16. Manage Marcom functions, including being the spokesperson for marketing, preparing promotional material based on branding and positioning messages, advertising, organizing trade shows, and preparing sales collateral.
17. Prepare and implement a customer service and support plan comprised of:
    - A support plan at product introduction over the first year
    - A long-term support and service plan, defining who (direct, distributors, or value-added resellers?)
    - A service and support value proposition and pricing (bundled with the product or sold as a separate package?)
18. Implement the marketing plan:
    - Achieve profitable market share and growth targets.
    - Partner with customers.
    - Lead the war against competition.
    - Advocate customers' requirements for total customer satisfaction within the company. Resolve escalating product, service, and customer satisfaction issues.
    - Manage internal and external interfaces through partnership and holistic involvement of engineering, sales and service (training, support), manufacturing (capacity and build plan forecast), suppliers, public relations, finance, and legal.
    - Own the products and manage the products' life cycles, including configuration management, CIP strategy, and common platforms for synergy and efficiency.
    - Manage the marketing, product development, and commercialization processes and:
      ○ Develop and implement market requirements specification (MRS).

      ○   Ensure compliance to the product development and commercialization process.

      ○   Set priorities during the product development process.

      ○   Resolve cross-organizational business process issues.

- Establish, track, and manage budgets for various marketing tasks.

3.3.1 Product Marketing Plan

To succeed, the "right" things must be done "well." Articulating the "right" product and charting how to develop it "well" are objectives of a product plan. Preparing and following the product plan improves the development team's effectiveness and accelerates reaching commercialization goals. Most serious mistakes are usually the result of poor planning—pursuing the wrong market with the wrong product at the wrong time.

An often-asked question is "Can a new high-tech product be planned?" Usually no model exists that can be followed for a new product in a new market, and too much uncertainty exists in a new technology to foresee the future. Nevertheless, a plan is needed to spell out the general direction a company should take and where it should end up. Details of the route can be identified during implementation. Plans almost never anticipate and address all of the major problems that a company will face. During execution of the plan, the team constantly learns about the market, the technology, and the product and must continuously update the plan. A good plan improves the chance of success, but a plan should never be trusted completely. Going through the process of preparing a plan, in most cases, is more important than adhering to the plan during the implementation phase. During the planning process, the team is "forced" to ask and to answer hard questions:

- What constitutes the *whole* product?
- What is the *right* market segment, business model, and timing?
- What is the *right* technology?
- What are the competitive SWOT?
- What is the new product success criterion?
- How can planned goals be achieved?
- What resources are available or needed?

A product marketing plan is the basic document which enunciates the marketing invention (the definition of the *whole* product); the commercialization plan, based on the external and internal environmental conditions (opportunities and constraints); and the approach for establishing the necessary market assets to achieve the business and the market strategy goals. Elements of a product marketing plan are listed below, constituting MRS as the guiding document in a new product development process. (*Note*: MRS is discussed in detail in Chapter 6.)

3.3.2 Product Marketing Plan Outline

A product marketing plan outline includes:

1. Strategic objectives—What are the firm's objectives for introducing this product, e.g., to enter a new market, to improve or revive a market position, or to complete a solution portfolio?
2. Market trends (emerging, growing, or declining market segments)
3. Targeted market segment characteristics (total available market, TAM; served available market, SAM; and growth rate of the target market)

4. Business plan (share of market, SOM; projections within a time frame, e.g., 3 to 5 years; projected revenue and profitability from the product)—The aim should be to achieve a commanding position in the target market with >25% share of SAM.

5. Customer population and characteristics in the target segment—Who are the customers in the segment, who is buying, and who are the end users? What customer problem (or need) does the proposed product solve? How will customers use the product? What is a customer's compelling reason to buy the product?

6. Competitive analysis (technology threat and competitors' SWOT)—Identify barriers to market entry and have specific strategy and action plans to overcome them.

7. Invention of a product—Describe the *whole* product and the services offered. Define the benefits of the proposed value. Identify applications for the product and prioritize them. Identify the initial commercialization application. Define the technical specifications for the product, the product life cycle roadmap, the product cost target, and the product development priorities based on the demand vectors.

8. Market penetration, product commercialization, and launch plans—Identify product introduction timing (and product development schedule) and beta customers. Identify marketing programs to communicate the product introduction to target customers (Marcom plan, collateral documentation, public relations, advertising, and internal communication).

9. Development plan for the necessary market asset/infrastructure

10. Sales strategy (direct and distribution channels)

11. Pricing strategy

12. Customer service and support plan

13. Execution of the plan (resources required to implement the plan, the plan to train the sales force, distribution channels, and support resources)—Assess risks, including a slip in product release date and a competitor's action (such as introducing their own new product).

14. Methodology to evaluate effectiveness of the marketing program including key indicators

3.4 THE MARKETING PROCESS—CHARACTERISTICS

Many marketing endeavors involve the use of art, rather than science—they are intuitive and mostly qualitative, rather than quantitative. Marketing must pay attention to attitudes, perceptions, and personal relationships. Engineers usually do not like the "softness" of marketing. Engineers are trained to be precise and quantitative. They want to analyze problems based on data, develop trends, and draw conclusions. The tendency to extrapolate observable data can be very misleading, even in R&D, when systems are nonlinear. Anticipating problems that will be created by a new invention that is intended to "change the world" is difficult. The past only establishes the initial conditions for the future, not a behavioral model.

The fundamental assumption in the engineering world is that the value of anything is a function of its objective utility. Yet there is a purely subjective value—of liking something just because it has a nice shape or a pretty color—that can affect a customer's purchasing decision.

This is true in both consumer and B-to-B markets. Attributes such as a supplier's management commitment, personal relationships, a customer R&D manager's commitment to a technology, and a customer's comfort factor with a new product and technology have a great impact on the customer's purchasing decision.

What is usually unclear to engineers and to marketing managers is the "*whole* product" that the customer experiences and from which value satisfaction is drawn. It is not enough to design and make the greatest widget. Benefits must be delivered to customers as *they perceive* "benefits." History has seen many great products, although *technologically* intriguing, which failed because they were not "*whole* products" and did not deliver sufficient benefits to prospects at the right time—within the window of opportunity.

A disconnect between the product and the market leads to unsuccessful application of technology to context. A disconnect may be in the product capabilities or in the time frame that the benefit is needed and valued by the market. That is why the role of marketing is so pivotal in business success. Marketing has to provide the connectivity between engineering, sales, distribution channels, and customers in:

- Defining market requirements to guide R&D
- Exploiting new technologies and products that are developed by engineering
- Developing markets
- Creating total solutions by leveraging corporate-wide capabilities
- Positioning products so that the sales force will understand what to sell, whom to sell to, and what differentiates the product from the competition
- Developing relationships to win customer loyalty
- Staying very close to the marketplace, monitoring change and leading the company in its timely response

In the development of a novel technology and a new product idea, the acceptance standards for the product are often vague and the risk of introducing the new product is too high. A novel product takes time for customers to become accustomed to using it and to accept the product as being part of their established habits and practices. Sometimes IC manufacturers evaluate new semiconductor process equipment or technology for several years before adopting it into their manufacturing process flow. The strategy for market acceptance must be developed and implemented concurrently with the product development process. Therefore marketing challenges should be confronted in a joint effort by all company functions, including engineering, manufacturing, sales, and strategic planning.

Oftentimes, engineering and marketing teams make dangerous assumptions, implicitly or explicitly, in the development and commercialization of a new product, leading to surprises, disappointments, or the downright failure of the process. These dangerous assumptions include:[3]

- Customers will buy the product because we think it is a great product.
- It is technically superior and will sell itself.
- Customers will run no risk in switching suppliers and in buying from us.
- Distributors will have no problem stocking and servicing the product.
- Sales people will believe that the product will benefit the customer significantly and in a differentiated way and will enthusiastically sell it.
- The project team will develop the product on time and within budget.

- We have and will continue to have the right mix of talent and quantity of resources.
- Competitors will respond rationally.
- We can offer the product at a low introductory price to capture market share and raise prices later for profitability.
- The rest of the company and management will support the team's strategy throughout its execution phase.

It is through well thought-out planning, flawless execution, anticipation of problems, and taking timely and proactive corrective action that a product development team will succeed. William Davidow has listed several attributes of an effective marketing program:[3]

- Does the plan comply with the strategic principle *that marketing must invent complete products and drive them to a commanding position in defensible market segments?*
- Does the team understand why customers will buy the product over competitors' products? What is the *compelling reason* to buy?
- Does the team have a crusade mentality? Is it reflected in the plan? Does it include *hard work, enthusiasm, confidence, and commitment (resources)?*
- Is customer satisfaction guaranteed—through support and service before and after sale?
- Does the product match the sales and distribution channels? *Developing the sales and distribution infrastructure to get the product to the customer is the responsibility of marketing (includes documentation, training, motivation, channel type decision, etc.).*
- Will the promotion program work? *Define the desired positioning of the product and promote it.*
- Is the product different? *Successful products are different from the competitors' products in significant ways to customers (a rule of thumb in industrial markets is >30% advantage in performance, productivity, or cost).*
- Is the marketing plan written down, communicated to everyone involved, and reviewed regularly? *The marketing plan must be a living plan and it must be updated regularly to reflect changes in the competitive landscape.*
- Is pricing fair? *Seek win-win for the customer and supplier.*
- Are marketing programs integrated? *Activities of product marketing, product management, Marcom, investor relations, product development in engineering, and field sales offices must be well orchestrated.*
- Is marketing "in touch" with the customer base? *Marketing people must always be probing for information and building close relationships with customers.*
- Does marketing respect sales and vice versa? *Teamwork is critical to target the product to a niche where it can sell.*
- Does marketing drive the organization? *Marketing must make engineering aware of customer needs and manufacturing aware of capacity and cost issues and plan the company's products.*
- Are products managed throughout their life cycle? *Maintaining a successful product throughout its life cycle is critical to customer satisfaction and the customer relationship and to profitability.*

- Is a forecasting system in place to *avoid opportunity losses and excess inventory problems?*
- Does the marketing process have quality control metrics? *Marketing must develop performance metrics for marketing effectiveness and then track them.*

The marketing management team, including the BU general manager, must energize and rally the entire company to execute the market strategy in the product development and commercialization process. The market strategy should be presented to the sales force to earn their support during sales or distributors' conferences and when they are doing road shows.

Top management's endorsement of the marketing plan and their commitment of resources are also critical. The plan must be communicated to all employees, particularly the product development team. The marketing manager must specify what employees are expected to do.

3.5 MARKETING MANAGERS—OUTPUT AND SUCCESS METRICS

Companies often view marketing as a nebulous activity and find that measuring the effectiveness of the marketing process and the performance of individual marketing managers is difficult. However, many high-tech companies find it convenient to define the success of *any program* based solely on overall business metrics such as revenue growth, market share, and profitability. These metrics are usually impacted by the collective work of a large number of cross-functional contributors and therefore they are excellent metrics for the overall performance of a team and a BU.

Although devising metrics to measure marketing success often requires creativity, the task is doable. To attract, develop, and motivate the top talent in a company, marketing must be viewed and developed as a professional discipline that is empowered by the BU general manager and has a clear reward-for-performance incentive system, including a clear career path.

Metrics and expected output that could be adopted to assess the performance of marketing/product managers in their area of responsibility include:

- Market share, customer satisfaction, and retention
- Segment vision, segment strategy (a list of customer value parameters versus specification, competition, and product tactics), and implementation milestones which are updated monthly
- Competitive strategy and implementation milestones—monthly update
- Portfolio analysis and action plan—quarterly update
- Product roadmap, technology roadmap, and market roadmap—quarterly update
- Product configuration management and life cycle evolution
- Pricing analysis and value option strategy—quarterly update
- Proactive market research and Marcom program (with sales team)
- Positioning strategy and actions—quarterly update
- Timely execution of product development tasks (MRS, beta customer management, product launch)
- Customer visits—quarterly or as needed

3.6 INVENTING THE *WHOLE* PRODUCT, ANCILLARY PRODUCTS, AND TOOLS

A product is the *totality* of what a customer experiences and as such has multiple dimensions. A product can be a physical object (hardware, food, and medicine) or software or a service and can include a number of other factors (such as mode of delivery) that make the product available, useful, and desirable to satisfy the customer's need. The packaging of a physical product, the ease of acquisition of a product, the user friendliness of software, the availability of testing equipment and diagnostic procedures for an industrial product, and after-sale support are a few examples of the factors that—together with the basic product—make a product a complete or "*whole* product." The definition of a *whole* product must be based on the characteristics of the target market segment, the phase of technology/innovation adoption life cycle, and the firm's value proposition strategy. Think about a few products and the totality of the experience that forms a customer's perception of value and satisfaction:

- For a restaurant, the total product is the sum of the food, ambiance, service, cleanliness, location, people who eat there, etc.
- At a supermarket, canned soup as a total product is the soup plus the can label identifying the brand, the store display, the store's cleanliness, and the type of store selling the soup. Canned soup is perceived to be a "high-quality" soup if it is sold at a gourmet food market, but it is perceived as a "low-cost and not very healthy" soup if it is sold at a gas station convenience store.
- The operating system (OS) for an embedded microprocessor as a total product is comprised of the OS software, development environment (hardware and software), user's manual, supplier's training program, supplier's service/troubleshooting capabilities, availability of drivers for peripheral hardware, and the supplier's future commitment and product enhancement plan.
- In the semiconductor process equipment market, a chemical vapor deposition (CVD) total product is the process recipe for the deposition of a thin film, plus the reactor design, wafer transfer platform, system software, process control hardware/software, system packaging, supplier's service and spares capabilities, supplier's ability/desire to continuously improve the product, operation and maintenance manual, presale demo quality, post-sale installation and qualification, and the customer's confidence in the supplier as a financially viable enterprise to whom he can entrust his operation.

A 1999 article in *Communications Magazine* cited the shortcomings of marketing strategy at Ascend Corporation as the main reason why competitors were taking market share away from the company. Although Ascend had some of the best products in the industry, its market position was in jeopardy. According to the article, "They introduce products as devices—'here is our sexy new box,' rather than 'this is our strategy for voice communication.' Customers did not understand the significance of a newly launched product."

Only the buyer or the user can assign value to a product from the function that it provides. Seldom do users of a facial cream refer to the product by its chemical formula. Instead, they refer to the product in terms of its need satisfaction, e.g., as a sun screen lotion. Similarly, IC manufacturers think of their CVD process equipment in terms of the thin film that it deposits on their wafers, not as a large complex piece of electromechanical machinery.

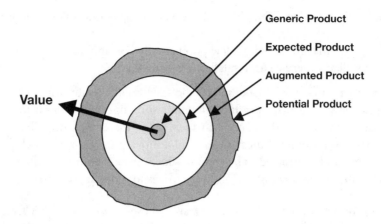

Figure 3.2. *Whole* Product Concept.

A product is a *cluster* of generic, expected, augmented, and potential attributes that are of value to the customer—what is called a *whole product* in this book. Figure 3.2 illustrates the *whole* product concept and its outward value vector.

Generic product. A generic product is the basic, substantive "thing" or "device." Without this product there is no chance to participate in a market. Generic products include:

- Contact lens in an optical store
- "For Sale" property in a realtor's office
- Cars in a dealership showroom
- Computers on a website
- A satellite TV antenna and receiver box in an electronics/appliances store

Expected product. An expected product represents the customer's minimal expectations, such as delivery conditions, installation services, post-sale services, spare parts availability, training, and packaging conveniences. For the above examples, expected products may include:

- Contact lenses with a protective case
- "For Sale" property and an agent who shows the property and gives honest advice
- Cars in inventory and in the showroom and a demo car to test drive
- Computers with the OS already installed in them
- A satellite TV antenna and receiver box plus a content delivery service contract (TV programs)

Expected attributes vary by customer and industry. They could be sources of product differentiation, depending on how well suppliers provide them.

Augmented product. An augmented product is an offering to the customer that is beyond what he/she expects or thinks he/she needs. For the above examples, augmented products may include:

- An optician who is willing to replace customers' lost contact lenses at night and during weekends and to deliver them to a customer's home
- A realtor who charges less than the customary 6% agency fee

- A car dealership that offers the final price at the onset and offers a floor mat at no charge
- A computer that comes with a few popular software applications already installed
- Free installation service for a satellite TV antenna

Augmentation is a means of product differentiation that might create customer dependency on the supplier. The downside is that product augmentation can educate the customer about what is reasonable to expect from the supplier, which raises the competitive "bar," turning augmented benefits into customer expectations (and a move into the inner circle in Figure 3.2). Not all customers can be attracted to by an ever widening circle of these differentiating "value satisfactions." Some customers may prefer lower prices to more augmentation.

Potential product. A potential product consists of everything potentially feasible to attract and keep customers. A potential product is anything that may remain to be done—and is possible—in the future. In high-tech markets, customers desire *extendibility* for the product so that the platform and basic technology can last over several generations of technology progressions. Such extendibility and future upgrades constitute potential products in an industrial market such as semiconductor manufacturing. In such markets, product roadmaps for life cycle evolution and continuous improvement with backward compatibility are important to customers.

In addition to the above examples, there are certain factors (in the *whole* product concept) that are more important in business markets than in consumer markets. For example, in industrial markets, more emphasis is usually on the function of the product; presale evaluation of the product (which sometimes takes over a year); post-sale support, customer training, and service; and customer risk in the purchase decision.

3.7 UNDERSTANDING STAKEHOLDER NEEDS AND PRIORITIES

If a product cannot be made to "work" by the customer, it is useless. Reasons might be that the product simply does not work; the user is not adequately trained and does not know how to use the product; the documentation telling the user how to install and operate the product is insufficient; or the product is not serviced and supported properly. *Important*: For a customer, the final measure of product *quality* and *value* is the product's *ability to meet the expectations* of the customer to fulfill his/her need.

In product development and commercialization, *not* underestimating the number of dimensions that a product must include to be considered *whole* is important. A *whole* product must be functional, i.e., it must employ the necessary technology and design to meet the desired specification. Furthermore, the product must be produced, i.e., construction materials and the tools of the manufacturing process and product assembly must be available. Additionally, the product must be delivered, serviced, and supported, i.e., distribution channels must be in place, the product must be serviceable, service tools and documentation must be prepared, and spare parts must be identified and delivered on a timely basis.

Successful application of a product in the use environment is often the most crucial proof of its functional utility. For example, process equipment for IC manufacturing is only useful if it can be integrated into the sequence of IC manufacturing process steps with the "right" process recipe that meets both unit and integrated performance requirements.

From an earlier discussion, remember that a product must be defined differently, depending on the targeted market segment's needs and wants and on the different phases of a new technology adoption life cycle. For example, for a new technology product, innovators (lead users) want to be involved in the supplier's product development phase. Innovators do not object to inadequate documentation or even a product that does not yet function fully. Conversely late majority adopters are conservative because the cost of a wrong purchase is often very high for them. Late adopters have no tolerance for malfunctions or documentation errors. Earlier, in the example of Ascend Corporation products, as Ascend grew and penetrated large customer markets, late majority customers were requesting a different "product" than Ascend had successfully marketed before—because the risk to these late majority customers was high. The purchase decision had to be made by the CEO and senior VPs of multibillion-dollar companies (such as GTE or Deutsche Telekom) who did not understand the technical jargon of Ascend engineers and were thinking in terms of solutions for *their* customers.

Yet development and commercialization of a *whole product* can be a source of competitive advantage. For example, the device that a company sells may not be particularly superior to the device of the competition, but if the *whole product* is better overall, no competitor can effectively challenge it. To position against competition, comparing *whole* products, not only generic products, is important. (*Note*: Consult Trout[14] for further discussion of product differentiation.)

Also important is understanding the evolutionary nature and content of a *whole* product throughout its life cycle. Marketers must renew a *whole* product in a proactive response to changing customer needs and the competitive situation and to the opportunities that arise for market extension with new applications. A *product idea* starts at the intersection of new technology capability and perceived market opportunity. The product idea takes shape during market research and the definition of MRS (market requirements specification) and becomes a reality as a result of the product development process, customer demonstration, and eventual commercialization. *Product definition* continues past product introduction through the discovery of new applications (which might not have been envisioned by the original developers) and continues further as the product "marches" through the technology adoption life cycle and is redefined for new groups of customers and as the company diversifies into new market segments and captures more market share.

When inventing a new product, marketing must understand the *vectors* of market demand. For example, the vectors of market demand in the semiconductor industry include the requirements of electronic devices and consumer products for power, mobility, speed, performance, application features, and cost. The degree of importance (or the size) of these vectors changes over time as markets evolve and mature. For example, in the semiconductor industry of the 1980s, power and mobility were less important than speed and performance, while in 2003, the reverse was true, as lower cost became more important.

Much is written and advocated about being responsive to the voice of the customer by marketing gurus. Although being customer centric is important, listening to the customer in a literal sense does not ensure long-term success—it could actually inhibit a supplier in perceiving future opportunities and threats in a timely manner. As noted earlier, customers may not always be able to articulate or even recognize their needs or to properly guide the development of new products. The ability of consumers is limited by their experiences. Moreover, customers may not be able to imagine what is made possible by new technology innovations or to recognize when their products and markets are threatened by disruptive technologies.

Yet it is crucial to get close to customers and to intimately understand a customer's operating environment and how the customer solves his/her problems. Only through such a "deep dive" into a customer's business can a supplier perceive opportunities (e.g., from a new technology innovation) to add value to the customer by making his business easier, less costly, and faster; by enabling the customer to do more and new things; and by improving the customer's competitive advantage.[15] Customers may be using new innovative products in a way that the designers did not originally intend the product to be used. Knowledge of this use could lead to opportunities for product improvement or differentiation and thereby to market extension in both business and consumer markets. In business markets, a supplier must stay close to the customer's customer as well and observe if product capabilities are exceeding the user's need. (*Note*: As modeled by Clayton Christensen, the latter is a ripe condition for a disruptive technology to create a business inflexion point.[16])

For example, by watching airline passengers struggle to open a package of peanuts, one can imagine how the packaging could be improved by changing the design or the material of construction to allow the package to be opened easily. As another example, when designing a new shopping cart, IDEO engineers sent "observers" to neighborhood supermarkets to observe customers using a shopping cart. They interviewed supermarket managers about their needs for a shopping cart.[17] This deep dive in the customer's operating environment enabled IDEO engineers to design a completely new cart that met the needs of shoppers and supermarket managers (the economic buyers of the cart.)

The following sections will discuss several methodologies that marketers employ in *inventing* a *whole* product. These tools should be selectively used in understanding, categorizing, and prioritizing the needs of the user and other stakeholders.[18] The most common methodologies include:

1. The Kano model
2. Conjoint analysis
3. The product value matrix
4. The lead user method
5. Quality function deployment—house of quality

3.7.1 The Kano Model

Named after Professor Noriaki Kano, the Kano method is used to determine the degree of importance of various customer needs. According to the Kano model (Figure 3.3), in satisfying customer needs, a product capability or a feature can be characterized into one of four groups:

- Must have—The must-have capability is expected by the customer. It is essential for need satisfaction. The extent to which the product falls short of fully satisfying this need contributes to the degree of customer dissatisfaction.
- Linear satisfier—More or better capability (or attributes) of the product results in additional customer satisfaction. For many linear satisfiers, there is a minimal threshold below which the capability or attribute of the product becomes a "must have." For example, there is a price ceiling above which the customer is not willing or able to purchase the product. The battery life of a laptop computer is a linear satisfier. The longer the battery lasts, the more satisfied the customer will be.

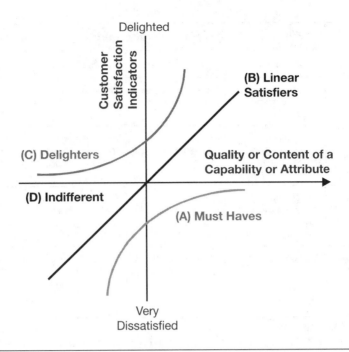

Figure 3.3. Kano Model.

However, the customer's expectation for an "acceptable" battery life might be 2 hours (based on prior experience with the competitors' products.) Therefore, the threshold of battery performance is 2 hours.

- Delighter—The delighter capability or attribute is not expected by the customer. If present, it will "delight" him/her. Conversely, if the delighter is absent, the customer is not dissatisfied. Delighters are great sources of product differentiation.
- Indifferent—Indifferent attributes or capabilities of a product are not important to the customer. Their presence or absence does not make a difference in the customer's purchase decision.

A fifth product attribute category exists that developers should be cognizant of—"reverse quality" attributes. These attributes are undesirable to the customer. They should be excluded from the product.

3.7.2 The Conjoint Analysis Method

Conjoint analysis is a statistical method for multiattribute preference analysis to assess the relative importance of user needs vis-à-vis product features and attributes. For example, marketers can use conjoint analysis to assess a new product concept compared to existing products of competitors. All combinations of the product's features and price options for each manufacturer's brand are listed. A survey of a representative sample of users is then taken to rank them. Statistical analysis of the responses guides the marketers to rank various product attributes and weigh them accordingly in design and commercialization of the product. Use of conjoint analysis is most appropriate for consumer products. It is often used by market research professionals.

	Stakeholder			
	Car Buyer	**Car Dealer**	**Mechanic**	**Future Society**
Purpose	Transportation of self, others, and cargo	Store, demonstrate, sell, and service	Repair and maintain car	Dispose of the remains of car
Physical	Opening door, seating position, temperature and other controls, etc.	Storage space required, brochures to aid sales	Tools for diagnosing and repairing easily; spares availability	Minimize interaction with waste created by car
Cognitive	Locating controls, knowing maintenance schedule	Knowledge of product, warranties, financing, and competitors	Knowledge of available tools for diagnosing and fixing	Knowledge of safe and sustainable environment
Aesthetics/ Emotion	Prestige, aesthetics	Prestige, brand value, quality rating	Satisfaction of making fast and accurate diagnoses	Pride in reuse and recycling

Figure 3.4. Product Value Matrix for a Car—Needs of Different Stakeholders in the Market Infrastructure. (Source: Adapted from Iansiti, M., Stein, E. *Understanding User Needs*. HBS Case 9-695-051. Boston: Harvard Business School Publishing; 1995 January 30.)

3.7.3 The Product Value Matrix

Product value matrix (PVM) methodology can be used to ensure that the plan for development and commercialization of a new product addresses the needs and preferences of all stakeholders in the value chain, including customers, distributors, suppliers, complimentors, after-sales service personnel, and end-of-life management needs. For industrial products, marketers and the sales team must intimately know all players inside the target customer organization and understand their mindset, value vector, and scaling coordinates. PVM can be used to develop the MRS for a new product, to select the required product design features, and to prioritize product development tasks. Figure 3.4 presents an example of a product value matrix for a car.

3.7.4 The Lead User Method

The innovator of a new product for satisfying an unfulfilled need is either the *user* or the *manufacturer* of the product. A user innovates when he/she expects to benefit by using the product, and a manufacturer innovates to benefit from making and selling the product.

User innovators are often the "lead users." They have new product or service needs that will become common in a particular marketplace, but they face them months or years before the bulk of the market. Because there is no "solution" available in the market, lead users innovate to satisfy their needs.

The lead user methodology, developed by Eric von Hippel, identifies these users for collaborative development and commercialization of a new technology.[19] When user needs are not understood or cannot be articulated, lead user methodology can identify emerging opportunities and application of new (breakthrough) technologies. The following steps are recommended for new product development with lead users:[20]

1. Specify a narrow product/market segment.
2. Identify important trends affecting this segment.
3. Identify lead users with respect to trend.
4. Developers and lead users jointly develop new product concepts and specifications.
5. Test acceptance of the product at the "means" of the market via traditional methods to determine if the new product concept appeals to routine users (early adopters and the early majority).

3.7.5 Quality Function Deployment

Quality function deployment (QFD) refers to building quality into the product design and manufacturing process from the onset of the product development process by relating the parameters that represent customer requirements and quality expectations to the technical requirements in engineering requirements specification (ERS). The methodology that graphically implements this approach is known as the "house of quality."[21,22]

The house of quality methodology follows the product development process sequence through development of MRS, ERS, design, process, and production and illustrates how the output of each step is linked to the parameters in the subsequent step. This "house" also prioritizes the requirements and establishes the dependency between the "what" and the "how" parameters in a correlation matrix.

Starting with the customer requirements (MRS) as the "what," the "how" of satisfying these requirements is established by developing the engineering specifications (ERS). In the next step, ERS parameters become the "what" that drives the product design characteristics. Next,

---

CASE STUDY—BUSINESS TRANSFORMATION—FROM EQUIPMENT PROVIDER TO SOLUTION PROVIDER

Setting. GE redefined value proposition, the business model, and the rules of the game in the "Jet Engine War." In the 1980s, suppliers of jet engines for commercial aircraft included GE Aircraft Engines, Pratt & Whitney (P&W), and Rolls Royce (RR). Business conditions were deteriorating for all suppliers and margins were diminishing due to the intense jet engine price war. The products of the three major suppliers were not differentiated. Price had become the primary factor in a customer's decision-making process.

Situation. To correct this situation, GE managers sought an out-of-the-box remedy to establish a differentiated value proposition and restore profitability. They created a paradigm shift away from the view of the airlines that a jet engine is merely a component of a plane that they buy from Boeing or Airbus Corporations.

GE devised a new business strategy to provide "power-by-the-hour" solutions to the airlines—by defining the engine as a power device to keep an aircraft in flight. This new value proposition required the assumption of total responsibility for the maintenance of the engines (including those of the competitors) by providing spare parts management, component refurbishment, and complete engine overhaul and maintenance.

Outcome. The new strategy changed the landscape and produced tremendous results in a short time. GE Aircraft Engines emerged as the winner, providing power-by-the-hour solutions for GE engines and for P&W and RR engines. In 2001, total business for GE climbed to $5 billion, while P&W business trailed at $1 billion and RR revenue was even less. The aftermarket service sector contributed 40% of the total revenue at GE Aircraft Engines and almost 100% of the profits. An additional benefit of the new strategy was stabilization of profitability at GE Aircraft Engines—by becoming less susceptible to the cyclic nature of the aircraft business.

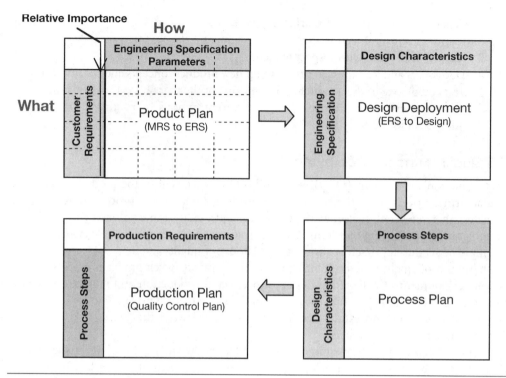

Figure 3.5. House of Quality Methodology Links Product Development Process Steps.

product design characteristics are related to the process steps which are then related to production requirements. The sequence of "houses" for these steps is shown in Figure 3.5.

The house of quality technique is not simple. However, it does ensure that all steps of product design, process, and manufacturing are directly linked and are driven by the customer needs. This methodology also helps team integration, collaboration, and common understanding among all team members of the requirements and priorities.

A more detailed representation that relates weighted customer requirements to product design parameters is shown in a correlation matrix in Figure 3.6. The correlation factors (CF) are estimated by engineers as the degree by which a design parameter (P) contributes to satisfying a given user need (CR). By summing the weighted correlation factors for each engineering parameter, the relative weight of each parameter in satisfying customer requirements is then calculated. The result of this analysis is used in product design tradeoffs. Often in developing a product, design engineers find out that some of the engineering requirements are in conflict with others. The calculated relative weight of the design parameters helps the designers to prioritize them and to resolve conflicts.

3.8 NEED SATISFACTION AND WINDOW OF OPPORTUNITY— CRITICALITY OF TIMING

The timing of the introduction of a new product to the market is a key element of commercialization success. Many new technology products are introduced "too early" and fail because they do not offer a compelling advantage to prospective buyers or they are not complete products.

		Engineering (Design) Parameters (Pm)				
Customer Requirement (CRn)	**Importance to Customer, Weight of CRn (wn)**	P1	P2	P3	...	Pm
CR1	w1	Correlation				
CR2	w2					
CR3	w3					
CR4	w4					
...	...					
CRn	wn					Correlation Factor of Pm with CRm (CFn)
	Raw Score	wn × CF1				Σwn × CFm
	Relative Weight (%)	Σwn × CF1/ Σwn × CFm				Σwn × CFn/ Σwn × CFm

Figure 3.6. QFD—Correlates Weighted Customer Requirements to Engineering Parameters of a Product.

Artificial intelligence and neural networks were introduced decades too early. Initially color copiers did not become particularly successful because no color printer was available to make the color originals widely used; later, color printing became very inexpensive and minimized the need for copying.

More often, however, a market opportunity is missed or significantly diminished because new products are introduced too late. The life of high-tech products is often short because of rapid changes in technology. Hence the window of business opportunity for a new high-tech product is usually limited. The Zip drive storage device for a PC had a limited window of opportunity between the 3.5-in. disk drive and the read/write compact disk drive (RW-CD) generations. Developing a new overhead projector in the year 2000 would have been unwise because the market was transforming away from transparency projectors to LCD projectors that connected to laptop computers.

Another factor that impacts the size and window of market opportunity for a new product is the timely availability of its complementors. Complementors are products and services that customers require to use in conjunction with the new product to satisfy their needs. For example, a new powerful application software can penetrate the PC market only if the complementary microprocessor and memory products are available (at the same time and at a reasonable cost) to provide the necessary computing power and memory capacity for the software to run satisfactorily. Market opportunity is also impacted by the factors that determine the ability of competitors to copy the product, including how much time is required, how much investment is required, how scarce are skilled resources, and how protected is critical know-how.

A study at HP (1990) illustrates the sensitivity of business profitability to time to market and the size of the market window.[23] The results of the study are depicted in Figure 3.7 and show the relative emphasis that must be placed on the timing of market introduction in the

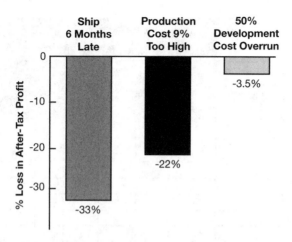

Figure 3.7. Sensitivity of Profitability to Schedule, Production Cost, and Cost of Product Development. Assumptions: 20% growth rate in market, 12% annual price erosion, 5-year product life. (Source: HP data. Adapted from Patterson, M. Accelerating innovation: a dip into the meme pool. *National Productivity Review* 1990 Dec; 9(4).)

development of a new product versus the costs of development. In this example, a 6-month delay in shipping the product results in a 33% loss in total profit after tax (PAT) that could have been realized over the 5-year life of the product. In contrast, a 50% cost overrun (i.e., 50% in additional investment) in the development effort results only in a 3.5% loss in PAT. Product production cost is also shown to have a significant impact on profitability—9% more in manufacturing costs results in a 22% loss in PAT.

3.9 S-CURVE MODEL AND GROWTH THROUGH SUCCESSIVE PRODUCT INTRODUCTION

Over its life cycle, the *differentiated value* of a high-tech product to the market (and corresponding product sale) takes the form of an S-shape as it goes through three phases:

- Slow penetration of new ideas in the market
- Rapid advance
- Leveling-off because of market saturation or product falling short of market needs

Progression of the S-shape is usually followed by a decline in product market share and revenue as substitution for the product by a new generation of technology occurs.

To sustain market momentum and business growth, creating a successive series of S-curves through the timely introduction of a series of new products and disruptive technologies is important (illustrated in Figure 3.8). Figure 3.9 illustrates the S-curve effect on four generations of product platforms at Lam Research Corporation over several decades. Lam, a supplier of etch wafer fabrication equipment for the IC manufacturing market, developed successive generations of product platforms to serve the market needs for increasing wafer size following Moore's law of semiconductor device technology. Figure 3.9 illustrates how the revenue from sales of each generation of platform has approximately a 10-year life cycle, following an S-curve to a peak and then subsequently declining to the end of life. Figure 3.10 illustrates how Lam, which understands the S-curve model, sustained its strong position in the poly etch equipment

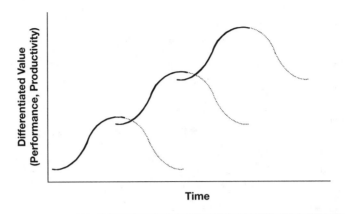

Figure 3.8. S-Curve Model of Product Value.

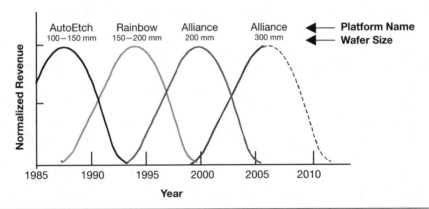

Figure 3.9. Life Cycle History of Successive Generations of Product Platforms at Lam Research Corporation.

market by introducing a series of successive products through technology innovation in platform and process application. The aggregate unit shipment of systems in the poly etch market segment (Figure 3.10) grew over the years by timing of the development and introduction of each new generation of product line such that the growth period of each new generation overlapped the declining phase of the prior generation.

Note: As Figures 3.8, 3.9, and 3.10 illustrate, the timing of the introduction of a new product and technology is critical to sustaining business growth. Too early introduction truncates profitability of the existing product line and too late introduction of a new generation product results in loss of market position, life cycle profitability, and return on investment (ROI.)

3.10 VALUE PROPOSITION

Value proposition is the description of the *differentiating benefit* of a product, which states target customers, the application, and the compelling reason why a customer should buy the product rather than an alternative offering. For example, the compelling reason for a customer of an industrial product to buy a product is to make his/her business successful by significantly reducing operating costs and enhancing competitive advantage. Typically, a good price/performance benefit for an industrial customer is more than 30% improvement in performance and productivity or a 30% reduction in costs over the customer's existing solution.

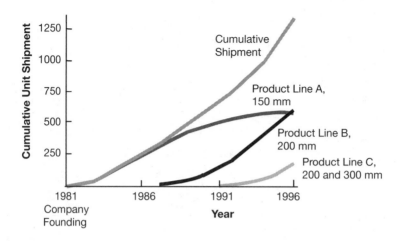

Figure 3.10. S-Curves at Lam Research Poly Etch Division—Product Life Cycle and New Product Commercialization Timing.

In developing a new product, the development team often has myriad choices in features, capabilities, and benefits that can be incorporated in the *whole* product offering. The responsibility of marketing managers is to prioritize the product capabilities and features by scaling their differentiating value to target customers in "must have," "should have," or "nice to have" categories. Team resources should be apportioned correspondingly. (*Note*: Chapters 7 and 10 will discuss the subject of prioritization of value in designing a new product in detail and present a holistic framework for such analysis.)

In order to prioritize opportunities, recognize that the product value scale applies differently to different people in a customer's organization in a B-to-B market. Players in a customer's company who are involved in the purchase decision include:

1. The initiator (recognizes the need)
2. The influencer
3. The decider (the ultimate decision maker)
4. The purchaser (authorizes the financial commitment)
5. The user

For example, in a semiconductor IC manufacturing company such as Intel, the players in the purchase of process equipment would include:

- The process application manager
- The process manager's peers (people who are impacted by the decision)
- The process integration manager
- R&D scientists (in component engineering and process technology)
- Fab managers, the "process equipment development committee" members (including equipment engineers, managers, and vice president)
- The purchasing agent and his/her managers
- The vice president of technology

The different players in the purchase decision process will perceive the value of the supplier's product differently according to their personal interest/preferences, the metrics by which their job performance are measured, and the impact of the decision on their power base in their organization.

For example, engineers tend to prefer a technology that "works" and they value product performance; a middle manager, who is taking a risk with a new technology or a new supplier, will have many concerns about the product because the decision to buy could be career limiting for him/her; the executive (e.g., a vice president), who is competing with other departments over budget issues, might prefer to extend the life of his/her existing installed base products and not buy a new equipment or to refrain from outsourcing (that results in less work for his/her own people) and do the work in-house; the CEO, on the other hand, will be excited about the vision of a bright future that is enabled by the supplier's new product technology and might be thinking about partnership and risk sharing with the supplier.

3.11 MARKET SEGMENTATION IN PRODUCT DEVELOPMENT

To develop a winning product, marketers must:

- Segment the market
- Identify the target customers
- Understand their characteristics
- Define a value proposition that captures the customer's imagination
- Develop a roadmap for the product
- Position the product in the mind of the customers with respect to competitors

These topics will be discussed in subsequent sections of this chapter.

A group of actual or potential customers who share common desires, needs, and buying patterns constitutes a *segment* in the market. These customers also reference each other. The marketing challenge is to identify the dominant characteristics of a particular segment and to create a product that satisfies the needs arising from those characteristics. A market can be segmented by industry, by customer application, by geography, or by other common buying behaviors.

For example, the semiconductor manufacturing equipment market is segmented by *front-end process* needs and *back-end packaging* needs. Front-end process equipment is in turn segmented by applications such as etch, deposition, lithography, and metrology/inspection equipment, each of which is further segmented by a specific technology application such as dielectric etch for interconnect applications or conductor etch for transistor gate applications. The equipment market is also segmented by countries or geographic regions such as the United States, Japan, Southeast Asia, and Europe. As another example, the microprocessor market served by Intel is segmented by hardware-oriented customers, software-oriented customers who use Intel's software, and software-oriented customers who want to write their own software.

Customers can belong to many segments. For example, global IC manufacturers are in all of the process application segments and in many geographical segments. Market segments may relate to each other. For example, dielectric and conductor etch market segments are related in the desire for commonality of product subsystems, spare parts, and service. Hence customers may prefer to buy both types of etch equipment from the same supplier, "collapsing" the two segments. Etch and CVD equipment is also interrelated in process integration needs. A film that is deposited by a CVD tool must be "etch-able" by the etch equipment. Another example of segment interdependencies is the digital dental X-ray market in which penetration into the segment of dentists depends on the insurance companies that accept the technology.

Customer buying behavior and market segments are formed by many attributes of the elements of the marketing mix such as product and technology characteristics (e.g., low-cost or high-end products, early adopters or the late majority in technology adoption, etc.), customer order size and purchasing power, geography, culture, and distribution channels. High-tech market segments shift over time as the industry and technology mature, which could create an opportunity for gaining competitive advantage.

Segmenting the market and understanding shifts and change are important in product development because they impact product definition (including ancillary products that are needed for delivering a solution to customers), product positioning, and the requirements and methods of supporting the product. Market segmentation also enables a product development team, including marketers, to focus their resources on a segment in which they can create a commanding position. By developing products that meet precise customer requirements, a firm can dominate (>50% market share) a specific niche market and use it as a base for expansion. Targeting a market segment will cause participation to be less costly (in R&D, marketing/sales, and other costs) and is particularly essential for start-up companies with limited resources. By focusing on a specific market segment, a small company can gain a large market share in the segment and discourage competitors from pursuing the business. In this way, a small company can match the resources of a much larger competitor.

An effective method of characterizing target customers is to use scenarios with different types of customers and applications. Envisioning the environment of different types of customers and what they will do with the product helps marketers to gain significant knowledge about the product requirements of customers, about the customers' skills in using the product efficiently, and whether a customer must change his/her behavior and operational process in order to take full advantage of the benefits of the product.

Assessing a customer's alternate choices in satisfying his/her needs helps to identify the differentiating benefits of the product and the features that offer a competitive advantage. "Living" in the customer's environment is important for the product development team and marketing, engineering, and support people—to learn the customer's language, think the customer's thoughts, and feel the customer's emotions. Team members can also learn a lot from service people who have first-hand experience with the customer's operating environment.

3.12 SEGMENT ANALYSIS

To assess and prioritize the market opportunity for a proposed product/technology, a marketing manager must perform a segment analysis to determine how well the product's capabilities and features satisfy the value parameters of customers compared to the competitors' products. Figures 3.11 and 3.12 illustrate frameworks for segment analysis.

The first column in Figure 3.11 lists market value parameters (or demand vectors) that customers use in making a purchase decision. These parameters could be the product's performance metrics, cost, ease of use, extendibility of the product, service, and support. The second column lists customer requirements for each of the value parameters to quantify the specification. In segment analysis, focusing on the future rather than the past is important. In other words, customer needs and the capabilities of competitive products in the future must be assessed against the new or enhanced product that marketing is planning to develop. Segment analysis must identify the segment market share goal. The product marketing manager must then prepare an action plan to achieve the objective (as shown in Figure 3.11). The action plan

Market Value (Purchase Decision) Parameters	Customer Needs/ Requirements (Specification)	Competitive Performance Today/ Future	Firms Current Product Performance	Firms Future Product Performance	Projects to Fill Gaps and Create Compelling Competitive Advantage
A (Performance)					
B (Productivity)					
C (COO)					
Branding and Positioning					
Others					

Market Segment: _____

Market Share Goal in 1 Year = ___%

Product Name:_____
Product Marketing Manager: _____
Date: _____

Figure 3.11. Segment Analysis.

1. Feature	2. Benefit	3. Competitive Advantage	4. Proof
Product capability or enabler	What value does the customer draw from this feature? What need or want does this feature fulfill?	What is the compelling advantage over competitive offering?	Quantify the benefit and delivery of the intended value (data, analysis).
1			
2			
3			

Figure 3.12. Product Description and Differentiating Benefits.

should identify product and market development tasks that, when completed, will ensure product competitive advantage and achievement of the market share goal.

Figure 3.11 is a tool for internal use and for guiding the product development effort. Figure 3.12, however, could be used in a presentation to a customer. Figure 3.12 is a framework that may be used to list the product's features/capabilities and the benefits that are of value to the customer and that form the basis for his/her purchase decision (columns 1 and 2). Column 3

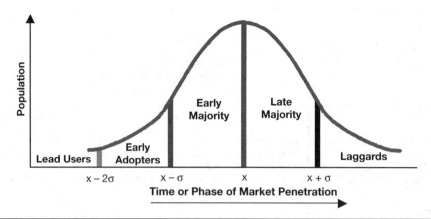

Figure 3.13. Diffusion of Innovation and Technology Adoption Life Cycle Model. (Source: Adapted from Rogers, E.M. *Diffusion of Innovations, Fourth Edition.* New York: Free Press; 1995 and Von Hippel, E. Lead users: a source of novel product concepts. *Management Science* 1986 July; 32(7).)

highlights the competitive differentiation of the product benefits and column 4 lists proof of the product's capabilities with data and analysis.

3.13 MARKET SEGMENTATION BY DIFFUSION OF INNOVATION AND THE TECHNOLOGY ADOPTION LIFE CYCLE

TALC (technology adoption life cycle) is a model for understanding the rate of acceptance of new high-tech products in a market. This model applies when a new product requires the customers to change their current mode of behavior and/or to modify other products and services they rely on. Change-sensitive products are often referred to as "discontinuous innovations" in contrast to "continuous innovations." Continuous innovations are improvements over existing products that do not require customers to change their behavior. Diffusion of innovation and TALC models describe the *market penetration* of a new high-tech product in terms of progression of the types of customers that the new product attracts based on the customers' perceptions of risk/reward of the new technology and their risk-taking tolerance.

Figure 3.13 illustrates a diffusion framework developed by Everett Rogers as the population of different customer groups over the penetration phases of a new technology product in the market.[24] According to the model, a new technology product is adopted in five phases, which are represented by five groups of customers—lead users or innovators, early adopters, early majority, late majority, and laggards. In Figure 3.13 wide acceptance of a new technological innovation depends on the rate of diffusion from left to right. The diffusion rate depends on a reference from an earlier group, the product quality in fulfilling the group's needs, and the effort of the marketing campaign.

Lead users (innovators). Lead users are technologists or technology enthusiasts (and the users discussed in Section 3.7.4). Lead users pursue new technology products aggressively, they are price insensitive, and, sometimes, they seek out a new technology product even before it is launched (released). Innovators buy because they like technology and want to explore the functions and possibilities of a new device. Innovators might be members of an R&D department of a high-tech company, who must always keep abreast of the latest advances in the supply chain. There are few innovators in a given market segment, but their endorsement reassures others that the product does work. Innovators are very valuable in critiquing a new product. They push/help a supplier to "get the bugs out" to make the product functional.

Early adopters. Early adopters are not technology enthusiasts, but they have some insight in matching emerging technology to a strategic opportunity. They imagine how the benefits of a new technology relate to solving their own problems, gaining competitive advantage (by differentiating their products), improving performance and productivity of their product, improving their services, and improving profitability by reducing operation cost. Early adopters are willing to take risks, believing that the rewards outweigh the newness risks of the technology. Early adopters make buying decisions with only limited data (for demonstrating performance of the new technology product) and rely on their own intuition and analysis. This group is crucial to the success of a new technology product because their reference influences the early majority, which represents the lion's share of a market opportunity. For example, in the semiconductor IC manufacturers industry, new entrants to the market and those who are in a weak competitive position are often early adopters. They seek competitive advantage through process technology innovation and work closely with equipment suppliers to co-develop new technologies and to be the first to deploy them in IC production.

Early majority. Early majority customers are somewhat driven by technology and are comfortable with handling a new technology product. They are primarily driven by a strong sense of practicality. Early adopters require a lot of data that demonstrates the performance of a new product before they buy. Early majority customers will only take a moderate amount of risk. Because there are many customers in this category, winning their business is a major step in product market acceptability and business growth.

Late majority. Late majority customers wait until a new technology has become an "established standard" in the market infrastructure and in the supplier's product portfolio. They tend to buy from large and well-established companies. Numerous customers are in this category. Their businesses could be very large and profitable because late majority customers buy in the maturity phase of a product's life cycle when the cost of manufacturing and support of the product is low.

Laggards. Laggards are not interested in and are skeptical of new technology. Laggards are the last group of customers to buy. Business buyers in this category often object to a new technology even when it is embedded inside a subsystem of the supplier's product. For example, in the IC manufacturing industry, laggards are either manufacturers of older low-tech commodity products or they are strong players who are market leaders and have weak competition. Strong players are risk-averse and try to leverage existing technologies in their next generation products for maximum operational efficiency. These customers only adopt a new technology when it is a "must have" enabler on their product roadmap.

3.14 IMPACT OF MARKET INFRASTRUCTURE ON NEW PRODUCT PENETRATION

New products in emerging markets require a mature enough infrastructure to enable the product experience to be acceptable and of value to customers. Therefore market infrastructure development must be an integral part of the market strategy and must be concurrent with

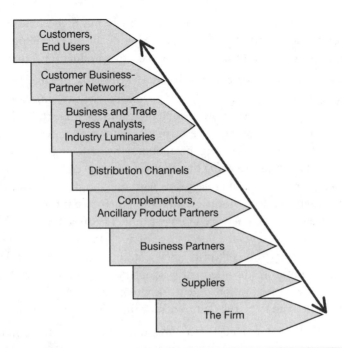

Figure 3.14. Path of Influence in Market Infrastructure.

development of the new product. Market infrastructure consists of the network of market stakeholders who influence the experience of value and purchase decisions of customers.

Marketing must create a map of market infrastructure and a path of influence as depicted in Figure 3.14. Early in the process of developing a new product, specific actions, such as establishment of alliances and co-development partnerships, must be planned with respect to each of the players in the path of market influence. An effective approach in charting the course of market creation, including market positioning, development of market infrastructure, and definition of the *whole* product, is to create a hypothesis and to test its acceptance among the stakeholders of the infrastructure on a real-time basis.[25] The following case illustrates the impact of market infrastructure on the commercialization success of a digital imaging product.

3.15 PRODUCT DEVELOPMENT AND COMMERCIALIZATION INVESTMENT

This section will briefly discuss the categories of fixed and variable costs that comprise the total investment required to get a product to the point of realizing a profit from its sale after market introduction. The total investment is significantly higher than the cost of engineering development of the product, particularly when the product is targeted for a market that is new to a firm. In high-tech markets, the costs of marketing, selling (distribution), and supporting the product are often more than the costs of manufacturing the product (e.g., the manufacturing cost of a software product is negligible). The nature of the investments in manufacturing, distribution, and support infrastructure may also change, e.g., from pilot production and soft tooling to volume production.

CASE STUDY—MARKET ACCEPTANCE OF IMAGIZER

Setting. In 1996 digital imaging technology had already created myriad new market opportunities in almost every industry. The founders of Image Science Corporation were banking on an opportunity in the dental healthcare industry. X-ray films were widely used in the industry for diagnostics by dentists, for preoperative authorization, and postoperative payment by insurance companies and transaction processing intermediaries. X-ray films of patients' teeth were taken at dental offices and mailed back and forth, physically, for pre- and postoperative processing.

Situation. The founders of Image Science invented a new product that would "digitize" dental X-rays at high speed, upload them into a computer, and attach them to a patient's database of records. Once the X-ray films were digitized, the films were filed away and not used again. The digital images were used by dentists on the large screen of a computer (compared to a 1.5-in. square transparency) in consultations with patients and then e-mailed to insurance companies and transaction processing centers.

Image Science knew that their new product (Imagizer) would substantially reduce transactional costs for all stakeholders, increase the speed of dental care (e-mail versus snail-mail), and improve the quality of care and patient satisfaction. The largest market segment for Imagizer was dental offices. Although insurance companies and transaction processing centers also needed Imagizer, the unit demand was much smaller. The viability of Image Science's business plan depended on Imagizer populating a large fraction of dental offices in the United States.

The founders soon found out, however, that the value of Imagizer to dentists strongly depended on product acceptance by the rest of the market stakeholders. These market stakeholders included claim assessors and reviewing dentists at insurance companies, insurance claim processing centers, distribution channels for dental equipment through which Imagizer must be made available and sold to the dentists, claim lawyers who had to be convinced of the safeguards for authenticity of digital images in contrast with a hard-copy X-ray film, and government regulators who had to be convinced that lawyers were happy!

Image Science Corporation had to steer the prevalent behavior of the players away from physical X-ray films to digital images. The marketing strategy for Imagizer had to include development of the market infrastructure and winning acceptance of digital dental images in diagnostics, processing, and financial transactions. Image Science had to have a multipronged market penetration approach with its limited resources.

Outcome. Three years later in 1999, the president of Image Science was frustrated with the slow pace of market acceptance for Imagizer. The market opportunity window was also being threatened by the advent of direct X-ray digital imaging technology that was destined to eliminate X-ray films all together!

Investments that must be made for delivery of the *whole* product to the market include:

1. Product development and commercialization costs
   - Marketing
   - R&D, engineering, prototyping (alpha and beta), development systems, and documentation
   - Product introduction, including evaluation prototypes and support
2. Market infrastructure development costs
   - Sales staff, distributors, reps, partners, and alliances
   - Support people and facilities near customers, training facilities, and products for training
3. Manufacturing fixed costs
   - Manufacturing infrastructure, facilities, tooling, and supply chain development

4. Manufacturing variable costs
   • Material, labor, and cost of inventory
5. Selling and support costs
   • Marketing and promotion
   • Selling and distribution
   • Sales support collateral, facilities, and demo units
   • Installation and warranty
   • Service and support, including labor, material, training courses, and spares inventory

Management cost, enterprise operational overhead, and the cost of capital should be added to the above items. Depending on the newness of the technology, product, and market, the confidence uncertainty band in the cost estimates should also be assessed—20 to 30% accuracy would be very good. (*Note*: Chapter 10 includes a detailed discussion of the subject of ROI in product development.)

3.16 THE PRODUCT ROADMAP

The purpose of a product roadmap is to elucidate how existing products will evolve and what new products will be developed and commercialized over the planned period. The evolution of an existing product line could include continuous improvement to gain market share, development of derivative products to extend the market and to enter into new segments, and cost reduction to grow market demand. The development of a new product might be in response to changing requirements of the target segment and be driven by the industry technology roadmap or it could be aimed at capitalizing on new market opportunities.

In the case of a new technology, the product roadmap should reflect the diffusion of the technology through TALC and should identify the evolution on the basis of competition and marketing mix components (i.e., product configuration, pricing, distribution, and positioning). When the market is technology driven, the firm's technology roadmap must also be developed in conjunction with the product roadmap, identifying the key milestones in technology development and exploitation corresponding with the product evolution.

The product roadmap consolidates the business, market, and technology strategies into a product and market development vision and guides the firm's product commercialization and marketing programs. The roadmap for a BU product line must be updated on a semiannual basis.

An example of a product roadmap for a Sony CNS product (car navigation system) is shown in Figure 3.15.[26] The CNS roadmap starts from the "infancy" of the CNS product when early adopters are targeted and extends to product "maturity" when it becomes a mainstream product and is installed in most mid- to high-end cars. Product model numbers for each phase of technology diffusion and customer group are also envisioned to ensure proper configuration management and branding. (*Note*: The Sony marketing team plan for the distribution channel evolving from direct sales and specialty aftermarket to OEM [original equipment manufacturing] contracts when CNS becomes a mainstream product.) The basis of competition (or the competitive criterion) also changes throughout the product adoption life cycle. The basis of competition starts as a *first mover advantage* for affluent early adopters and ends at *cost* when the product has matured as a commodity in the mainstream market. The price target for each segment is also shown on the roadmap in Figure 3.15.

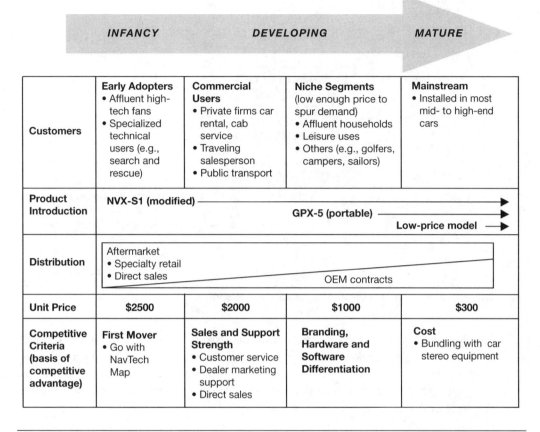

Figure 3.15. Sony CNS Product Marketing Roadmap, United States Market. (Source: Adapted from Quelch, J.A., Fujikawa, Y. *Sony Corp.: Car Navigation Systems*. Case Number TN-5-598-082. Boston: Harvard Business School; 1998.)

When developing the product roadmap, marketers must be cognizant of interdependencies between technology and the product roadmaps of other players in the supply chain. An industrial product in a high-tech B-to-B market is often a subsystem/component of a customer's product or is an enabler of customers' manufacturing processes:

- When Sony's CNS penetrates the mainstream OEM market (see Figure 3.15), it will be driven by the product roadmap of the target car manufacturers.
- In the supply chain of semiconductor products and the IC manufacturing process, a radio frequency generator is integrated as a subsystem onto a thin film etcher that is used in a factory for the fabrication of integrated circuits. The product roadmap of one supplier is driven by and is dependent upon the roadmap of other high-tech players in the supply chain.

The responsibility of marketers is to ensure that their product roadmap integrates the customers' and the suppliers' roadmaps and to drive the supply base, in addition to his/her own development team, to meet the planned milestones on the roadmap. The following examples are from the semiconductor process equipment market:

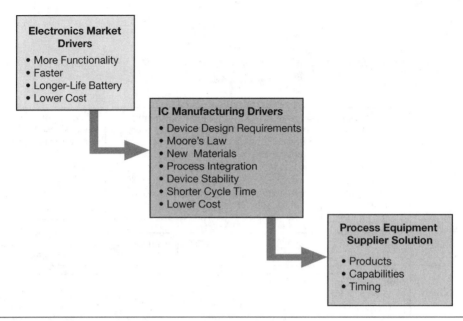

Figure 3.16. IC Industry—Drivers of Technology and Product Roadmap.

Example 1. Figure 3.16 is an illustration of the drivers of technology and a product roadmap in the electronic market of cell phones, handheld organizers, and digital appliances. The market for these products demands faster performance, a longer-life battery, and lower cost. These requirements drive chip design and manufacturing suppliers, which in turn drive the process equipment supply chain.

Example 2. Figure 3.17 depicts the technology roadmap for IC device packaging, which integrates a cascade of technology and product drivers in the supply chain.

Example 3. Figure 3.18 illustrates the product roadmap for an IC manufacturer that spans several technology node generations. Manufacturing technology development and the production ramp plan drive process equipment development (at the suppliers) through the identified time spans for equipment evaluation and selection. Note the long process of evaluating and selecting process equipment at each IC technology node. Marketing managers at process equipment suppliers use a customer roadmap such as the one in Figure 3.18, not only for the development of their product roadmap, but also for planning their business and forecasting sales. Based on IC manufacturers' timing of ordering equipment for volume production, their planned fab capacity, and annual investment plan, marketing managers can forecast revenue following the format of Figure 3.19.

Example 4. Figure 3.20 illustrates an example of a product roadmap for CMP (chemical mechanical planarization) equipment that is used in IC manufacturing to planarize deposited copper thin films prior to lithographic patterning. The CMP product roadmap in Figure 3.20 is based on IC manufacturing technology and production roadmaps such as those in Figures 3.16 and 3.18. Figure 3.20 depicts a 4-year roadmap that shows the progression of device design rules (technology nodes) per the industry's roadmap (Moore's law), IC production schedule

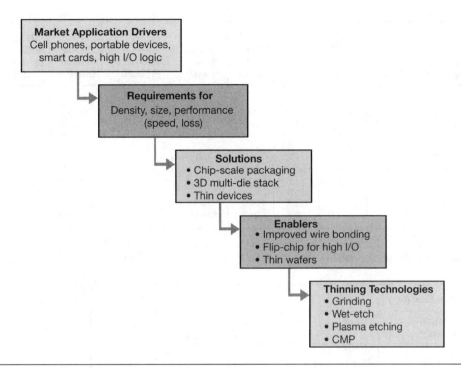

Figure 3.17. IC Device Packaging—Technology Roadmap.

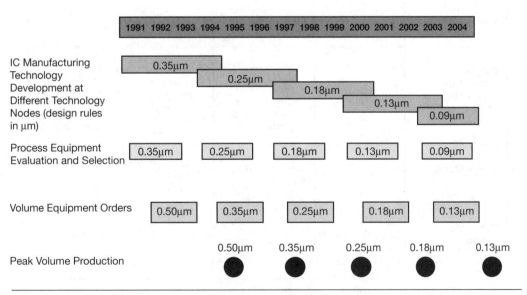

Figure 3.18. Timing of IC Manufacturing Technology Drives Process Equipment Development.

Customer/ Fab Line	Investment ($M)			Wafer Size (mm)	Design Rule (nm)	Customer's Product	Firm's Product Offering	Sales Potential (in Units and $)
	2003	2004	2005					
Customer A: • Fab 1 • Fab 2	200 300	1000 200	400 1900	200 200/300	180 90	Foundry manufacturing	List of products	
Customer B: • Fab 1 • Fab 2	100 200	300 300	400 900	200 200	180 130	Logic devices	List of products	
Customer C: • Fab 1 • Fab 2	2000 600	950 2000	3000 800	300 300	130/90 130/65	Microprocessor	List of products	

Figure 3.19. Manufacturer's Investment Plan and Process Equipment Sales Forecast.

Feature Size (nm)	130	90	70	40
Production Ramp Year	2002	2003	2005	2007
Underlying Dielectric Film Roadmap	Fluoro-Silicate Glass	Carbon Silicate Glass	Ultra-Low Dielectric Organic Film	?
Copper Recess and Dishing Requirement (Å)	<400	<350	<250	<150?
Supplier Technology/ Product Solution, (to be developed in time)	Process Formulation X	Second-Generation Polishing Head Design, Advanced Process Control Algorithm	Low Mechanical Down Force (<3 psi) and High-Speed Rotation of Polishing Pad (>400 rpm)	New Platform Design and Process for "Mostly Chemical" Removal of Cu
Competitor A Solution	Current Solution	Redesigning Current Product for Improved Reliability	Next-Generation Polishing Head and Platform	?
Competitor B Solution	New Revolutionary Design	?	?	?

Figure 3.20. Product Technology Roadmap—Copper CMP Equipment.

timing, and requirements for the critical CMP process parameters at each node. Figure 3.20 also shows how the CMP supplier is planning to meet the market requirement by developing the necessary CMP technology and product platforms. The product roadmap of the top two competitors is also shown for identifying any emerging competitive threat or opportunity.

	Requirement/Target	2003	2005	2007
Application and Devices	Technology Generation, Design Rule (nm) • Microprocessor • Memory (DRAM)	90 X-GHz 1 Gb	65 Y-GHz 4 Gb	45 Z-GHz 16 Gb
	Number of Metal Levels in Logic Devices	7	9	11
	Wafer Size (mm)	200/300	300	300
Aluminum Sputtering Process	• Temperature Control • Low Cost	Product A CIP	Product A CIP	?
Copper Plating Process	• Void-Free Fill • Minimum Pattern Dependence • Stable Microstructure	Product B CIP	Product C	Product D
Platform and System for all Applications	• Low Cost • Throughput (wafers per hour) • Wafer Size (mm)	Platforms A and B: 75 200/300	Platforms B and C: 75 300	Platform C: 75 300

Figure 3.21. Technology and Product Roadmap—Aluminum Sputtering and Copper Plating.

Question marks (?) or open fields in the figure highlight gaps in the supplier's understanding of market needs, in its technology portfolio, and in competitive intelligence.

Example 5. Figure 3.21 is another example of a semiconductor process equipment roadmap. In this example, the company has two product lines, aluminum sputtering and copper plating equipment. The figure lists the technology generations and device applications of the served market segments, namely, memory (DRAM) and microprocessor device manufacturing. The roadmap depicts the evolution of the process technology as well as the platforms of the two product lines. "Platform and System" refer to subsystems of the products that transport wafers and interface to IC production fab. The platform roadmap is intended to meet the wafer size, cost, and productivity needs of device manufacturing.

Example 6. Figure 3.22 illustrates an example of a flat panel display (FPD) manufacturing market roadmap that depicts the manufacturing capability needs to capture ever increasing market opportunity for FPDs in obsolescing cathode ray tube (CRT) monitors and televisions. This example is for the liquid crystal thin-film transistor (TFT) technology in fabrication of flat panel displays.

The primary market drivers are increase of FPD size and cost reduction. FPD market segments include:

- Consumer products, including digital cameras, mobile phones, global navigation systems (GNS), digital devices, and appliances
- Laptop computers
- Workstation monitors
- Televisions

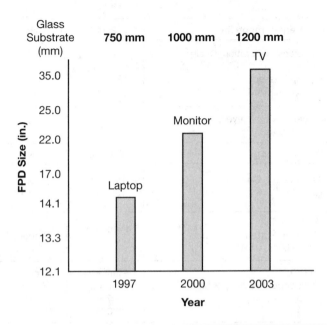

Figure 3.22. Manufacturing and Market Roadmap—Flat Panel Display.

The requirements shown in Figure 3.22 drive the roadmap for process equipment used in FPD manufacturing. Suppliers of processing equipment must develop ever-larger glass-handling capability, improve productivity, and lower manufacturing costs. (*Note*: By 2004, advances in equipment and manufacturing technology had enabled FPD to make impressive inroads into replacing CRT products in the huge computer and television markets.)

3.17 POSITIONING STRATEGY

A brand position is the prospect's "state of mind" about a supplier and its product. Factors that create a particular position for a brand in a customer's mind include the customer's experience, references from external sources (such as other users and competitors), and the supplier's efforts to communicate the value proposition and its differential advantage to the customer. A customer positions a brand in three dimensions—the company, the product, and the market status.

Product marketers must establish a positioning strategy, identifying the desired position and the action plan that creates this position in the customer's mind. A positioning strategy should start with a positioning *statement* that articulates the value of the product to the customer (in fulfilling her/his needs) and its comparative advantage to competitors. An effective positioning statement captures the customer's imagination. It is concise, simple, believable, defendable, and memorable.

In positioning a new product, customers must easily recognize the *name* and *category* of the product, the target user (*who*), the purpose of the product (*what*), the *competition*, and the provider (the *company's* name, financial strength, and staying power). To a customer, the degree of importance of each part of this information varies based on the phase of technology diffusion and the market acceptance of the product. For example, in a technology adoption life

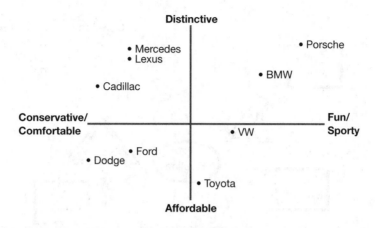

Figure 3.23. Perpetual Map—Positioning of Different Brands of Cars.

cycle, innovators are only interested in the product technology and what it does, but the late majority wants to know about the competition and the company.

Geoffrey Moore has proposed documenting a positioning strategy by filling in the blanks of a format.[4] This format articulates the value proposition of the supplier in delivering a product with differentiated advantage to the target customer segment:

- *For* (target customer)
- *Who* (statement of the need or opportunity)
- *The* (product name) is a (product category)
- *That* (statement of the key benefit, i.e., the compelling reason to buy)
- *Unlike* (primary competitive alternative)
- *Our product* (statement of primary differentiation)

To develop a positioning strategy, marketers must first understand the current state of their product in prospects' minds. To assess the existing position of a brand in comparison to the competitors' brands, a variety of attribute-based methods can be used. A few of these methods and formats are discussed below and illustrated in Figures 3.23, 3.24, 3.25, and 3.26. Some of these methods use qualitative attributes and dimensions that are important to the target customers, while others use quantifiable customer value metrics. Using these tools, marketers can assess the gap between the current position of their product and the desired position and create a marketing action plan to fill the gap. The action plan might include development of a new product, improvement of an existing product, a Marcom initiative to inform and educate the customers, or a new pricing strategy.

3.17.1 The Perpetual Map

A perpetual map plots the relative position of the different brands of a product against the attribute coordinates that are important to buyers. Figure 3.23 depicts the positioning of various brands of cars in two coordinates: affordable to distinctive and conservative/comfortable to fun/sporty. Note that a depicted position of a brand is not necessarily what the supplier desires, but what the buyers (generally) believe. The coordinates of a perpetual map do not represent the relative goodness of a position or an attribute. This map is merely a tool to assist marketers to target customers and to reinforce or alter their belief systems through appropriate marketing actions.

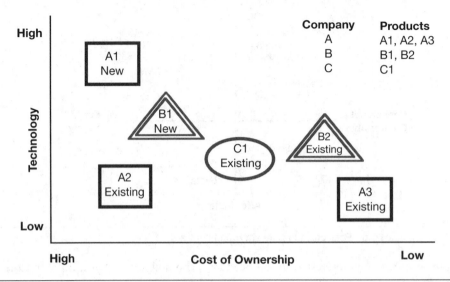

Figure 3.24. Positioning of Semiconductor Process Equipment Manufactured by Companies A, B, and C.

Figure 3.24 is another example of a perpetual map. Figure 3.24 depicts the relative position of products from three suppliers of process equipment in the semiconductor fabrication market. The dimensions of value to the buyers in this market are technology (performance) and cost of ownership in IC manufacturing.

3.17.2 The Bingo Chart

A bingo chart is a graphic illustration of a product's acceptance by target customers. It is particularly useful in a high-tech industrial market and in assessing penetration into key accounts. Figure 3.25 depicts an example from the semiconductor manufacturing equipment market. In Figure 3.25, the positioning status of the various product lines of a supplier is shown. The chart shows whether the key account customers have made the decision to use the supplier's product in production or not. In semiconductor industry jargon, a product is considered to be the "production tool of record" or PTOR if it has been qualified by the customer for production. A box with an **O** on the bingo chart in Figure 3.25 indicates that the firm's product has a PTOR status; a box with a **C** indicates that competition has claimed the PTOR position; and a box with an **S** box indicates that the customer has either decided to split the order or has not yet made a decision—and hence, there is a short-term opportunity for action.

3.17.3 The Market Print (Spider Map)

A spider map is an effective tool for assessing the competitiveness of a firm's products (in attributes that are of highest value to customers) in meeting customer requirements. Figure 3.26 is a spider map for etch equipment in the semiconductor manufacturing industry. The concentric circles represent the layers of customer requirements at the present and in the future, corresponding to different IC technology nodes from 0.18 micron (μm) to 0.09 μm.

To make a spider map easy to interpret, the spikes are scaled such that the outward direction (away from the center) represents the direction of increased *goodness* for all the parameters on the map. Customer requirements for each technology node are noted on the

Positioning Code:			Competition (C)	Split (S)	Ours (O)

		Key Accounts							
Market Segment	**Product Line/ Application**	**Intel**	**IBM**	**TSMC**	**UMC**	**TI**	**ST**	**Toshiba**	**Samsung**
CVD	ILD	C	C	O	O	O	O	S	S
	STI	S	C	O	O	C	O	O	O
Etch	Dielectric	C	C	S	O	S	C	O	O
	Conductor	S	C	C	S	S	S	C	C
CMP	Dielectric	O	C	O	S	O	C	O	O
	Copper	S	C	O	C	S	C	S	S

Figure 3.25. Bingo Chart—Key Account Positioning in Semiconductor Process Equipment Market. ILD, inter-layer dielectric; STI, shallow trench isolation.

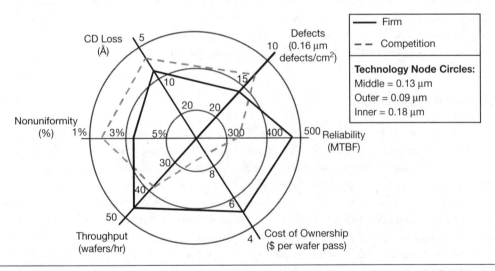

Figure 3.26. Spider Map (Market Print)—Competitiveness of Etch Process Equipment in Semiconductor Fabrication Market; MTBF, mean time between failures.

corresponding circle along the spike of the attribute. The actual performance of the firm's products and competitors' current products is plotted along each spike, and the points are connected with straight lines.

Figure 3.27 is another example of a spider map. This example illustrates how a spider map can be used for decision making in product development. In Figure 3.27, the strength of alternate platforms is assessed to select the best for designing semiconductor process equipment. In

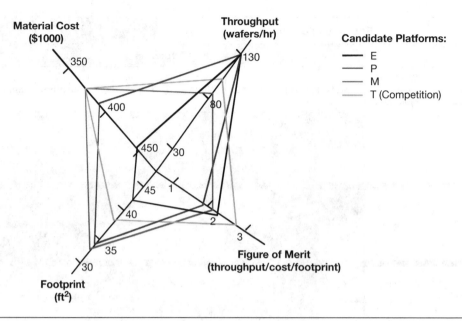

Figure 3.27. Spider Map Ranking Alternate Product Platforms in Product Development.

a selection analysis, each platform's material cost, throughput, and physical dimensions (footprint) are chosen as the critical parameters because they impact the product profit margin, productivity, and fab clean room space utilization, respectively. A figure of merit, as the ratio of throughput to cost and footprint, is shown as an aggregate metric in comparing the different platform options. The attributes of a competitive platform are also shown on the map to ensure that the selected platform is superior in the supply chain.

3.18 VALUE PRICING

The price of a product is what a customer is willing to pay for the value received. The Roman (Syrian-born) mimeographer, Publius Syrus said in 100 B.C., "Everything is worth what its purchaser will pay for it." Philip Kotler defines price as "the consideration, usually money, that is exchanged for the product or service offered."[27]

To create a customer value model, one must begin by generating a comprehensive list of customer value factors. Value factors are product attributes and features that fulfill customers' needs and wants and attributes and features that customers are willing to pay for. For example, for a business customer, value factors enhance the customer's competitiveness and lower the cost of doing business (and of manufacturing a product). Value factors can be technical, economic, support, psychological (uncertainty and fear), or social (trust and relationship). Value factors also include the exclusivity effect and accessibility of alternative solutions. For example, the exclusivity of a value factor might be created by a protected intellectual property (IP) or by capacity constraints in the supply chain. Value factors often include the customer's life cycle experience with the *whole* product, including the product's cost of ownership, installation cost, ease of use, post-sale service and support, and the characteristics of the supplier (branding, relationship, and longevity).

A monetary value can be assigned to each of the factors to create a "value model" for the worth of the product to a customer. In order to create the customer value model, the supplier must fully understand the customer's:

- Needs and wants
- The operating environment in which the product is utilized
- Alternate choices
- Business objectives and success factors
- The business model, in which the supplier's product is considered as an operating expense (for services) or a capital item
- The business process in acquiring the supplier's product, including key customer players in the process (influencers, the economic buyer, the decision maker, etc.)

Such deep understanding of the customer can only be achieved through a very close relationship with the customer and mutual trust. Often, business customers do not permit suppliers to have significant visibility into their R&D projects and business operations because they prefer to protect their IP and market-sensitive information, to not give one supplier an unfair advantage over another, and to not weaken their own position in price negotiations with the supplier.

3.18.1 Customer Pricing Decisions

Factors that affect a customer's pricing decision (and a supplier's consent) can be grouped into five categories:

1. Customer factors
   - Reference price
   - Perceived quality/value
   - Psychological price point
   - Psychology and negotiation process
   - Budget (constrained by operation and business models, business condition, and competitiveness)
2. Competitive factors (customer's choice)
3. Market conditions
   - Power of buyer versus supplier
   - Supply condition and exclusivity
   - Elasticity
4. Supplier's pricing strategy
   - Competitive insulation
   - Skim
   - Penetrate
   - Market positioning*
5. Product factors

---

*Value chain positioning is an important consideration in the strategic pricing of products, which is illustrated by the experience of a leading process equipment supplier in the semiconductor industry. A marketing manager summarized the experience as: "We give big discounts to large and strong foundry customers who place large orders and sell at high prices to small customers. This practice drives the small customers out of the business of manufacturing their own ICs and forces them to outsource to the big foundries, which in turn become even bigger (foundries) and stronger customers. Our gross margin gets further eroded as the order mix becomes even more biased toward the big customers!"

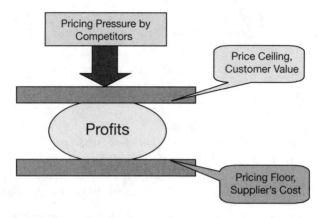

Figure 3.28. Simple Pricing Model.

- Differentiation in value factors
- Life cycle stage
- Cost (of manufacturing the product)

A simple model of pricing is depicted in Figure 3.28. The supplier's profitability is constrained by the cost of producing and marketing the product (the floor) and the value factors that the customer is willing to pay for (the ceiling). The ceiling is influenced by the customer's reference price, i.e., the price of rival products or the cost of alternate methods of satisfying the customer's needs (e.g., an in-house solution). A brief discussion of pricing theory and value pricing is presented in the next section.

3.18.2 Pricing Theory

A customer's *economic value* is equal to the *reference value* plus the *differential value*. The *differential value* could be positive or negative, depending on pricing factors (see Section 3.18.1). Figure 3.29 provides a model of customer and supplier pricing economics. In this example, the customer's economic model is based on the product's cost of ownership (COO) or the sum of the purchase price (P), the installation/start-up costs (IS), and the operation and maintenance costs (OM) over the life cycle of the product. The COO for the reference product A and the supplier's product B is designated by a subscript corresponding to the product's name (A or B). The price that the customer is willing to pay is equal to or below the customer's economic value.

The supplier's model for pricing the product (Ps) is based on the product's cost of goods sold (COGS) and the supplier's business model for contributed margin (CM). The contributed margin must be large enough to pay for future R&D investments and for marketing/administration costs and to generate an acceptable level of profit (e.g., the level that is expected by investors). The supplier's latitude in price negotiations with the customer is in the product's differential value generated by its competitive advantage. If the product is inferior to the reference product, the differential value is negative and the supplier must price his product below the reference price, resulting in a lower CM and loss in profitability. When the differential value is positive, the supplier might choose to price the product below the customer's economic value

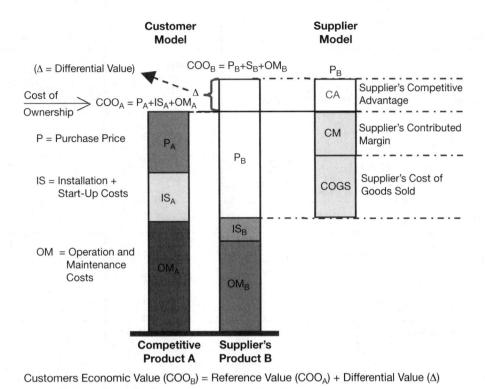

Customers Economic Value (COO$_B$) = Reference Value (COO$_A$) + Differential Value (Δ)

Figure 3.29. Customer and Supplier Pricing Models.

for other reasons such as market expansion (if the market is elastic), competitive insulation, and to raise the barrier for new entrants.

The differential value of the product is enhanced by improving the *value frame* of the product and the service offering. The value frame is what a customer perceives as the gain or loss incurred by selecting the product. Value frame is based on the relative importance and the competitive advantage of the product's attributes (in satisfying the customer needs or wants.)

In price negotiations, customers frame the value in a way that is most advantageous to them and highlight the negative differentials such as shortcomings in product functionality and productivity. *Real values* are usually not disclosed to the supplier. The supplier, on the other hand, must frame the value in the context of differentiated benefits that satisfy the customer's needs and wants. (*Note*: Nagle and Holdem [1995] and Anderson and Narus [1998] contain in-depth discussions of pricing strategy and tactics.[28,29])

3.18.3 Value Pricing

In order to extract the best value from a customer, the supplier should adopt a value model that begins in the product development phase and apply value pricing in negotiations with the customer. Understanding the customer's value factors (i.e., product attributes that are of value to the customer) and the ranking of the value factors in importance to the customer enables the firm to develop a product that is differentiated in what is important and to demand a price that captures the maximum value.

Product Name:				Firm		Competitor	
Value Category	Value Factor	Market Requirement (Magnitude)	Importance to Customers	Rating, Compliance to Market Requirement	Score	Rating, Compliance to Market Requirement	Score
Process Performance	Uniformity	<1%	1	3	15	5	25
	Defects	<10	2	2	8	3	12
	Category Total				**23**		**37**
Productivity	Throughput	>50 w/hr	3	4	12	3	9
	Reliability, MTBF	500 hr	2	3	12	3	12
	Category Total				**24**		**21**
Brand	Past Performance, Resources, Technology Leadership	N/A	2	4	16	3	12
Overall Score					**63**		**70**

Figure 3.30. Framework for Competitive Scoring of Prioritized Value Factors. MTBF, mean time between failures; w, wafers. Definitions—Importance to customer = 1 to 5, 1 being most important; Rating in meeting requirements = 5 to 1, from excellent to poor, 5 being best; Score = (6 – Importance) × Rating, higher is better (categories are considered of equal weight).

Figure 3.30 illustrates a framework for establishing the customer's value factors and computing a competitive score for each factor. The example in Figure 3.30 is for process equipment in the semiconductor fabrication market. For this product, the value categories are process performance, tool productivity in production, and supplier's brand equity. In each category, the value factors, market requirements, and importance to the customer are listed. The relative rating of the supplier's offering against competition is estimated and a total score is computed for each value factor (according to the formula in Figure 3.30).

The analysis in Figure 3.30 provides a guide for focusing product development resources on high-priority customer value factors and on product weaknesses that are relative to the competition. In pricing a product and in negotiating with customers, this analysis also helps to identify the product's differential value. At the point of sale, subjective parameters that are not included in the analysis, but affect the customer's pricing decision, must also be considered. These factors include the customer's psychology, culture, and relationships with the firm.

3.18.4 Option Pricing and Continuous Improvement

Suppliers often price their "baseline" product and product options separately. Often product options are features and capabilities that enhance the product, allow a certain degree of customization, and further improve the product's competitive advantage over the customer's expectations.

Important: Improving a product or its options does not necessarily result in capturing an added value. Even if an improved function or feature of a product is desirable, a customer may not be willing to pay for it. Understanding this reality is an important consideration in prioritizing CIPs during a product's life cycle. An exception is if the purchased product does not meet the customer's expectations or a contractual specification. In these cases, the supplier might be obliged to improve the product for compliance to the specifications and for maintaining the customer's relationship and loyalty.

3.19 THE SELLING PROCESS

This section will briefly discuss the key elements of the selling process in a B-to-B industrial market and highlight the necessary competencies of a sales person. Whether an industrial product is sold directly or through a distribution channel, in most cases the sale is made on a personal level. If the product or technology is new, the buying process is usually long and includes a rigorous evaluation of the product and the supplier by the customer.

3.19.1 Key Elements

"Selling" is a promise and "delivery" is the fulfillment of that promise. Good sales people promise only what they can deliver. In the eye of the customer, the sales person is the "supplier." The sales person is the person who the customer must trust to deliver the promise. In fact, the sales person is often considered to be a part of the supplier's offering to the customer.

A successful sale is the result of a combination of a recognized need (or problem), a motivated customer, and available funds. The sales person must listen carefully to identify the highest-priority problem that the customer is trying to solve and to discern if the product price fits into the customer's budget. A sales person must follow through in every step of the selling process, starting with the first call and continuing on to delivery of the product (ensuring that the customer's expectations have been met) and then to the subsequent "keeping-in-touch" communications. To win the customer's loyalty, the sales person must ensure a timely delivery on commitments, provide reliable information, be consistent, champion the customer in the company, and ensure that senior management in the company has visibility and a high level of interest in the customer. The sales person must view the issues in the selling process and in post-sale support through the customer's eyes.

To make a profitable sale, a sales person must develop a selling strategy before beginning the process. The selling strategy should be developed through a team effort of key resources in all stages of the selling process, the delivery of the product, and the post-sale support. The team could include members of account management, marketing, business development, product management, engineering, service, manufacturing, finance, and senior management. The selling strategy must include qualification and prioritization of the business opportunity, analysis of customer influencers in the buying decision, and an action plan that leads to a win. Figure 3.31 illustrates a tool for the preparation of a selling strategy. This tool helps to assess the supplier's position with customer influencers and decision makers and to plan winning actions. The example illustrated in Figure 3.31 is for selling semiconductor process equipment to a production fab of an IC manufacturing company.

Customer Account: CSM		Product: Dielectric Etch		Revenue Potential: $30 Million	Date: 6/10/1996
Customer Personnel Influencing the Purchase (Name, Title, Organization)	Role (Economic, Technical, User, Executive, Advisor)	Buying Decision Impact (High, Medium, Low)	Key Winning Factors (According to Customer)	Rating of the Firm's Competitive Position (1 to 5, Weak to Strong)	Action (What, Who, When)
Manager, Engineering	T, U	M	Process Performance	5	
Director, Purchasing	E	M	Price, Contract T&Cs	3	
Manager, Equipment Selection Committee	T, A	L	Specification Roadmap	1	
VP, Technology	T, A	M	Technology Roadmap, Process Performance	3	
VP and Fab Manager	U, Ex	H	Reliability, Quality, COO,COC, Support	2	
Executive VP and Chief Operating Officer	Ex	H	Firm's Longevity, Commitment, and Breadth of Product and Technology Portfolio	4	

Figure 3.31. Selling Strategy—Analysis of Customer Influencers in a Buying Decision and Planning Winning Actions. COC, cost of consumables; COO, cost of ownership; T&C, terms and conditions.

3.19.2 The Sales Person—Attributes and Competencies

Essential attributes and competencies of an effective sales person include:
- Knows the products and services, the company's strengths and weaknesses, and the customer's perception of them
- Knows the industry
- Knows the customer's business drivers, products, technology, and timing of satisfying the needs, critical success factors, priorities, psychology, and biases
- Knows the customer's buying behavior and process, the decision makers and their priorities, and the customer's budget and investment plan
- Champions the customer
- Knows how to map the customer needs and wants onto the firm's available offerings; identify solution opportunities among the product portfolio; articulate unique values of the firm's products and services

- Knows the competition, their strengths, weaknesses, and selling strategies
- Has superior selling skills, including customer screening, engagement, SPIN selling (situation analysis, problem definition, implication for the customer, need clarification),[30] probing, responding to objections, recommending and gaining commitment, closing, and follow up
- Has interpersonal skills to influence, overcome resistance, reach agreement, and make persuasive presentations
- Has negotiation skills
- Has management skills
  - Is results oriented (short and long term)—forecasts sales and meets commitments
  - Obtains timely customer information
  - Manages field subordinates
  - Sets and manages priorities—knows how to accomplish tasks with limited resources
  - Manages stress and loss
- Networks within the account and inside the firm
- Is a team player, who is a professional and constantly strives to be better

3.20 MANAGING CUSTOMER RELATIONS

An excellent customer relationship underpins total customer satisfaction and loyalty. The relationship with a customer of a high-tech product must be intimate and lasting because customer requirements change frequently, products are complex, and the buying cycle is long and costly (for both the customer and the supplier). Customers in an industrial market do not just buy a product. They expect to enter into a relationship with the supplier that starts long before the purchase order is issued and extends long into the life of the product once it is in use at the customer's site.

According to Theodore Levitt, "When a customer buys a product, for the seller it is the end of the process, for the buyer the beginning."[1] This statement is particularly relevant in a B-to-B market in which the customer buys a component or a production tool for his/her own product.

A supplier must make a large investment to develop, market, sell, and demonstrate a product over a long period before a customer makes his/her decision. A supplier must support installation of the product, warrant it, train customer operators, and support, maintain, and continuously improve the product's performance over the product's life at a customer's factory. In return, a supplier expects to be reimbursed for the product and the services rendered and to receive repeat orders from the customer.

For a customer, a buying decision is a risky endeavor that must be undertaken very carefully. The customer's business success and the decision maker's career will be impacted by the purchase decision. The customer will become dependent on the supplier for the performance of the product and for the supplier's ability (and willingness) to support and resolve problems in a timely manner.

For an industrial customer, purchase of a product is usually part of a large investment (e.g., building a new factory or an enterprise communication infrastructure), which is dependent on the supplier's performance for success. Yet the customer's leverage over the supplier will diminish as soon as the purchase order is placed. So the customer negotiates diligently and strives to get the best contractual agreement possible before saying "yes." The customer's/buyer's anxiety builds up after the purchase decision is made—will the supplier fulfill his promises? Is this supplier, product, technology, or solution, the best there is? Did we/I pay too much for it?

The above are realities for both suppliers and customers. They create an interdependence which, if constructive, can lead to a win-win outcome. In the win-win paradigm of constructive interdependence, the supplier becomes an extension of the customer's operation and the needs of both parties are satisfied.

Constructive interdependence is a learning relationship between both parties that is nourished through their interactions. These interactions span a broad range of engagements—to share strategies and roadmaps; to conduct joint projects for technology and product development; to deliver a quality product on time; to support the product; and to share product performance data within the customer's operation. By informing the supplier of its needs and preferences, and thereby "teaching" the supplier how to improve the product, the customer increases its commitment to the supplier. Key customer individuals (engineers, buyers, managers) develop allegiances to the supplier (or even become the supplier's champion). As the success of an individual/customer becomes more dependent on the supplier, the stronger the customer's desire will become to ensure that the supplier is successful. A loyal customer provides a competitive advantage to the supplier in a "run-off" situation between competitors by providing information about his priorities and by assigning resources for timely evaluation and development of the supplier's product.[31]

Customer loyalty is the most important indicator of success for a marketing organization. A loyal customer:

- Places repeat orders—Sustained business success depends on repeat customers.
- Wants the supplier to succeed—Loyal customers will spend their own resources to *help* a supplier succeed, before and after the purchase decision is made.
- Will be tolerant of a supplier's shortcomings in product performance, delivery, or service
- Will give time and resources to solve product problems
- Will give a supplier a chance to catch up with competitors who produce a "better" or cheaper product—Loyal customers do not switch at the first opportunity.
- Trusts the supplier—Stealing a trusting customer is extremely difficult for a competitor.
- Serves as a great reference to other buyers
- Provides timely forecast of potential orders
- Will not force a supplier to be the "lowest-cost supplier"
- Shares strategies and roadmaps with the supplier
- Offers ideas for new products and applications
- Teams with a supplier to develop new products and technologies
- Is cooperative in problem situations
- Maintains confidence in a supplier as long as there is a steady progress toward delivery of promises and fulfillment of expectations

The worst thing that can happen is losing a loyal customer.

3.20.1 Customer Expectations

Customer satisfaction is the congruence of the supplier's performance with the customer's expectations. Customer expectations are shaped by the promises that a supplier makes during the selling process, in the process of building and nurturing the relationship, and when communicating the value proposition and branding. The customer's expectations might be in the form of a written document or merely be the state of the customer's mind. In B-to-B markets, written expectations are often set (in response to the customer's RFQ). Frequently the supplier is asked to specify its current and future capabilities and to make contractual commitments for future service and continuous improvement of the delivered product. Making verbal commitments and/or implying that the initial purchase price covers the cost of future support and product enhancements will be remembered by the customer as an expectation of performance by the supplier.

Who pays for the "yet-unfulfilled expectations" might not be the biggest issue in the relationship between the supplier and the customer. The major consequence of the supplier's commitment (as perceived by the customer) is that the customer will plan his/her business operation or manufacturing plant around that expected performance. For example, the customer's production capacity and plant design will be based on the "expected" output capability of the supplier's product. Fab managers will plan their factory layout, business model, and ROI based on their expectations, written or implied, of the supplier's product performance. The career success of many individuals might be impacted by set expectations.

Start-up entrepreneurs are more likely to promise the "moon" because of their enthusiasm about their new technology and product and their limited experience with similar situations. They commit to the (perceived) potential of their new product before they have had time to demonstrate it. On the other hand, an interested customer interprets the supplier's enthusiastic promise as a commitment for timely development of the new product (to the expected level of performance) at the supplier's expense. The root cause of overenthusiastic promises is often the fact that the start-up entrepreneurs make promises for performance and delivery based on what they *think* is possible, *if* the necessary resources are available, instead of what is the *most likely* scenario.

The most important factor in managing customer expectations is having an understanding of "what has been promised" as perceived by the customer. An effective approach is to clarify the customer's expectations in writing and to have the document signed and dated by the customer. The next step is to meet the documented commitments and thereby attain complete customer satisfaction.

Marketing and sales managers must manage the customer satisfaction process by ensuring that all organizations within their firm commit to the timely accomplishment of what they are supposed to do. For this process to work effectively, the performance metrics and associated rewards of sales, marketing, manufacturing, engineering, and service personnel must be aligned with the objective of fulfilling the customer expectations. For example, if the sales commission is paid when the customer places a purchase order, a sales person has minimal incentive for committing his/her time to post-sales activities such as on-time delivery and flawless installation and start-up of the product. He/she would rather pursue the next sales opportunity. If the manufacturing manager is only measured by meeting the quarterly build plan and the unit shipment target, customers are more likely to receive defective products. The preferred approach is to pay the sales person's commission when the customer is satisfied and has fully

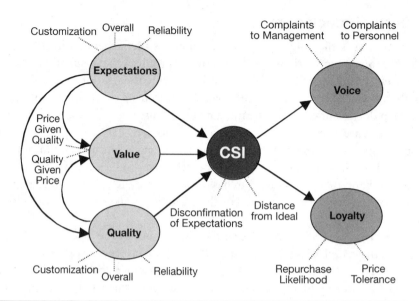

Figure 3.32. CSI Index Model. (Source: Adapted from Anderson, E.W., Fornell, C. In *Handbook of Services Marketing and Management*. Swartz, T.A., Iacobucci, D., Eds. Thousand Oaks, CA: Sage Publications; 1999.)

paid the supplier's invoice and to assess the manufacturing performance against compliance to a zero-defect and on-time delivery target, as determined by the customer.

A customer satisfaction model has been proposed by Anderson and Fornell (1999). The model is illustrated in Figure 3.32.[32] In this model, the customer satisfaction index (CSI) relates customer expectations to product quality and price. Customers express their response as either loyalty or by voicing complaints based on the CSI alignment of disconfirmation of expectations and distance from the ideal.

3.20.2 Managing Customer Relationships

The relationship with a customer must be managed continuously. It must be managed in every interaction with the customer, before and after the sale is made. At all times, the supplier must be vigilant of the customer's perceptions of the supplier's product, company, people, and the relationship. Probing the customer frequently by asking questions is important:

- "How are we doing?"
- "Is the relationship improving or deteriorating?"
- "Are your expectations fulfilled in a timely manner?"
- "How does our relationship compare to the competitors?"
- "How can we improve our technology, products, and services and how we do business with you?"

One sure sign of a deteriorating customer relationship is the absence of customer "complaints." No news is bad news! No news does not mean that everything is perfect. No news often means that the supplier's product is not important to the customer any more, the customer has given up, the interdependence bond has been broken, or the customer has replaced the supplier's product with that of a competitor.

A customer's relationship must be assessed at all pertinent levels of the customer's organization, including engineering, purchasing, middle and top management, economic buyers, and technology users. If a supplier's sales person has an excellent relationship with the customer's engineers, but a competitor's CEO strikes a strategic deal over a golf game with the customer's division general manager (GM), things may not go your way for long! The opposite approach of only tending to top-level relationship management is not sufficient either. The customer's GM may think highly of the supplier's technology and its future potential, and may enjoy the tennis games that you keep losing, but if the customer's engineer dislikes your product's unreliable performance and the support he is receiving, he may spend most of his time developing the competitor's alternative.

Building and maintaining excellent customer relationships and fulfilling customers' expectations transcend the marketing manager's job and extend to the entire organization. Sales and service people are on the front line, but the supplier's CEO, engineers, manufacturing staff, shipping dock personnel, the receptionist in the lobby, and the janitor who keeps the conference rooms tidy all contribute to building the relationship with the customer. Marketing's job is to advocate total customer satisfaction throughout the organization and take ownership of CRM. Relationship management requires caring for little things and big things. What customers care the most about, however, is that their expectations are understood and that you as their supplier will create an action plan for delivering these expectations in a time frame that is acceptable to them. You must also be sensitive to the customer's feelings, needs, and changing requirements.

A supplier's firm must have a total customer satisfaction culture and a management system that measures employees' performances based on their fulfilling of customer expectations. Relationships build up over a long time, but they can deteriorate over a short time. Relationships must be nurtured, maintained, strengthened, and justified.

3.20.3 Customer Satisfaction Improvement Programs

To build customer loyalty, the supplier must sustain the customer's satisfaction over time. In B-to-B markets, having a proactive improvement program that documents customer expectations, identifies gaps, and manages an action plan to fulfill expectations is important. The marketing manager must interview customers and document the level of understanding of the customer's expectations. Understanding and using the indicators and metrics that customers use in assessing the supplier's product and performance are also important.

A "customer score card" is a type of table that is a useful tool for documenting the supplier's current performance against customer expectations, identifying gaps, and listing actions for meeting the expectations. Numeric satisfaction scores can be assigned by the customer for each indicator of performance relative to competing supplies. The customer score card should be jointly prepared by the supplier and the customer and be reviewed on a regular basis.

Another useful tool in managing customer satisfaction programs and resolving outstanding noncompliance to customer specifications is a problem-solving chart (PSC) (Figure 3.33). The PSC in Figure 3.33 presents an example for a program to improve the reliability and support of equipment in an IC manufacturing fab. The PSC identifies the current product performance, the customer's expected performance or requirement, the root causes of noncompliance, supporting data, and the action plan to resolve the issues. (*Note*: PSC methodology is further discussed in Chapter 8.)

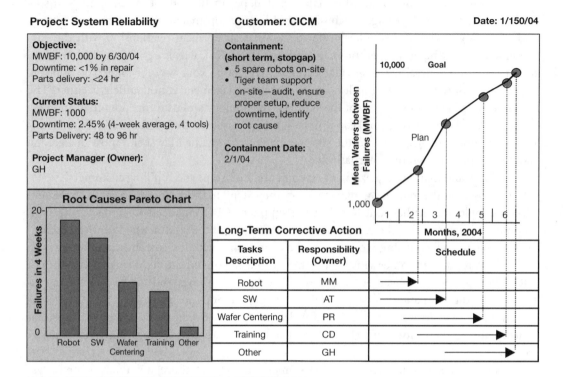

Figure 3.33. Problem-Solving Chart.

Comment: A comprehensive program of CRM has been developed and practiced at HP.[35] The reader is also encouraged to consult the resources provided in the *Additional Reading* section at the end of this chapter.

3.21 CASE STUDY AT IPC—MFS—A DISRUPTIVE PRODUCT WITH COMMERCIALIZATION CHALLENGESS

This case study relates the internal and external challenges encountered in turning a vision into a reality. It discusses a company's efforts in product invention and product development and also discusses development of a winning market and business strategy. The case study also includes selling the concept internally to rally the resources behind an investment for the future and the market response to a proposition that would upset the status quo.

3.21.1 Background

Semiconductor integrated circuits are manufactured through a sequence of steps performed by discrete process, lithography, and metrology equipment (see Chapter 11). In the late 1990s, Innovative Process Corporation (IPC), a leading equipment supplier in the semiconductor manufacturing market, had grown into a successful, billion-dollar company with a diversified portfolio of wafer processing and metrology products. Taking advantage of its strength and

---

CASE STUDY—CUSTOMER LOYALTY IMPACTS BUYING BEHAVIOR

Situation. The CVD division of Innovative Process Corporation (IPC) faced an uphill battle to keep its archrival, Company X, out of 90-nm production fab at MDT Corporation in the United States. MDT, a large global IC manufacturer, has a recognized leadership role in the industry and therefore has tremendous influence over other IC production houses.

The IPC product family InoDep has been the PTOR at MDT fabs for the last 5 years and for two generations of technology nodes. Additionally, IPC technologists have an intimate relationship with the MDT R&D organization and work closely with the director of R&D to qualify the new revision of InoDep for 90-nm production.

Company X claims that HiPro, their new product, has many technological advantages over the aging IPC product line. Although the InoDep process is more mature, HiPro incorporates several design innovations that promise significantly higher reliability and productivity than InoDep.

To broaden their supply base and to enhance their buying power, MDT production managers wanted to give Company X a chance. The main reason for the interest of MDT production engineers in Company X is that several of the MDT engineers once worked at Company X and were members of the HiPro development team. These engineers believed in the potential of HiPro and had some degree of ownership and loyalty to the product.

Outcome. According to the customer's business process, the MDT central R&D organization initially has an upper hand over MDT production engineers in selecting process equipment for the next tech node. However, final responsibility for IC manufacturing is with the production engineers. The internal fight between R&D and production engineers at MDT went on for several months before the fab manager could "convince" R&D to bring in the HiPro tool for 6-month evaluation. Customer loyalty had paid off for Company X!

---

moving up the value chain by offering an integrated solution to its traditional customers was an attractive growth opportunity for the company.

The prospective solution included a cluster of process equipment to build a microstructure (a portion of an IC device) by integrating a few successive steps in the IC manufacturing process. The integrated solution contrasted with the traditional single-step discrete process equipment solutions that IPC and its competitors had been offering, but left process integration to the customers. IPC was one of a few equipment suppliers that had a broad enough product portfolio to be able to offer an integrated solution. If such a value proposition were attractive to the customers, it would greatly enhance product differentiation, competitive strength, and profitability at IPC.

The challenge for IPC was to create a compelling value proposition, to build the engineering expertise to develop the product, and to implement a marketing strategy for overcoming market barriers and winning customer acceptance. To enable this vision, the company invested hundreds of millions of dollars in product development and in building an R&D infrastructure (development laboratories) and engineering skills over subsequent years.

3.21.2 MFS—An Integrated Solution

The integrated solution was given the name "microstructure fabrication solution," or MFS, and was defined as "a *whole product* comprised of multiple unit-process equipment and an associated process sequence that are integrated to manufacture a microstructure of a semiconductor device for a specified function." Figure 3.34 illustrates the difference between the traditional

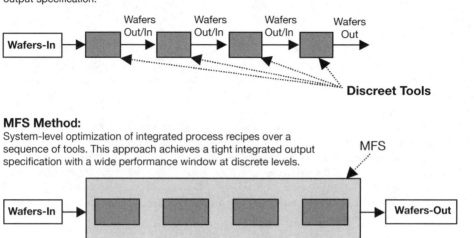

Figure 3.34. Integrated Solution—MFS versus Traditional Offering of Discrete Tools (IC Manufacturing).

discrete equipment process flow and the integrated MFS approach. Manufacturing optimization benefits of MFS are also noted in Figure 3.34.

The success criteria for MFS (as with any new product) are if it solves a real customer problem and if it offers a compelling advantage over the alternate choices that are available to customers. For example, solving technological challenges of copper interconnect at <100-nm geometries, or significantly reducing the time to market for copper transition, or drastically reducing IC manufacturing costs would capture the attention of customers.

The MFS value proposition is illustrated as layers of capabilities and benefits built into the model of a *whole product* concept in Figure 3.35. Figure 3.35 also depicts the outward historical shift of IC manufacturers' value expectations (from equipment suppliers). By the year 2000, with maturing of the IC manufacturing industry, customers were demanding the capabilities of the "Expected" layer from equipment suppliers. The promise of MFS was to offer the "Augmented" and "Potential" capabilities illustrated in Figure 3.35 and to deliver a set of pre-qualified equipment and integrated process formulations that would build an IC microstructure according to a customer's performance specifications.

3.21.3 MFS—Market Segmentation and Customer Adoption Behavior

The MFS value proposition was a significant departure from the traditional discrete tool offering, which required a reassessment of the market segmentation and customer buying behaviors. For discrete equipment, the market was usually segmented into foundry, DRAM, and microprocessor/logic device manufacturers. In segmenting the market, MFS marketing managers noted that the purchase of MFS amounted to IC manufacturers outsourcing work that had traditionally been done in-house, i.e., the integration of discrete equipment and associated process recipes for building microstructures onto a semiconductor chip. MFS customers could be segmented based on three criteria that established their buying behavior:

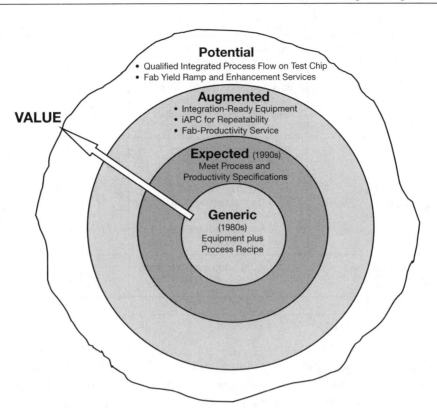

Figure 3.35. MFS and *Whole Product* Concept—IC Manufacturing Equipment Market. iAPC, integrated advanced process control.

- Customers' business needs according to the markets that they served (and the needs of the customers' customers)
- Customers' bases of differentiation and competition in their markets, defining their value vector
- Customers' outsourcing strategies and the tasks, knowledge, and competencies that they considered to be the core (versus context) of their business operation

Figure 3.36 depicts possible market segments for MFS products. The middle column lists the core competency and the basis of competitive differentiation for each customer group. Although customers assess MFS value along these dimensions, they would not want it to level the competitive playing field. The last column identifies the major customers in each segment in order, from early to late adopters. The early adopters were targeted as co-development and initial penetration candidates.

The next challenge facing the IPC team was preparation of the MFS product development plan and market penetration strategy. MFS represented a family of products for IC manufacturing, including fabrication of a gate structure, a copper wiring interconnect, or other microstructures of a device. Marketing managers had to decide where to focus the company's limited resources for maximum return on the investment. IPC management wanted to introduce the first MFS product in the shortest possible time (with minimal resources) to gain credibility and to create a customer reference for the concept. Team members, both marketing and technologists, also knew that they were new to the IC manufacturing integration business and that there was much to learn.

Segment	Core Competency and Basis of Differentiation	Early-to-Late Adopters
1. Foundry	**IC manufacturing technology and know-how** for efficiency/flexibility in mixed-product manufacturing	SMIC, Tech Semi, TSMC
2. Chip supplier with manufacturing capability	**IC and chip set design:** Maintain manufacturing capability for: <ul><li>Protecting design IP</li><li>Historical reasons, moving away from IDM strategy</li><li>Building prototypes to qualify design and process</li></ul>	AMD, Motorola, Sony
3. Vertically integrated companies (IDM)	**IC design and manufacturing technology**	Toshiba, TI, Intel

Figure 3.36. Market Segmentation—MFS Product Line.

The key parameters in making the product's priority decision were technological complexity, availability of engineering and scientific resources with the right skills, and the probability of success with early adopters in each market segment. Figure 3.37 illustrates a framework for the product line and commercialization decision. The horizontal axis lists the potential MFS products in order of technological complexity, availability of expertise, and development time and the vertical axis shows the technology adoption sequence from early to late adopters. To maximize the probability of success, the product development and commercialization sequence had to follow the direction of the arrow on Figure 3.37.

The MFS BU selected deposition/etch (Dep/Etch) and copper wiring (Cu-Wiring) at the 130-nm technology node as the first two MFS products for development. They also targeted the early adopters for product introduction. The PMD product, which is shown as having the lowest technological complexity barrier, was not pursued because it was deemed noncritical to customers. The selected product strategy also called for successful positioning of the Dep/Etch and Cu-Wiring products for the 90-nm node in 1 year and for the 65-nm node in 2 years following "alpha-release" of the 130-nm product. The BU general manager believed, and company top management concurred, that it was possible to grow the MFS business to 15% of the company's total revenue in 3 years. This was set as the revenue goal for the MFS BU. The MFS product and market and business strategies went through many trials and tribulations at IPC from 1997 to 2003, when the strategy for commercialization of MFS was finally abandoned and the BU was dissolved.

The following sections will discuss the factors that drove the MFS strategy at IPC and the customers' responses to elucidate the strengths and weaknesses of the MFS concept and the IPC implementation strategy. First the IPC perspective will be presented, including the impetus for developing and commercializing MFS and the benefits that were to capture the imagination of customers and fuel commercialization success. Then the customer's perspective will be presented, including perception of risk and expectations of the scope and benefits of MFS.

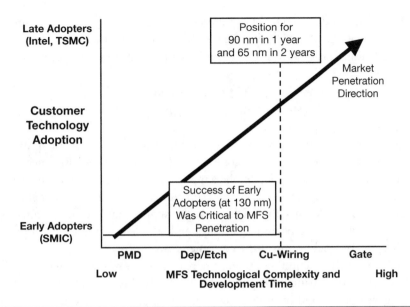

Figure 3.37. MFS Market Penetration and Product Development Strategy Business Objective—Achieve $300M in MFS Revenue in 3 Years.

3.21.4 MFS Strategy—The IPC Perspective—Impetus for IPC and Benefits for Customers

Impetus for the MFS strategy at IPC includes:

- The wafer processing equipment market was maturing in the late 1990s and IPC was experiencing gross margin pressure.
- The CEO knew that IPC needed a disruptive product that would not be subject to the likely commoditization of traditional product lines in the following decade. MFS seemed to be an invention that could buck the commoditization trend and improve company's leadership position. MFS would move the company up the value chain and away from competitors and would change the rules of the game.
- IPC was the only company with a breadth of equipment portfolio to offer an integrated solution and it had the financial strength to afford the high costs of R&D.
- MFS would reduce the company's vulnerability to the challenging cycles of the capital equipment market through a "continuous" revenue stream from the manufacturing services that has been built into the value proposition (see Figure 3.35)

According to IPC, MFS strategy offers several benefits for customers, including:

- Reduces R&D costs for customers (see Figure 3.35)
- Reduces the time to market for customers at each technology node by 6 to 12 months—Between the suppliers and customers, traditionally 18 to 24 months are required to develop and qualify an integrated set of equipment and process steps for IC production at a new technology node. The long development cycle was comprised of a serial sequence of tasks that started in the suppliers' R&D facilities with the development of equipment and a process recipe according to a customer's specification. Several tasks were subsequently conducted by IC manufacturers:

- ○ Evaluation and selection of equipment suppliers—Usually several suppliers are evaluated and at least two are selected for the next two steps.
- ○ Installation and qualification of equipment and process recipes at customer R&D
- ○ Development of the integrated process in R&D
- ○ Qualify-to-yield testing of the final equipment set and integrated process sequence in the production fab
- Creates an opportunity to collapse many of the serial tasks into overlapping parallel tasks and to shorten the overall cycle time—For example, the integrated process development will be performed by the supplier (IPC) in parallel with the development of discrete equipment recipes. This substitutes the integration task at the customer R&D. To make this approach work, the supplier and customer must work collaboratively from the beginning at the supplier's facility all the way to the MFS qualification and yield ramp at the customer's fab.
- Reduces customer's technological and financial risks in moving down the path of Moore's law—Increasing technological complexity, below 100 nm, causes the timely development and commercialization of new products to be out of the reach of many IC manufacturers. Many semiconductor providers, small and large, form industry alliances to share technological and financial risks. The financial risk reduction offered by MFS could be in the form of leverage on the customer's capital utilization and cost/performance sharing in the actual fab operating environment, in which the supplier would guarantee the specified output of "good" wafers.
- Offers technological benefits that are inherent in MFS design and delivery:
  - ○ Improves repeatability of manufacturing process (i.e., higher C_p and C_{pk})
  - ○ Ensures that discrete equipment is well integrated with the adjoining process steps and the integrated process is qualified at the supplier site before delivery to the customer fab and start of the manufacturing ramp
  - ○ Protects against production process excursions in real time

Comment: The customer benefits of MFS appeared compelling. Yet, IPC failed to turn MFS into a successful business, in spite of many years of engineering and marketing effort and an investment in excess of $250 million. Reasons for the failure of the MFS initiative can be detected from the perspective of customers.

3.21.5 MFS Success Issues and Risks—From the Perspective of Customers

According to customers, MFS was a discontinuous innovation and the *whole* product concept and the value proposition were not clearly understood:

- Customers perceived a great risk in allowing IPC to take responsibility for the integration of device microstructures because customers did not trust the technical and operational capabilities of IPC and were concerned about the lack of experience at IPC in IC manufacturing.
- Customers believed in their age-old proven methodology of best-of-breed equipment selection to buy the best technology at the lowest price among competing suppliers. MFS, to them, meant having one or more pieces of equipment that were not the "best" in the supply chain.

- The description of MFS as "a collection of equipment performing a certain function" was not consistent with the actual fab operating environment. First, the output capability (throughput and reliability) of individual tools did not usually match. To achieve a given manufacturing capacity, customers acquired different numbers of each tool. With the MFS approach, however, it appeared that customers had to buy multiple MFS equipment sets and therefore ended up with too many of the slower tools. Second, a given tool usually had the capability of performing more than one process function. Fab managers, therefore, used a piece of equipment at two or more process steps in the fabrication sequence and maximized equipment utilization. For MFS configuration, the number of each piece of equipment on delivery and how it matched the customer's operating environment was unclear. In fact, customers interpreted this lack of clarity as IPC having a poor understanding of the business they were getting into!
- Customers perceived the device integration capability to be an "underperformer" in the manufacturing process and hence a competitive differentiator. They were not willing to outsource a core capability.
- In early 2000, there was no other viable MFS supplier besides IPC. If successful, IPC would have become a sole-source supplier. This scenario posed an unacceptable level of risk to the customers. When marketers in the MFS BU warned that competitors were getting into the business, the CEO of IPC frequently responded with "Competition for MFS is a blessing. You can never succeed in a market unless you have competition, i.e., unless customers have an alternative to chose."
- MFS would change the power structure in the supply chain. Customers were not willing to allow IPC to gain (at their expense) more power than it already had as one of the largest equipment suppliers.
- The R&D cost of device manufacturing technology had become very large, reaching hundreds of millions of dollars at each technology node. Larger IC manufacturers with deeper pockets considered the higher R&D cost to be a barrier to new smaller entrants in emerging markets such as China. The MFS offering by IPC would level the playing field, enabling new entrants and smaller contenders and increasing the number of IPC customers. This would create new players and weaken the market position of big manufacturers and erode their power position in the value chain.
- Customers' R&D organizations perceived MFS as a threat to their "purpose in life" because MFS would replace most of what they were currently doing. An MFS contract amounted to outsourcing a portion of IC manufacturing development engineering. Therefore customers' R&D engineers would not collaborate with IPC and would use all their "ammunition" to prove that IPC was incapable. This situation proved to be true even at smaller IC manufacturers who were considered to be early adopters because their need for MFS was greater.
- IPC could not clearly define deliverable value guarantees and did not have a compelling business model that was attractive to customers. Lack of a clear business model made the product untenable to the IPC internal financial community as well. One of the main reasons for the lack of a crisp business model was the unwillingness of IPC to change the business paradigm from the old equipment-selling model to a highly service-content MFS business. Internal financial business processes for MFS were lacking, and management was unwilling to take the necessary risks of

playing a new game. MFS also resulted in a change in the rules of the game for customers' economic buyers, which brought about associated resistance.

- In the 1990s and early 2000, customers were trying to reduce their investment and technology risks by forming industry alliances and sharing risks. This new reality diminished the value of MFS as a risk reduction instrument. IPC did not proactively pursue participation in any of the customer alliances that would have increased its learning of the device integration technology and know-how. IPC did not recognize this opportunity and did not pursue it out of the fear of alienating the rest of the customer base and of being hindered in collaboration with the other customers outside the alliance.

3.21.6 What Actually Happened

IPC struggled to articulate a clear value proposition, a compelling advantage to customers, and a win-win business model. The MFS pricing model consisted of a two-tier proposal—make an upfront payment for the MFS tool set at a reasonable price and close to the market value of discrete equipment; and sign a 3-year contract and pay per wafer for fab productivity enhancement services during the factory ramp and in production. Because IPC did not have access to customers' proprietary test structures, integration of a sequence of steps and process qualification of the equipment set were of limited value to customers and could not entirely substitute for their in-house development.

Additionally the scope and benefits of the proposed fab services were not specified. Customers did not understand what they were paying for and what assurances of yield enhancement they would receive. IPC marketers produced myriad presentations and benefit statements that were primarily firm-centric and did not capture the imagination of customers. The presentations actually backfired because customers interpreted them as a confirmation of the lack of deep understanding of customer operating environments and customer economics at IPC.

Not only could IPC not sell any MFS contracts, but the initiative worked against IPC and raised customers' expectations of individual tool performance. IPC was asked to continue selling individual equipment, as before, but with a higher capability, including robust integration testing of individual tools and optimization of process recipes before shipment. The company's impressive accumulation of MFS engineering talent and investment in R&D facilities also contributed to raising the bar of customers' expectations. Customers began demanding the added integration capability of process equipment in their purchase specification without having to pay a premium price, which lowered the IPC profit margin. MFS had created the opposite of the intended result!

3.21.7 MFS Benefits—Case Studies of Two Early Adopters

Two customers of IPC did see the process integration capabilities of IPC as having benefits that could help them to reduce risks and the time to market for next generation products. One was MTI, a global leader in the semiconductor industry, and the other was ChinaSemi, a new entrant to the market from China. These customers expressed interest in teaming with IPC and using the impressive MFS labs at IPC to qualify process integration of copper interconnects in their new devices. Such a team approach was also of great value to IPC because it would provide opportunities to sharpen the definition of the MFS value proposition and business model; to significantly deepen understanding at IPC of the new business; and to provide a valuable early adopter reference for the product.

3.21.7.1 Customer 1—MTI Corporation

MFS REDUCES TECHNICAL RISK, COST OF DEVELOPMENT, AND TIME TO MARKET, ALLEVIATING THE COMPLEXITY OF INTERNAL POLITICS

Setting: MTI was considering a technology transition to copper (Cu) interconnects in 130-nm flash memory manufacturing. In 2001, MTI was not sure of the benefits of transition to Cu and wanted to evaluate the risks and benefits of the technology before making a commercialization decision to use Cu in flash memory.

Situation: Joe Donaldson, vice president of R&D at the central development lab at MTI, was in charge of bringing new IC products to market faster than the competitors and on a low budget. He had an excellent track record and a reputation for being a no-nonsense technology executive. The standard business process for purchasing mass production equipment at MTI was to first evaluate the products of alternate suppliers and next to develop integrated manufacturing processes at the MTI central R&D labs.

Life was very hectic in the summer of 2001 for Joe Donaldson:

- He was behind schedule in evaluating the benefits of Cu in flash memory. He also knew that the archrival company of MTI was 6 months ahead of him.
- Because of recent layoffs due to a market downturn, his engineering resources were stretched to the limit. He did not have the capacity for another new project in addition to his long list of existing development projects.
- Outsourcing of technology development was usually not considered as a viable option in alleviating resource crunch in the technology-centric IC manufacturing business.

Furthermore, Joe's engineers were loathe to outsource new technology development or even to "acquire" existing new technologies (such as Cu MFS from IPC Corporation) because they did not want to lose "power" or cause themselves to become redundant by outsourcing their core function. Theoretically, Joe was the ultimate decision maker in developing the strategy for new product development, including acquisition of a new technology—assuming that he could convince his engineering staff, which he thought he could.

However, life was also not simple for Joe within the large, global MTI Corporation. Joe was under the influence of many strong power centers in the company when making a major product technology decision such as transition to Cu. The relationship between Joe's central R&D organization and the other worldwide centers at MTI are illustrated in Figure 3.38. Joe had to heed the input from all of the players and collaborate with them in decision making to ensure the success of his new product initiatives. Figure 3.38 also shows the MFS product offering from IPC as an outsourcing (partnering) opportunity that Joe was seriously contemplating.

To Joe, the MFS appeared to be attractive. He wanted to give it a chance and do a first-order viability evaluation of the technology. So he planned a Cu-interconnect development project that was divided into three phases.

Phase 1 was deposition and characterization of a "metal-1" Cu layer on wafers that were patterned with an MTI device mask. He decided to give IPC a chance to perform the first phase using MFS technology. To gain confidence in IPC and to mitigate risk, Joe decided to also run the first phase at his own lab in parallel with IPC. He thought that early parallel development at his own labs would establish a basis for side-by-side evaluation of MFS technology with his own technology and help to gain confidence in IPC and thereby win the support of his engineering managers for outsourcing the remaining two phases to IPC. Although Joe was still committing some engineering resources, the investment was small in comparison with a full-blown project in which he would have to bring in a complete tool set (that he also had no money or time for) and spend much more engineering resources. Also, Joe felt good about not discouraging his own engineers—they would be judging the adequacy of IPC solution and thereby feel empowered. The Phase 1 evaluation went quite well for IPC. By late 2001 the MFS results proved to be superior to the in-house work at MTI.

Outcome: Phase 2 required a major contractual commitment from IPC before Joe would be confident enough to "put all of his eggs in the IPC basket." That never came to pass! Risk aversion and a faint-hearted commitment to MFS at IPC plus internal politics at MTI led to a withering-down of the project at both IPC and MTI.

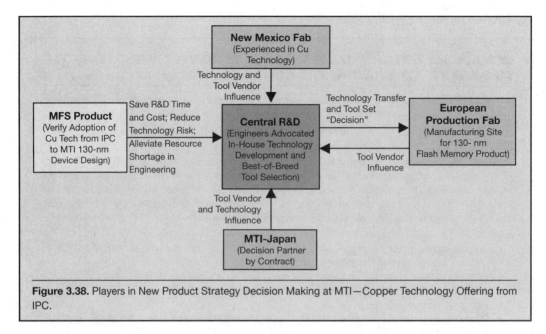

Figure 3.38. Players in New Product Strategy Decision Making at MTI—Copper Technology Offering from IPC.

3.21.7.2 Customer 2—ChinaSemi

THE PROPOSAL—RELUCTANCE OF IPC MANAGEMENT TO GUARANTEE PERFORMANCE

Setting: ChinaSemi, a small semiconductor foundry with limited R&D resources, was a new entrant to the market in 2001. ChinaSemi was planning a new 200-mm fab for 130-nm technology and was aggressively evaluating equipment suppliers. The main focus at ChinaSemi was having low equipment costs and speed in bringing the fab to full production capacity. MFS marketers at IPC thought that their Cu-interconnect technology and extensive in-house R&D capability could enable ChinaSemi to adopt the technology into production rapidly without needing to go through a long and expensive in-house learning and development effort.

Situation: Business development managers in the MFS BU at IPC prepared a proposal for Cu-interconnect MFS for the new fab. The proposed contract was comprised of:

- Collaboration by ChinaSemi and IPC scientists to qualify MFS Cu-interconnect technology to ChinaSemi's design rule at IPC development labs in 3 months
- Delivery of the integrated set of MFS equipment to the new fab for a 10,000-wafer-per-month production capacity 6 months later
- On-site support by IPC engineers for rapid production ramp in the new fab
- Product yield enhancement support by IPC engineers for the first year of production

Outcome: The proposal was well received by ChinaSemi, but was rejected by IPC top management as being too risky. This was the first time in the long history of MFS that the product deliverables, pricing, and payment method were well defined and the benefits for the customer and supplier were delineated. The proposed customer benefits included a lower initial capital burden and fab productivity risk sharing through a "good wafers out" guarantee by IPC. The benefits to IPC were a higher equipment market share in the new fab, higher revenue (equipment plus services), and a higher profit margin over the 3-year contract. The risk to IPC was that it had to guarantee the output capability of MFS (good wafers out) on a specified test chip structure. Although the risk of ensuring fab output capability is normally assumed by IC manufacturers, it was perceived unacceptable to IPC management.

3.21.8 What Could IPC Have Done Differently?

Before and after the ChinaSemi proposal was prepared, many discussions were held about what IPC should do and what strategic options IPC had for success. Several conclusions emerged:

Enable weaker and emerging customers as a baseline strategic focus. Dan Fong, marketing strategist at IPC, said, "MFS strategy should enable competitors of our strong customers. That is what Intel did when IBM resisted using the 386 microprocessor. Intel helped Compaq to become a strong PC maker against IBM (which was the dominant player)." (*Note*: Another Intel strategy that is applicable to MFS was Intel's decision to enter the PC motherboard business. Intel did not make money in the motherboard business. In fact, the motherboard strategy actually hurt Intel's core microprocessor business. However, Intel developed the motherboard design for two reasons—to help the competitors of strong customers, particularly new entrants into the PC business, to increase their customer bases and to weaken the strong ones, e.g., Intel enabled Gateway to make gains against Dell; and to facilitate integration of Intel's microprocessor chip into the PC system design.) Dan Fong continued, "To apply Intel's model to MFS, IPC should focus on offering equipment integration services to smaller customers and the new entrants who are strained by resources and are under time pressure. This would help the weaker customers to become viable players against stronger customers." IPC was somewhat obsessed with "first-tier" companies such as TSMC (the largest foundry) and Intel (the largest semiconductor manufacturer) and interpreted penetration at these customers as the real proof of the "goodness" of MFS and the key indicator of success. Applying the diffusion-of-technology model to MFS would have directed IPC to focus on "second-tier" customers (e.g., MTI and ChinaSemi) that were much more willing to take a risk with MFS for the benefit of gaining competitive advantage over the larger first-tier competitors.

Allow best-of-breed equipment selection. A major issue facing MFS marketers was how to address the desire of customers for best-of-breed equipment selection and how to overcome their objections that MFS forced them to use an all-IPC tool set even if a piece of equipment was not the "best" in the supply chain. The question was should IPC offer the "best" solution to customers even if it meant using a competitor's equipment (e.g., similar to the strategy that IBM adopted in their service solution business). Top management at IPC was adamantly against this idea because of a fear of weakening the discrete equipment business which was and would remain the predominant source of revenue for a long time to come. Dan Fong suggested working with the competitors to re-brand their products under the IPC brand. However, the "old ways" were too strongly ingrained to seriously entertain that idea!

Create a revenue stream in the form of dollar-per-wafer pricing in production. One of the strategic benefits of the MFS business is its potential to create a stable stream of revenue for the company in the form of dollar-per-wafer pricing during fab production. The per-wafer charge was modeled partially for the fab productivity services rendered by IPC and partly for amortization of deferred initial capital to purchase the MFS equipment set. In addition to growing the market opportunity, the MFS dollar-per-wafer revenue had the benefit of dampening the cyclical nature of the traditional capital equipment business. However, customers reacted negatively to the dollar-per-wafer wafer pricing model. Customers would have been more open to this pricing model had IPC been willing to assume a measured share of fab operational risk to ensure good-wafer-out capacity. As noted in the ChinaSemi case, IPC management was unwilling to take on such a risk. (*Note*: This doubt about the dollar-per-wafer pricing mode at IPC was reinforced by the experience of other companies such as Microsoft and Oracle who had failed to sell software on a per-use charge basis.)

Develop the necessary tactics for a winning strategy. Top- and middle-level executives at IPC pursued the MFS endeavor for 5 years with a strategy that was "high-level, firm-centric, and complex" and a tactic that was "diffuse, high-level, and top-down selling." The outcome was unsuccessful and costly. Trout and Reis (1990) advocate tactics-driven strategy development, particularly for a new high-tech product and market.[34] A supplier should become inspired by customers to discern the "real value." In a tactics-driven strategy, applying the paradigm of *vision-tactic-strategy-result* to MFS means focusing on the tactic of creating an intimate partnership with an early adopter such as ChinaSemi and learning the new business. Through this tactic, IPC would enhance its understanding of a customer's operating environment and the base of the customer's competitive advantage, qualify the *value of* process integration and fab productivity services that MFS offered, and be able to articulate a simple "compelling reason to buy." After the successful implementation of such tactical steps, IPC would be able to develop marketing and organizational-capability strategies around the "qualified value." However, as already discussed, adopting such a tactic required a bold and risk-prone business undertaking approach that IPC management was unwilling to take.

Create demand through customers' customers. A potential strategy was to market MFS to customer's customers and co-develop the microfabrication process flow for the critical layers of new devices by "fab-less" companies. In the semiconductor industry, the number of fab-less companies has been growing for several years since the required investment in a new fab exceeded the resources of most companies. Fab-less companies design integrated circuit devices and outsource manufacturing to foundries around the world. Fab-less companies either sell chips or, in most cases, use them in their own electronic products. Some large fab-less companies have in-house R&D fabrication capability to qualify and ensure manufacturability of their new designs. If fab-less companies were to partner with IPC, the MFS development and qualification platform could be used by a fab-less company to develop their new products with minimal in-house investment in R&D equipment. In turn, because the larger fab-less companies exert a significant degree of influence on the foundries, they could require the foundry to acquire MFS to ensure rapid production ramp of the new chip design.

Surround the customers. The MFS strategy was to offer enabling capability (an integration-ready equipment set, integrated process, integration R&D services, and fab productivity/yield support) and to capture value through a win-win business model (an initial reduced capital payment and subsequent regular payments structured in dollars-per-month and dollar-per-wafer charges for process integration and fab services). This baseline strategy is depicted in Figure 3.39a, with MFS being one-stop shopping for customers to acquire the capability for manufacturing an IC microstructure. As noted before, the barriers for success of this business proposition proved formidable. For customers, MFS was too new and risky, its benefits were ambiguous and unproven, IPC had no track record, IPC had no competition, and the product would create too much dependence on IPC. After the unsuccessful proposal to ChinaSemi, the MFS BU general manager was convinced that the baseline MFS strategy was

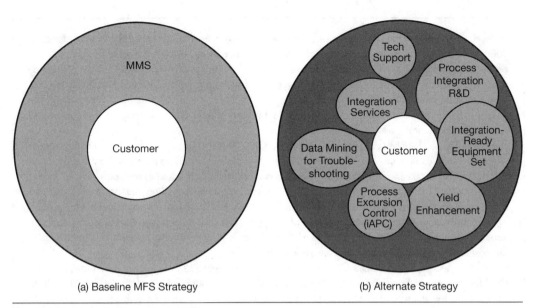

(a) Baseline MFS Strategy (b) Alternate Strategy

Figure 3.39. Alternate Strategies to MFS.

dead. He devised an alternate strategy to accomplish the intended market and business objectives of MFS. The alternate strategy was designed to "surround the customer" with IPC products and services—accumulation of these services amounted to the MFS package (shown in Figure 3.39b). By diversifying its product portfolio and marketing "bits and pieces" of MFS separately, the GM thought IPC could gradually gain the sought-for credibility in process integration and fab services know-how. This approach allowed customers to have selection freedom through competitors' solutions at the individual offering level. If IPC excelled at the individual product offering, it would achieve a gradual move up the value chain and a "natural" progression toward the total-solution offering of MFS.

3.22 CASE STUDY—BUSINESS STRATEGY AND A PRODUCT ROADMAP

CASE STUDY—NELA CORPORATION—BUSINESS STRATEGY AND PRODUCT ROADMAP

This case study is about value distribution in the supply chain of CMP (chemical mechanical planarization) for an IC fabrication process. To an IC fab manager, the cost per wafer of a CMP step, or the cost of ownership (COO), is comprised of the depreciated cost of the CMP equipment plus the cost of consumables per wafer pass.

Situation Analysis

Market and product. NELA had a strong market position as a CMP process equipment supplier in the semiconductor manufacturing market. The CMP product line had over a 60% share of the overall market in 1999. The largest competitor, ESL Corporation, had only a 25% market share. NELA had achieved this commanding market position through a broad product portfolio covering all CMP application steps in the IC fabrication process, including copper (Cu), inter-layer dielectric (ILD), pre-metal dielectric (PMD), tungsten (W), shallow-trench-isolation (STI) dielectric, and poly silicon films, for both 200-mm and 300-mm wafer fabs. Product reliability, however, had been a major weakness of NELA products, resulting in a significant competitive advantage for ESL (which was known for its reliable products). By early 2000, product reliability had been significantly improved by CMP engineers as a result of an intensive high-visibility project. The challenge for the CMP division GM was not reliability improvement or market share gain anymore, but how to take advantage of this commanding position and improve business profitability and shareholder value.

Supply chain. The CMP process in IC manufacturing is not unlike the process of a chemical plant in which chemical consumption and the consumable parts are major contributors to the total production unit cost. In an IC fab, the manufacturing unit cost is measured and tracked in cost-per-wafer-pass and is called COO. The major consumables in a CMP process include the polishing pad, polishing slurry, pad conditioner, and various other polishing components. In 1999, a few suppliers controlled a large portion of the consumable market, mostly through their strong IP position. Some companies were traditional large chemical companies and others were medium-sized companies that had gained an attractive market position through innovation and strong patent protection.

NELA. In early 2000, the COO of Cu CMP was approximately $23 per wafer in a 300-mm fab. The CMP tool (equipment) depreciated capital cost was only $5 per wafer or 22% of the total CMP COO. In other words, the value position of NELA in the market was weak in spite of its dominating market share position. The lion's share of CMP value was going to consumable suppliers. Figure 3.40 illustrates the value distribution in early 2000 in terms of cost per wafer of the Cu CMP process in a 300-mm IC fab. The "baseline" bar in the chart represents the situation that the CMP BU faced in early 2000. The "system depreciation" contribution to the overall COO was calculated by amortizing the CMP equipment cost over its 5-year life and taking into account its anticipated wafer utilization. The equipment output capability or throughput (in wafers per hour) used in the calculation is also plotted in Figure 3.40 as a line against the right vertical axis. The CMP BU had planned a CIP to reduce the overall COO by extending the life of consumables and increasing system throughput. The anticipated reduction in COO and the corresponding throughput improvements are shown on Figure 3.40 as Revisions 1 and 2. The CIP project was planned for implementation over the following three quarters of calendar year 2000. At the completion of the project, NELA was forecasting to reduce customers' COO from $23 per wafer to $16 per wafer. Although this project benefited customers greatly, it did not improve the position of NELA in capturing value with respect to other players in the supply chain, notably consumable suppliers.

Value Capture and Competition

Power position. The power position in the supply chain, from customers (the end users) to subsuppliers, determines where the money goes. In the CMP business, the power to demand a bigger share of the total profit pie depends on a number of factors:

- Degree of commodification of products in the supply chain—IC chip manufacturing was commodifying as multiple sources of supply (foundries) sprang up in Southeast Asia and China. Conversely, process equipment design and the manufacturing of CMP consumables (pads, slurry, etc.) were becoming more complex, were underperforming, and had limited sources of supply.
- Switching cost to the customer—If customers cannot readily define/verify the desired product performance and a long time is required to qualify a new supplier, the switching cost is high. CMP equipment and consumables had a high switching cost. Specifying the precise performance requirements of a polishing pad was difficult. Pad performance could only be assessed indirectly by evaluating the performance of the entire CMP system in how well it polished a wafer, i.e., measuring the precise contribution of a pad to the final condition of a polished wafer was difficult.
- Control of interface to the customer—NELA did not provide a one-stop shopping, total-CMP solution. Consumable suppliers sold their products directly to IC manufacturers for production. This created a situation in which NELA had no influence over consumable pricing and the IC manufacturers established the relative value of equipment versus consumables in their total COO budget for the CMP step in IC production.

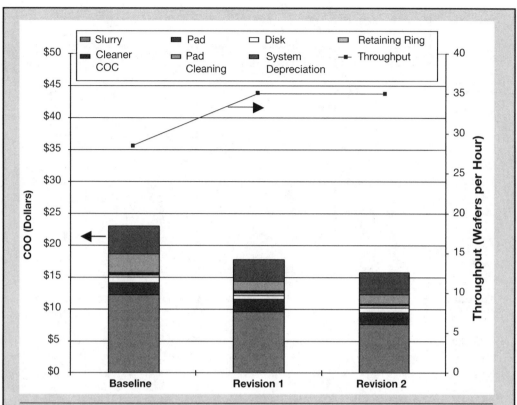

Figure 3.40. COO and Throughput for Copper CMP. COC, cleaner cost of consumables; D, disk; P, pad; PC, pad cleaning; R, retaining ring; S, slurry; SD, system depreciation; throughput, —■—.

- Control of interdependent product interfaces—NELA did not control the interfaces to critical consumables (such as pad and slurry), and suppliers "dictated" the corresponding equipment design interfaces. For example, NELA had to adapt the design of their equipment to accommodate the available pad specification and to design a delivery system that was suitable for supplier-specified (or customer-specified) slurry.
- IP position in the differentiators and enablers of value parameters in the CMP process (quality of wafer polishing)—The protected IP of critical process technology, equipment design, and the manufacturing process was shared by customers, consumable suppliers, and NELA.
- Core competency in process R&D and product development—NELA, through its extensive R&D resources and access to expensive CMP equipment, had a comparative advantage over consumable suppliers in integrating the consumables with process equipment. A few of the consumable suppliers, however, were chipping away at this advantage by purchasing CMP equipment from NELA and investing in R&D facilities and integration know-how.
- Core competency in manufacturing technology and manufacturing processes of consumables—The position of NELA was weak in consumable manufacturing technology and could not easily substitute suppliers' products. Know-how, protected IP, and the large capital investment had raised the entry barrier and limited the supply of consumables to a very few companies.
- Channel control—As noted above, IC manufacturers purchased critical consumables directly from suppliers and the position of NELA was weak.
- Strength of market position via market share and brand equity—The position of NELA was strong.

Supplier/ Product	Total Score	1 Commodity/ Differentiated Product	2 Switching Cost	3 Customer Interface Control	3 Product Interface Control	5 IP Position in Differentiators	6 Core Competency in Product Development	7 Core Competency in Manufacturing	8 Channel Control	9 Market Position
NELA, Equipment	45	9	9	1	6	3	8	1	1	7
Company A, Pad	72	9	6	9	5	9	9	8	9	8
Company B, Pad	47	10	6	1	1	4	9	10	5	1
Company C, Pad	68	10	10	2	7	10	10	10	5	4
Company D, Slurry	67	7	8	9	5	8	8	8	7	7
Company E, Slurry	64	7	6	8	5	9	9	8	6	6

Figure 3.41. Value Chain Power Ranking—CMP Consumables. Rating scale—1 to 10, 1 being the weakest.

A numerical ranking of the strength of various players in the CMP value chain based on the above power factors is presented in Figure 3.41. The rating is from one (weak) to ten (strong). The total score in Figure 3.41 indicates the relative weakness of NELA in the value chain. Something had to be done to improve profitability.

Outcome. To improve the value position of NELA in the supply chain, the marketing director at the CMP BU used the above assessment factors and devised a new market strategy. The BU set a goal of capturing 75% of the value in the CMP step of IC fabrication process (see Figure 3.40). The new strategy called for offering a "total solution" to the IC manufacturers for cost-effective planarization of copper interconnects. The deliverables of the total solution would include CMP process equipment, CMP consumables (pad, slurry, and other components), and an integration-verified process recipe. The strategy also called for competitive COO pricing and a superior copper planarization result on the wafer.

The critical enabler of the new marketing plan was a proactive consumable strategy consisting of several elements:

1. Develop a CMP pad and slurry with alternate new suppliers to broaden customer choices and to "commoditize" the consumables.
2. Strengthen the protected IP portfolio in consumable technologies through aggressive co-development with new consumable suppliers. Acquire IP as needed.
3. Enhance in-house core competency in consumable design and manufacturing technologies.
4. Enhance control of consumable distribution channels through aggressive distribution agreements with existing and emerging worldwide suppliers. Use the internal service BU at NELA to deliver and service consumables at customers' fabs.
5. Enhance control of the customer interface by co-developing consumables with customers as a total-solution provider.
6. Enhance control of interdependent product interfaces by designing value-added and differentiated features onto consumables that are provided by "commodity" suppliers. NELA must take advantage of its unique equipment design and integration capabilities and develop proprietary features into consumables, such as new sensors, a metrology window in the pad, and a slurry delivery module.

APPENDIX I. OUTLINE OF A BUSINESS PLAN FOR A NEW PRODUCT

The following outline for a business plan can be used as a reference for practitioners. Elements of the plan are discussed throughout this book.

1. Executive Summary
   - Business and Market Opportunities
   - Mission and Strategy
   - Objectives and Success Criteria
   - Key Actions and Milestones
   - Executive Team
   - Funding Requirements and Return Factor
2. Business Scope and Customer Needs
   - Business Purpose, Category, and Scope
   - Value Proposition and Differentiation
   - Impact on Customers
3. Business Strategy
   - Industry Characteristics and Market Trends
   - Segmentation
   - Demand Forecast—Total Available Market (TAM) and Served Available Market (SAM)
   - Competition and Market Barriers
   - Company Strategy:
     - Technology and IP
     - Market Assets
     - Competitive Insulation
4. Product Strategy
   - Product Development Focus
   - Key Success Factors
   - Market Penetration and Initial Target Customers
5. Business Model
   - Financial Model and Pricing
   - Sales Forecast
   - Cost Structure
   - Key Assumptions
6. Financial Plan
   - Proforma P&L
   - Balance Sheet
   - Cash Flow Statement
   - Funding for Growth
7. Operation Plan and Required Investment
   - R&D, Marketing, Sales, and Support Headcount
   - Critical IP and Protection
   - Manufacturing and Materials Plan (Outsourcing, Capacity)
   - Enterprise infrastructure (IT) and Facilities
   - Logistics
   - Partnerships

- Investment Dollars Including Capital
- ROI and Shareholder Value Growth

8. Implementation Plan
   - Management Team
   - Internal Alignment
   - Schedule Milestones and Accountability
   - Risk Analysis and Mitigation Strategy

REFERENCES

1. Levitt, T. *The Marketing Imagination.* New York: Free Press; 1993.
2. Drucker, P. *Post Capitalist Society.* New York: HarperBusiness; 1993.
3. Davidow, W.H. *Marketing High Technology.* New York: Free Press, 1986.
4. Moore, G. *Crossing the Chasm.* New York: HarperBusiness; 1991.
5. McKenna, R. *The Regis Touch.* Boston: Addison-Wesley; 1986.
6. Light, L.S., Goldstein, J. What high-tech managers need to know about brands. *Harvard Business Review* 1999; July–August.
7. Shanklin, W.L., Ryans, J.K., Jr. Organizing for high-tech marketing. *Harvard Business Review* 1984; November–December.
8. Homburg, C., Workman, J.P., Jr., Jensen, O. Fundamental changes in marketing organization: the movement toward a customer-focused organizational structure. *Journal of the Academy of Marketing Sciences* 2000; 28: 459–478.
9. Moorman, C., Rust, R.T. The role of marketing. *Journal of Marketing* 1999; 63: 180–197.
10. Srivastava, R.K., Shervani, T.A., Fahey, L. Marketing, business processes, and shareholder value: an organizationally embedded view of marketing activities and the discipline of marketing. *Journal of Marketing* 1999; 63: 168–179.
11. Lehmann, D.R., Jocz, K.E. *Reflections on the Futures of Marketing: Practice and Education.* Cambridge, MA: Marketing Science Institute; 1997.
12. Paul Sherlock, P. *Rethinking Business to Business Marketing.* New York: Free Press; 1991.
13. Lehmann, R.W. *Product Management, Second Edition.* New York: Irwin/McGraw-Hill; 1997.
14. Trout, J. *Differentiate or Die.* New York: John Wiley & Sons; 2000.
15. Leonard, D., Rayport, J. *Spark Innovation Through Empathic Design.* HBR Reprint 97606. Boston: Harvard Business School Publishing; 1997 November–December.
16. Christensen, C.M. *Innovator's Dilemmas, When New Technologies Cause Great Firms to Fail.* Boston: Harvard Business School Press; 1997.
17. IDEO Corporation. Video: *Deep Dive.* ABC *Nightline*; 1999.
18. Iansiti, M., Stein, E. *Understanding User Needs.* HBS Case #9-695-051. Boston: Harvard Business School Publishing; 1995 January 30.
19. Von Hippel, E. Lead users: a source of novel product concepts. *Management Science* 1986 July; 32(7).
20. Thomke, S., Nimgade, A. *Innovation at 3M Corporation (A).* HBS 9-699-012. Boston: Harvard Business School Publishing; 1998. Available at: http://harvardbusinessonline.

21. Hauser, J.R., Clausing, D. *The House of Quality.* HBR Reprint 88307. Boston: Harvard Business School Publishing; 1988 May–June.

22. Ashihara, K., Ishii, K. Paper No. IMECE2005-81956: Application of quality function deployment for new business R&D strategy development. In *Proceedings of IMECE 2005.* Orlando, FL: International Mechanical Engineering Congress and Exposition; 2005 November.

23. Patterson, M. Accelerating innovation: a dip into the meme pool. *National Productivity Review* 1990 Dec; 9(4).

24. Rogers, E.M. *Diffusion of Innovations, Fourth Edition.* New York: Free Press; 1995.

25. Menjo, H., Carpenter, P. *Diamond Harvard Business.* 1995 (a Japanese publication, translated by Regis McKenna Inc.).

26. Quelch, J.A., Fujikawa, Y. *Sony Corp.: Car Navigation Systems.* Case Number TN-5-598-082. Boston: Harvard Business School Publishing; 1998.

27. Kotler, P. *Marketing Management.* Upper Saddle Ridge, NJ: Prentice Hall; 2000.

28. Nagle, T.T., Holdem, R.K. *The Strategy and Tactics of Pricing.* Upper Saddle Ridge, NJ: Prentice-Hall; 1995.

29. Anderson, J.D., Narus, J.A. *Business Marketing: Understand What Customers Value.* HBR 98601. Harvard Business School Publishing; 1998 November–December.

30. Rackham, N. *SPIN Selling.* New York: McGraw-Hill; 1988.

31. Pine, B.J., II, Peppers, D., Rogers M. Do you want to keep your customers forever? *Harvard Business Review* 1995; March–April.

32. Anderson, E.W., Fornell, C. The customer satisfaction index as a leading indicator. In *Handbook of Services Marketing and Management,* Swartz, T.A., Iacobucci, D., Eds. Thousand Oaks, CA: Sage Publications; 1999.

33. Kincaid, J.W. *Customer Relationship Management* (Hewlett-Packard Company). Upper Saddle Ridge, NJ: Prentice Hall; 2003.

34. Ries, A., Trout, J. *Bottom-Up Marketing.* New York: Plume/Penguin Group; 1990.

ADDITIONAL READING

Baird, M.L. *Engineering Your Start-Up.* Belmont, CA: Professional Publications; 1997.

Brandenburger, A., Nalebuff, B.J. *The Right Game, Using Game Theory to Shape Strategy.* HBR Reprint 95402, J-A. Harvard Business School Publishing; 1995.

McKenna, R. *Real Time.* Boston: Harvard Business School Press; 1997.

Porter, M.E. *Competitive Strategy: Techniques for Analyzing Industries and Competitors.* New York: Free Press; 1998 June.

Ries, A., Trout, J. *Marketing War-Fare.* New York: McGraw-Hill; 1986.

Ries, A, Trout, J. *The 22 Immutable Laws of Marketing.* New York: HarperBusiness; 1993.

Stolze, W.J. *Start Up, Fourth Edition.* Franklin Lakes, NJ: Career Press; 1996.

Wallace, J., Erickson, J., Erickson, J., *Hard Drive: Bill Gates & the Making of the Microsoft Empire.* New York: Harper Business; 1993.

Watkins, W.M. *Technology and Business Strategy, Getting the Most Out of Technological Assets.* Westport, CT: Quorum Books; 1998.

4

PRODUCT PLATFORM AND KNOWLEDGE INTEGRATION

This chapter addresses several fundamental concepts that are essential to understanding the nature of products and processes and in making managerial decisions in the product development process. The product and process platform concept, design architecture, product modularity, types of products, and integration of knowledge in developing a product are discussed. (*Note:* Subsequent chapters will discuss the process of developing and commercializing a new product, including the sequence of tasks and best practices in project execution.)

A commercially successful product satisfies a multitude of requirements, including functional, cost, competitive differentiation, value creation, after-sale supportability, and life cycle extendibility. To a large extent, the potential for life cycle success of a product is often established at the design development stage. A developer's choice of the product/process platform, modularity of the architecture, and the selection of technologies and how they are integrated have the largest impact on the commercial performance of the product's life cycle. These design decisions are strongly dependent on the type of product and the context in which the technology is applied.

In order to focus the discussion in this chapter on product commercialization success, the chapter will begin with clarifying the goals of product development. Product development decisions about platform design, architectural modularity, the choice of technologies and how they are integrated, commercialization timing, tradeoff priorities, and risk-taking must all be made to further achievement of product development goals.

4.1 PRODUCT DEVELOPMENT GOALS

Product development is the process of applying technology to transform customer needs into a differentiated solution. Successful products match a technology to the target application context and produce optimal system performance at the lowest cost of production, delivery, and ownership.

The success of a product development project must be measured by the indicators that represent various dimensions of its purpose. These indicators should encompass the effectiveness of the process as well as the final product and service, including:

- The development process
- The product's performance in improving a user's experience
- Product market leadership
- Product profitability
- Return on investment

Table 4.1 provides metrics that can be used to measure the effectiveness and efficiency of a product innovation, development, and commercialization process. The practitioner should adopt the categories pertinent to his/her particular market, product, and organizational context and select the metrics accordingly. Important to note, however, is that the success metrics (set according to the guidelines of Table 4.1) should be measured against the established specifications and expectations of external and internal stakeholders. For example, manufacturability and serviceability of the design should be assessed against specifications from the manufacturing and service organizations, respectively.

4.2 KNOWLEDGE—GENERATION, RETENTION, REUSE, AND INTEGRATION

In product development, a team must ensure that the wide varieties of technologies that are incorporated in a product are well integrated so that the overall product (system) performs its intended function. An optimal product solution simultaneously meets all stakeholder requirements, including customer performance and experience needs, manufacturability, maintainability, time to market, and the product's production cost target. Simultaneously meeting all stakeholder requirements is only possible through an integrative approach and by performing multivariate tradeoffs for an optimal outcome. This chapter and subsequent chapters will expound upon this concept.

Applicable technologies are integrated through design modeling, simulation, and prototyping. High-risk design concepts and technologies are developed and integrated using bench-scale prototypes in the early stages of product development (during the exploration and feasibility or E&F phase). System-level integration issues are debugged and verified by using full-scale system prototypes later in the development process (as explained in Chapter 5).

The performance of a product's integrated technologies must be demonstrated within the intended application environment. During the product development process, performance of the integrated technologies should be simulated by imposing (on the system) appropriate boundary conditions which represent a realistic operational variability that the product is likely to encounter in the application context.

The context is comprised of the needs and wants of the product stakeholders in the marketplace and in the application (use) environment. For example, a product that is targeted for a low-volume manufacturing application such as a job shop has different automation technology needs than one that is targeted for high-volume manufacturing or an assembly line. The end user characteristics and skill levels, and how the product is transported and stocked in the

Table 4.1. The Metrics of Efficiency and Effectiveness of the Product Innovation, Development, and Commercialization Process

	Category	Purpose	Possible Metrics
1	Innovation and Matching Technology to Context	Perceiving market opportunities and capitalizing on technological possibilities	Percent of revenue and bookings from products developed in the last 2 years (firm or BU)
		Productivity in invention of products and technology	Number of disclosures and patent filings and awards
		Product performance compliance to market requirements	Key value factors, market requirement metrics, competitive standing, and firm's comparative performance
2	Commercialization and Life Cycle Leadership	Market penetration agility	Time to first customer satisfied or time to money
		Market position	Share of market 1 year after product introduction and penetration at key customers
		Business momentum, as a leading indicator of market positioning	Rate of change in market position
		Competitive advantage	CAP—number of years during which a firm can generate economic profits by creating and sustaining competitive advantage
3	Customer Experience	COO	Purchase price, installation, operation, and maintenance costs; product productivity, reliability, maintainability and cost of consumables and spares
		EHS	Metrics of EHS best practices, codes, and standards
		User friendliness and simplicity	Ease of operation, GUI ease of functionality, intuitiveness, self-diagnostics and troubleshooting, etc.
4	Business Objectives of Firm	Cost structure	Product production cost (manufacturing fixed and variable costs, including tooling, material, labor, overhead); R&D cost as percent of revenue, R&D fixed asset utilization, number of employees to revenue ratio
		Value capture	ASP, gross margin, profitability, ROI
		Environmental sustainability	1. Compliance to worldwide standards and treaty requirements 2. Resource efficiency in supply chain and zero-waste manufacturing 3. Ability to recycle at end of life
5	Effectiveness and Efficiency of the Development Process and the Implementation Project	Product quality	1. Compliance to MRS metrics 2. Compliance to customer expectations
		Project management	1. Actual schedule versus plan 2. Actual project cost (investment) versus budget
		Following the PDCP	1. Quality of documentation for manufacturing, suppliers, and service organizations according to users 2. Compliance to product development process checklist 3. Knowledge generation and integration by development phase and exit per established success criteria 4. Knowledge retention and reuse metrics

Note: BU, business unit; CAP, competitive advantage period; COO, cost of ownership; EHS, environmental, health, and safety; GUI, graphic user interface; ASP, average selling price; ROI, return on investment; MRS, market requirements specification; PDCP, product development and commercialization process.

distribution channel, all impose different requirements on product technologies and their integration scheme.

In short, in defining contextual requirements, having a comprehensive view of the stakeholders, including end users (customers)—manufacturing operation, distributors, customer service organization, project team members, firm's strategic IP requirements/constraints of the firm, suppliers, alliance members, and finally the community (environmental, labor, and cultural issues)—is important. In the early stages of a product development process, characteristics of the context must be well delineated in the MRS (marketing requirements specification) and be translated into engineering and technology requirements in the ERS (engineering requirements specification) (discussed in Chapter 5).

The needs and wants of stakeholders, however, may not be known—even by the stakeholders themselves! In high-tech industrial markets, customers frequently develop their own products and technologies concurrently with a key supplier that is developing a subsystem of the product. In this case, the customers' detailed technological requirements might not be known *a priori* and might evolve during the exploration phase of product development. Precisely specifying the interface to the supplier's subsystem might not be easy or even possible when a technology is new and interdependence of the supplier's product to the other components of the system is strong (depending on the location of the subsystem interface). An example of this situation is discussed in Section 4.8 of this chapter (in the case of a RF generator for a semiconductor etcher).

When there is a high degree of uncertainty in the technology and in the market requirements, the product development team should adopt a flexible process and emphasize frequent iterations throughout the cycle of system specification/component design/system testing. Frequent interaction and integration with customers and other stakeholders, experimentation in all dimensions of the development process, and assessment of the scope of the project are all critical to successful product development. A flexible process also mitigates risk and allows rapid adjustments in product development decisions. Although a flexible process is highly desirable, it must be well controlled. At each phase of development, the project should be replanned by considering the changing priorities of the firm and reaffirming the viability of the project.

Knowledge *generation, retention, reuse, and integration* form the foundation of the product development process. Knowledge is generated at the project team level through research, analysis, modeling, experimentation, prototyping, and system integration and verification testing by various stakeholders. Knowledge is retained by organizational learning across a diverse base of experience. An effective product development process captures and applies systematic knowledge of technologies, manufacturing, market conditions, and other contextual requirements as well as knowledge of the interactions between the subsystems and components of the product. The characteristics of the interactions or system dynamics may not be known or predictable at the onset. Extensive modeling, experimentation, and trial and error might be required to understand interactions between the technologies and the behaviors of various subsystems.

ERS must take advantage of and include the knowledge generated from previous projects and the experiences from production, marketing, and other parts of the organization. The company must have a way to retain and draw from previously generated knowledge. The product development team must also use new and retained knowledge proactively to guide its technology choices and design decisions.

**EFFECTIVENESS IN RETAINING AND REUSING KNOWLEDGE—
A SMALL VERSUS A LARGE COMPANY**

For a small company, retaining and reusing knowledge might not be particularly difficult, as was the case at Lam Research in 1984. Lam had just gone public after developing and commercializing an initial start-up product successfully. Knowledge capture from the first product development experience and reusing it for developing Rainbow, a second-generation product, was relatively easy. Lam had only 100 employees, who could communicate easily with each other. Although the second-generation team members were mostly new to Lam with little or no background in the initial product, they were not inhibited by a not-invented-here (NIH) constraint. The new team leader collected knowledge from the first-generation team members in engineering, manufacturing, marketing, and process technology by conducting interviews and gathering archived documents. The collected knowledge was documented in the MRS and ERS for the new product in the form of design constraints, reference material, design criteria, and test requirements.

Yet for larger companies such as Applied Materials with 23,000 employees who were developing 95 new products over a span of 2 years (in 2000), knowledge retention, sharing, and access was much more difficult. A formal system for retaining knowledge and a culture that promoted the reuse of existing knowledge was required. Creation of such a system and establishment of this type of culture proved to be challenging for management.

4.3 DIMENSIONS OF KNOWLEDGE INTEGRATION

The integration of knowledge in product development must occur in four dimensions:

- Integration of a variety of technologies and designs to achieve the desired performance in a component or a subsystem of the product, particularly in the E&F phase of the product development process—For example, technologists in a new product development team at a CMP equipment supplier must evaluate numerous technologies and integration concepts in the development of a new wafer polishing pad. The essence of the challenge is the feasibility of integration of the alternate concepts and the manufacturability of the final CMP pad design assembly. The new pad requires the integration of mechanical design, electrical design, and new manufacturing technologies to embed conductive fibers onto a dielectric pad that has the desired polishing properties.

- Integration of multiple components and subsystems into a system, in a holistic manner, in which their interactions are understood and optimized for overall system performance—The arrangement of components and subsystems and the definitions of their function, interfaces, and interactions constitute the product architecture and modularity (to be discussed in the sections that follow).

- Integration of a multitude of (often competing) requirements in the implementation phase of a new product development effort—Trade-off decisions and prioritization must be made between production cost and performance, features, and reliability; project scope versus budget; and time to market versus confidence level in the system performance before commercialization (how much verification testing and data collection is necessary?); etc.

- Integration of team members (across the supply chain) and the tasks of product development, including integration of the knowledge and contributions of team

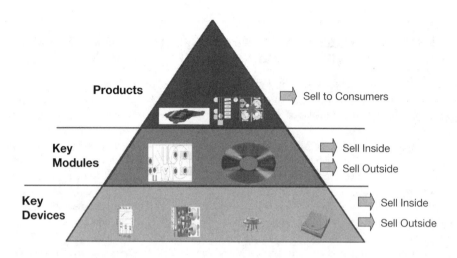

Figure 4.1. Vertical Integration in the CD Business at Sony. (Source: Data from Sony Corporation.)

members and integration of team interactions with the all company functions which provide resources or are impacted by the team—An example of such integration challenges is often encountered in software development in which various pieces are being designed concurrently by different engineers. Coordination of unit and system testing and sequencing and experimentation in the design concepts all become critical.

Vertical integration in the compact disc (CD) business at Sony provides an example of a systems approach in product integration and marketing (Figure 4.1). In Sony's systems approach, a multitude of devices are developed, manufactured, and integrated into modules, which in turn are integrated into various product lines such as audiovisual players and data storage products. At Sony, key components (devices) and modules are sold independently to Sony internal divisions and to external customers in the consumer electronics industry. Modular system design architecture, reuse of common technology and components, and integration of myriad technologies into multiple application contexts enable Sony to create a strong portfolio of products.

4.4 KNOWLEDGE INTEGRATION ACROSS THE VALUE CHAIN AND VIRTUAL TEAMS

Effective knowledge integration in all of the four dimensions discussed above requires a holistic view of the product and the product development team—a view that crosses all boundaries within the firm and across the value chain. A systems approach encourages experimentation and iteration to enhance understanding of the interactions and embraces a diversity of ideas and risk-taking to turn constraints into differentiating benefits. Key aspects of a systems approach and its success include:

- Effectiveness of the systems approach is predicated by the firm's organizational structure, business processes, and culture. The team, business unit (BU), and corporate-level management and leadership capabilities and decision-making processes strongly impact the success or failure of integration in a product development endeavor.

- The development of technology, components, subsystems, production processes, development tools, and ancillary products must all occur concurrently and across a *virtual* team in the supply chain. Members of this virtual *integrated worldwide cross-functional* team include internal members (from marketing, engineering, sales, manufacturing, materials procurement, field services, customer support, and finance), outsourced engineering and manufacturing resources, key suppliers, co-development customers, and industry partners.

- A systems approach in product design necessitates seeking the design requirements and constraints from all sources within the context of the project (as discussed in Chapter 3, Section 3.7). Requirements could come from early adopters and customers who drive the technology, from suppliers who drive manufacturability and manufacturing cost considerations, and from sales and distribution partners who drive product packaging, configuration, and pricing.

- Innovators, early adopters, or lead users are excellent customers to team with and to set up a joint development project (JDP) for product development. A JDP provides a risk-reduction opportunity in development of high-tech products, although there is a downside in exposing the early "weaknesses" of a developing product to a key customer and in becoming too biased by the input of only one customer.

- Increasing complexity of products and technologies and business risk in high-tech markets has created a strong dependency among the players in value chains. Seldom does one company have all the resources and technologies to develop a new product in a timely manner and with an acceptable return on investment (ROI). A firm must leverage concurrent development with suppliers, industry organizations, peers, and strategic partners and integrate technologies and products across networks of development organizations. To develop a new product, a firm must take advantage of technological possibilities created by others, even from outside its own industry. Strategic alliances must be established from the beginning to acquire the necessary technology, people expertise, or market assets. The strategic partners must be involved in the product development process from the onset. (The subject of strategic alliances is discussed in more detail in Chapter 7.)

Participating and driving the standards groups and organizations in an industry is also critical in developing a product that will be widely accepted and can take advantage of a network effect.

4.5 TIME VALUE OF KNOWLEDGE AND SHORT TIME TO MARKET

Time to market defines a product development schedule. Time to market has a first-order impact on the commercialization success of a product. The schedule is always a point of contention for an RD&E team. There is seemingly never adequate time to do the *whole* job "right." Engineers always feel pressured to heed time-to-market requirements—and that they are compromising quality in product design and characterization testing by doing so.

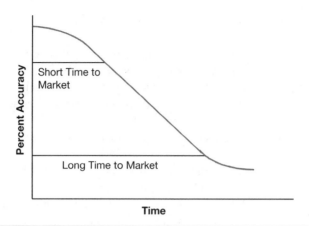

Figure 4.2. The Accuracy of Estimating Market Conditions.

In high-tech product development and commercialization, the benefits of a short time to market are many and far reaching. They include:

- Improving the chance of defining market requirements[1]—Market conditions and the needs and wants of customers change because of changes in the economy, advances in technology, and the actions of competition. The stability of product definition and the accuracy of estimating market conditions diminish the longer the look is into the future of a high-tech market (illustrated in Figure 4.2).
- Providing market information—A new product introduction is a powerful *sampling technique* to obtain market information from the feedback of customers. In addition, new opportunities are often identified by customers, who apply the product in new ways that the supplier had not perceived. A higher sampling rate via frequent new product releases results in enhanced knowledge generation.
- Increasing product life cycle revenue, profitability, and ROI (as shown in Figure 3.7 in Chapter 3)
- Providing first-mover advantage in market penetration and positioning
- Improving the chance of becoming designed into an industrial customer's new production process or product by concurrent development with the customer
- Increasing the technological gap over competition as noted by Clark and Wheelwright (1993)[2] (illustrated in Figure 4.3)

In the final analysis, the most important and often the only differentiator of a new technology product is the time-to-market advantage over competitors. Sooner or later, competitors will catch up in technology and product design, even if a firm has a protected (patented) technological position.

4.6 TYPES OF PRODUCTS AND DEVELOPMENT PROJECTS

The scope of a development project, the required competency of resources, the required investment, and the potential risks of the new product development endeavor all depend on the type of product that is being developed. Therefore, a product development and commercialization

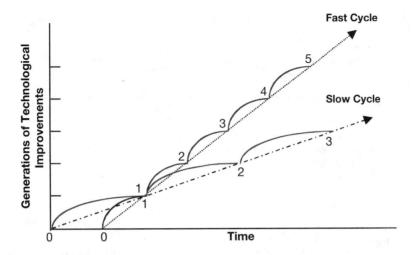

Figure 4.3. Fast-Cycle Developments and the Technological Gap. Similar amounts of technology are incorporated in each generation of product in both cycles. (Source: Adapted from Clark, K.B., Wheelwright, S.C. *Managing New Product and Process Development*. New York: Free Press; 1993.)

process should be scaled and tailored to the particular product type. In defining product types, the interdependent nature of a product and the process for its production and use should first be reiterated.

In the development of a new product, often new manufacturing processes have to be developed too. A new manufacturing process might be for building a component, a subsystem, or the assembly of a *whole* product. For example, the new product might require a new method of assembling a printed circuit board, a new packaging technology, a new method of fabricating specialty materials (e.g., silicon carbide-coated graphite), or a new formulation of the padding material that is used in polishing a silicon wafer, etc.

Some products may be intended as a manufacturing process tool for a user (the customer). For example, a welding robot is a product that is used on an automobile manufacturing line. Wafer process equipment is a product that is used in fabricating integrated circuits (ICs) in the semiconductor industry. In wafer process equipment, product development must include not only an automated piece of equipment that handles silicon wafers and performs certain function of the IC manufacturing process (such as etching a pattern or depositing a thin film), but it must also include the integration of its function with other process steps (before or after) in an IC fabrication process.

In short, for many new products, product development must be inclusive of process development, processes for manufacturing of the components of the product, and processes for the user's application. In the remainder of this chapter, the term *product development* will be used in this broader context to include the development of the production processes.

The type of a product in a category, as it relates to the development effort, is usually defined with respect to the characteristics of the target market, the product technology, and the firm. As proposed by various researchers and practitioners in the field, a few examples of product type classification are shown in Figures 4.5, 4.6, 4.7, and 4.8.

Alignment with an existing market and creation of a new market. Leonard and Barton classify a product according to its alignment with an existing market and the creation of a new

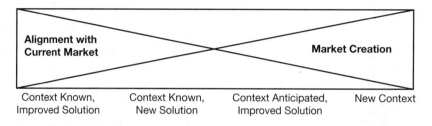

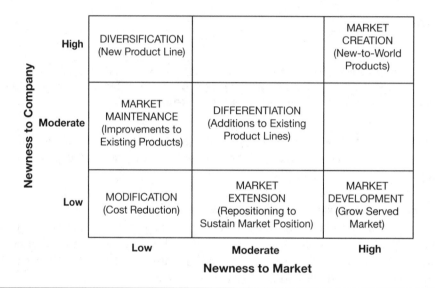

Figure 4.4. The Newness of Products and the Market. (Source: Adapted from Leonard-Barton, D. *Wellsprings of Knowledge*. Boston: Harvard Business School Press; 1995.)

Figure 4.5. Product Categories Based on Newness to the Market and the Company.

market (Figure 4.4).[3] In this classification, knowledge of the market context and the type of solution (new or an improvement over an existing solution) characterize a new product and the associated development project.

Newness to a market and to a company. As suggested by many researchers, products are also categorized according to their newness to the market and to the company (Figure 4.5). A different development and commercialization plan is required for each product category (type). For example, if an existing product is introduced into a new market segment (market development), the scope of the product development project is generally small, depending on the degree of customization required in meeting the needs of the new segment. On the other hand, when the product is new both to the company and to the market (market creation), a development and commercialization project is often faced with significant challenges and risks.

Nature of the technological innovation. Products and development projects are categorized by the nature of a technological innovation (Figure 4.6). Type A products are based on a mature technology and are developed through a low-risk continuous improvement project

Type A	Type B	Type C
Mature Technology	**Leading-Edge Technology**	**Disruptive Technology (Discontinuous Innovation)**
• High Production Worthiness • Good Profitability • Shrinking SAM • Project — CIP	• Competitive Advantage in Performance • Good Production Worthiness • Good Gross Margin • Project — New Product Development	• Redefines Market Through Breakthrough Innovation • High Growth Potential • Project — E&F

Figure 4.6. New Product and Project Types by Technological Innovation.

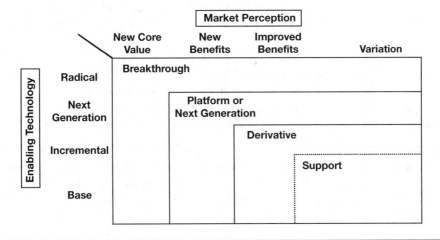

Figure 4.7. Types of Product Projects According to the Nature of the Technology and Market Perception. (Source: Adapted from Iansiti, M. *Technology Integration: Making Critical Choices in a Turbulent World*. Boston: Harvard Business School Press; 1997.)

(CIP.) The purpose of a CIP is to sustain the market position and improve profitability. Type B products are developed with leading-edge technologies and represent the next-generation product line for a BU. A Type B product creates competitive advantage and improves the product line market share. The development scope and risk of a Type B product are moderate. A Type C product is based on a disruptive technology that creates a new market or redefines an existing market. This product type has high growth potential and creates a compelling competitive advantage by redefining the playing field. Development risk of a Type C product is high. The firm may need new competencies in engineering and marketing and a paradigm shift in its business model. Usually the scope of a Type C development project is large.

Enabling technology and market perception. Based on the work of Clark and Wheelwright,[2] Marco Iansiti[4] classifies product development projects by the dimensions of enabling technology and market perception (Figure 4.7). The model in Figure 4.7 classifies product projects as *breakthrough, platform/next generation, derivative,* and *support.*

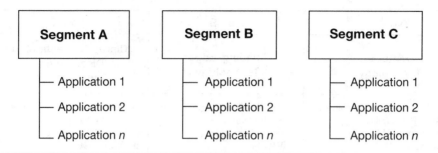

Figure 4.8. Varieties of Markets and Applications Served by a Product Platform.

- Breakthrough projects often create new product categories and require new technology R&D in the E&F phase of the product development process.
- Platform/next generation projects result in a new product line and build a substantial commercial presence in a market or enable market share gain in an existing market. Platform/next generation projects follow the new product development process (see Chapter 5).
- Derivative projects develop new applications or improve productivity and competitiveness of an existing product line. Derivative products generally enable reaping profit from prior investments in technology and market creation.
- Support projects are in a CIP category and are intended to improve customer satisfaction, enhance reliability, and lower the cost of an existing product.

The framework for classifying project types in Figure 4.7 does not include path-finding R&D projects for which the product application and commercialization target has not yet been identified. It does, however, include breakthrough technology projects for which the target application is identified, whether the application is in an existing market (a new core value) or it is a perceived opportunity in an emerging market.

4.7 PRODUCT PLATFORM AND ARCHITECTURAL DESIGN CONSIDERATIONS

A framework for the definition of a *product platform* must encompass the product's life cycle factors, including target market characteristics and the variety of technologies, within the dimension of time—a product platform must be designed based on how markets and technologies will evolve over the product's life cycle. A platform integrates the common technological capabilities and modalities of the product/technology to enable penetration into multiple market segments (target/potential) with one or more product lines and applications over an extended period of time.

Platform architecture should be extendable, i.e., allow the future addition of required capabilities without actually designing them in from the outset—because designing them in from the outset often results in overdesign of most segment applications. Therefore a platform design should *not exclude* the future addition of necessary features and capabilities for the success of the product over its life cycle and across its target segment applications. Over the product life cycle, a platform should be able to serve multiple applications within a range of market segments (an example is illustrated in Figure 4.8).

4.7.1 Product and Process Platforms—Definitions

A *product platform* is a collection of common elements, especially the underlying defining technology, which is implemented across a range of products.

- A product platform is the lowest level of relevant common technology within a set of products or a product line.
- A product platform is the foundation upon which multiple products that are related by common technology are built. Yet a platform is not a product; it does not necessarily perform a specific function; and it is not saleable.
- A product platform establishes the cost structure, potential capabilities, and differentiation for the subsequent products that are built on it. Based on a common platform, new products implement different features and functions for specific market segments and distribution channels.

Defining the product platform is one of the most important strategic decisions that a firm can make when developing a new product. Focusing on the product platform simplifies the product strategy process. A well thought-out platform enables a firm to rapidly develop several successful derivative products over the platform life cycle without having to make frequent major decisions. Leveraging the platform as a foundation also reduces product development and manufacturing costs.

A *process platform* shares most of the characteristics that are enumerated above for a product platform. A process platform is a collection of common elements, especially the underlying defining technology, implemented across a *range of processes*. It is the lowest level of relevant common technology within a set of processes.

4.7.2 Defining a Product Platform—Guidelines

Based on the above platform framework considerations and definitions, several guidelines should be adhered to in defining a new platform:[5]

- Firms must have a robust theory or framework—a thought process that can unambiguously guide managers in deciding what part of a product platform constitutes the core that may be leveraged and that will alert them when their historical definitions and structuring of platforms are no longer appropriate.
- Platforms must be flexible and extendable to spawn derivatives at a relatively low cost.
- Platforms often leverage the elements of development and commercialization that are the most costly to replicate, e.g., elements such as product architecture, process technology, components, or brand positioning. As a result, competitors may define their product platforms differently.

A platform definition should be changed when underlying or supporting technologies change and make the existing platform lose the above characteristics and when changes in the nature of market segmentation and demand across these segments alter the relevance of a certain definition of the platform.

4.8 PRODUCT ARCHITECTURE AND MODULARITY

The market strategy for winning a strong power position in the value chain and for creating a compelling competitive advantage is strongly linked with the choices that developers make in the product platform and design architecture and in the sourcing of components from suppliers. Before discussing these linkages, design terminologies will be defined that, in addition to the product platform (see Section 4.7), establish the fundamental characteristics of a product.

- *Architecture* identifies the subsystems and components of a product and defines their functions, interfaces, interactions, and communication.
- *Standards* set design rules, communication protocols, and how subsystems perform relative to one another.
- *Structure* is the makeup of a module or a product and how it is constituted.
- *Function* is what a product or module does and the purpose that it serves.
- *Module* can be defined in several different ways. Baldwin and Clark define a module from a structural viewpoint: "A module is a unit whose structural elements are powerfully connected among themselves and relatively weakly connected to elements in other units . . . In other words, modules are units of a larger system that are structurally independent of one another, but work together."[6] According to the *Merriam-Webster's Dictionary*, a *module* "is an independently operable unit that is a part of the total structure" and *modular* is "constructed with standardized units or dimensions for flexibility and variety in use."

Modularity may exist in the design functionality in which different modules perform distinctive functions and are independently operable units. *Modularity* may also be defined and built into a product from a structural point of view for manufacturability, in which an assembly can be built in an independent work cell and be readily integrated with other modules and assembled into the *whole* system. In this context, *architecture* is a framework that allows independence of the structure and integration of the function of different modules.

4.8.1 Modularity in System Design

A modular product design enables designers to establish "well-defined" interfaces between the modules of a system in which one module can be potentially replaced by another "equivalent" module. The degree to which a module can be replaced, the degree of equivalency, and the precision of the definitions of the interfaces between one module and the other modules can be the basis of value distribution in the architecture of a product.

Design engineers (hardware or software) usually think of a modular architecture in terms of *function*. Manufacturing engineers usually think of a module in terms of its *structural independence* for ease of assembly with other modules. In a complex high-tech product, the two definitions co-exist for engineering, manufacturing, and service reasons as well as for the fuzzy interdependence that exists when technologies/functions are underperforming. When a product technology is new and it is underperforming against the customer's needs (specifications), function is the basis of competition. In this case, the modularity is usually in the function. As the basis of competition changes, the product and process architecture becomes modular in structure. As the interfaces between the subsystems become well defined, outsourcing of the design or manufacturing of a module would not jeopardize the retention of a differentiating function, core technology, or IP.

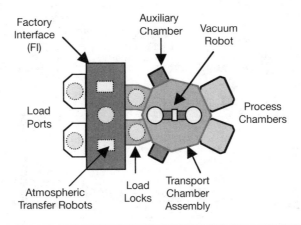

Figure 4.9. A Process Equipment Architecture.

Modularity in system (product) design is desirable because it improves manufacturability, reduces cost, increases economy of scale, improves the opportunity for outsourcing, enables concurrent development, and improves maintainability and service. Drawbacks of modularity in system design (structure) are reduction in the system's optimized performance, migration of value, and diffusion of IP to the suppliers of independent subsystems, which lowers the barriers for suppliers to move up the value chain and to become subsystem and eventually system integrators.

In a modular system, the interface control documents (ICD), application programming interface (API), and the attributes of various subsystems must be well defined. Whoever defines and controls these interface specifications has the opportunity to control the subsystems' "value."

To clarify this discussion, modularity concepts in an IC manufacturing process equipment will be examined and the historical transition and shift in customer value among the subsystems will be noted.

4.8.2 Modularity and IC Manufacturing Process Equipment

The architecture and major subsystems of typical process equipment used in the fabrication of IC are illustrated in Figure 4.9. Details of the process chamber assembly and the associated subsystems/components are shown in Figure 4.10. The basic system architecture and the process chamber design structure have not changed significantly over the past 20 years, in spite of many advances in IC manufacturing technology. However, subsystem and component designs, process formulations (recipes), and manufacturing technology have progressed significantly, in pace with the needs of IC fabrication technology and Moore's law. Furthermore, the number of system integrators and suppliers of major subsystems has reduced dramatically since the early 1980s, and value distribution among players in the equipment industry shifted substantially.

For example, examine the gas panel that delivers a precisely controlled flow of an ultra-clean gaseous chemical mixture to the process chamber (see Figure 4.10). In the early to mid 1980s, gas panel assembly technology was a source of competitive differentiation in system performance. The architecture of the gas panel design, the performance of individual components, and the manufacturing technology of the assembly were all underperforming, constituting the basis of competitive advantage. Most system providers shied away from outsourcing

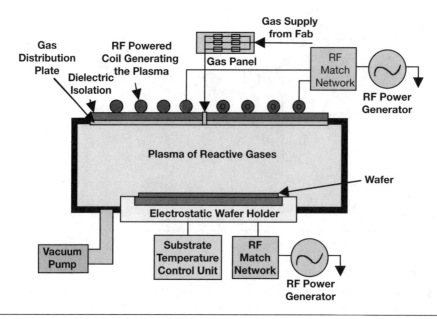

Figure 4.10. A Process Chamber Assembly and Associated Subsystems.

gas panel manufacturing, fearing that suppliers would level the playing field among system providers. By early 1990, the design and performance of gas panels had converged industry-wide and were meeting IC manufacturers' specifications. The basis of competition for the gas panel had shifted to size (smaller was better) and cost. Profit margins were depressed and most system integrators (process equipment suppliers) outsourced their gas panel assembly manufacturing. The gas panel had become a commodity! Important to note is that the gas panel was both structurally and functionally modular and its interfaces to the system (including the reaction chamber) could be precisely defined even when the *whole* assembly was an underperformer.

In contrast, consider the case of the RF (radio frequency) power generator assembly (see Figure 4.10). An RF generator provides RF energy to ionize a low-pressure gas mixture in the reaction chamber and to create a chemically reactive plasma environment that, through a surface reaction, deposits or etches thin films on the surface of a wafer (see Chapter 11 for more detail on IC manufacturing techniques). As early as 1983, independent suppliers were emerging from related industries to design and manufacture RF generators (because most process equipment system suppliers lacked the technology). Additionally the RF generator function was a critical underperformer in 1983. (In spite of much progress, it was still underperforming 20 years later!)

A major problem facing system integrators was that the functional specification for the generator and its functional interface to the reaction chamber could not be precisely defined. Over the two decades from 1983 to 2003, the number of generator suppliers remained small, and the product did not commoditize to the point of cost being the main differentiator. An RF generator is supposed to deliver a specified forward power to the reaction chamber. However, the ability of a generator to deliver a specified forward power is dependent on the reaction chamber impedance. The reaction chamber impedance is a variable, changing as a function of the gas mixture, wafer surface conditions, and other parameters that are purposefully varied in production, depending on the IC product that is being built by the system. However, "fixing" the interface of a generator to the system was necessary so that the interface could be specified and the generator could be qualified as an independent module. The clever solution to the interface specification problem was to fix the output impedance of the generator to 50 ohms. In order to do this, equipment system suppliers designed an interface device between the generator and the reaction chamber that—irrespective of the changing impedance of the chamber—always produced a 50-ohm interface to the generator. This interface device was called an "RF match network" (see Figure 4.10). Because of its critical functionality, the RF match network became proprietary IP and a differentiator of equipment system performance.

Although the RF match network technique worked well, it compromised the integrated performance of the generator and the chamber. Nevertheless, because system suppliers had maintained control of the interdependent interface (with the RF match network), they retained the market value.

In 1995, one of the system suppliers invented a new technique (in conjunction with a generator supplier) in which the match network was eliminated and the generator design was modified to always deliver the desired load power into the chamber irrespective of its impedance. This optimized, integrated design provided a superior system performance that had not previously been possible. However, the generator performance could no longer be precisely specified or measured independently of the reaction chamber. Multisourcing of the generator also became more difficult because the generator and the chamber formed a single integrated module with a strong interdependent "fuzzy" interface. In the new design, the value shifted from the system integrator to the generator supplier that controlled the interdependent interface.

In a reaction chamber assembly (see Figure 4.10), many other components and subsystems went through a similar evolution. The temperature control unit and vacuum pump followed a similar path to that of the gas panel, while the electrostatic wafer holder (ESC) remained a differentiator because the ESC was highly interdependent with the functions of the chamber. Most system suppliers designed the ESC assembly such that its components could be outsourced to different contract manufacturers while the critical assembly remained a proprietary design. Again, with the ESC, control of the interdependent interface stayed with the system supplier and so did the market value.

By outsourcing the ESC assembly or the RF match network, control of the interface shifts to a component supplier who could demand a change in the chamber structure, assembly, or even function. Also, as subsuppliers learn about the chamber construction and function, they are more likely to move up the value chain and become a competitor of the system (and chamber) supplier, shifting the value further away from the system supplier.

The reaction chamber design and process recipe are perceived by IC manufacturers (the customers) to be the heart of process equipment and where the most value resides. The process technology and reaction chamber design fit the definition of a "core technology" that must be protected by an equipment supplier and must not be outsourced as a module. The reaction chamber assembly is usually designed and tested as a "functional module," while for ease of manufacturing, it is broken into structural modules such as the lower and upper assemblies. Outsourcing the structural modules to contract manufacturers that do not have system engineering/integration capability does not risk shifting value to suppliers.

As noted in the examples, product architecture, modularity strategy, and the location of interfaces (between the modules) have a first-order impact on product commercialization success. A proper definition of the system architecture enables a firm to outsource areas in which technology performance has exceeded customer needs (i.e., the commodities) and to "in-source" (and allocate appropriate product development resources) and control high-value subsystems (underperformers, modules that are highly interdependent and possess a high degree of technical uncertainty, etc.). By protecting the modules of higher value with exclusivity, a firm can enhance its competitive insulation.

4.9 STRATEGIC OUTSOURCING AND PRODUCT ARCHITECTURE

Outsourcing strategy for product development must be integrated with the design of system architecture and subsystem interfaces in order to control what is core and of high market value to the firm. When subsystems are strongly interdependent and their performance requirements cannot be precisely specified (as demonstrated by the examples in Section 4.8), several guidelines should be followed in designing the system architecture and in implementing the outsourcing strategy:

- Wherever possible, design-in commercially available "commodity" subsystems or components that have multiple sources of supply.
- Design functional and structural modules that can be "standardized" with precisely defined specifications and interfaces and that can be outsourced to multiple suppliers.
- Specify the necessary functionality of every subsystem (and module) as a stand-alone unit, but verify the interfaces and qualify the performance of each subsystem according to the overall system integration and functionality metrics. For example, in the case of the RF generator in semiconductor process equipment, specifications for the generator would establish the required peak output power, frequency range, and interfaces to the rest of the equipment (including the physical and electrical and communication interfaces). In addition, the specifications would stipulate that generator performance is acceptable only if certain process results on the customer's wafers are achieved when the generator is integrated with the reaction chamber. (*Note*: The ERS document that is discussed in Chapter 5 is appropriate to frame the design rules, specifications, and acceptance criteria for each subsystem.)
- Control the interface. In designing a modular system and outsourcing its manufacturing, whoever controls the interface to the customer captures the highest value over time—which is why solution providers usually capture the highest value in the supply chain. For example, in the case of IC process equipment in Figure 4.9, the factory interface (FI) module is the interface to the customer's wafer supply and automation management in a fab. The system supplier has to exercise caution in outsourcing the FI to a third party. If the fab customer can directly buy from the FI supplier, the system supplier will lose the opportunity to stay close to the operating environment of the IC manufacturer and over time will lose the fab integration value.

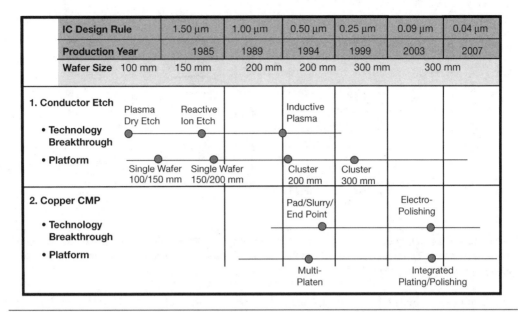

Figure 4.11. Evolution of Platforms and Technology Breakthroughs in the Semiconductor Process Equipment Industry.

CYCLES OF BREAKTHROUGH INNOVATION AND INTRODUCTION OF NEW PLATFORMS IN THE SEMICONDUCTOR PROCESS EQUIPMENT INDUSTRY

Different product project types are usually encountered at vastly different frequencies (see Figure 3.10). Review of the following example from the semiconductor process equipment industry provides an instructive illustration.

Evolution of product platforms and breakthrough technologies in the semiconductor manufacturing equipment industry over a 20-year span are depicted in Figure 4.11, which shows etch and CMP applications in the sequence of process steps for fabrication of an IC. Note that new platforms and new breakthrough technologies for either etch or CMP were introduced only once every 8 to 10 years—despite the fact that IC geometry (or the design rule) had been shrinking 2-fold every 18 months (according to Moore's law). In other words, derivative products of a generation of technology and platform had been adequate to follow Moore's law over several generations of device nodes.

The need for a new equipment platform, in addition to the enabling of a new process technology, was driven by a desire to increase wafer size for fab productivity improvement, which also occurred every 8 to 10 years, although the two drivers did not always coincide. In summary, the majority of development projects at suppliers of etch and CMP equipment had been for derivative products. Only every 8 to 10 years did they have to develop a new technology or a new platform.

4.10 PRODUCT LIFE CYCLE

A classic product life cycle model is illustrated in Figure 4.12 in which cash flow is plotted against time. Cash flow is negative in the beginning as the firm invests in the development of a new product and peaks in a latter interval of the project. A typical product goes through

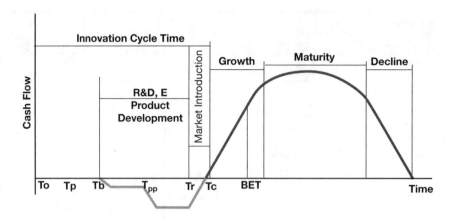

Figure 4.12. A Classical Product Life Cycle. **To** = opportunity **o**ccurs; **Tp** = opportunity is **p**erceived; **Tb** = proj-ect **b**egins (Phase 1); **Tpp** = **p**roject **p**lan (Phase 2); **Tr** = product **r**elease to manufacturing (Phase 4); **Tc** = pos-itive **c**ash flow; **BET** = **b**reakeven time.

periods of growth, maturity, and decline of revenue generation before it reaches its "end of life" and becomes obsolete.

In Figure 4.12, key events before and after the start of a product development project (at Tb) are illustrated. To is when the opportunity for a new technology/product occurs—when end users' needs are unsatisfied with existing offerings in the industry. Tp is the time when an opportunity is perceived by marketers. The closer the times To, Tp, and Tb are, the better the chance is for commercial success of a new product.[1] In other words, marketers perceiving a market opportunity (in applying technology to context) as early as the opportunity occurs at To and starting a product development project (Tb) without delay are critical.

Figure 4.12 also depicts a few other critical milestones that can be used as key performance indicators (KPIs) in monitoring and controlling the effectiveness of a product development process (or PDCP, which is discussed in Chapter 5). These milestones include Tp, completion of the project plan (Phase 2); Tr, product release to manufacturing (completion of Phase 4); Tc, the time when cash flow turns positive and the market introduction phase is "concluded;" and finally, BET, the investment break-even time. (*Note*: Chapter 10 will discuss a "return map," which is a more comprehensive framework for measuring the success of a PDCP and a prod-uct's ROI.

4.11 CONTINUOUS IMPROVEMENT OF A PRODUCT

The decline of product revenue that occurs in the period following the maturity phase (see Figure 4.12) is often averted through a series of continuous *improvement* projects (CIPs) that extend the product's life (shown in Figure 4.13). CIPs can serve a variety of strategies in extend-ing product life:

- Product upgrades to meet new customer requirements and maintain competitive advantage—Upgrades are released into the forward manufacturing builds and are also sold to the installed base as "upgrade kits."
- Improved product reliability to maintain customer satisfaction and lower warranty cost

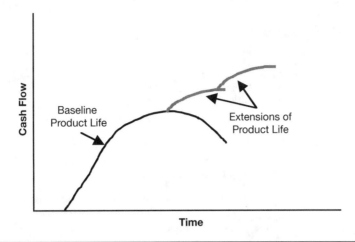

Figure 4.13. Extension of Product Life with Continuous Improvement Projects.

- Lower product fabrication cost to maintain profit margin as product price erodes over time
- Customization as a new model or a product revision to diversify into a new market segment
- Overcoming product shortcomings in compliance to specifications which were committed to by the company at the time of sales—Shortcomings could be in safety features that cause product liability (e.g., in automobiles) or in contractual obligations for the performance of industrial products. Contractual performance obligations are usually required to obtain an industrial customer's final sign off on the product and to receive payments withheld from an invoice. CIPs for product compliance result in what is known as "retrofit" hardware and software.

4.12 BASELINE AND DERIVATIVE PRODUCTS

As noted earlier in this chapter, a breakthrough technology and a new platform create a baseline product to serve a target market segment. Derivative products enable a firm to satisfy the changing needs of a served market (over time) and to maintain or improve the firm's market position. Additionally, derivative products enable diversification into new segments to increase the size of the served market. Derivative products add features and capabilities to the baseline and are developed and commercialized through a series of incremental innovation steps (shown in Figure 4.14).

In a continuous *innovation* process, marketers are often faced with the dilemma of how much of the known features and capabilities should be included in the MRS for a baseline product and its derivatives. Marketers and engineering managers are often tempted to include "everything" in the baseline and go for a "home run" product that satisfies the needs of more than one market segment and enables broad-based market penetration and a rapid growth of business.

In the semiconductor equipment market, a "home run" would be an etch product that meets the needs of DRAM, microprocessor, and foundry manufacturing at a new technology

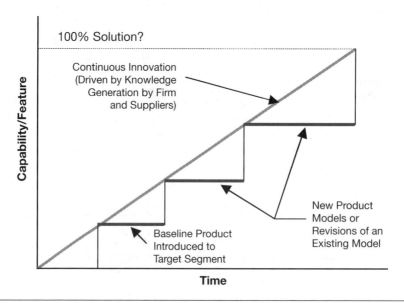

Figure 4.14. Incremental Innovation and Strategy for Introducing Derivative Products.

node for both front-end and back-end applications. However, such an approach is often too risky and does not deliver commercial success. The scope of a project that incorporates "all capabilities" becomes too large for timely market introduction, product cost becomes too high for competitiveness and profitability in most segments, and the product becomes too complex to be user-friendly and serviceable. In short, a "home run" product that can serve all market segments is often non-optimal in most market segments. Best is to have a series of product models that serve different segments.

Figure 4.14 illustrates how an RD&E team continuously develops features and capabilities through incremental innovation (the straight line) and marketing introduces a series of derivative products and new models by bundling selected features and capabilities (the stair steps). This approach enables a company to meet a short time-to-market objective with the baseline product and thereafter to introduce a series of new (derivative) products to maintain market momentum and competitive advantage.

Managing the frequency of introducing new revisions or new models in a given market segment is important. For example, the business of industrial customers is disrupted if a supplier informs the customer about new upgrades, derivative products, or new models too frequently. Best is to bundle a set of capabilities and features together and introduce them collectively at an appropriate time. For a new technology or a new platform baseline, the frequency of introducing derivative products or product upgrades in a given segment should diminish as time passes from the initial baseline release (see Figure 4.14). In other words, although more frequent upgrades and revisions are acceptable in the first year after a baseline release, a supplier should stretch out the introduction of upgrades and derivative products in the second and third years.

REFERENCES

1. Patterson, M.L. *Accelerating Innovation*. Hoboken, NJ: Van Nostrand Reinhold; 1998.
2. Clark, K.B., Wheelwright, S.C. *Managing New Product and Process Development*. New York: Free Press; 1993.
3. Leonard-Barton, D. *Wellsprings of Knowledge*. Boston: Harvard Business School Press; 1995.
4. Iansiti, M. *Technology Integration: Making Critical Choices in a Turbulent World*. Boston: Harvard Business School Press; 1997.
5. Christensen, C. HBS Teaching Note #698-056 (HBS 5-698-056). Boston: Harvard Business School Publishing; 1998.
6. Baldwin, C.Y., Clark, K.B. *Design Rules, Volume 1, The Power of Modularity*. Cambridge, MA: The MIT Press; 2000.

5

THE PRODUCT DEVELOPMENT PROCESS

According to the Software Engineering Institute at Carnegie Mellon University, a *process* is a sequence of steps performed for a given purpose. A *process* integrates people (with skills and motivation), tools, tasks, and procedures (which defines the relationship of tasks).

This chapter is devoted to the process of product development. The various phases of product development are discussed. Guidelines for the key tasks of new product development are also presented, including the content of key documents and the roles and responsibilities of core team members. Because of their unique characteristics, additional sections are devoted to a discussion of new process and new software development.

A brief review of selected product development processes that are reported in business literature and practiced by leading global companies is presented in Section 5.2. Subsequently the recommended process for development and commercialization of a new product (PDCP) based on cited best-known methods and the author's experience is outlined. [*Note*: Consult Kahn (2005),[1] Belliveau and Griffin (2002),[2] and Belliveau, Griffin, and Sommermeyer (2004)[3] for additional information.] Chapter 5 concludes with sections discussing product release and life cycle change management.

A product development process is comprised of several distinct phases (E&F, alpha, beta, and gamma). Each phase accomplishes an important objective toward an end goal of commercial success, and the roles of key players change during each phase change, including marketing, engineering, manufacturing, suppliers, and management. (The goals of a product development process are discussed in Chapter 4. Figure 4.1 provides metrics that can be used to measure the effectiveness and efficiency of a product innovation, development, and commercialization process.)

PDCP implementation methodology is strongly dependent upon the type of product that is being developed. A process can be sequential, with clear gates for exiting one phase and starting a new phase, or a process can be flexible and iterative, with overlapping phases. (See Section 5.8 for a discussion of the phases of PDCP.) Product types and the market conditions in which one implementation approach is more appropriate than another are also discussed.

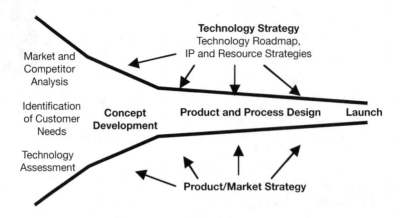

Figure 5.1. Framework for a Product Development Process.

To make the development process of a new product successful, a development team must employ effective project management methodologies. Most importantly, a team must be able to establish and verify the project success criteria. Whether the product is an application of a new breakthrough technology or an incremental innovation of an existing product, the team must establish appropriate success (or exit) criteria for each phase of the development process. In other words, the team must be able to clearly answer: "How will I know that the project or a phase of it is complete?" (*Note:* Best practices in project management are discussed in Chapter 8.) Because a project to implement a PDCP may be preceded by a screening or product selection process that assesses the commercial viability of the proposed product, commercial viability is also discussed in this chapter (also see the discussion in Chapter 10).

5.1 THE PRODUCT DEVELOPMENT FRAMEWORK

Wheelwright and Clark,[4] Iansiti,[5] and Christensen[6] have discussed a "funnel" framework for product development. In the funnel framework in Figure 5.1,[4,5] the market/competitor analysis, target customer needs, and technology assessment establish the basis for concept development—the first phase of the process. The next phase is the product/process design, which leads to the product launch and commercialization phase.

The technology, market, and product strategies at a firm play key roles throughout the development cycle in guiding the effort (as shown in Figure 5.1). Remember from Chapter 2 (Figure 2.13) that a firm's product portfolio strategy and aggregate project plan lie at the intersection of its business, market, and technology strategies. The objective of product strategy is to define the target market segment, the breadth and depth of the product line, the market assets (including the distribution channels), and the value proposition. The technology, market, and product strategies must be established prior to initiation of a new product development project. Furthermore, throughout the product development process, these strategies must be updated regularly to capture the new realities of the market and competitive situations and any advances in technology.

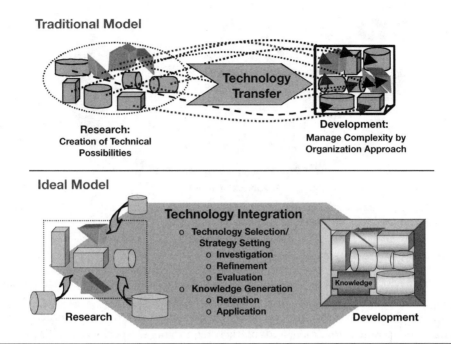

Figure 5.2. Evolution of the Research and Development Process at Toshiba. (Source: Adapted from Toshiba Corporation material; 2002.)

5.2 THE PRODUCT DEVELOPMENT PROCESS AT LEADING COMPANIES

5.2.1 Toshiba Corporation

At Toshiba the process of technological knowledge generation and product development has evolved from the "traditional model" to an "ideal model" as illustrated in Figure 5.2. In the traditional model, the Toshiba corporate R&D organization created a portfolio of technical possibilities that were then given to product development teams through a "technology transfer" process. The development teams then selected technologies from the R&D portfolio for commercialization. In the ideal model, however, research, knowledge generation, technology selection, and product applications are integrated with market strategy through a process of investigation, evaluation, and refinement.

5.2.2 Sony Corporation

An integrated product development process, or "process of R&D to business," at Sony is shown in Figure 5.3. This process comprises a sequence of phases from development and design to production and sales. The process is integrated with research results and market information through various feed-forward and feedback loops. The knowledge generated in research is fed into all phases of the development process; future market trends and opportunities are fed into the development phase; and post-sales market learning is fed back to the design phase for continuous improvement and development of derivative products. *Note*: Kamath and Liker (1994) provide additional information about product development in Japanese companies.[7]

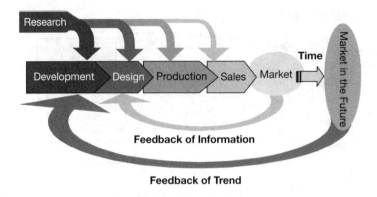

Figure 5.3. Process of R&D to Business at Sony Corporation.

5.2.3 Applied Materials Corporation

The product development process at Applied Materials, a leading supplier of semiconductor fabrication equipment, has four phases—concept and feasibility (C&F), alpha (α), beta (β), and gamma (γ). Market opportunities identified at the onset drive the entire process via two documents—the product roadmap and market requirements specification. Product and process designs are developed through the C&F and alpha phases until the customer evaluation or beta phase, when the design is frozen. The gamma phase is dedicated to qualification of the manufacturing process and field support procedures and results in the production release of the product. Note that the product/process design is concurrent with the manufacturing and field support design efforts to ensure manufacturability and serviceability of the product.

The competitive pressure of the maturing semiconductor equipment market has forced Applied Materials to modify the above process in order to accelerate the time-to-market introduction of new products. The accelerated process, shown in a shaded box in Figure 5.4, moves several of the beta phase tasks forward into the alpha phase and allows higher risk taking by shipping the alpha version of the product to selected customers for evaluation. The early customer evaluation phase is concluded with a "customer release" authorization that enables the

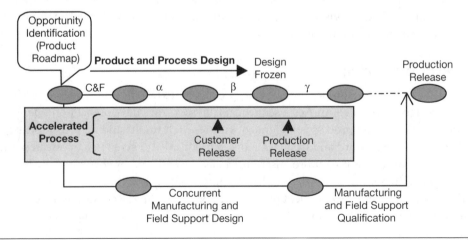

Figure 5.4. Product Development Process at Applied Materials Corporation. C&F, concept and feasibility.

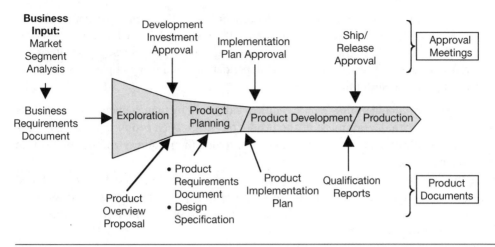

Figure 5.5. Product Development Process at Intel Corporation in 2002.

firm to ship the product for sales on a limited basis. Field support and manufacturing qualification tasks are also accelerated through a tight, concurrent cross-functional team effort in the alpha phase.

5.2.4 Intel Corporation

The overarching objective of the product life cycle process at Intel is to optimize synergistic planning (and concurrent development) with suppliers, to improve development efficiencies, and to accelerate time to money (TTM). The new product development process at Intel is depicted in Figure 5.5. Intel's process consists of four phases and is driven by a business requirements document that is generated at the onset. The business requirements document incorporates business input resulting from a market segment analysis. The development process starts with an exploration phase followed by the product planning and product development phases that lead to the production phase. At the conclusion of each phase, a product document summarizing the outcome of the phase is prepared and an approval meeting is held to authorize proceeding to the next phase.

The initial market segment analysis and the business requirements document constitute the market strategy for a product line and establish the firm's desired market position in the target segment. The first or "exploration" phase is carried out by a cross-functional team of marketing, engineering, and finance to develop the concept and the definition of a specific product. The output of this first phase is a product overview proposal and a business plan that includes a return on investment/net present value (ROI/NPV) analysis, target customers, high-level product requirements, major risks, an estimate of resources needed, a preliminary schedule, and an estimate of the technical and timing feasibility of the product development plan.

The next or second phase is "product planning," which is intended to produce two documents:

- Product requirements—In this document, in addition to a listing of the complete product requirements, sufficient architecture, design, and quality plans are specified to enable due diligence planning. Design specification is also required to describe how product requirements will be realized.

- Product implementation plan—This document is a program plan for developing the product throughout subsequent phases. It rolls up functional area plans and includes a detailed program schedule and resource plan, program success criteria, a risk assessment, internal and external dependencies, and product plans for quality, support, and sustaining.

Exiting from the "product planning" phase requires a decision by management about whether (or not) to proceed with development of the product as it has been proposed. The "go" decision is a mutual commitment—by management to provide the resources and by the team to deliver according to the plan.

In the third or "product development" phase, the product is engineered, developed, and evaluated against the requirements. The responsibility of project management is to meet the phase success criteria, to prepare qualification reports, and to obtain ship/release approval at the conclusion of this phase.

The fourth or "production phase" of the product life cycle includes manufacturing of the product for sale, customer support, and sustaining engineering to maintain customer satisfaction. The production phase ends with a product discontinuance approval for end of life.

5.3 THE NEW PRODUCT DEVELOPMENT AND COMMERCIALIZATION PROCESS

A generic process for the development and commercialization of new high-tech products (NPDCP or new product development and commercialization process) is illustrated in Figure 5.6. In this process, knowledge generation and integration proceed through a series of phases (each with a distinct purpose) until the product design and the process are qualified as satisfying the target market needs and as meeting business objectives. The PDCP is linked to the firm's product strategy (at the intersection of business, market, and technology strategies as discussed in Chapter 2) and starts with a product development proposal. A cross-functional team, led by marketing, prepares the proposal based on market segment analysis, business requirements, technology strategy, and R&D input.

Before commitment to product development and commercialization, R&D projects for new and breakthrough technologies are often carried out within "incubators" and by "skunk works" in medium- to large-size companies. The approval of a proposal coming out of Phase 0 of a PDCP is the first step in management's commitment to developing a new product. The actual product development process starts in Phase 1, E&F (exploration and feasibility), as shown in Figure 5.6. In this phase, alternative technologies, designs, and process concepts are explored, the feasible (and optimal) approach is selected, and its market and commercial viability is assessed. The next three phases are product project planning (Phase 2), design/process development and characterization (Phase 3, alpha), and manufacturing and customer qualification (Phase 4, beta). Phase 5 (gamma) is the unrestricted production ramp and commercialization of the product. As the product enters the commercial growth stage of its life cycle (see Figure 4.13 in Chapter 4), a series of CIP projects is often initiated to improve the product line competitiveness and profitability and to extend its life.

Although the purpose, overall scope, expected output, and success criteria of each phase of a generic PDCP are presented later in this chapter, important to mention now is that the

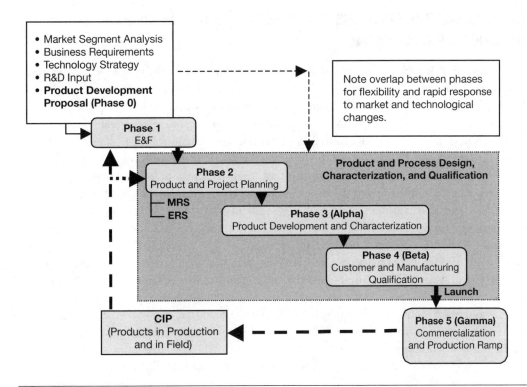

Figure 5.6. Product Development and Commercialization Process. CIP, continuous improvement projects; E&F, exploration and feasibility; ERS, engineering requirements specification; MRS, market requirements specification.

project task list in each phase and the extent of overlap between the phases must be tailored to the *specifics* of the proposed product, including the market conditions, product project type, and resource availability. A product development project may be large or small depending on the project scope and product complexity. Nevertheless, if the initial product concept and technology are immature and the product platform is new, careful planning and execution of all phases are necessary. If the product is a CIP of an existing product and its impact on the market and the firm's resources is small, a *scaled-down* PDCP is advisable. If the scope of the CIP project is small, an *engineering change management* process by the firm might be all that is required. (The methodology for scaling a PDCP is discussed in Section 5.4.)

The understanding of the context and the needs and wants of the product's stakeholders, including customer needs, manufacturability and serviceability requirements, distributors' constraints, environmental and societal requirements, and the firm's strategic and business needs, are documented in the MRS (market requirements specification). A Phase 0 proposal includes the product concept and a preliminary MRS. At the end of the E&F phase, the MRS is revised to capture the knowledge gained during E&F about the product concept, the technological risks, and the commercial viability of the concept in "matching the technology to the context." The "final" MRS is developed during the product project planning or Phase 2. Because market conditions and technologies rapidly change in a high-tech market, the MRS must be frequently updated throughout the development cycle (Phases 2, 3, and 4) and necessary midcourse adjustments must be made to the project approach and priorities.

5.4 SCALING THE PROCESS AND THE DYNAMIC NATURE OF PRODUCT DEVELOPMENT

An efficient PDCP includes organizational structures and tools that facilitate fast decision-making and continuous improvement of the process itself. This chapter presents a generic PDCP, but the practitioner should customize this generic process to her/his specific product type and market environment by identifying and implementing the relevant value-added steps in each phase of the generic process (in design, manufacturing, and testing)—a practice known as *scaling* the PDCP.

During the process of developing a complex, high-tech product, technological possibilities, market needs, and company priorities frequently change due to the usually long development cycle and the turbulent nature of high-tech markets. A development team must be vigilant of environmental conditions during the development process and adjust their process to current realities by continuously redefining what is "right" to do, including the objectives, the strategy, and the plans, as necessary. Canceling a project or a product might even become necessary if matching the technology to the target context is no longer feasible. Important, however, is not allowing vigilance and responsiveness to contextual change to result in a lack of focus and indecision in product development. The leadership challenge is maintaining a balance—keeping the effort focused and changing the requirements or the approach only when the change is essential for success.

As already noted, a product development process must be scaled *at the onset* according to the type of the product and complexity of the development project. Furthermore, a resource plan must be prepared to assess potential gaps in technical competency at the firm and in funding for project execution. In scaling the product development process, questions to ask include:

- Are all of the steps in the *generic* product development process (from Phase 0 to 5) necessary?
- Should the phases of the product development (E&F, alpha, and beta) be overlapped to accelerate the time to market and to accept the potential risk?
- Should a structured "stage gate" approach be adopted in which the exit criteria of one phase is achieved before starting a subsequent phase? *Note*: A structured (and less flexible) approach is more pertinent to situations in which the market condition is not turbulent, but the technology integration risk is high or the required investment is substantial.

Scaling of the product development process and resource considerations, based on the project type, must be captured in the three main documents of the product development process, namely, the MRS (market requirements specification), the ERS (engineering requirements specification), and the aggregate project plan. The contents of these documents are discussed in detail in the remainder of this chapter.

Rangan and Bartus have enumerated the "common mistakes" in commercializing new products.[8] These "mistakes," include dissonance in the customer-supplier perceptions about the product type, gaps in the firm's technical competency, and poor project execution, which result in missed market opportunities and in the development of a product that has no market demand.

Whether the technological innovation in a new product development is of a breakthrough or an incremental nature, the essential ingredients of commercialization success are intimacy with the market and customers, imaginative application of the technology, and flawless project management (with proper scaling of the product development process to the project type). Three examples illustrate scaling a PDCP:

5.4.1 Scaling a PDCP

As already discussed, the firm's resource situation, product type, and state of technological maturity and newness to the company should be considered in scoping the phases of a product development. The generic process for product development in Figure 5.6 should be "scaled" and adapted to the exigencies of the situation. For example, when developing a derivative product that has minimal technological risk, it might be best to combine Phase 0, the E&F Phase, and even Phase 2 (planning) into one phase. The following examples describe a few situations that marketers and engineers face in scaling the product development process.

5.4.1.1 Example 1—A Breakthrough Technology and a New Platform that Require Full Implementation of a PDCP

The semiconductor industry roadmap calls for integration of an insulator with very low dielectric constant (κ) in IC devices at and below the 65-nm technology node. Very low κ materials usually have low structural strength and cannot be well integrated into other traditional steps in the IC fabrication process. For instance, the traditional CMP approach of planarizing copper over these insulators would not work because the force applied during the CMP process damages these low-strength films.

The company has a skunk works team that has identified a novel electropolishing technique that offers a potential planarization solution over "very low" κ insulators (i.e., a new methodology that is significantly different from the past methods and "solves" the problem). The team's investigation has been primarily theoretical, based on modeling, and therefore the technique had to be proven experimentally. The team leader (also the principle inventor) recognized that an E&F phase was required and had asked company management to approve his Phase 0 proposal. Many technological challenges had to be overcome and successful device integration had to be demonstrated before the team could embark on a new product development. Furthermore, many product management and marketing issues had to be investigated and resolved during the E&F phase. Some of the questions facing the marketing team were:

- Should the new technology be integrated into an existing CMP platform or into a new platform? What are the market positioning implications of this choice?
- Should the new planarization technology be integrated with the copper plating process to offer an integrated copper deposition/planarization solution? Traditionally, the copper deposition (by plating) and copper planarization steps are performed on two independent pieces of equipment.
- What is the right point in time to introduce the product—at the 90-nm or 65-nm node? Introduction at 90 nm would upset the playing field in favor of the company and blunt a potential threat from a start-up company that had been working on an integrated copper deposition/planarization product. However, the 65-nm node was widely recognized as being the appropriate choice at a time when the market *needed* the new dielectric material and the new planarization technology. Introducing the new technology while it still was immature might confuse the

customer base and potentially hurt the market position of the company's existing successful CMP product.

In this example, the E&F phase was critical to the overall success of the new product development and commercialization endeavor. All the technology, product, and marketing issues had to be investigated and resolved before embarking on the costly Phase 3 and 4 implementations.

5.4.1.2 Example 2—A Product with Relatively Small Design Scope and Low Technological Risk, but with Significant Market Penetration and Market Infrastructure Development Challenges

John was a senior technologist in a medium-size company. He had identified an opportunity in the dental market to replace X-ray dental films by taking advantage of then-recent advances in digital imaging technology. Learning that his employer would not invest in developing the proposed product, John decided to leave and start his own company in partnership with an experienced design engineer and a business person. John was weighing two product concepts for the new company. The first concept was to design a device that captured a dental image directly inside the patient's mouth, eliminating the need for X-ray films. The first concept faced a significant competitive challenge. Two other companies were already offering the direct digital imaging product to the market and had established limited brand recognition. The second concept was to develop a product that would create a digital image of an existing X-ray film. The second product concept offered several advantages:

- It would improve the quality of patient care in a dental office by providing an ability to present dental images to patients on a large computer screen versus traditional viewing on 2-inch-square film.
- e-Mailing digital images versus snail mailing of X-ray films would lower costs and increase the speed of transactions between dentists, insurance companies, and transaction-processing intermediaries.
- The concept was easier to productize. The scope was relatively small and could be done faster and with less investment than developing a direct digital imaging product.
- A device that digitized X-ray films would make transaction efficiency benefits available to the large archives of patient X-rays that were present in every dentist's office.

John prepared a proposal and presented it to a few venture capital investors. His project plan did not include an E&F phase. It showed that the entire design development through alpha phase could be done in 3 months. John's proposal, however, lacked an attractive business model and a clear strategy for market infrastructure development and market penetration. The investors gave John a less than enthusiastic response to the proposal, so John and his partners decided to develop the product with their own funding.

The alpha phase objectives were met in 3 months, as planned, but as John and his partners found out the hard way, dentists' network externalities and acceptance of the product by all players in the market infrastructure (insurance companies, dentists, and intermediaries) were imperative for success. Although one major payer (an insurance company) showed interest in the product as a beta customer, and even purchased a few units, dentists were not enticed to purchase the product, and they did not attempt to make X-ray-less transactions the standard in processing claims. The provider market, with over a hundred thousand dentists in the

United States, represented the bulk of market demand. This market was critical to the business. Dentists who generally did not have extra funds to invest in new equipment or who were under pressure from other players did not find the quality care benefits of the X-ray imaging product to be compelling enough to entice them to spend a few thousand more dollars.

5.4.1.3 Example 3—Phase 0 Proposal for Partial Funding of Product Development by a Government/Industry Consortium in a Competitive Bidding Process

Lam Research Corporation was considering entering the flat panel display (FPD) manufacturing equipment market. In 1995, the Defense Advanced Research Program Agency (DARPA) formed a consortium with the industry to fund development of a FPD manufacturing capability, including process equipment in the United States. DARPA was concerned that U.S. manufacturers were losing out to their Japanese competitors. Lam was a successful supplier of etch process equipment for the semiconductor fabrication market. However, concerned about being a single product line company, Lam was striving to expand its product portfolio. In the early 1990s, Lam attempted but was unsuccessful in developing a synergistic thin film deposition (CVD) product line based on its already strong technological capabilities, brand recognition, and global customer support infrastructure. Lam was also looking for an opportunity to diversify into other equipment markets to reduce its vulnerability to the cyclical nature of the semiconductor equipment business.

In 1995, the FPD consortium issued a RFP (request for proposal) for development of a new etcher for FPD manufacturing, stipulating that the consortium would fund 50% of the effort. To management at Lam, the RFP looked very attractive to enable the company's strategic objectives. The RFP provided a springboard for Lam to diversify outside the semiconductor market with its unique and patented inductive plasma etch (TCP) technology and to leverage the consortium's 50% funding. A formal proposal had to be submitted to the consortium by Lam.

The proposal team at Lam carried out an intensive theoretical and conceptual R&D during the proposal phase and assessed the feasibility of scaling up the TCP technology from 200-mm round silicon substrate wafers to much larger 1000-mm and square glass substrates for FPD manufacturing. The proposal team partnered with scientists at the Xerox Research Center in Palo Alto, California and at the University of Wisconsin. The proposal laid out a product development plan that included an E&F phase with a formal exit criterion before entering the design/development alpha phase. The objective of the E&F phase was to demonstrate the proof of concept that had been theoretically established during the proposal (or Phase 0) for a full-scale prototype reaction chamber.

The Lam proposal won the competitive contract and the team developed a successful etcher for manufacturing FPDs on 1000-mm substrates.

5.5 KNOWLEDGE GENERATION AND INTEGRATION IN PDCP

The concept of knowledge generation during product development as the process marches through the various phases is illustrated in Figure 5.7. The horizontal axis shows the duration of each phase sequentially. The vertical axis (from the bottom) illustrates how knowledge accumulates in the process. Knowledge generation starts in the E&F phase, which produces

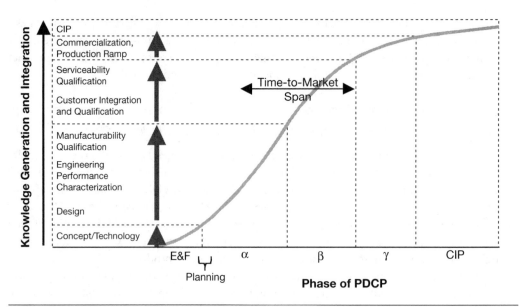

Figure 5.7. Knowledge Generation and Integration and Time to Market.

knowledge about the feasible technology and the commercial viability of the concept. During the next phase (alpha), product design and process are generated, and knowledge of its performance is attained through characterization testing. Building knowledge requires experimentation and prototyping through several cycles of learning in the alpha phase. Next, knowledge of the manufacturability of the design is generated through the manufacturability qualification steps in the alpha phase.

Knowledge acquired from the beta phase (through customer qualification testing) is used to determine whether (or not) the product/process satisfies the customer's needs in the use environment and how well it integrates within the customer's production process. Further learning in the beta phase concerns the serviceability of the product. The gamma phase generates commercialization knowledge, the product's large-scale market acceptance, and the firm's ability to meet market demand.

The critical knowledge that must be generated in a PDCP is *integration* knowledge. The success of a development project depends on how well the varieties of technologies integrate in performing the intended overall product performance and how well the knowledge of market opportunities and the competitive threat (from the MRS) are integrated into the project management decisions and the commercialization strategy.

Both the manufacturing and the end-user exigencies must be considered in an integrative fashion, by resolving their complex interactions through many cycles of iteration and learning. Integration of knowledge is enabled through proactive team interactions and a tight project management practice. (Effective project management methods are reviewed in Chapter 8.) An efficient PDCP not only integrates the new knowledge, but also captures and integrates the knowledge retained from prior experiences through a diverse base of team membership, inclusion of experienced people in the team, and proactive use of the best-known methods (BKM), existing solutions, and designs.

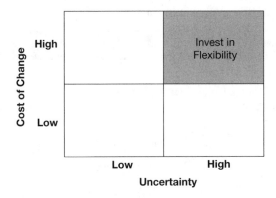

Figure 5.8. Flexibility Framework—Uncertainty Cost Matrix. (Source: Adapted from Thomke, S., Reinertsen, D. Agile product development: managing development flexibility in uncertain environments. *California Management Review* 1998 Oct; 41(1): 8–30.)

5.6 FLEXIBILITY IN PRODUCT DEVELOPMENT

Flexibility is an ability to adapt to changed conditions normalized by the costs of adaptation. Thomke relates flexibility to the "economic cost of change" and defines the flexibility index (FI) as a metric of flexibility.[9] According to Thomke, FI is the ratio of "delta" variable to "delta" cost. Figure 5.8 illustrates a framework for flexibility as an uncertainty cost matrix. Investment in building flexibility is advisable when both uncertainty and the cost of change are high.

Flexibility is an imperative of success in high-tech markets in which the ability to accurately forecast future conditions is severely limited. The technological rate of change is high, customer preferences shift rapidly, and competitors' actions are unpredictable. Having a high degree of flexibility obviates the need for long-term forecasting and allows a firm to quickly respond to new conditions. Flexibility can be built into several different dimensions of a product development environment, including flexibility in:

- Product design architecture
- Choice of technology
- Business processes and structure of the organization
- Product development process

Having a well thought-out product platform and architecture and a forward-looking choice of technologies enables a product to be flexible—to be quickly adaptable to the changing needs of customers; to rapidly fend off competitive threats through small design changes; and to penetrate new market segments with minimal investment. Product development process flexibility is essential to adjusting course in midstream when market conditions shift and/or the basis of competition changes. Process flexibility can be achieved through sequencing the development of product modules, freezing some things early, and leaving others for later decisions, e.g., after some degree of learning has been generated through integration or from alpha/beta customer feedback. An example of a flexible process, with overlapping phases and iterative approach, in contrast to the traditional sequential or stage gate model of product development, with its implied "measured pace" of activities, is shown in Figure 5.9.

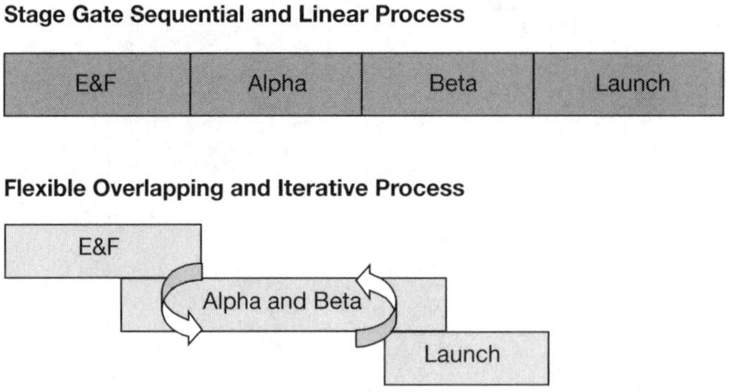

Stage Gate Sequential and Linear Process

E&F	Alpha	Beta	Launch

Flexible Overlapping and Iterative Process

Figure 5.9. Stage Gate Approach versus Flexible PDCP.

Important to note is that the success of the flexible approach is contingent upon ensuring that the objectives of every phase of the generic process (see Figure 5.6) are met and that critical interactions and integration issues are resolved. In other words, do not circumvent the necessary knowledge generation steps illustrated in Figure 5.7. Development objectives and critical integration issues in a PDCP include compliance of the design and process to the MRS, engineering validation of the design, and qualification of the product performance in manufacturing and customer use environments.

The flexible approach of Figure 5.9 requires effective risk management and tight project management. Risks in the flexible process stem from inefficient knowledge integration and frequent changes during iteration cycles. Project management challenges include reconciling the competing needs of a short time to market, compliance to performance specifications, steering a high-quality product through the turbulent waters of changing contextual conditions, and the necessary midcourse corrections. The success of the flexible approach is dependent upon the ability of the team to proactively, and in real time, capture systemic knowledge of the product, user, and production environments and to execute rapid iterations in system specification, design, and system testing.

The extent to which the flexible approach can be employed depends on several factors, including the stability of the market environment, the maturity of technology, the product type and complexity, the extent of interdependence among various product modules and technologies, and the risk tolerance of the team and the firm. A framework for adoption of flexibility in the product development process is presented in Figure 5.10.

5.7 MARKET REQUIREMENTS SPECIFICATION

MRS (market requirements specification) is an acronym representing the requirements for a product to be commercially successful in a target market and to have a winning strategy to achieve competitive success. An MRS must be prepared by marketing before product design development starts. An MRS defines:

- The target market segment and customer applications
- The *whole* product concept and value proposition
- Competitive and market asset strategies

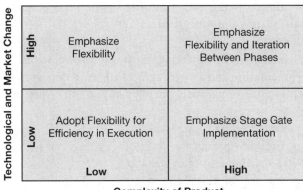

Figure 5.10. A Change/Complexity Framework for Flexibility in Product Development.

- Product architectural and performance requirements for engineering design of the product
- Serviceability, maintainability, and manufacturability requirements
- Market and environmental constraints, including regulatory obligations
- Product production costs and price targets
- Market introduction timing
- Product life cycle roadmap
- Product baseline configuration and application at launch (the basis for a family of derivative products)

MRS is based on market segment analysis and forecasting, competitive analysis, and technology assessment. MRS must be a living document, and therefore be reviewed and updated regularly because customer requirements and priorities change during a product development process and because the understanding of the technology and its new possibilities or limitations is enhanced as the team moves along the product development path and generates new knowledge. This new knowledge/learning may necessitate a change in the product commercialization plan and positioning strategy.

MRS is not required for the development of all CIP and derivative products, but MRS is required for all breakthrough and new platform products and for derivative products that incorporate a significant change to an existing product line. *Significant* change means a product change that alters a customer's manufacturing or operation processes or the product cost by more than 30%. Change is also significant if an implementation project takes more than 3 months, which implies a significant degree of complexity.

The following outline provides the content of an MRS document. This outline should be followed from the onset of a PDCP. At the beginning of the process, there is usually not enough information available to fill in every detail of the document. However, the MRS should be updated and more details should be added to the outline as the process moves from the initial proposal stage to the E&F and project planning phases.

Contents of an MRS
1. Executive Summary

2. Economic Conditions—Macro and industry trends by geographic regions; trends that impact the planned product line

3. Market Analysis:
   - Market Characteristics—Emerging, existing, growing, stable, or declining?
   - Market Segmentation and Target Segment Characteristics—Vision for the segment, segment size and growth, buying patterns and target applications in the segment
   - Emerging and Declining Usage Models
   - Customers' Unfilled Product and Technology Needs and Issues—Performance, productivity, cost, and cost of ownership
   - Customers' Application Contexts
   - Technology Trends Assessment—Customers' technology roadmaps, technology drivers, emerging technological enablers
   - Technology Context—Including IP and other issues
   - Firm's Context—SWOT (Strength/Weakness/Opportunity/Threat), constraints, and preferences
   - Competitive Analysis—Competitors' SWOT, now and in the future; firm's desired position relative to competition; areas in which the planned product will create or strengthen the firm's competitive advantage; threats of substitution and new entrants
   - Business Opportunity Potential—TAM (total available market) and SAM (served available market) size and growth in 3 to 5 years; market share target and product growth strategies and gaps; price target at introduction and at volume production

4. Market Penetration Strategy:
   - Competitive Advantages and Differentiators of the Product—In technology, capability, price, timing, brand, etc.; compelling reasons for the customer to buy the product
   - Product Capability Priorities—Listed by price point and application model
   - Timing—Window of opportunity timing and market introduction timing, e.g., beta schedule, product launch date, sensitivity of opportunity to timing
   - Initial (First Year) Commercialization Approach—Beta customers, differentiator by customer and by competitors, product launch and marketing communication (Marcom) plan
   - Competitors—Responses and planned counter measures

5. Product Performance Requirements:
   - Product Description—Name, basis, functional designators
   - Targets—Target applications, product baseline configuration and options, platform and modularity requirements, hardware/software/process performance capabilities, customer interface specification, requirements for reliability, productivity, manufacturability, maintainability, environmental and safety; target cost and cost of ownership at introduction and at volume production; areas of weakness in past products and new differentiators to gain market share; key constraints (backward compatibility, interoperability, commonality, etc.)
   - Differentiators and Priorities—Highlights compelling differentiators and priorities

- Other Requirements—Future needs and "nice" features of lower priorities
6. Execution—Required schedule to meet the window of opportunity; key program milestones, critical deliverables, and dates; first year milestones, beta criteria, product introduction market share and profitability targets; key resources.
7. Business Plan—Pro forma P&L, unit sales and balance sheet, ROI and profit margin requirements (hurdle rates), pricing strategy, assumptions and risks (The business plan must be updated regularly, e.g., every 6 months, based on the learning from feedback from the product development process and throughout the product life cycle after the product is launched.)
8. Product Life Cycle Roadmap—Evolution of the product line over time (served market characteristics, basis of competitive advantage, product models, pricing, market assets and channel strategy)
9. Key Assumptions—Used in the above items, vis-à-vis economy, market, technology, customer, competition's response, threat of substitution, resources
10. Risk Analysis:
    - Risks—In order of severity in key assumptions, introduction timing, resource availability, etc.
    - Sensitivity of Business Plan and ROI to High-Risk Items
    - Mitigation Strategy

Numerous tools and sources can be used by marketers to perform market research and to collect information about market opportunities, technology drivers, customer needs and preferences, customer operating environments and buying behavior, and competitive intelligence. In addition to the secondary sources from myriad Internet-based databases, several primary market research methods can be deployed. These market research methods, listed in order from being "deep/flexible" to "shallow/structured," include immersion; ethnography (the study and systematic recording of cultures); observation; conversations; interviews; focus groups; and surveys and questionnaires. In industrial business markets there is no substitute for customer intimacy and a close relationship with all key customer personnel in gaining a deep understanding of the customer's needs, behavior, and decision-making process. (See Section 3.20 of Chapter 3 for a discussion of customer relationship management.)

5.8 PHASES OF THE PDCP

The purpose, scope, and expected output of each phase of the PDCP as illustrated in Figure 5.6 are described in this section.

5.8.1 Phase 0—Proposal

Phase 0 identifies and documents the opportunity for matching a technology to an application context. Technological advances can take place at myriad places, including in a firm's RD&E organization, in the R&D organizations of other players in the industry value chain, and at research universities and institutes. Synergistic technological opportunities might even be identified in unrelated industries. Market opportunities also arise from myriad drivers and fulfillment of global needs, including an industry roadmap for evolution of the market vis-à-vis technology (e.g., Moore's law of the semiconductor industry), an emerging market enabled

CASE STUDY—DEVELOPMENT OF AN ORGANIC DIELECTRIC DEPOSITION PRODUCT AT SPEQ CORPORATION—IMPACT OF IMPROPERLY FOLLOWING A PRODUCT DEVELOPMENT PROCESS

Setting. At the time that SPEq Corporation began to design a new product to deposit a breakthrough organic film, IC manufacturing customers were using a proven fluorine-doped silicon oxide (FSG) film in the production of 180- and 130-nm devices. SPEq had a competitive FSG product with a strong market position. SPEq also had two new derivative products for depositing carbon-doped silicon oxide (CSG) films in various stages of technology development. The CSG films were called CSG-1 and CSG-2. CSG-1 was being qualified for production at several customers' pilot production lines for 130-nm and 90-nm nodes. CSG-2 was still in the alpha phase of development in the process lab at SPEq. CSG-2 was being evaluated at a leading R&D customer for 65-nm node application, but it had encountered several device integration issues in the early phases of evaluation at the customer's labs.

Situation. Disappointing results of the CSG-2 evaluation had caused management at SPEq to be quite anxious and fearful of losing the company's edge in technology leadership. Hence, management decided to embark on development of the breakthrough organic film technology and to leapfrog the CSG-2 and other silicon dioxide-based films.

An organic film was already widely known in the industry for having superior properties (i.e., very low dielectric constant) and for being potentially the only solution for the 45-nm technology node and beyond. This film was also known to pose many unresolved technological challenges that had to be fully characterized and overcome before the film could be adopted into IC production. However, these concerns did not cause SPEq management to waver in their resolve to leapfrog the industry and to be the first company with an organic deposition product. A high-level, talented team of scientists and engineers was assembled and charged with the ODD (organic dielectric deposition) product development. The project team was directed to move quickly to gain first-mover advantage in introducing the new breakthrough organic film technology for the next-generation IC manufacturing at the 65-nm technology node (or perhaps even for 90 nm).

Among a number of available alternatives for 65-nm devices, customers were not sure which one was the "right" technology choice. Most IC manufacturers were certain about their approach for 90 nm as being an extension of the FSG or CSG-1 type films. However, the integration issues of an organic film were poorly understood, and organic film was considered to be a high-risk option. Additionally, development of a new thin material and resolution of the integration issues in IC manufacturing usually took several years. Therefore IC manufacturers were very cautious in adopting a discontinuous change into production. Transitioning from the traditional and proven silicon dioxide-based films to the organic film was certainly a major step in IC manufacturing that IC companies did not take lightly.

Outcome. The ODD product development at SPEq went through two sequential trials in a span of 3 years! The first product concept constituted a "vertical track wafer handling" design, with a central robot traversing vertically and serving many stacked deposition chambers. The engineering team moved very quickly and developed an intriguing system architecture—three new robots, a new control system and software, and a new reactor design.

The system platform and processing reactors had been designed without first going through the E&F phase and exploring alternative process technologies, chemical sources, operating regimes, film properties, and the feasibility of new film integration into an IC device. Although an E&F technology evaluation could have been done on a very low-cost experimental reactor placed on an existing platform in the development lab, instead the team started the project in the alpha phase and developed an expensive system complete with wafer handling, controls, and software. The project was done on a very high-priority basis, with the GM of the division promising a sizable bonus to team members if they finished the alpha phase within 6 months.

The design was abandoned after building two prototypes at a total project cost in excess of $7 million! The viability of the new ODD technology still remained elusive.

A second product concept was developed shortly after the first system design was assessed as being too complex and having too many new components to be production worthy and cost effective. The second system architecture was the integration of two existing platforms in the company's portfolio, with a small degree of modification. Again, the engineering team started in the alpha phase, moved quickly, and developed a product design in 7 months. The team was recognized by the company's top management for pioneering the adaptation of a new product development methodology that had been advocated by a consulting firm to reduce the time to market and to improve product profitability. The design methodology was shown off in many large company meetings and with much political fanfare to other engineering teams as being exemplary reuse of existing subsystems and enhancing product commonality across the company.

After spending another $5 million, the second project was also cancelled. The concept and feasibility of depositing an organic film that could be used in IC device manufacturing had still not been established.

Both of these designs were scrapped because the market was not ready for an organic film. The costly hardware and platform designs were developed unnecessarily before demonstrating the feasibility of the technology. In short, the team did not follow the PDCP in Figure 5.6.

The development timing of the ODD product was many years ahead of its time. The expensive investment in ODD was wasted. The company also lost other important opportunities because it misdirected valuable resources.

While the two ODD projects were in full swing, the CSG-1 and CSG-2 development teams were making steady progress in meeting customers' needs for 90-nm and 65-nm devices. They discovered a simple treatment technology and improved the CSG-2 film's structural integrity and dielectric constant and made it viable for integration into 65-nm devices.

Comment. This case illustrates the consequences of rushing too quickly into full implementation of a new product development project without evaluating the proposed breakthrough technology and assessing its technological and commercial viability. Company management, rather than directing the team to follow the PDCP and to make decisions based on strict criteria for success for each phase, rewarded action-oriented behavior instead. Achieving results, as measured by the commercial success of the new product, was not a metric of performance.

The case also demonstrates the costly impact of not following the PDCP. The team did not include the E&F phase to assess the viability of the new proposed technology and its ability to be integrated with the customer's process before embarking on an expensive, resource-intensive, and complex hardware and software design in the alpha phase. Another root cause of the problem, which is commonplace in many "big companies," was the availability of *too much money in* the R&D budget! A small start-up company would have been much more judicial in making investment decisions—or it would not have survived two successive cycles of unsuccessful product development.

by technological advances (e.g., the advent of the bioindustry), and an application of technology to improve operational efficiency of a business in the value chain. During Phase 0, the proposal team identifies the technology/market opportunity, performs a market segment analysis, identifies the product line capabilities that would capitalize on the opportunity, develops an attractive business model, and prepares a preliminary MRS and business plan for commercialization.

The output of Phase 0 is a formal proposal that is presented to company management for approval and authorization to start the product development process. This is akin to the proposal prepared by a start-up company to venture capital investors for initial funding of the enterprise. The proposal content should include the proposed vision, business opportunity, MRS, product business plan, market segment analysis, and product line concept. In reviewing the proposal, company management must ensure that the proposed product marketing strategy and business plan meet the firm's business, market position, and ROI objectives. If the proposal meets the firm's strategic and investment criteria (hurdle rate), a product development project is formally established to start the E&F phase. (See Chapter 10 for more detail about the Phase 0 process for assessing a product's viability.)

5.8.2 Phase 1—E&F

- Purpose of the E&F Phase:
  - To conduct path finding and evaluation of candidate design concepts and technologies and selection of the optimal approach
  - To demonstrate the feasibility of the proposed technology and product design prior to product (development) commitment; to define the *whole* product concept
  - To assess the viability of the market and the proposed business model for the product (Marketers must establish what is being sold, i.e., the *whole* product/service, and how the company will be paid for the product/service and will extract market value, including the initial price, licensing fee, consumable income stream, transaction fee, advertising fee, pay for performance or others.)
  - To ensure alignment of the proposed product and business model with the firm's product portfolio strategy/roadmap, investment priorities, and business strategy
  - To gain management approval for the product concept and business before committing a significant level of resources and accruing a substantial investment
- Scope of the E&F Phase:
  - To form an E&F project team, develop alternate product architecture and design concepts, build bench prototypes (BP), and test candidate designs; to establish selection criteria and identify the optimal solution; to determine the desired product features
  - To conduct speculative research (Speculative research can happen during the E&F phase. However, speculative research is best done prior to E&F to the extent that an opportunity for "matching technology to context" is clearly identified and a proposal for product development can be prepared in Phase 0.)
  - To prepare the preliminary MRS and commercialization strategy (Establish the commercial viability and ROI models for the product. Obtain data and perform ROI and investment risk analyses of the proposed product.)
  - To perform product portfolio and aggregate resource analyses vis-à-vis the proposed product
  - To assess the scope of the product development project based on the technology and market knowledge gained in this phase
- Output of the E&F Phase:

- An E&F report demonstrating feasibility of the selected technology and design concept and identifying pertinent product scaling issues (The report should include a conceptual design of critical subsystems and technical risks and their mitigation strategy.)
- A preliminary MRS, assessment of product differentiators and the product's competitive advantage; commercial risk analysis and mitigation strategy
- A portfolio analysis report confirming the firm's intention to invest in the product versus other opportunities and to commit resources at a high priority level (i.e., the product will be put on the business unit's product roadmap and portfolio)
- An Investment approval report documenting the minutes of management review and approval sign-off for authorization to proceed to Phase 2

5.8.3 Phase 2—Product and Project Planning

- Purpose of the Planning Phase:
  - To prepare a detailed project plan for developing and commercializing the product
  - To develop detailed requirements for the product functions, features, and capabilities and strategy for competitive advantage
  - To identify the overall project schedule, cost, and resource requirements, rolling up all cross-functional staffing plans
  - To finalize the market requirements specification (MRS), including target product costs, target sales price, and market potential (Considering the planned project cost and schedule, ensure an acceptable ROI and a timely market introduction.)
- Scope of the Planning Phase:
  - To finalize the MRS and establish the product development and project objectives, including target markets, commercialization strategy, and project SOW (statement of work) (The scope of a project plan is discussed in detail in Chapter 8.)
  - To prepare the ERS (ERS translates the MRS requirements into engineering specification and design criteria for the product performance, reliability, manufacturability, and serviceability; see discussion in Section 5.8.4.)
  - To perform platform and system-level conceptual design studies and to identify the product architecture and modular structure
  - To develop an engineering characterization test plan, including test objectives and success criteria
- Output of the Planning Phase:
  - A detailed project plan, final MRS, ERS, platform and system conceptual designs, and product production cost target
  - Exit (success) criteria for the alpha and beta phases
  - Customer co-development partnership and beta strategy
  - An operational plan, including the outsourcing strategy (This plan identifies co-development suppliers, outsourced engineering partners, and material and manufacturing sourcing approach.)

- Formal approval of the plan by the company management (This approval is a commitment by management to invest in development of the product, and to provide resources, and a commitment by the team to attain the project objectives.)

5.8.4 ERS

An ERS is generated by the R&D/engineering team and *translates* the MRS requirements into engineering specifications/criteria/guidelines that engineers can use to design and develop a product that meets the MRS. Although the MRS focuses on "what," the ERS emphasizes the "how" of product development. ERS defines:

- System and subsystem descriptions, theory of operation, operating modes, applications, performance metrics, and targets
- Product hardware design, software design, and process requirements
- SRS (software requirements specification) as a subset of the ERS to cover the issues unique to software, such as operating system, coding language, coding standards, graphical user interface (GUI) design, security, maintainability, and troubleshooting guidelines (Methodologies for developing software products are discussed later in this chapter.)
- Criteria for design tradeoff studies
- Design constraints such as backward compatibility, commonality with other products, and packaging constraints
- Interoperability requirements across target applications
- Reliability metrics, targets, and associated "budgets" for all subsystems and major components
- Serviceability requirements
- Product system and subsystem cost targets
- Applicable codes and standards, including safety, regulatory, and environmental requirements

An example of an ERS for IC process equipment is outlined below. The figure illustrates the system layout for reference.

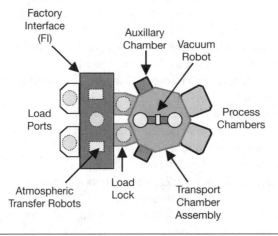

System Layout of Typical IC Fabrication Process Equipment.

1. Product Description and Overall Operating Features—What it does and how it does it
2. Prioritized List of Product Capabilities and Features—According to customers and the differentiating features of the product
3. Systems Engineering:
   - Product hardware and software architecture, including the system layout (if not available, specify requirements); system block-diagram depicting subsystems and interfaces
   - Product design life—If a new platform, a design for a 10- to 15-year life
   - System electrical single-line diagram
   - P&ID (system process and instrumentation diagram depicting all fluid lines, control signal lines, instrumentation locations, and parameters)
4. Modularity Requirements—For product performance, competitive advantage, value chain positioning, and IP protection in outsourcing
5. Module and Subsystem Interface Definition—If available, include hardware ICD (interface control documents) and software API (application programming interfaces). Subsystems and interfaces include:
   - Factory interface, wafer transport, chambers, vacuum system, gas delivery, RF power, AC power, controls, facilities interfaces
6. Process specification, including materials and structures to be processed (e.g., to be etched or deposited), requirements, and methodology for measuring the parameters in testing and verification
7. Defect Control Requirements and Design Guidelines
8. Controls:
   - Theory of operation, controls architecture, microprocessor, I/O requirements, data acquisition, and storage requirements
   - Pressure control subsystem—Pressure range and accuracy; type of manometers
   - APC (automatic process control) requirements
   - Hardware and software safety and security interlocks for the whole system and for each subsystem
   - Remote sensing and display of peripheral equipment status and faults
9. Software O/S, Language, Architecture, Performance Specification, and UI (User Interface) Guidelines:
   - Real time control response latency
   - Error diagnostics and recovery
   - Factory communication specification (General Equipment Model) including factory control interface and protocol (operational commands, wafer sensing, status reporting, others)
10. System Throughput = 50 wafers/hour, with three-chamber configuration
11. Subsystems Performance—Characteristics, design criteria, and reliability budgets:
    - Wafer transport subsystem
      - Theory of operation
      - Performance specification—Overall wafer transport limited throughput (zero process time) = 125 wafers/hour; speed of transport between different

stations; sensing and diagnostics requirements; vacuum level; pressure control requirements

- Wafer size—200-mm and 300-mm capability with a simple conversion kit and software setting
- Wafer orientation and mapping capability
- Accuracy of positioning wafers in different stations, including the input wafer loading containers (or FOUP), transfer station, loadlocks, and process chambers
  - Loadlocks
    - Specification for vacuum level, preheat of wafers in loadlocks (including the temperature range and time rate of heat up and cool down); isolation valve opening size and actuation speed
  - Vacuum system—Base pressure, leak integrity (rate of pressure rise); pressure gauge specification; vacuum pump size and type
  - Reaction chambers
    - Theory of operation (how it works, metrics of its performance)
    - Volume and geometric constraints, functional parameters, and operating range
    - Wafer temperature control—Range, uniformity, heat-up speed
    - RF power range and frequencies
    - Electrodes spacing, range and control
    - Lower electrode—Theory of operation, electrostatic wafer holding (chuck) with wafer-present sensing; chuck and de-chuck time <1 second
- Chamber housing temperature range and control, view ports, cleaning access
- Instrumentation—Controls and data acquisition; end point detection
  - RF power supply subsystem
    - RF generators specification
    - Chamber impedance matching design guidelines
  - Process gas and liquid delivery subsystem
    - Type of fluids, flow rates, and flow control accuracy
    - MFC (mass flow control) specification, chemical compatibility, size, and cost
12. Component Selection Guidelines:
    - Specify company's standard components and libraries to select from, including pumps, MFCs, electronic and electrical connector types, fittings, valves, tubing, o-rings, etc.
13. Materials of Construction, Purity, and Impermissible Materials
14. Surface Finish Specifications—Includes anodization and painting
15. System and Subsystems Cost Budgets:
    - Total system cost per MRS = $1265K for a three-chamber system
    - Factory interface (FI) = $120K
    - Wafer transport (WT) = $130K
    - Chamber assembly, including RF supply, vacuum pumps, and controls = $300K each
    - AC power supply = $20K
    - System controller = $20K

- Process fluid delivery = $25K per chamber
- Budget for consumables, replacement parts, and frequency of change to meet COO target of the MRS

16. Subsystem Reliability and Productivity:
    - System reliability, mean wafer between failure (MWBF) = 5000
    - WT = 15,000, software = 100,000, chamber assembly = 7,000 each
    - Component life cycle testing criteria at alpha exit to be set at 80% confidence level

17. Serviceability Specification—Mean time to repair (MTTR) and unscheduled downtime

18. Safety and Environmental Specification:
    - Toxic chemicals, electrical, and thermal to meet industry and customer specifications, including SEMI and European CE mark
    - List other applicable codes and standards for design such as pertinent sections of IEEE, NEC, and NFPA

19. Peripheral Equipment Specifications—Temperature control unit, remote vacuum pump, AC power supply, vacuum line sizes

20. Facilities Interface Specification—Water, air, process fluids, power drop location, and ratings

21. DFx (Design for x) Guidelines

5.8.5 Phase 3 (Alpha Phase)—Product Development and Characterization

- Purpose of Product Development and Characterization:
  - To implement the ERS into the product hardware and software design
  - To develop the process
  - To characterize the system design and process performance at subsystem and system levels; to characterize the system operating window/stability, security, robustness, and compatibility
  - To qualify the system performance against the ERS
- Scope of the Alpha Phase:
  - To generate the product detail design and software code with sufficient documentation to procure, build, and test the alpha-build units (i.e., the engineering prototypes)
  - To seek input from co-development customers and incorporate their feedback in product design and process to ensure seamless integration into the customer's operating environment
  - To seek and implement suppliers' guidance on how to reduce cost, improve manufacturability, and reduce lead time and cycle time
  - To hold a series of design reviews, including detailed, critical, and alpha exit design reviews; to identify the design and performance gaps against the MRS and ERS and implement corrective action plans (Reviewers should represent cross-functional expertise and evaluate the product DFx for performance, cost, safety, environmental sustainability, reliability, manufacturability, testability, and serviceability.)
  - To identify the risks in meeting the ERS with simulation, modeling, analysis, and component/subsystem testing in-house and at suppliers' sites.

- To modify the product design and process by implementing the corrective actions from the design reviews and risk analysis
- To build and test the alpha units (or EPs) by an integrated team of engineering, manufacturing, suppliers, and customer support staff
- To finalize product configuration and documentation incorporating lessons learned from the alpha builds and characterization testing
- To verify system design and performance compliance to the ERS
- Output of Product Development and Characterization:
  - Detailed design documentation (to procure, build, and test beta units)
  - Software design and documentation
  - A baseline process
  - Alpha exit test reports satisfying Phase 3 success criteria to proceed to Phase 4 (The report should demonstrate how the design complies with the ERS and identify risks and their mitigation plan.)
  - Revised beta customer list, plans, and beta exit criteria
  - An operations plan, including manufacturing and packaging sourcing and a build plan
  - A plan for operations and maintenance manuals, training of support/service personnel, and spare parts

5.8.6 Phase 4 (Beta Phase)—Customer and Manufacturing Qualification

- Purpose of Customer and Manufacturing Qualification:
  - To qualify the performance, ability to integrate (compatibility), serviceability, and cost of ownership of the product at customers' use environments, including installation, user-friendliness, and troubleshooting; to demonstrate production worthiness of the product; to verify compliance to MRS
  - To qualify product manufacturability and cost at the production environment of the firm
  - To release all product documentation (hardware design, software, process recipes, and installation/service manuals) for production and commercialization
- Scope of Customer and Manufacturing Qualification:
  - To update detail plans, schedules, and responsibilities for manufacturing build verification, beta testing, and release of the product
  - To build-verify the design in pilot manufacturing
  - To proactively participate in beta customers' evaluation testing of the product and support the customers for a flawless execution of the beta programs
  - To incorporate necessary changes in product documentation as a result of the build verification and customer qualification
  - To release the product for production and commercialization; to identify deviations and risks in complying with the product release criteria (The release criteria must be established along four vectors; see Section 5.14.1 for more details.):
    - Product performance quality in compliance to MRS
    - Time to market according to the market penetration plan

- Operational readiness, including materials availability, supplier readiness, manufacturing infrastructure, and service training
- Profitability criteria for meeting the product gross margin target
- Output of Customer and Manufacturing Qualification:
  - Release of product documentation for manufacturing ramp and product commercialization launch
  - Beta qualification and exit compliance report
  - Report of product compliance to the MRS and ERS

5.8.7 Phase 5 (Gamma Phase)—Commercialization and Production Ramp

- Purpose of Commercialization and Production Ramp:
  - To launch the product with controlled availability
  - To ensure an agile production ramp at the firm and at suppliers' production factories
  - To ensure an agile production ramp at the customers' production factories
  - To develop market assets for rapid market acceptance and revenue generation
  - To demonstrate revenue, market share, and profitability objectives
  - To monitor and identify product performance and volume manufacturing improvements for CIP projects
- Scope of Commercialization and Production Ramp:
  - To implement the product launch project (as described in Section 5.9)
  - To finalize volume production tooling and the training program for the production and service workforce
  - To monitor preferred customers (early adopters, early majority) to identify shortfalls in competitive advantage
  - To develop and expand distribution channels and other market assets
- Output of Commercialization and Production Ramp:
  - A revenue, market share, and profitability demonstration
  - An updated product business plan and positioning-statement
  - A product verification report comprising the level of ECR (engineering change request) activity, field problems (RMA, FA), and customer feedback
  - A product life cycle roadmap and implementation plan, including CIP goals for a series of derivative products, product enhancements, and value added options

5.9 PRODUCT LAUNCH

A new product launch during Phase 5 of a PDCP is an important undertaking that requires the formation of a dedicated project, which is headed by the product marketing manager. The launch project scope and implementation approach depend on the importance and impact of the product. Accordingly, launch projects can be classified into three categories:

- Category A—Launch of a major new product that changes the competitive order with a new platform and breakthrough technology; enables entering into a new

business area; and creates a significant business opportunity (a dollar value threshold can be set depending on the company or BU size)
- Category B—Launch of a line extension or a new model product with a moderate business opportunity
- Category C—Launch of a CIP product or a new application of an existing product in a small market segment

5.9.1 Launch Criteria

A product is ready for a formal launch if the following items have been completed:
- A business opportunity and impact analysis—Update the product business plan, including pro forma 3- to 5-year revenue, market share, and profitability.
- Product pricing—Describe the business model and pricing strategy at launch and throughout the commercialization phase for the baseline configuration and major options.
- Product positioning and differentiation:
  - Make a positioning statement articulating the value proposition and the target user.
  - List the key customer benefits.
  - Identify the problem that the product solves for the customer.
  - List the product differentiators versus competition.
  - Describe impact on the firm's product portfolio—How is the new product different from the company's existing products in the same family or in other product lines? Will the new product replace or augment an existing product? Will the new product erode the market share of other products?
- Product naming and trademark search:
  - Is this a new product line family? If yes, name it.
  - Has the proposed name been cleared for trademark availability?
- Launch implementation plan:
  - Identify the audience (early adopters, all customers), venue (trade show, TV, special launch event, Internet), communication method (Internet venues, advertisements in trade journals, direct mail, press release, customer seminars, PR giveaways, analysts event, technical articles), collaterals, sales training, and internal communication.
  - Prepare a launch roll out plan with major events and a time frame for each including prelaunch activities, formal launch activities, and postlaunch events.
  - Estimate launch budget.
- Identify the project leader and team members, including marketing manager, product manager, division and corporate Marcom, corporate affairs and PR officer, and investor relations manager.
- Launch plan approval (timing, scope, and budget)—Understanding the required level of management approval for each launch project category is important. For example, approval from the company president might be necessary for a Category A launch, while a product line general manager might be the highest level required for a Category C launch.

5.9.2 Contents of a Product Launch Plan

1. Cover Page—New product category and name, BU, launch manager, and date; also includes required approvals for launch (names and organizational level)
2. Business Opportunity—Impact (external and internal), business model, pricing, and positioning statement
3. Product Naming—New product or product family name; trademark search
4. Target Launch Date
5. Launch Budget
6. Launch Project Team Members
7. Prelaunch, Launch and Postlaunch Tasks and Events
8. Launch Milestone Timeline

5.10 CROSS-FUNCTIONAL RESPONSIBILITIES AND DELIVERABLES IN PRODUCT DEVELOPMENT

Cross-functional tasks of the members of a development project by phase are provided in Table 5.1. Table 5.1 can be used as a checklist by a program manager and task leaders to monitor progress and compliance to a PDCP. Table 5.1 can also be used by functional managers to plan project resources.

Each phase of a PDCP should have well-defined exit criteria that identify the key metrics and their target values for a successful completion of the phase and attainment of its purpose. For example, the technical feasibility and market viability of a new product concept must be established in the E&F phase by overcoming a well-defined and quantified set of hurdles before proceeding to the product planning phase. The responsibility of the project team is to demonstrate that phase exit criteria are satisfied. Marketing must call phase reviews and together with the project management team decide who attends phase reviews and who approves advancing to the next phase. At each phase of the development process, the product business plan must also be updated to verify the continued commercial viability of the new product.

5.11 DELIVERABLES CHECKLIST

Based on the tasks in Table 5.1, the project manager and task force leaders should develop a checklist of deliverables from each cross-functional task. The checklist should identify the deliverables (in the form of plans, models, design documents, test reports, physical prototypes, etc.), the responsible organization and person, and the internal customers who receive the deliverables. The checklist should be used as a program management tool to ensure accountability and timely completion of all tasks.

The deliverables and the product development team members should be defined broadly to include a virtual team of suppliers, strategic partners, channel members, and other players in the value chain that make the product development, production, and delivery to the customers possible. *Strategic alliances* should be established and *partners* should become involved from the beginning of the product development process. Although market requirements come from customers, manufacturability and manufacturing cost considerations should be sought

Table 5.1. Product Development Task List and Responsibilities

Functional Organization (Across the Value Chain)	PDCP Phase 1 Exploration and Feasibility	PDCP Phase 2 Product and Project Planning
Management (product line manager, BU general manager, division or company president)	Assign E&F manager Allocate resources Approve phase exit and authorize next phase	Monitor progress Allocate resources Approve phase exit and authorize next phase PDCP project manager to create the product project plan
Marketing	Develop preliminary MRS Determine commercial viability	Finalize MRS Clarify project priorities Develop product business plan Develop co-development and beta customer plans
R&D, Engineering (hardware, software, process)	Prepare E&F proposal Determine Phase 1 tasks and deliverables Create preliminary ERS Define product architecture Create conceptual design and DOE approach Perform modeling, simulation and tradeoff studies Design, build, and test BPs Conduct E&F and phase reviews	Determine tasks and deliverables of subsequent phases Finalize ERS Create project task plan Prepare preliminary design Conduct preliminary design review Generate preliminary alpha test plan Prepare product cost breakdown Perform risk analysis Conduct phase review
Manufacturing, Operations, and Supplier Management	Support BP builds as required	Prepare manufacturing plan for product development and production ramp Prepare materials and supplier sourcing plans

PDCP Phase 3 Product Development and Characterization	PDCP Phase 4 Manufacturing and Customer Qualification	PDCP Phase 5 Commercialization and Production Ramp
Monitor progress Allocate resources Approve phase exit and authorize next phase	Monitor progress Allocate resources Approve manufacturing and supplier plan, including build plan Approve phase exit and authorize next phase	Approve PLC roadmap
Update product business plan Develop product release and launch strategy Select beta customers and prepare agreement	Manage beta projects Define product baseline configuration, models, and options Publish product specifications Prepare launch project plan	Launch product Manage product cost, COO, profit margin, and market penetration Validate profitability and market share targets
Update Phase 3 tasks and deliverables Prepare detailed design documentation Conduct critical design review Finalize alpha test plan and exit criteria Characterize alpha design and prototypes versus ERS Conduct alpha design review Update design documents and finalize BOM Create preliminary spares parts list Prepare preliminary beta test plan and exit criteria Conduct phase review	Update Phase 4 tasks and deliverables Prepare product configuration tree Support beta qualification tests Identify and implement design changes Release product documentation to Manufacturing Conduct phase review	Update phase tasks and deliverables Support Marketing, Customer Support, Manufacturing, and Materials teams as required
Procure and build alpha units with Engineering Develop manufacturing facilities and tools Verify supplier's design and performance Assess product manufacturability Prepare product should-cost estimates with Engineering Develop suppliers and negotiate contracts Finalize packaging, assembly sequence and flow layout Update manufacturing and sourcing plans Prepare detailed manufacturing documentation (e.g., flow sheets and sequence of events)	Build and test beta units Perform build verification Finalize manufacturing and sourcing plans and contracts Finalize product should-cost estimates	Manage MRP Manage pilot production run Execute manufacturing plan Execute sourcing plan Validate cycle time, quality, and cost targets to MRS Maintain customer support (includes RMA and FA)

Table 5.1. Product Development Task List and Responsibilities (Continued)

Functional Organization (Across the Value Chain)	PDCP Phase 1 Exploration and Feasibility	PDCP Phase 2 Product and Project Planning
Customer Support, Field Operations, and Sales (assuming that Customer Support reports to Sales)		Provide input to product business plan MRS and ERS Prepare customer support, training, and field operations resource plan
Finance	Support product business model	Support product business plan Create financial model Review and approve project budget
Environment, Health, and Safety; Quality and Reliability Assurance	Review MRS and ERS to ensure compatibility with laws, company and industry codes/ standards, and sustainability	Update EHS and reliability requirements Prepare detailed reliability assurance and quality plans
Legal	Patent application IP portfolio management	

from suppliers, and packaging, configuration, and pricing requirements and constraints should be solicited from the sales force and distribution channels.

Innovators and early adopters are excellent customers to team up with and to set up joint development projects (JDPs) at the onset of the product development cycle. A JDP provides an excellent opportunity for mitigating risk in the development of high-tech products. A development team should integrate technologies and products across a network of development organizations in the industry, taking advantage of technological possibilities created by others, including subsystems and software modules developed by suppliers.

Leveraging resources across the multiple functions of the firm and across the supplier and partner chain alleviates the resource crunch that is often felt by new product development teams. Just as outsourcing across the globe has become a common practice in production, outsourcing can accelerate a product development process too. Furthermore, a PDCP team should strive to improve quality of execution and to maximize efficiency in resource utilization by adopting the best project management and design practices. (Chapters 6, 7 and 8 are dedicated to this subject.)

The market and profitability potential of a new product is shaped early in the development process and is impacted throughout by the quality of the design and the efficiency of project execution. Figure 5.11 illustrates the basic elements of product profitability and how they are impacted by the quality of execution in the product development process. Product excellence (in performance and in differentiated value to the customers) can demand premium prices. An

PDCP Phase 3 **Product Development and Characterization**	PDCP Phase 4 **Manufacturing and Customer Qualification**	PDCP Phase 5 **Commercialization and Production Ramp**
Support business plan update Support beta site selection Assess and confirm serviceability Manage field documentation (spare parts list, O&M manuals) Provide alpha test resources	Finalize field documentation Complete product training Provide resource and participate in beta qualification project Provide feedback to Engineering and Marketing	Support customers Implement product traceability program Prepare and publish technical notes Maintain field documentation
Support product business plan Finalize financial model Monitor project spending versus budget and drive corrective action	Monitor project spending versus budget and drive corrective action Support business model	Monitor project spending versus budget and drive corrective action Support business model
Assess alpha units for EHS and compliance to reliability requirements Execute to quality plan	Evaluate reliability compliance Execute to quality plan	Disseminate lessons learned and best-known practices Monitor reliability performance Execute to quality plan Support RMA/FA tasks
Customer agreements Supplier agreements Patent application and IP portfolio management	Customer agreements Supplier agreements Patent application and IP portfolio management	Review product and technology roadmap

excellent design results in a product that can be manufactured and maintained, i.e., is reliable, and that has low costs of production and support and hence delivers a high profit margin. Higher profitability results in higher ROI and makes more funding available for R&D investment in future products. R&D investment in future products enables sustainable growth for the firm. [*Note*: A more detailed analysis of design impact on product ROI (return factor) is presented in Chapter 10; see also Figure 10.1.]

5.12 PROCESS DEVELOPMENT METHODOLOGY

Development of a product design must be concurrent and well integrated with the development of associated manufacturing processes for component fabrication, packaging, assembly, and volume production of the product. For example, a new gas turbine cannot be properly designed and manufactured unless the blade material and the fabrication technique for the blade are developed concurrently.

The process performed by a piece of industrial equipment that is a tool in the user's (customer's) manufacturing operation, and represents one or more steps of the user's manufacturing flow, must be developed concurrently with the equipment. For example, in the semiconductor industry, IC manufacturing is comprised of a series of process steps that are performed by various pieces of equipment in a fab. The process performed by each piece of

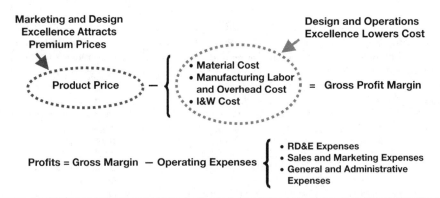

Figure 5.11. Basic Elements of Product Profitability—Excellent Product Development Improves Profitability and Makes More Funds Available for R&D. I&W, installation and warranty.

equipment (such as deposition or etching of a thin film) must be developed by the equipment supplier. Each process and each piece of equipment must be able to be integrated with the other steps in the fab to produce the final customer product. Equipment design, therefore, must be done concurrently with the development of an equipment-level process that is production worthy at the user's factory.

The product might be a material whose manufacturing process is based on a platform that was developed from research and a subsequent E&F phase. Development and commercialization of the material must be concurrent with the development of a production-worthy process beyond the bench prototype samples and proof of material properties. In short, manufacturing process technology must be an integral part of a product development and commercialization process.

The E&F phase (Phase 1) or the early part of an alpha phase should be dedicated to the investigation of alternate process technologies and material choices and to the assessment of the product operating capability in meeting the MRS and ERS. Subsequent steps in a process development should include a definition of a "baseline" process flow and characterization testing of the baseline to assess its window of operation. Following the baseline process characterization, a development effort should move to process integration in which the impact of each step on adjacent process steps (before or after) is assessed. Process integration tasks must be carried out in the alpha phase and assessed against the corresponding success metrics in the phase exit criteria. In a development project starting in the E&F phase, giving the production worthiness of the product (i.e., the stability and predictability of the integrated process) high priority on par with the process capability is important.

5.13 SOFTWARE PRODUCT DEVELOPMENT

Software products and technology have produced great economic value in every aspect of human life and have created enormous markets. Software technology has enabled advances in communication, computing, productivity enhancement, and e-business through a wide range of applications—from embedded capability in consumer and industrial products to myriad user-interactive applications.

Software technology is ubiquitous in the design and production of virtually every high-tech product. For example, in the semiconductor IC manufacturing industry, software technology enables Moore's law for the low-cost production of advanced sub-100-nm ICs. Software is becoming a competitive differentiator for IC fab suppliers by enabling several capabilities:

- Process equipment real-time control, wafer transport, process application, a GUI, and tool/factory connectivity software
- Enhanced robustness, fault tolerance, and auto-error recovery in process equipment
- Productivity enhancement of process equipment by throughput optimization
- Web-based remote monitoring, control, diagnostics, and troubleshooting of process equipment
- Fab automation in materials handling and information management for factory job management and cycle time reduction and yield enhancement
- Automatic process control (APC) for tight control of multivariate processes across process tools in the manufacturing of nano-scale IC devices
- Integrated metrology, data collection, and analysis
- Automated testing in manufacturing
- e-Business in the IC manufacturing supply chain

In spite of the enormous impact of software, however, the product development process for software in most high-tech firms has not reached a high level of maturity. The result has been less-than-desirable software quality.[10] With that issue in mind, this section will now adapt the PDCP in Figure 5.6 to encompass the unique attributes of software products and products with significant software content.

Rapidly changing high-tech market conditions and technological advances in software necessitate the adoption of a flexible process in software product development (see Figure 5.9). Yet collecting customers' requirements in sufficient detail for many new software products (such as office applications, games, and even an industrial user interface) is difficult at the onset. In this situation, customers can provide useful input to developers if a framework is made available to them to use for feedback (e.g., for an initial software product).

During a software development project, when customers are developing new products concurrently with a supplier, the definition of market requirements is fluid and may change frequently for the supplier. In this situation, the use of multiple beta sites can help capture input and clarify the market requirements of customers (Figure 5.12).

In a flexible software product development process, the team will engage several key customers early and co-develop the product with them. The development team should make frequent "beta" releases to capture market feedback and to perform rapid experimentation with parallel development of competing technologies. As Figure 5.12 illustrates, feature design and coding are concurrent with the system software design and integration occurs through a series of iterations in testing and redesign.

Software products are generally subject to several constraints that the developers must heed for commercial success. Often, software products must be backward compatible with an older revision application and maintain the older "look and feel" of the user interface (UI) to which customers are accustomed. Occasionally, legacy products impose constraints on the

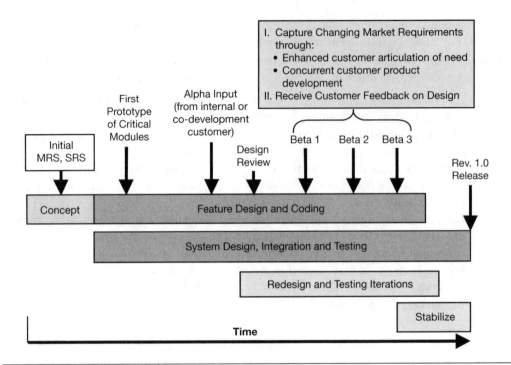

Figure 5.12. Flexible Software Development Process with Iterative Beta Evaluations and Learning Cycles. MRS, market requirements specification; SRS, software requirements specification.

choice of coding language and development tools because of time-to-market pressure, the team's experience base, and backward compatibility requirements.

5.13.1 The Software Development Process—Description of Tasks and Events

Figure 5.13 depicts the detail process flow in Phase 2 and Phase 3 of the PDCP for a new software product. Note that a software-specific engineering requirements document (or SRS) is created at the onset based on the MRS and in conjunction with preparation of the ERS. The ERS and the SRS form the integrated system engineering requirements. In a hardware product, the systems requirements including process control, automation control, and safety interlocks must be defined as input to the SRS.

As shown in Figure 5.13, having an independent software engineering team (a team that has not been involved in writing the software) perform the integration, characterization, and alpha phase exit testing of the software product is strongly recommended. (This independent team approach is also recommended for a hardware product, although doing so is not as critical as it is for a software product.) Additionally, a reliability and quality assurance team should perform the final (alpha-level) evaluation of the product performance against the alpha exit criteria independent of the product design team.

The process flow in Figure 5.13 emphasizes software configuration management because this area is usually a major source of development inefficiency, software defects (bugs), and customer dissatisfaction. Holding formal reviews with proper documentation at the comple-

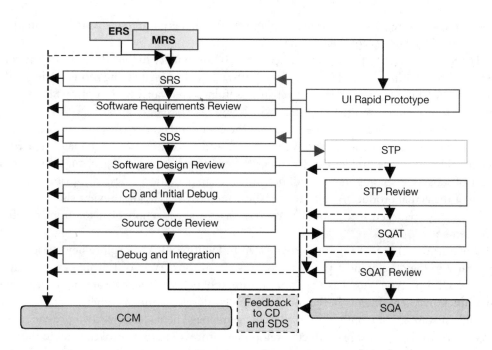

Figure 5.13. Process for Software Development. CCM, configuration and change management; CD, code development; QA, quality assurance; SDS, software design specification; SQA, software quality assurance; SQAT, software QA test; SRS, software requirements specification; STP, software test plan; UI, user interface. (Source: Adapted from Sandia National Laboratories.)

tion of every major task in the development process, including preparation of the SRS, design specification, software coding, and test planning, is also important.

The purpose of a software requirements review is to verify that it meets the MRS. The responsible software engineer, SQA (software quality assurance) manager, software engineering manager, project manager, and marketing manager should attend the review. From the SRS review, a report stating any deficiencies in complying with the ERS and the MRS must be produced. The project should not be authorized to proceed until the SRS is formally approved.

SDS (software design specification) defines the major building blocks of the software architecture, the interfaces between these building blocks, and flow of information through the system. The SDS describes how product requirements are met. The SDS should be in sufficient detail for someone other than the designer to develop the code. Changes to the SDS after it is approved should be authorized through a change control process.

The purpose of a software design review is to identify and correct any software defects and errors prior to code development. The software design review is a peer review, including software engineering experts, which should ensure that the software design can be easily translated to code and that it satisfies the SRS.

The software code must be reviewed in conformance to the coding standards of the firm and the industry and to the software design specification. The code should also be reviewed for readability.

The debug and integration task is the responsibility of the engineer who does the coding. The debug test plan must test all limits and boundary values and be documented. The output of the debug and integration task is the *baseline software* that is given to the configuration manager and the SQA for system level testing.

The STP (software test plan) is intended to verify compliance to the SRS and to verify software traceability using system-level test cases. Software quality engineering should generate the test plan. The STP should be reviewed to ensure usefulness, relevance to the critical SRS parameters, and thoroughness of the test cases.

Quality assurance testing must ensure that the code meets every aspect of the SRS. When defects are detected, a cognizant software engineer and the configuration management engineer should correct the problem and manage the change as required. Performing simulation testing of subsystems, components, and the entire system operation is desirable prior to system testing of the actual product. A software question and answer (QA) test review should be held by the quality manager, who should also create a corrective action plan for implementing improvements.

The purpose of the UI rapid prototype step in Figure 5.13 is to explore new design concepts early in the development process and to perform short cycle-of-learning experimentation. The UI prototype is used as a communication tool between the software engineering and other functional departments in the company and co-development customers.

The software CCM (configuration and change management) team has two primary functions—to control the software product development process and to control changes to the software product and maintain product integrity and traceability throughout its life cycle. The CCM team releases the software product to internal users and to customers. The configuration management of software should encompass all parts of the software whether they are developed internally or licensed from external suppliers. The CCM manager should enforce strict configuration management discipline both internally and with suppliers. The scope of CCM work includes management of the release notes, the executable and source codes, simulators, compilers, editors, and development tools. CCM should also create software backup and manage disaster protection.

The methodology for software configuration management and the release process during the product life cycle (including the initial software development) is illustrated in Figure 5.14. The baseline release branch (R.n) is the software that is delivered to customers. New capabilities and enhancements (to the baseline product) can be developed concurrently and are first built into an independent integration branch (such as R.1i.1, R2i.1, etc.). After QA qualification, they are integrated into the baseline product (through the feeder lines) and then are released as a new revision of the software (such as R.1, R.2, etc.)

An important feature of a software product is the UI design that is usually a major determinant of customer's experience with the product. UI design guidelines that developers will find helpful in designing software include:

- The software engineer should know the users and their operating environment well and should recognize that users are likely not developers.
- A software engineer must know the product well in its entirety, including the system design architecture, the subsystems, and their intended functions.
- The look, feel, location, and function of icons, call outs, and buttons should be consistent, simple, and intuitive. *Note: Intuitiveness* is dependent on the users' cultural attributes and experiences in the target market segment.
- Keep the UI simple, neat, and organized.
- Minimize the number of steps between the user and a desired action or location.

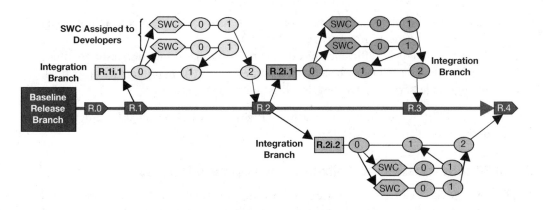

Figure 5.14. Product Life Cycle—Software Configuration Management and Release. SWC, Software Changes.

- The user should always know what is happening. The user should control the system.
- Every mistake made by the user should be recoverable and not be catastrophic. Provide a graceful way to reset, exit, and start over.
- Error messages should be meaningful to the user, i.e., in the "user's language," and tell the user how to fix the problem. The "help" instructions should correspond to the actual situation that a user is experiencing!
- Features and capabilities that are important to a software engineer in a help menu might be quite different from those that are "helpful" to the user of an application.
- Allow easy customization of the UI by users to fit their preferences.

5.13.2 Managing the Software Development Process

Efficient software development requires a keen understanding of the requirements of customers and the dimensions of value for customers. These requirements should be documented in the MRS, ERS, and SRS. A software development team should prioritize the requirements based on the dimensions of value in order to maintain focus and to meet schedule requirements. The development process should also be continuously monitored to assess the efficiency, effectiveness, and quality of the process and the product and to take corrective actions as necessary to improve the process.

This section will review the guidelines for prioritizing customer needs and discuss the indicators of effectiveness of a software development process that a development team should monitor during the project. It should be noted that the customer prioritization guidelines in this section are a subset of the broader discussions in the earlier sections of this chapter and in Chapters 3, 4, and 10.

5.13.3 Software Product Development—Prioritizing Customer Needs

A model developed at Hewlett Packard Corporation defines customer requirements in measurable terms and establishes their priorities.[11,12,13] The model is known as FURPS:

- Functionality (feature set, capabilities, generality, security)
- Usability (human factors, aesthetics, consistency, documentation)

- Reliability (frequency and severity of failures, recoverability, predictability, accuracy, MTBF or mean time between failures)
- Performance (speed, efficiency, resource consumption, throughput, response time)
- Supportability (ability to be tested, extended, adapted, maintained, compatible, configurable, serviced, installed, localized for non-English users)

Grady (1992, 1997)[11,12] and Grady and Caswell (1998)[13] may be consulted for a detailed discussion of this model and the indicators in the software development process.

5.13.4 Effectiveness of the Software Development Process

The Carnegie Mellon University Software Engineering Institute (SEI) has developed an excellent model that is recommended for assessing the quality of a software development process in an organization.[14] The SEI model defines five levels of maturity in the process capability of a software organization:

- Initial—Few processes are defined and success depends on the heroic efforts of individuals.
- Repeatable—Disciplined project management processes are in place.
- Defined—A consistent set of standard engineering and management processes are in place.
- Managed—A predictable process is in place and the process and product quality metrics are measured and tracked.
- Optimized—The process is continuously improved.

A software manager can use this model to assess the maturity level for software development in his/her organization and can identify corrective actions that are required to move up the maturity scale.[15]

Critical elements in developing a reliable software product and the recommended guidelines include:[16]

1. Adherence to a Software Development Process:
   - Identify the factors that impact software reliability and determine how to measure them. These factors and how they are measured depend on the application type (real-time software or not), the company's software organizational structure (does it include independent departments for testing, quality assurance, and configuration management?), the size and complexity of the software product (number of modules and lines of code per module), the software language, the development tools, and the project schedule.
   - Track the project and the software quality metrics, including the number and types of defects, the size and complexity of the software product, and the resources expended over the project schedule.
   - Prepare the SRS with a checklist of guidelines and establish clear exit criteria for each phase of the development cycle. The guidelines should include instructions for designing the software with instrumentation that enables testing, rapid troubleshooting, and root cause analysis.
   - Prepare the project plan for each phase, including a resource plan (people and tools).

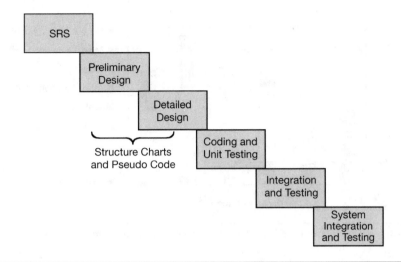

Figure 5.15. Software Development—Waterfall Model. SRS, software requirements specification. (Source: Adapted from Grady, R.B. *Practical Software Metrics for Project Management and Process Improvement.* Upper Saddle Ridge, NJ: Prentice Hall/PTR; 1992.)

- Establish the appropriate software development model for the specific product/project. Can the phases of the development cycle be sequential (the waterfall model in Figure 5.15)? Can the functionality be partitioned into increments that can be implemented in their order of priority (the incremental model)? Are the interface requirements unstable and likely to change? Can changes not be foreseen except through a series of prototypes and iterations (the spiral model)? The waterfall model is the traditional product development model (see Figure 5.15).

2. Proper Testing and Verification of Software Reliability and Compliance to SRS:
   - Employ structured methods for unit testing, including path, logic, math, domain, and functional testing.
   - Employ structured testing methods for system testing, including functional, performance, configuration, security, and recovery testing.
   - Perform regression testing any time that a change occurs in a revision under change control. Acceptance testing must be performed before delivering the product to a customer (internal or external).

3. Effective Version Control and Configuration Management—A change could be a new feature, an upgrade to an existing feature, a defect correction, preventive maintenance and restructuring, or a documentation change. A delivered version must first be baselined, and all changes must be documented with a description. An approval process must exist for change control, baselining, and delivering the software to a customer.

4. Failure Reporting, Analysis, and Corrective Action System (FRACAS)—Establish a FRACAS to provide accurate and timely defect data for the developer and the customer, to measure baseline software reliability, to develop defect profiles, and to provide data for statistical analysis. A FRACAS should be deployed during the product development cycle as well as after the product is delivered to a customer.

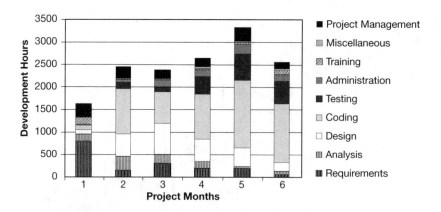

Figure 5.16. Software Development Project—Hours Used by Category per Month.

Software engineers, quality assurance engineers, and testers are responsible for deploying FRACAS tasks.

The distribution of time that software engineers and managers spend in performing the various tasks of a development effort is an excellent indicator of the team's effectiveness in following a PDCP. Figure 5.16 depicts an example over the first 6 months of a software development project at Lam Research Corporation in 1996. The project scope was extensive and included the design of a new software platform, controls application, and UI. The project team followed the PDCP guidelines in Figure 5.13. In the first month of the project, the team spent very little time in design or in writing code. During the first month, many hours were spent on defining requirements and project management planning. Note the subsequent trend in design, coding, and testing hours over the 6-month period—the level of effort in coding and testing increased and the hours spent on requirements and design diminished. The project was quite successful. A relatively small team of engineers produced quality software on time.

5.13.5 Software Quality and Reliability Indicators

A software development team should track several metrics to assess a product and the process quality and reliability. The team should establish a target level of performance for each indicator and implement corrective actions to reach the target:

- Software defect trend—A plot of defects as a function of time, indicating the number of discovered, closed, and remaining defects (Remaining defects should be measured as a cumulative backlog of open defects.)
- Software reliability in MTBI (mean time between interrupts)
- On-time delivery (adherence to schedule)—Days early/late per version and per delivered configuration to customers

5.13.6 Defect Tracking

A defect tracking system is comprised of a prioritized database of defects (bugs) that has been created based on input from all stakeholders, including development team members (design-

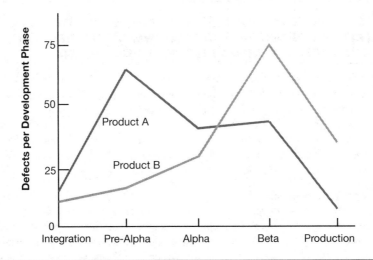

Figure 5.17. Profile of Software Defects by Development Cycle—Management of Project A Compared to Project B.

ers, developers, and test engineers), internal users, beta customers, commercial customers, customer support engineers, and marketing. The database should identify the priority of each defect and the engineer who is assigned to fix the defect and report the status of resolving the problem. A defect status might be reported as:

- Will be solved in Rev. X
- Is being worked on and is scheduled for Rev. Y release
- Will work on defect, but currently not resourced/scheduled
- Will not be worked on

The defect database should be made available to cross-functional team members and internal stakeholders.

Figure 5.17 depicts two examples of a software defect profile during the phases of product development, including integration, alpha tests, beta tests, and production. An efficient development process that starts with a high-quality SRS and executes the design, coding, and testing flawlessly catches most of the bugs (defects) earlier in the process. In the examples illustrated in Figure 5.17, Product A is better executed than Product B. The cost inflicted on a firm by a software defect depends on when in the product development cycle the defect is discovered and fixed. A software defect that is discovered by commercial customers of the software is several orders of magnitude more costly than a defect that is detected and fixed by the development team prior to exiting the alpha phase.

Oftentimes, software engineers and managers are frustrated with reported defects that they do not perceive to be bugs, but rather new features and capabilities desired by the user. This common occurrence is usually rooted in poor customer expectation management and education or perhaps due to customer dissatisfaction with the product's design when the software does not function to their liking. A careful analysis of a reported "defect" enables the team to direct their corrective actions to fixing the root cause and to preventing future recurrences of similar complaints.

CASE STUDY—FACTORY AUTOMATION SOFTWARE DEVELOPMENT AT NATL CORPORATION, A LEADING SUPPLIER OF IC MANUFACTURING PROCESS EQUIPMENT

Background. Semiconductor processing equipment communicates with the host computer of an IC manufacturing fab for materials and information management within the fab. The host downloads information about the material being loaded into the process equipment and downloads the processing recipe to be used by the equipment. In turn, the host receives information about the equipment's operational status, the state of the wafers being processed, and process data such as equipment operating conditions and metrology data. The software within the equipment that manages the interface between the equipment and the factory is called factory automation (FA) software.

Situation. In January 1992, Kevin Gardner, NATL software director, faced severe customer dissatisfaction with NATL FA software. The products were always delivered late and ridden with bugs. Kevin was very frustrated because his baseline software product did not meet customer needs and required customization for every customer. Company executives were seriously contemplating bringing in a new software director, but decided to give Kevin one last chance. The company president asked Kevin to present a remedial plan in 1 week. Kevin garnered all his expert resources and spent significant time preparing his presentation for the company executives. He wanted to describe the market environment, to state the problems and root causes, and to delineate an aggressive corrective action plan. Kevin knew that this could be his last presentation at NATL.

A week later, Kevin presented the following information to the company president and his staff. Details of the data that he presented in support of his statements are left out for brevity.

THE PRESENTATION

A. Problem and Situation Analysis:
- NATL products have severe FA software problems with numerous bugs at many customer sites.
- Fab designs are not standard across the customer base. They interface differently with process equipment. IC manufacturers use a variety of equipment to load the wafers into process equipment and to transport them within the fab. There are numerous suppliers for the load and transport equipment in the industry, and they are chosen by IC manufacturers to suit their particular fab design and operational strategy. The situation is made more complex because the software interface protocol between the material handling equipment and the process equipment varies significantly between suppliers and fabs. Therefore, NATL must customize its software and hardware interfaces for each fab. There is an industry standard known as SECS/GEM that defines the communication protocol between the fab and process equipment. Unfortunately, customers interpret these standards differently and therefore require different types of information to be transmitted to the host computer.
- Customers provide the FA specification to NATL at the time the order for the equipment is placed. Customers expect the delivered product to work flawlessly the first time. This expectation is difficult to fulfill because the initial customer specification for a new fab often lacks the necessary detail required for NATL engineers to proceed quickly with the customization project. New fabs often use a third-party software company to develop their factory management software (i.e., CIM or computer integrated manufacturing) concurrently with their NATL orders. Therefore, details of specifications become available to NATL after the receipt of order and they can change midstream.

- Customization varies. To demonstrate the degree of customization from one fab to another, Kevin mapped elements of his FA software for two different fabs of a customer in Japan. The mapping showed that only 40% of FA software requirements for the same piece of equipment were common, i.e., a 60% variation from one fab to another, even for the same customer.
- Integration of equipment FA software with the fab CIM and the host computer usually happens many months after fab start-up because new fabs first qualify their product flow and technology integration in a small batch mode. After gaining confidence in achieving the desired device performance and yield, they then move to automating the factory. This strategy prevents NATL FA engineers from testing their software in the fab during the start-up mode. FA software installation and integration occurs too late when there is little time for troubleshooting and fixing bugs. Yet when the fab is ready to produce product, everything must work flawlessly.
- Fab automation (CIM) engineers and managers at customer sites are different than fab process engineers/technologists. NATL sales staff and process equipment engineers usually talk to the fab process engineers/technologists because they are the primary decision makers in selecting an equipment supplier. Furthermore, there is very limited FA expertise among NATL field personnel. FA spec negotiations are usually an afterthought, occurring late in the process by software engineers from headquarters (in California), which results in a poor understanding of the technical details, timing, and priorities of the customer's FA.

B. Shortcomings of the FA Software Development Process at NATL—Kevin understood that the software product development process in his organization was grossly flawed and was inadequate for the existing complex market situation. He identified "inadequate software integration and qualification testing" as a key shortcoming in the software development process. To illustrate his point, Kevin made a step-by-step comparison with the product development process that the process engineering department at NATL used. His figure illustrates the differences between the two development processes. Note that the FA software development process lacks two critical steps in developing a production worthy software—integration testing of software in-house and at the customer's fab.

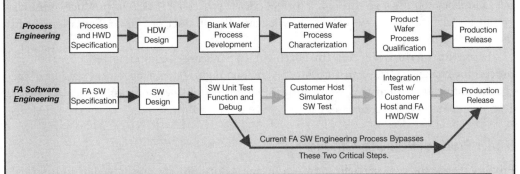

FA Software Development at NATL Corporation, a Leading Supplier of Process Equipment for IC Manufacturing—Comparison of FA Software and Process Recipe Development Processes. FA, factory automation; HDW, hardware; SW, software.

C. Proposed Remedial Plan—Kevin recommended several actions to alleviate the crisis in the short term and to win customer satisfaction over the long term:
- Work closer with FA and CIM customer engineers and managers to initiate FA specifications negotiations early in an order cycle.

- Obtain a host simulator from the customer (or co-develop one if it does not exist) for in-house testing prior to customer delivery.
- Develop a FA software test plan with customers at the beginning of projects.
- Plan for the project's schedule to include time for factory software integration testing.
- Develop a host-interface "translator" that will link the standard NATL product to customer's special command set.
- Develop a FA "suitcase" of software products/options/utilities that customers can chose from.
- Develop working relationships with third-party integrators and material-handling product suppliers and proactively develop interface software for their products.
- Develop FA expertise in NATL field engineers so they can negotiate specifications, write customized software, and support the customers.

Outcome. Kevin's plan was approved by company management and he began implementation immediately. A year later, the situation at NATL was much improved. Reflecting on the situation, Kevin was convinced that maintaining a closer relationship with customers, understanding the details of customers' fab automation strategies, and having face-to-face negotiations of specifications with CIM engineers early in the purchasing cycle were the most important factors in improving customer satisfaction.

5.14 PRODUCT RELEASE AND POSTRELEASE MANAGEMENT

Releasing a product (which is the last step in the product development process) means making the product available for sale to customers. The decision to release a product authorizes marketing to introduce and launch the product, manufacturing to build and ship the product, and sales to distribute, sell, and generate revenue.

A product release must be decided formally, based on established criteria. Often, over the life cycle of a product, many revisions and derivative models are developed to extend the product's life. They too must go through a formal release process. A "released-product" must also be put under formal revision control to safeguard the product design configuration against unauthorized changes.

Successful product life cycle management (postrelease) requires an effective business process for change control and tracking, product configuration management, and customer change notification. Managers must ensure that such a business process is in place before authorizing a new product release.

5.14.1 Product Release Criteria

Product release for commercialization is a business decision. The business decision must be based on release criteria that integrates input from product development stakeholders, including engineering, manufacturing, marketing, sales, customer support, finance, and quality assurance. Release criteria assess the *readiness* of a new product according to three release *vectors*—performance, time to market, and operation support:

- Product readiness—The extent of product compliance to specifications (MRS) and to launch criteria (see the PDCP Phase 5 discussion)
- Time-to-market readiness—Timeliness of the release for capturing the target business opportunity

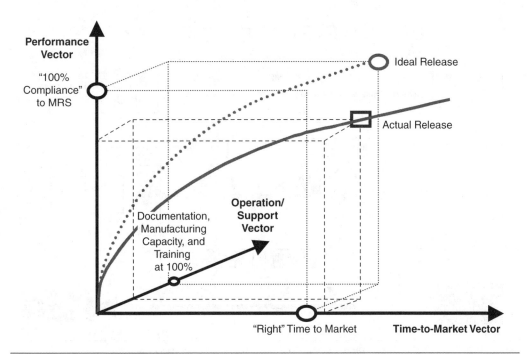

Figure 5.18. Product Release Vectors—Actual Release versus Ideal Release Conditions.

- Operational/support readiness—The firm's ability to manufacture, deliver, and support the product and to meet market demand (Metrics of this criterion include product documentation, personnel training, market assets, supplier readiness, manufacturing capacity/cycle time, and product cost/gross margin.)

When developing new high-tech products, tension always exists between the release vectors. Simultaneously achieving a desirable level of readiness according to these three vectors is challenging. In high-tech global markets short time to market is of the utmost importance; engineering development of a complex product is exigent, risk prone, and time consuming; and operational/support readiness requires timely financial commitment and global reach. Business managers are often faced with compromise and must take risks when making a release decision. The business environment may dictate that the company should make a new product available to customers (i.e., release it) under time-to-market pressure, even if, for example, performance and support criteria are not met. Figure 5.18 illustrates the three release vectors for a product and how the "ideal" release (when all three criteria are fully met) is compromised by an "actual" release based on an imperative of time to market when the product development project is behind schedule. Note that at "actual release" product performance and operational readiness are subpar.

5.14.2 Product Configuration Management

Product configuration management is a process to:
- Define the product configuration throughout its life cycle, including the *standard* (baseline) and *options*

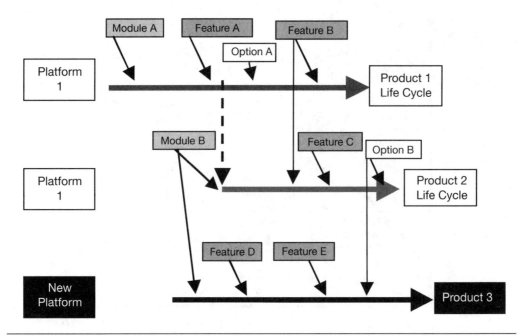

Figure 5.19. Product Life Cycle—Product Line Extension and Naming Strategy Decisions.

- Define the strategy for customization of a product—Would we (and under what conditions) customize a standard product to a particular customer's demand?
- Manage change, including the process of justifying, implementing, and controlling change
- Classify, name, and market product revisions (as retrofits, optional upgrades, derivative versions, or new product models?)
- Notify customers

To preclude proliferation of options and confusing customers, a standard product configuration should be comprised of design features and capabilities that are necessary to meet more than 80% of the target market requirements. Product options (offered at an additional cost) should be decided based on a strategy for market segmentation and breadth of customer reach.

Any strategy for customizing products is strongly dependent on business and market characteristics and on the basis of competitive advantage. In most consumer markets, customization is not desirable or even practical, although the advent of information technology, the Internet, and CIM has made mass customization possible (e.g., the practices of National Bicycle, Anderson Windows, and Levis Strauss have been widely reported). In industrial markets, customization might be necessary for competitiveness, e.g., when the product is a production tool for a large customer. Customized products are usually priced on a case-by-case basis, depending on a customer's needs, the extent of customization, and the size of the business opportunity.

Effective product configuration management is critical to the operational efficiency, financial performance, and profitability of a firm. Product configuration impacts the demand forecast (for standard configuration and options), inventory level, manufacturing cycle time, sales negotiations, product warranty, and customer service. Although forecasting demand for a standard configuration is a challenging part of product marketing, forecasting options is usually more difficult.

Over a product's life cycle, as product configuration is revised through CIP projects, marketing managers must also manage revisions to the product's name. Figure 5.19 illustrates an example of a product line extension and a naming strategy when certain features and options are "bundled" together and added to the baseline platform and when modules and features of an existing product are incorporated onto a new platform.

5.15 PRODUCT CHANGE MANAGEMENT

Product change is modification of a released product that affects the product's form, fit, or function, including the product's performance, functionality, quality, reliability, manufacturability, safety, maintainability, serviceability, UI software, configuration, interoperability, and interchangeability of parts. Product change also constitutes altering the product's design or modifying the manufacturing process, including changing a raw material. Modification of a manufacturing process can occur by merely changing the supplier of a component or changing a contractor who packages the product, even if the design specification did not change.

The primary objective of change control is to ensure that a comprehensive analysis of the proposed change is performed to validate its benefits (to customers and the firm) and to identify risk mitigation plans before implementing the change. To assess and justify customer benefits, product marketing managers should perform a "segment analysis" using the template in Figure 3.11 in Chapter 3.

If product change is not controlled and properly disseminated, customers will be surprised when they receive a product that has been changed unexpectedly. Nothing can be more damaging to a customer relationship—especially if the change has a significant impact on the customer's operation or the product's performance.

Without proper change control, repeat and multiple shipments of the "same" product will not be possible. (*Note*: Intel corporation has a copy-exactly doctrine, which demands that suppliers of process equipment ship "identical" products when multiple units are ordered for Intel fabs.) Without proper change control and accurate records of product configuration in the installed base, customer support will be very difficult, e.g., when ordering the right spare part and when installing the right hardware and software upgrade.

Another important factor in change management is the frequency of change introduction. If too many changes are introduced too frequently, customers become confused, production inventory management becomes difficult, obsolete inventory increases (lowering profitability), and extra manufacturing rework results in a longer cycle time and lower quality. In short, product change management is critical to customer satisfaction and profitability.

Note: Product documentation and configuration change management are not "necessary evils" in large companies only. Small entrepreneurial start-ups must manage product configuration and change as well.

5.15.1 Configuration and Change Management Responsibility

A product manager is the "product owner." A product manager is responsible for the product's configuration and change management. Every change must be carefully examined and justified, based on its contribution to enhancing customer benefits, competitive advantage, BU market share, and profitability. A product manager must ensure that product changes are consistent with the product's CIP roadmap for market penetration and line extension. Timing of the introduction of product revisions to a market must also be carefully planned. Too frequent and too many revisions to a product are disruptive to customers' business operations and create confusion.

A product manager must devise a strategy for the market introduction of product revisions and new models. Bundling changes into major revisions and tailoring the frequency of their introduction to situations in the market is advisable. For example, a product revision that solves a critical customer problem must be introduced urgently. Yet, when revisions are for continuous improvements that enhance market share and profitability, revisions should be introduced in very orderly fashion, with adequate advance notice and consultation with customers.

5.15.2 Backward Compatibility and Change

Product managers must ensure that changes are backward compatible in industrial and commercial markets. Backward compatibility is critical to a customer who has incorporated the last revision of a product into his design, production, or operation. Any change that is not backward compatible with established interfaces is highly undesirable, for example:

- A new revision to a computer operating system (OS) that cannot access data files generated with an older revision of the OS is not acceptable to most users.
- A new model microprocessor that cannot run legacy OS or application software is highly undesirable.
- New control hardware in the semiconductor process equipment industry must have drivers that are compatible with legacy OS software.

Intel has successfully practiced the backward compatibility principle in the company's new product development process. Andy Grove, founder and chairman of Intel states: "We (Intel) are determined that all our new microprocessors will be compatible with the software our customers bought for their earlier microprocessors."[17] This philosophy caused Intel to develop the 486 chip based on older CISC (complex instruction set computing) design architecture rather than switching to the faster and cheaper RISK (reduced instruction set computing) architecture that Intel's competitors and industry gurus were touting at the time.

Backward compatible improvements have an added benefit of allowing a firm to sell product upgrades into its ever-growing installed market (i.e., the after-sales market). Product managers in industrial and commercial markets should make backward compatibility a design constraint in the implementation of change.

5.15.3 SEMATECH—Guidelines for Product Change Control

SEMATECH's recommendations for process equipment change control in the IC manufacturing industry are summarized in this section.[18] An effective change control system incorporates:

- Identification of all changes with reference to an established product baseline configuration (particularly in reference to the configuration that the customer possesses (in the installed base), including design specifications, drawings, and manufacturing process

CASE STUDY—NATL CORPORATION—NOT DOING THINGS RIGHT THE FIRST TIME CAUSES PAINFUL AND COSTLY CHANGE MANAGEMENT

Setting. In 1999 NATL Corporation, a leading manufacturer of semiconductor equipment, had been developing its next-generation product family for 300-mm wafer fabrication for 3 years. The 300-mm family was based on a new platform for wafer handling known as Millennium-300 or M-300. M-300 was being developed by the central corporate PEG (platform engineering group) and was intended for use on multiple products in four product divisions (BUs) of the company.

By mid-1999, the M-300 platform had met most of the alpha requirements and had been given authorization to enter the beta phase. One notable exception was the material cost for M-300, which was 75% over the MRS target. According to the business process at NATL, PEG was the internal supplier of the platform to the BUs, which integrated their process modules with the platform and offered the entire system for sale to IC manufacturers. For the PEG, BU integration was the "beta" testing phase of the platform.

Situation. During beta evaluation of M-300, many problems, including poor reliability and several serviceability issues, had surfaced. The BUs, the internal customers of the PEG, had exerted significant pressure on the M-300 development team to resolve these issues expeditiously and to reduce the cost of the platform to the target level. PEG engineers together with their BU counterparts chartered a course of action to resolve these problems.

A decision was made, based on consensus among the technical team members and with direction from a key BU general manager, to solve all of the problems through a radical change to the M-300 platform. Only interfaces to BU process chambers and to customer fabs were kept intact. The changes were so significant that the platform had to be renamed as A-300 and re-qualification was required by the BUs.

While A-300 was in development and alpha testing, the BUs were busy shipping the M-300 to several beta and pilot production customers that were pioneering transition to 300-mm IC manufacturing. The BUs had no choice but to ship their product with an inferior M-300 platform because A-300 was not ready. The BUs had to aggressively penetrate the infant 300-mm market or risk missing out on market momentum and fall behind. By mid 2000, the installed base of M-300 had spread to all major customers and had grown to 50 units, in spite of its performance shortcomings.

The A-300 passed alpha testing in June 2000, but it encountered major internal customer acceptance challenges from the BUs. The A-300 marketing manager had anticipated this problem, arguing that it was manageable and necessary "pain" for the sake of the benefits provided by the A-300. He argued that the 300-mm platform was expected to have a 10- to 15-year life and was in its infancy in 2000. Hence, solving all of the M-300 problems as early as possible rather than letting them proliferate in the field and hurt customer satisfaction and product profit margin for many years was important.

The BUs raised many objections to adopting the A-300 platform—performance risk was too high; the BUs did not have enough resources to undertake another project to qualify the A-300; their customers would consider the A-300 platform to be a major change and would also have to re-qualify their products and hence would not accept the A-300; and the benefits of the A-300 over the improved M-300 were not compelling enough to make the switch.

The A-300 was well designed and looked attractive, but now it was quite late in the commercialization cycle. Because changes were significant, the A-300 platform had to be re-qualified by the BUs and their beta customers. Another complication was that while A-300 was being designed, BUs were putting tremendous pressure on the PEG to not abandon the M-300, but to carry out aggressive CIP projects to improve the cost and reliability of the M-300. In the 9 months required for design and alpha testing of A-300, the M-300 revisions were paying dividends.

Outcome. Switching most of the BUs to the A-300 took 2 years, although not all did. The company was forced to support both the M-300 and A-300 platforms for several years to come, at very high engineering, operation, customer support, and product management costs!

- Recording, forecasting, and tracking of all changes on a planned implementation schedule
- Investigation of all changes to assess impacts, risks, and benefits to the customer
- A change evaluation committee, which is chartered to validate change benefits, manage the change implementation plan, and update equipment design documentation
- Communication of the above information to the customer

5.15.4 Customer Notification

Customers in industrial and commercial markets must be notified about *planned* or *pending* changes to a product. The purpose of a change notification is to receive the customers' reactions to the planned change (Does it add value to the customer's business? Will the customer accept the change or prefer to stay with an older product configuration?) and to provide sufficient time for customers to integrate the change in their operations.

A formal change notification process must be established. A formal change notification process should cover different categories of change based on customer impact. A likely change categorization scenario includes:

- Category 1—Changes the function of the product and is likely to change the performance of a customer's product, process, or operation
- Category 2—Improves product performance (e.g., reliability), but is expected to have minimal functional impact on the user
- Category 3—Minor or aesthetic change, with no change to product performance (e.g., a change that improves product assembly)

Requirements for change and notification of them can vary. For example, Ford Motor Company requires notification from Motorola, a supplier of IC chips used in automobiles, to occur 6 months in advance of incorporating any change to the *design* or the *manufacturing process* of Motorola chips. Intel has a "copy-exactly" policy when buying process equipment from suppliers for manufacturing a specific microprocessor generation. Intel policy requires that successive units of equipment models, which are ordered and delivered over an extended period of time (typically longer than 1 year), are identical in every respect, including minor parts such as fasteners.

This copy-exactly policy is in support of Intel's methodology for the development of a microprocessor manufacturing process (at every technology node per Moore's law). The Intel methodology includes qualification of suppliers' equipment in conjunction with the device manufacturing process. Production ramp, following process qualification, to full capacity often extends to several Intel fabs worldwide. All fabs are required to adopt the released manufacturing process and to use the qualified equipment configuration. Although equipment suppliers often change their products through CIPs during this period, Intel will not be receptive to any of these "improvements" because they would result in re-qualification of the equipment and change to the released fab manufacturing process. The change management process at suppliers of equipment to Intel must be also able to handle multiproduct configurations. Additionally, a flexible manufacturing flow is required to handle mixed product configurations.

REFERENCES

1. Kahn, K.B., Ed. *PDMA Handbook of New Product Development.* New York: John Wiley & Sons; 2005.
2. Belliveau, P., Griffin, A., Somermeyer, S., Eds. *The PDMA Toolbook for Product Development, Volume 1.* New York: John Wiley & Sons; 2002.
3. Belliveau, P., Griffin, A., Somermeyer, S., Eds. *The PDMA Toolbook for Product Development, Volume 2.* New York: John Wiley & Sons; 2004.
4. Clark, K.B., Wheelwright, S.C. *Managing New Product and Process Development.* New York: Free Press; 1993.
5. Iansiti, M. *Notes for a Product Development Course.* Harvard Business School Note. Boston: Harvard Business School Publishing; 1997.
6. Christensen, C. *Improving the Product Development Process at Kirkham Instruments Corporation.* HBS Case #9-697-058. Boston: Harvard Business School Publishing; 1997 January 2.
7. Kamath, R.R., Liker, J.K. *A Second Look at Japanese Product Development.* Harvard Business Review Reprint #94605. Boston: Harvard Business School Publishing; 1994 November/December.
8. Rangan, V.K., Bartus, K. *New Product Commercialization: Common Mistakes.* Harvard Business School Case #9-594-127. Boston: Harvard Business School Publishing; 1995 March.
9. Thomke, S., Reinertsen, D. Agile product development: managing development flexibility in uncertain environments. *California Management Review* 1998 Oct; 41(1): 8–30.
10. Mann, C.C. Why is software so bad? *Technology Review;* 2002 July/August.
11. Grady, R.B. *Practical Software Metrics for Project Management and Process Improvement.* Upper Saddle Ridge, NJ: Prentice Hall/PTR; 1992.
12. Grady, R. *Successful Software Process Improvement.* Boston: Pearson Education; 1997.
13. Grady, R.B., Caswell, D.L. *Software Metrics: Establishing a Company-wide Program.* Boston: Pearson Education; 1998.
14. Carnegie Mellon University/Software Engineering Institute. *The Capability Maturity Model, Guidelines for Improving the Software Process.* Boston: Addison-Wesley; 1995.
15. Persse, J.R. *Implementing the Capability Maturity Model.* New York: John Wiley & Sons; 2001.
16. SEMATECH. *Tactical Software Reliability Guidebook.* Austin, TX: SEMATECH Technical Publications; 1995.
17. Grove, A. *Only the Paranoid Survive.* New York: Doubleday; 1996.
18. SEMATECH. *Equipment Change Control.* TT 93011448A-GEN. Austin, TX: SEMATECH Technical Publications; 1993 January.

6

EXCELLENCE IN DESIGN AND PRODUCT RELIABILITY

Selected best-known methods for product design, prototyping, and testing as well as topics in product reliability are discussed in this chapter. The chapter is intended to provide design guidelines for practicing engineers and to provide a broad knowledge of design rules for management personnel, including business unit (BU) general managers, vice presidents of engineering, and program mangers, who are responsible for guiding product development teams to success in product development and commercialization. A number of references providing more in-depth coverage of the subject are also cited.

Design for excellence is satisfying the myriad requirements that success in product development and commercialization entails. Some of these requirements are briefly reviewed:

Design. Successful products are usually built on an expandable platform architecture, have a modular design, and deploy synergistic common technology and design knowledge to continuously expand the business of a firm by commercializing new applications and derivative products. Sustained product leadership at Sony (compact discs) and Intel (microprocessors) over several decades is a testimonial to having this winning strategy.

Reliability and robustness. Product reliability and robustness are critical to customer satisfaction and the perception of quality in consumer and industrial markets.

Low-cost production. Designing a product to have a low cost of production improves profitability and enables flexibility in pricing to gain competitive advantage. A new product should be designed to the target cost so that its "should cost" is equal to the target cost of the MRS. The target cost must be achieved at the engineering prototype level (in the alpha phase) through collaboration with material and component suppliers. Toyota follows this approach in car manufacturing by working with suppliers to design to cost for a win-win outcome.

Product development and commercialization. Fierce global competition in high-tech markets demands efficient implementation of the product development process and timely commercialization of the product. Reuse of common subsystems/components and best-known solutions; application of solid modeling in design, systems engineering, and rapid prototyping;

Design Parameters	A	B	C	D
A				x
B	x			
C		x		
D	x		x	

Figure 6.1. Design Structure Matrix.

deployment of e-business in PDCP; and excellent program management must be standard practices.

Value. A product design approach must emphasize customer value and a firm's desired position in the value chain through creative modular architecture, discriminating interface definition, and careful choice of product features and capabilities.

Customer and stakeholder requirements. Excellence in design requires not only a thorough understanding of the customer and other stakeholder requirements, but also a deliberate effort to meet these requirements by incorporating the necessary design concepts and attributes from the beginning of a PDCP.[1]

6.1 PRODUCT DESIGN—GUIDELINES FOR EXCELLENCE

Adhering to certain guidelines will significantly improve the quality of design in product development. Engineering managers and program managers should discuss these requirements periodically at staff and project meetings. Engineers should be required to demonstrate adherence to these guidelines to engineering and program managers at design reviews. The guidelines include:

- Customer needs and benefits to the customers are paramount considerations in design. Give priority to customer *needs*, not to customer *wants*.
- Understand the *purpose* and the *why* of an engineering specification before designing to specification.
- Take a risk *if* success results in a product differentiator.
- Do what the competition cannot!
- Design-in provisions for a long product life and an opportunity for market extension. Consider modifying the design, without compromising compliance to the ERS, to extend the product utility in a different application.
- Elegant, aesthetically pleasing, and simple designs are good designs. A product must look (at least) as good as it is claimed to perform. The design must look state of the art (per the principle of suggestiveness).
- Benchmark the design practices of other companies, outside and inside your industry. Take advantage of other people's clever designs and build on them.
- Past practices ("we have always done it that way") are not a good justification for a design approach.

- Doing less than one's best should not be tolerated.
- Cost and schedule requirements are no justification for a less-than-quality design. The only allowable compromise is in the number of features that are designed into the product, i.e., the scope of the project. Better design does not necessarily take longer or cost more money.
- The primary drivers of product cost are the design *concept* and the *capabilities* of the design.
- In a detailed design review, assess what component or subassembly can fail and design-in an improvement. Ask: What is insufficient in the design?
- Use of one part in many different subsystems and for different applications may appear to be attractive (for minimizing the number of parts and for economy of scale), but doing so might be an expensive compromise. Some companies have tried to find (or, even worse, to design) a "universal" component that will have application in multiple subsystems or product lines in the company. Except for the single use for which the universal component was optimized, for most applications, such practices result in a poor and costly design.
- Design parts so that incorrect assembly and incorrect installation will be impossible (i.e., poka-yoke techniques).
- The design should not require special tools to assemble or to repair the product.
- Minimize the use of special components (except for machined parts). Use standard catalog components.
- Excellent designs do not require any adjustments, alignments, or calibrations to assemble, set up, or operate properly.
- In a CIP (continuous improvement practice), do not change ("improve") the original design until the reasons (the whys) behind the original design are fully understood. Lack of attention to this guideline leads to the creation of new problems.
- A product development team can use a DSM (design structure matrix) to establish relationships and interdependencies among the design parameters in a system or in a module. A DSM is a table-like chart that lists the parameters of a design in the rows and also in the columns of a square matrix.[2] To show the dependencies among the design parameters, an "X" is put in a box that is at the intersection of the column of a parameter that is an input to the parameter in the intersecting row (Figure 6.1). For example, in Figure 6.1, parameter A is an input to parameters B and D.

A DSM can also be used for project management in product development (see Chapter 8). The tasks of the project are listed instead of the design parameters. Reading across the row of a task (e.g., D), the DSM shows all tasks whose output is required to perform that task (D). In project management, a DSM helps identify and analyze task dependencies. (*Note*: Project management application software such as MS Project can also create a DSM through PERT charting.)

6.2 DESIGN FOR EXCELLENCE

DFx (design for excellence) is a generic designation for excellence in meeting a multitude of requirements in a design—"x" might stand for manufacturability, serviceability, and maintainability; safety; environmental sustainability; reliability and robustness; etc.

The following sections discuss each of these requirements and recommend design practices for excellence. A more detailed section is devoted to reliability and robustness. The important subject of design for environmental sustainability (DFES) is treated only briefly. A number of references are cited, however, that the reader is encouraged to consult.

6.2.1 Design for Manufacturability

DFM (design for manufacturability), design for lean manufacturing, and design for assembly are common (and synonymous) terminologies that are used to indicate "designing a product that can be manufactured most efficiently." The primary metrics of efficiency are product manufacturing cost, manufacturing defects, and production cycle time.

To achieve the objective of efficiency, a product development team must understand well the manufacturing processes by teaming with manufacturing engineers, value engineers, and supplier engineers during the design process. For example, a DFM necessitates a careful assessment of design tolerances (so they are not made too tight) and a careful selection of product components to maximize usage of commercially available parts (instead of special designs or parts that require special processes to fabricate). Value engineering of a product *after* the design is complete and released to production is often too late and is the equivalent of a *rework* of the design.

Lean manufacturing is eliminating waste at all steps of material flow in the production process. Lean manufacturing achieves low overhead, short cycle time, high inventory turns, high labor productivity, low defects, and on-time delivery. Common manufacturing wastes that must be eliminated include:

- Wait time (people waiting for material or machines, machines waiting for material or people, material waiting for people)
- Transportation waste (multiple moves of material due to layout or process design, multiple transactions, and return of unused material)
- Walking around to get parts and tools
- Lack of proper tools and fixtures, inadequate maintenance of tools and machines, long setup time
- Defects in material and assembly at the input to and output of any stage
- Large inventory (incoming, in process, and finished goods) causing excessive material and space cost, obsolescence, extra people and paperwork
- Overproduction and overcapacity

A product that is designed for lean manufacturing facilitates elimination of these wastes through efficient plant design, proper production planning, ergonomic work stations that are safe and efficient, continuous housekeeping, and Kaizen.

A common practice of manufacturing is to employ statistical process control (SPC) methodologies to minimize variability in production. The product design can play a pivotal role in the production process control by making the function of the product insensitive to variability in the manufacturing process. Design engineers must also build poka-yoke into the product design. Poka-yoke, or "error proofing" in Japanese, makes the product difficult to assemble incorrectly and the assembly mistakes obvious.

6.2.2 Design for Serviceability and Maintainability

DFS (design for serviceability and maintainability) is designing a product that has a predictable frequency of maintenance (required) and that can be serviced and put back into operation quickly. DFS ensures minimal unscheduled and unpredictable downtime.

Intelligent systems "alarm" for pending failures before a catastrophic breakdown and notify the operator about an upcoming scheduled maintenance. For example, many modern automobiles have an early warning capability for scheduled maintenance and are instrumented to alarm pending critical failures. Design for ease and speed in maintenance, whether it is scheduled or unscheduled, is an important element of the serviceability specification (if an unscheduled failure occurs, can it be easily diagnosed and its root causes identified?). In other words, the product hardware and software should have adequate instrumentation for serviceability.

An unscheduled failure results in poor predictability in system performance and is highly undesirable and costly in a business operation, including the manufacturing plant operation and the enterprise IT system. An unscheduled failure (or downtime) of equipment in a manufacturing plant causes damage to the customer product in production, backs up the work in progress (WIP) inventory, delays delivery of customer products to the customer's customers, and lowers customer productivity.

Training service personnel to troubleshoot and maintain the product is also critical in minimizing downtime. Furthermore, training users of the product to operate the product is important to minimize downtime caused by operator error and to make the customer's experience satisfying. A user-friendly, error-free, and complete product operations and maintenance (O&M) manual is a requirement of serviceability. The Q&M must be delivered with the product.

6.2.3 Design for Safety

Personnel and equipment safety must always be treated as the number one priority in product and process design. DFS (design for safety) means ensuring the safety of all stakeholders of the product, including the user, development engineers, manufacturing and plant personnel, service personnel, and the suppliers, and safety in transportation and in the community at large. The product ERS should call out, in detail, the product and process safety requirements to comply with local, national, and global safety laws, codes, and standards and customer-specific requirements. The firm may have more stringent safety requirements of its own that should be included in the ERS as well. The best DFS practice is to apply the most stringent safety requirements uniformly worldwide—even if certain regions of the global market have less restrictive local regulations.

6.2.4 Design for Environmental Sustainability

DFES (design for environmental sustainability) has become an imperative of business sustainability in the twenty-first century and hence a crucial requirement in product development. *Environment* refers to air, water, soil, and all other natural resources of the earth (including raw material) that are endowed for the well being of living species (people, animals, and plants) locally, globally, at present, and in the future. *Environmental sustainability* refers to being in harmony with the ecological system of the earth, ensuring that manufacturing resource utilization and effluents do not harm the ecosystem equilibrium.

The engineering team must design a product and develop a manufacturing process that meets the environmental laws and standards, global protocols, and the company's internal safeguards for leadership in environmental protection and sustainability. Designing for maximum efficiency and for minimal waste (in the usage of process consumables, manufacturing material, and packing material) is environmentally and economically sound. The use of reusable packing material and shipping crates should be a standard practice. The product should also be designed for environmentally sound end-of-life management, including an ability to be recycled and a minimal need for disposal in landfills.[3] A sustainable product does not include hazardous material or material that cannot be recycled; is designed for disassembly; has a long life; and can be manufactured by means of a sustainable process.

To meet the DFES requirement, the product design must start with a life cycle analysis (LCA) that assesses the environmental impact of the product throughout its life cycle, starting with raw material extraction, manufacturing, use, and end-of-life disposal. DFES minimizes environmental impact throughout the cycle. Reviews of DFES practices may be found in Klostermann (1998),[4] Manahan (1999),[5] and Graedel and Allenby (1998).[6]

6.3 DESIGN FOR RELIABIITY, PREDICTABILITY, AND ROBUSTNESS

Product *reliability*, according to the Japanese Industrial Standards (JIS), is the probability that the product satisfies the required functions during the specified time period and under the specified conditions.[7]

Predictability of product performance is the variability (dispersion) in the expected performance (or the output) of one unit from another or of a given unit over a time period. A system is stable when it has a consistent and predictable output over time.

Robustness of a system is the tolerance of its performance (or output) to variability in the specified conditions of the operating environment, including the initial and boundary conditions, environmental state, and system constraints.

When a product is said to be *fault* tolerant that means its function is not interrupted by faults and that the product has the ability for self-diagnostics and auto-recovery from a fault condition.

Availability is the percentage of time, during the period of operation, that a product is in a condition to perform its required function.

The commonly used metrics of product reliability are mean time between failures (MTBF) and failure rate (FR). FR is the inverse of MTBF. "Shorter" failures are sometimes referred to as "interrupts" and are specified in mean time between interrupts (MTBI). The product reliability goal in MTBF must be specified in the exit criteria of the alpha and beta phases of a PDCP and should include the acceptable confidence level in demonstrating conformance to the goal. The confidence level is the measure of how well the test data conforms to the statistical probability of failure in a real (customer) operating environment.

Reliability of a complex system depends on the reliability of individual components and subassemblies and the interactions between them. Design and process characteristics, manufacturing quality, service quality, and product operability all contribute to the reliability of a system and must be considered in the product design for reliability. The product design must then be tested for reliability at both the subsystem and system levels. An inadequate design for reliability results in higher cost of quality assurance, warranty, and service. Lower reliability of industrial products also increases the customer's operating cost.

Availability of a product depends on its reliability and the time to repair should the product fail. The time to repair a failed product is measured in mean time to repair (MTTR) and directly impacts the product's downtime.

6.3.1 Reliability and Robustness—Guidelines

The following guidelines must be followed in the alpha phase of a product development process:

1. Clarify product reliability requirements (MTBF, MTBI, confidence level, availability, predictability, and MTTR) and specify guidelines for design in the ERS (engineering requirement specification) document.
2. Understand well the operating environment of target customers. This is usually the weakest link in design for reliability. Although the reliability requirements (MTBF, availability, etc.) are usually specified, design engineers often do not fully comprehend the customer's operating environment and its variability. They do not understand how and under what conditions the customer might operate and maintain the product. This situation often occurs when an existing product is modified for use in a different market segment and for a different application. In such a case, a proven, reliable product fails because it does not "match" the new application environment. For example, robotic products and components that had been designed and successfully used in automotive applications over a long time failed when they were introduced into the semiconductor manufacturing environment. Robot suppliers facing this problem learned about the new application environment the hard way—through many redesign cycles of learning. Design engineers should visit the customer's use environment and familiarize themselves with the customer's operating scenarios. The engineering team should then review their level of understanding with the customer.
3. Select parts according to their recommended application.
4. Use off-the-shelf proven components when possible.
5. Select suppliers who have a reputation for reliable products.
6. Select a part such that it is operated at less severe stress conditions than the conditions for which it is rated.
7. Add redundancy by using parallel components when possible.
8. Design-in simplicity and minimize the number of parts through combining functionality.
9. Use sensors to detect failure or prevent catastrophic failures (e.g., a thermal switch fuse or a temperature sensor could prevent major damage to the equipment and even the operator).
10. Use automated process control (APC) techniques with feed-forward/feedback control to reduce variability in the product performance.
11. Make a list of reliability problems with similar products in the past and identify design actions that would prevent their recurrence. A library of existing knowledge gained through experience and the corresponding design guidelines should be referenced in the ERS. Include industry standards for reliability.

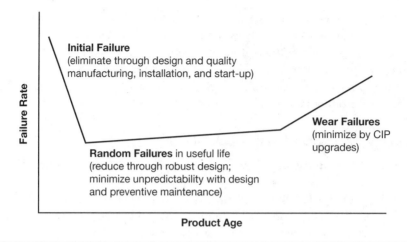

Failure Rate (y-axis)

Product Age (x-axis)

Initial Failure
(eliminate through design and quality
manufacturing, installation, and start-up)

Wear Failures
(minimize by CIP
upgrades)

Random Failures in useful life
(reduce through robust design;
minimize unpredictability with design
and preventive maintenance)

Figure 6.2. A Typical Life Cycle Reliability Model. CIP, continuous improvement projects.

12. Train a serviceperson who can readily troubleshoot and service products that integrate varieties of technologies and components. Products with integrated technologies and components are often complex and difficult to troubleshoot and maintain. Training a serviceperson who can readily maintain such products will be difficult. To improve maintainability, capabilities that must be designed into the product include:
   - Modularity, in which functions of the modules can be independently tested
   - Fault detection and status monitoring functions
   - Fault diagnostics and rapid fault localization
   - Fault recovery, preferably an auto-fault recovery
   - Alarm indicators and useful help descriptions
13. Evaluate the reliability of *new* technologies and components as early as possible. New parts are usually the weakest link. Reliability testing of a new technology and a newly designed part must be carried out first at the component level. If successful, the new component should be tested within the entire system to evaluate its interactions with other components.
14. Develop the test tools and methods for measuring and verifying product reliability and robustness and for implementing failure corrective actions.
15. Test subsystem and system reliability at the design point and over the planned range of operational envelope. Furthermore, test the system for robustness in a simulated customer environment over the entire range of input parameters and extreme conditions of the operating environment.
16. Develop a reliability test plan and include:
   - Test objectives for alpha and beta phases
   - Required resources (people, equipment, measurement tools)
   - Sample size, test length, and required confidence level
   - Test environment for robustness
   - Test procedure and schedule
   - Data collection scheme (DOE, IRONMAN, or marathon methods)

- Data analysis and modeling methods [Use reliability modeling to predict product reliability and to identify subsystem reliability (budget) requirements.]
- A test report and a corrective action project put in place based on the test results

6.3.2 Corrective Action Plan

Based on analysis of the failure data, engineers should develop hypotheses about the failure mechanism, identify the root causes, and verify the hypothesis by reproducing the failure. Corrective actions should follow to improve the design and the manufacturing process. Often engineers rush to implement a corrective action based on the data analysis and a hypothesis for a root cause, bypassing the verification step. This usually results in "fixing" the wrong problem.

Note: If you do not reproduce the failure, you cannot be certain that you have correctly identified the root cause of the failure or that you fully understand the exact failure condition.

6.4 RELIABILITY PROFILE OVER THE PRODUCT LIFE CYCLE

A typical reliability profile over the life cycle of a product is illustrated in Figure 6.2. The initial failure rate (which is typically high) can be eliminated through excellence in design, manufacturing quality, and flawless product installation and start-up. Random failures (past the initial failures and during the product's useful life) create undesirable downtime and unpredictability. Random failures can be eliminated through designing robustness into the product, improving its maintainability for low MTTR, and an excellent preventive maintenance schedule.

6.5 RELIABILITY ASSURANCE BEYOND THE DESIGN PHASE

Reliability assurance in the manufacturing, quality inspection, and sales and service stages is also important to maximizing product reliability and predictability as experienced by the customer. In high-tech products, often the manufacturing technology is not well understood and the relationship between the manufacturing parameters and the product performance cannot be accurately specified. This situation can result in unacceptable deviations in product performance. In such a case, documenting the best-known manufacturing process conditions precisely and strictly adhering to the process of record might be the only solution.

An example of such case in IC manufacturing was encountered by a supplier of equipment for etching polysilicon in the manufacture of transistors. Polysilicon etching was done in a plasma reactor and was known to be quite sensitive to the properties of the electrode in the reactor. The electrode was made of high-purity aluminum and was coated by a thin layer of aluminum oxide through an anodization process. The etch results were quite sensitive to the anodization process. However, the relationship between the behavior of the electrode in the reactor and the manufacturing process to anodize the aluminum was not understood. The yield in making "good" electrodes was quite low. After a long and painful investigation, the equipment supplier and the anodization shop decided to precisely document the "good anodization" process (that resulted in a "good" electrode) and to strictly adhere to it in the shop operation. The documented process of record included all of the people, machines, and materials that came in contact with an electrode. Anodization yield improved drastically.

Sales personnel can contribute to the customer's experience of product reliability by ensuring that they understand the application environment, sell the product to an appropriate application, and manage the customer's expectations. The training level and responsiveness of service personnel in installation and maintenance of a product greatly impact the customer's experience. Knowledge of the product and proficiency in troubleshooting and problem solving by service personnel are highly critical in reducing equipment downtime. Also, timely communication of the field data to the engineering team enables rapid corrective action and resolution of reliability problems.

6.6 RELIABILITY DESIGN—RELIABILITY MODELING AND OTHER TOOLS

Numerous methodologies and tools are available in the literature that can be applied to predict system reliability, to reduce product life cycle failures, and to improve a product's useful (reliable) life. This section will briefly review some of these tools. (*Note*: The reader may consult the resources in the *Additional Reading* section for a comprehensive treatment of the topics in this overview.)

6.6.1 Reliability Modeling

Reliability modeling, as a tool of product development, can be used to:
- Improve understanding of a product by quantifying the effect of variability in a subsystem on the overall system
- Allow evaluation of design alternatives
- Identify critical subsystems, components, and their interactions
- Apportion product system reliability goal into individual subsystem/component budgets
- Assist in planning reliability tests to verify compliance to the ERS

A reliability model is particularly useful in predicting reliability when the system is complex and consists of a large number of interacting subsystems.

6.6.2 Mathematical Methods—Series and Parallel Models

Mathematical methods such as raptor and empirical block models predict system reliability by modeling the system as an assembly of blocks (subsystems and components) that are connected in series or in parallel. A reliability model is usually based on the input from a system reliability block diagram and a fault tree (see Figure 6.4), which depicts the system components and subsystems that affect its reliability and the failure rate of components and subsystems, for every failure mode and distribution. Most reliability models use Monte Carlo methods to generate a large sample of the system in the analysis.

Reliability of a system with independent failure modes is designated as:

$$R_{system} = f (R_1, R_2, ..., R_n)$$

where,

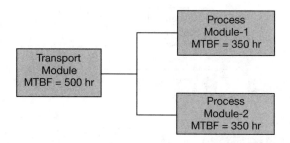

Figure 6.3. IC Process Equipment—Series/Parallel System. MTBF, mean time between failures.

R_i is the reliability of component or subsystem i

$$R_i = e^{-(\lambda_i)t}$$

where,
λ_i is the failure rate of component i
t is the interval of operation
The failure probability or unreliability of component i over time interval t is:

$$F_i = (1 - R_i)$$

The function f depends on the interdependence of the components and the system and on the distribution of the failure rates. In a series model, failure of one component results in system failure, while in a parallel model, all components in a group must fail to cause a system failure. The following is the formulation of system reliability for the series and parallel models:

Series system. A series system is a system in which all subsystems and components are so interrelated that the entire system will fail if any one of its components fails. The probability that the system will fail is given by the special rule of multiplication for probabilities or the series product law of reliabilities, i.e.,

$$R_{system} = \Pi R_i, \text{ or}$$

$$R_{system} = \Pi e^{-(\lambda_i)t} = e^{-(\Sigma \lambda_i)t}$$

λ_s, the failure rate of the entire series system, is equal to the sum of the failure rate of its components:

$$\lambda_s = \Sigma(\lambda_i)$$

Since MTBF = $1/\lambda$, the series system MTBF is:

$$MTBF_{series} = 1/(1/MTBF_1 + 1/MTBF_2 + \ldots + 1/MTBF_n)$$

$$= 1/(\lambda_1 + \lambda_2 + \ldots + \lambda_3)$$

Parallel system. A parallel system is a system in which all "n" subsystems and components are connected in parallel and the system will fail to function if all n components fail. The unreliability of component i is $F_i = 1 - R_i$. Applying the special rule of multiplication for probabilities:

$$F_{parallel} = \Pi F_i = \Pi(1 - R_i)$$

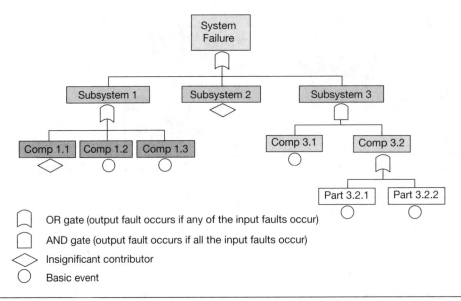

Figure 6.4. Construct of a System Fault Tree.

Using the product law of unreliability, the system reliability will be:

$$R_{system} = 1 - \Pi \, (1 - R_i)$$

The MTBF $(= 1/\lambda)$ for the parallel system is:

$$MTBF_{parallel} = 1/(\lambda_1) + 1/(\lambda_2) - (1/(\lambda_1 + \lambda_2) + \ldots$$

If the failure rates of all n components are the same, the MTBF of this "redundant system" will be:

$$MTBF_{parallel} = (1/\lambda) \times (1 + 1/2 + \ldots + 1/n)$$

Example: Figure 6.3 illustrates a system of semiconductor process equipment that is comprised of three subsystems—a transport module that is in series with a cluster of two process modules that are in parallel. The reliability of the individual subsystems is noted in the figure. The overall system reliability can be computed using the above equations as follows:

$$MTBF_{System} = 1/(1/500 + 1/ (350 + 350 - (1/ (1/350 + 1/350)))) = 256 \text{ hr}$$

6.7 FAULT TREE ANALYSIS

FTA (fault tree analysis) is intended to describe and analyze all failures—their rates, their causes, and the possible design failures of a system. The first step in the FTA process is to list all system failure events. Next is to determine the various ways that a given failure can occur and to identify the potential subsystems and their components whose failure can lead to the system failure.

This methodology results in a tree of subsystems and components in which the fault might initiate and lead to a system failure. Based on the fault tree, an equation for system failure is constructed as a function of subsystem/component failures. Figure 6.4 depicts an example of a fault tree. Note the designation of the dependency of the system failure to the fault conditions of its subsystems and components. The OR and AND gates (see legend in figure) signify series or parallel dependencies, respectively, in the hierarchy of the "significant" contributors. The tree is constructed downward from the system level failure to the "basic events" at a subsystem or component level.

6.8 FAILURE MODES, EFFECTS, AND CRITICALITY ANALYSIS

FMECA (failure modes, effects, and criticality analysis) *examines* all of the components of a system to identify how they might fail and the results of these failures; *prioritizes* the failures; and *plans* corrective actions. FMECA is best conducted using a table with columns that contain the following information:[8]

1. Part name (subsystem or component)
2. Part function
3. Potential failure mode
4. Effects of failure, both local and system level
5. Severity (assign a number from 1 to 10, with 10 being the most severe)
6. Potential causes of failure
7. Likelihood of occurrence (assign a number from 1 to 10, with 10 being highly likely)
8. Current design verification
9. Design detection number (assign a number from 1 to 10) (A low number means failure is detected, reduced, or prevented. A high number means the failure is not detected or stopped.)
10. RPI (reliability priority index), calculated as the product of "severity," "likelihood," and "detection number" from columns 5, 7, and 9, respectively (The RPI range will be from 1 to 1000.)
11. Root causes and recommended actions (Prioritize and assign resources based on the RPI ranking.)

6.9 DESIGN OF EXPERIMENTS

DOE (design of experiments) is a statistical method for determining the relationship between the factors affecting a process and the output of that process. A factor of an experiment is a controlled independent variable whose "levels" are set by the experimenter.

6.10 PASSIVE DATA COLLECTION

PDC (passive data collection) is a test procedure to establish process stability. PDC accumulates data for a specified time period without any process or equipment adjustment (i.e., under normal operating conditions).

6.11 ACCELERATED TESTING AND SCREENING

Accelerated testing is intended to establish a relationship between environmental factors and system lifetime. These tests include environmental stress screening (ESS) and highly accelerated life testing (HALT).

6.12 WEIBULL ANALYSIS

Weibull analysis uses the following equation to predict the expected number of failures as a function of time:

$$N(t) = (1 - e^{-(t/\alpha)\beta})\, n$$

where,
t is time
n is the population
α and β are Weibull constants corresponding to *scale* and *shape* parameters, respectively

Using the experimental data of past failures, one can calculate the Weibell parameters (α and β) and use the above equation to forecast the expected number of failures in the future.

6.13 THE DUANE GROWTH MODEL

The Duane growth model uses a relationship between the cumulative test time and the cumulative failures to develop a reliability growth profile. The Duane model allows a user to assess the effectiveness of proposed and implemented reliability improvement fixes. A Duane chart is a log-log plot of cumulative MTBF versus cumulative test time.

6.14 RELIABILITY GROWTH TESTING

The reliability growth testing method is the continuous testing of a system to detect failures (under test conditions), to implement corrective actions, and to continue with the test. One such method is called IRONMAN (**i**mproving **r**eliability **o**f **n**ew **m**achine **a**t **n**ight) developed by Motorola Corporation in partnership with semiconductor equipment suppliers.

6.15 ROBUSTNESS AND PREDICTABILITY OF PERFORMANCE

A product must be designed for the "real world" context of the target application, i.e., the conditions of the stakeholders' environments that it comes into contact with. Variability in the input parameters should not cause undesirable excursions in product performance.

A system or subsystem has two types of input parameters. First are the input parameters at the interface of one subsystem or system to another that are designed to change for achieving the desired performance of the system (or subsystem). These parameters and their operating ranges are usually determined by the product designer and set by either the manufacturer or the user. For example, the interior temperature of a passenger car is set by the driver and the temperature of the engine coolant is set at the factory.

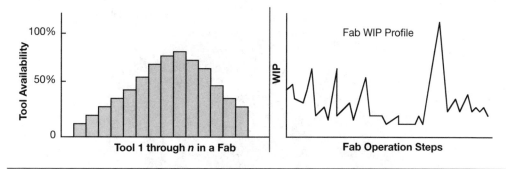

Figure 6.5. Impact of Process Equipment Availability on an IC Manufacturing Fab Operation. WIP, work in process.

Second are the input parameters from the conditions of the environmental within which the system operates. These parameters are either kept "constant" or are expected to have minimal impact on the performance of the system (subsystem). For example, the temperature and humidity of an office or a hospital operating room are the environmental parameters within which a computer or an X-ray scanner must properly operate.

An example of the first type of parameter or system variable is radio-frequency (RF) electrical power in an etch system in the IC manufacturing process. The RF power level is set at different levels by the user to achieve a higher or lower etching rate. The second type of parameter in an IC fab is the utility AC voltage level (normally 110 or 220 volts). The utility AC power energizes the etcher to generate the user-set RF power level and to operate the etching reactor.

A robust system (or subsystem) has a predictable and controlled response (i.e., not very sensitive) to the variability in the input parameters of either type. In other words, a robust system is *tolerant* of inaccuracy and imprecision in the input variables. Achieving a higher degree of accuracy and precision in input variables is usually costly and increases the system's complexity.

The etcher in the above example is not a robust system if a random deviation from the set point (e.g., a fraction of 1%) in the output of the RF generator results in a significant change (e.g., more than 10%) in the reactor etching rate. Moreover, if a random "voltage sag" in the fab utility power caused a catastrophic damage to the etch equipment, the system is not robust.

Predictability of performance of a product is often as important to a user as its reliability and availability. Predictable downtime is undesirable, but manageable; however, unpredictability is disruptive to the user's operation and could be very costly, which is true for consumer and industrial products. A random crash of a computer operating system or a desktop application software can be catastrophic (or at the least annoying) for a sales person in a conference with a customer.

Predictability of performance of an industrial product in a customer's production environment is often more critical than its MTBF because predictability of performance impacts the customer's manufacturing work in progress (WIP) and the overall factory output in an unplanned way. Figure 6.5 illustrates an example of how an IC fab WIP profile is impacted by dispersion in the availability of process equipment (tools) in the fab. (*Note*: The unbalanced fab line in Figure 6.5 has downstream effects that constrain fab operation and lower fab output.)

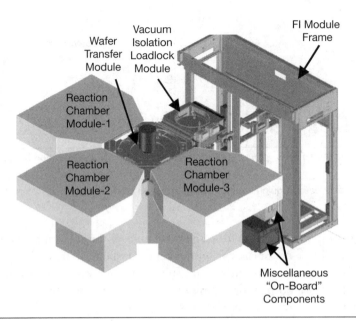

Figure 6.6. Architecture and Subsystems of Semiconductor Processing Equipment. FI, fab interface.

6.16 TERMINOLOGY IN PRODUCT DESIGN AND DEVELOPMENT— DEFINITIONS

This section defines common terminologies for several key tasks and events in product development to clarify the scope of these tasks and to provide a common communication framework for team members. The definitions in this section are not intended to be universal or precise. They are merely a framework for establishing a common language and for managing the product development project. These definitions should be tailored to the specific needs and preferences of a product development team based on the firm's established business processes, the nature of the firm's business and the product, and historical practices.

Important for a product development team is that it has a clear definition and common understanding of the scope of the various tasks and their success criteria. Oftentimes the lack of a common response to questions such as "what is a conceptual design," "what should be the scope of alpha testing," "what does a product release entail," and other similar questions reduces the efficiency of the product development team and causes confusion and frustration among team members.

To elucidate the concepts in this section, the layout in Figure 6.6 of process equipment in semiconductor manufacturing is used as a reference product.

6.16.1 Design Stages

The design of a product usually undergoes three stages of evolution—conceptual, preliminary, and detailed design. In general, the conceptual design is carried out in Phase 1 of a PDPC and the preliminary and detailed designs are done in Phase 3 (alpha phase).

Different subsystems and components of a product, however, can be in different stages of design and go through different evolutionary paths during the PDCP. For example, if a new product incorporates an existing component of another product, that component is already at a detailed design stage (from the beginning of the PDCP). On the other hand, in Phase 1 (E&F), in which alternate concepts for a high-risk component are evaluated, the design must be carried out to the detailed stage in order to fabricate and test the component—although this design might be modified a few times during the same phase or in subsequent phases as new knowledge is generated during the development process and through multiple cycles of learning. A new product, including all its components and subsystems, must reach the detailed design stage before the product can be released for commercialization in Phase 3 (beta phase).

6.16.2 Designs—Scope and Output

The scope and expected output of each design stage are outlined below. Some of the examples of their content are specific to the system in Figure 6.6:

Conceptual Design:
- System architecture (hardware, controls, and software)
- System layout, identifying various modules and their interfaces
- Subsystem arrangement, on-board and off-board of the product
- Controls and software design approach
- Overall system performance modeling and calculations, such as throughput, fluid flow, heat transfer, structural stress, power distribution, signal communication timing and latency, etc.
- Subsystem sizing and performance calculation, such as controllers, robotic arm (reach, speed, and loads), temperature control unit, vacuum pumps, power generators, gas delivery system, and others
- Detailed subsystem and component performance budgets that add up to meet the overall system requirements per MRS (defect contribution, robotic transport overhead, power consumption, reliability, and availability)
- System conceptual cost estimate
- ERS (engineering requirements specification)

Preliminary Design:
- Component sizing
- Component selection and supplier identification (user interface, pumps, mass-flow controllers, robots, control units and microprocessors, application software, software development system, power generators)
- Materials of construction and manufacturing methods for all components and system packaging (Certain manufacturing techniques may have to be determined to meet the performance requirements of a component or subsystem. For example, a high vacuum chamber in Figure 6.6 may have to be machined out of a solid block of aluminum rather than forged to attain a desired "low" leak rate.)
- Layout of the subsystems (For the Figure 6.6 example, the subsystems include reaction chamber module, wafer transfer module, robotic arm assembly, vacuum manifolds, FI module, and various printed circuit boards.)
- ICD (interface control document) for all hardware modules (subsystems) and API (application programming interface) for all software modules

- System-level drawings and documents, including assembly tree, signal list, P&ID (process and instrumentation diagram), and electrical single-line diagram
- System preliminary cost estimate
- Updated ERS (engineering requirements specification)

Detailed Design:
- All drawings, documentation, and specifications of the product and manufacturing tools necessary to manufacture the product
- Software source and executable codes and documentation for installation, use, and troubleshooting instructions
- BOM (bill of materials)
- Fabricated parts drawings and specification
- PCB (printed circuit board) designs, layout, routing, and components
- System frame and packaging design
- Electrical schematics
- Power and signal cable harness routing and terminations
- Specification sheets of all supplier components
- Assembly drawings and procedures
- Updated system documents (assembly tree, signal list, P&ID)
- Facilities installation package, including tooling and software

6.17 PRODUCT DOCUMENTATION

Output of the engineering effort in developing a new product is a set of documents that serves the needs of all stakeholders (internal and external to the firm) and informs them of the product performance characteristics (product specification data sheets). The product stakeholders and their needs include customers who use the product; sales personnel who configure the product and quote a price; manufacturing and supplier organizations who buy parts and build the product; service organizations that install the product, support the customers, and maintain the installed base; engineers who continuously improve the product; and marketing/product management who forecasts demand for the product, manages change throughout the product life cycle, and identifies opportunities for business development and for extending the product's life.

Product documentation should include the items listed above (in *Detailed Design* output) and the following items:

- Process recipes
- System and subsystem theory of operation
- Manufacturing sequence of events and method sheets
- Manufacturing parameters and control methodologies for all components and subsystems except for off-the-shelf items (Although external suppliers of components and subsystems might protect such information as proprietary, the product development team must ensure that such information is available and is under revision control.)
- System test plan for manufacturing qualification and for troubleshooting

- Subsystem and system test and calibration procedures
- Design specification of special tools and equipment
- O&M (operation and maintenance) procedures, including tools and diagnostics software
- Shipping assembly
- Installation instructions, including software
- Spares parts list and recommended stock
- Product sales documents such as system configuration software
- Marketing collaterals and brochures
- Training documents for application engineers, customer process engineers, and the Manufacturing, Customer Service, and Marketing and Sales departments
- Product specification (specifies the product from the customer's viewpoint, including product performance, its intended use, interfaces to the customer's operating environment, such as signal communication protocol, physical dimensions of the product, and facilities interfaces)

Comment: Engineers usually do not like to *complete* the product documents listed above because the documentation process is considered to be boring and not creative. Yet the completeness, accuracy, and usefulness of product documents are paramount to the product commercialization success, including profitability and customer satisfaction. The best practice is to document the mechanical, electrical, controls, and software designs "as you go."

6.18 PROTOTYPING

Knowledge generation by experimentation through cycles of learning is a crucial element of new product development. Experimentation can be done via modeling, analysis simulation, and prototyping. The objective of prototyping is to learn the interaction among various modules/subsystems, verify the design, learn design shortcomings, and characterize the performance of subsystems and the system as a *whole* in applicable use environments.[9]

Prototypes can be built in full scale or in subscale. Usually, a subscale prototype is built to save cost and time. However, experimentation through subscale prototyping is only effective if the scaling laws of design and performance are understood.

Prototyping occurs in all phases of the PDCP. Prototypes can be built for a component, a subsystem, or the entire system. In Phase 1 of the PDCP, in which the objective is to evaluate a new technology and to assess alternative design concepts, building a prototype of only the subsystem (module) under evaluation is generally more economical. This practice is known as building a "bench prototype." Interaction of the subsystem developed in Phase 1 with the other modules, and its performance within the system as *whole*, is learned in Phase 3 by testing a prototype of the entire system (known as an "engineering prototype"). Customer testing and a manufacturing evaluation of the product are carried out in Phase 4 by building a "preproduction prototype."

Descriptions of the different types of prototypes are presented in the following sections. The prototype purpose, characteristics, and timing during a PDCP are highlighted.

6.18.1 Bench Prototype

Purpose. The purpose of a bench prototype (BP) is to evaluate and demonstrate the feasibility of proposed technologies and design concepts; to evaluate high-risk components and modules; to perform life cycle testing of high-risk subsystems; and to identify early life reliability and performance issues. A BP mitigates overall project *schedule risks*. BP test results can be used as a basis for the technology and design "go/no go" decision in Phase 1.

Characteristics. A BP usually operates manually; is a realistic (full scale?) representation of the function of the final design; performs a "single" function (as much as possible); is heavily instrumented; and is highly flexible to permit rapid experimentation of ideas and improvements.

Timing. A BP should be built as early as possible in Phase 1 of a PDCP. The BP design/build/test should be scheduled into the project plan to allow for timely evaluation and learning. BP evaluation requires resources for the design/build/test and impacts the overall project schedule and cost. Required resources are usually overlooked by project managers, causing schedule and cost variances.

6.18.2 Engineering Prototype

Purpose. The purpose of an engineering prototype (EP) is to evaluate the integrated system performance, including hardware, process control, and software; to develop the process; to learn about the interaction between various modules; to identify performance and design integration deficiencies of the subsystems with the system; and to establish the final design of the system packaging (including cable harness routing and piping).

Characteristics. An EP should be designed as the "final product" for volume production as if the EP were the team's last chance. For example, Japanese car manufacturers emphasize that the first EP should be fully functional and in some cases complete in appearance, down to surface finishes, because the EP is the ultimate test of how the entire system fits together. If there is a significant difference between the EP and the later volume-production parts, the alpha-phase test and the refinement of the design will be rendered irrelevant. Unlike a BP, no special design provisions (e.g., one-time instrumentation) should be required for an EP. To accelerate the development schedule, the EP could forego inclusion of "second-order" and low-risk features and capabilities of the product that can be integrated during the subsequent beta phase. Data collection and storage capability in IC process equipment are examples of second-order features.

Timing. EPs are built in Phase 3 (the alpha phase) of a PDCP. A development team is often faced with the question of how many EPs to build. The "right" number depends on the nature and complexity of the product and the extent of testing that is called for in the alpha exit criteria. For example, for IC process equipment, a minimum of two EPs is often desirable—one dedicated to developing the process and a second dedicated to verifying the hardware and software performance against the ERS. For a flash-memory card of a digital camera, several hundred EPs might be required to gather statistically valid verification data. Budget and project schedule constraints, however, often play a decisive role in how many EPs can be built.

6.18.3 Beta (Preproduction) Prototype

Purpose. The purpose of a beta or preproduction prototype (PPP) is to qualify the product for customer use and for manufacturing before its release for production and commercialization; to characterize the function of the product in-house and at the customer's environment (under "battlefield" conditions!)

Characteristics. A PPP should include the design modifications (for improvement) that were identified in the alpha phase after evaluation of the EP. A PPP should also include all product features and capabilities that are intended for *initial* product introduction such as packaging and provisions to install the product at the customer's operating environment. A PPP should not be *conceptually* different from the EP. If, as a result of the alpha (EP) testing, the system architecture or its design concept was found to be inadequate (in meeting the ERS and MRS), the PDCP has to revert to the beginning of Phase 2 to reassess the viability of the product design, technology, and market timing.

Timing. A PPP is shipped to a selected group of beta customers for evaluation during Phase 4 of a PDCP. One or more identical units of the product should be kept in-house for manufacturability verification, finalization of manufacturing process and tooling, and for customer support through rapid resolution of issues identified by beta customers.

6.18.4 First Article Production

Purpose and timing. The purpose and timing of a first article production run is to develop volume manufacturing procedures and tooling in the Phase 5 production ramp (gamma phase). The product design and documentation modifications resulting from the beta evaluation should be incorporated in the design before the first article production run.

Comment: Depending on the nature of the product and the structure of the PDCP, the first article production run and the beta prototype (PPP) could be synonymous.

6.19 PRODUCT CHARACTERIZATION TESTING

The testing to validate a new design and characterize its performance is a critical task of product development. Testing is required in Phase 1 of a PDCP to select the optimal technology and design concept, in Phase 3 to learn the interactions between the subsystems and components of the product, and in Phase 4 to validate the system performance against the MRS.

In each phase, the tests must be carefully planned, carried out, and their results analyzed. Specifying the objective of a testing program and articulating the planned output and knowledge that the team is expected to learn are important. A detailed test plan, including how to conduct testing, the required tools and instrumentation, and the methodology for data collection and analysis, should be carefully prepared and reviewed before starting testing. After the tests are completed, a test report must be prepared detailing test conditions, test method, collected data, data analysis, and conclusions that are derived from the results and observations stating whether the test objectives have been satisfied.

In Phases 3 and 4, planning a testing program that measures the performance parameters that are pertinent to demonstrating whether the product has satisfied the success criteria of the phase is important. If the product performance falls short of the goal (in any critical parameter), test engineers must identify the root cause of the problem and, in collaboration with design engineers, implement a corrective action plan.

Usually, too many variables exist, preventing the performance of all of the possible experiments. Therefore a subset of the experiments must be run, with a focus on the most efficient combination of experiments to permit gathering system information. One such approach is the design of experiments by Genichi Taguchi. Refer to Taguchi, Chowdhury, and Wu (2004)[8] and Taguchi and Clausing (1990)[10] for a full discussion of this approach.

In Phase 4 of a PDCP, beta customers should participate in setting the test objectives and in preparing the test plan for the phase (see Section 6.20).

6.20 CUSTOMER PARTICIPATION IN PRODUCT DEVELOPMENT

In high-tech markets, customer intimacy is critical in all phases of product development, from the onset in preparing the MRS to execution of the beta phase and product launch. Notwithstanding the concern for IP protection and the risk of exposing an immature product and technology to key customers, consulting customers in Phases 0 and 1 and having selected customers participate in the alpha phase as co-development partners are desirable. The beta phase, however, must include active participation by several key customers to qualify the viability of the product in meeting their needs.

The purpose of a customer joint development project (JDP) in the alpha phase is mitigation of development risk through early and deep learning of the customer's application needs and priorities. A JDP customer might also assist in evaluating the technology through active participation in test planning and execution. The engineers from a JDP customer could reside, at least part time, at the manufacturing company's premises and provide expertise, the user's viewpoint (realistic applications and expectations), testing material (such as wafers in the development of IC process equipment), and other resources.

The purpose of customer participation in the beta phase is to assess product performance qualification against the requirements by the customer in his/her operating environment. The goal is to test the product in the "battlefield" environment of the customer, to receive installation and maintenance feedback (including requirements for spare parts), and to assess the product's user friendliness and robustness.

The desired (or optimal) number of beta customers is highly dependent upon the technology, product, industry, and firm's resources (in personnel and budget). For example, in the development of process equipment in the semiconductor manufacturing industry, three is the optimal number of beta customers, whereas to qualify new application software, Microsoft Corporation might have several hundred beta customers.

Critical is that beta customers are selected carefully and a formal agreement is signed with them that specifies the objectives and mutual expectations. A successful beta program is also dependent on having a dedicated beta project team. Because beta customers are usually early adopters of the new technology and are interested in making the product successful, supporting beta customers with the best resources during a beta program must be the number one priority of a product development team.

6.20.1 Selection Criteria—Beta Customers

Four criteria should be used in selecting beta customers:

- Customer's level of interest and excitement for the product in satisfying an unfilled and high priority need—Does the product capture the customer's imagination about its future possibilities? The firm's technology and the product should enable the beta customer's business success and enhance the beta customer's competitive advantage.
- Competitiveness of the new technology and the product in the beta customer's application—Is there a compelling differentiating advantage over the customer's alternative solutions?
- Customer's strategic significance to the firm, as measured by the potential business opportunity, and the customer's market position and influence as a reference to assist the firm to successfully penetrate the market
- Resource availability to make the beta project a resounding success—Adequate skilled resources in technology, engineering, support, operations, and project management are essential for success. Doing fewer beta projects well is preferable to doing many poorly.

6.21 QUALITY

The subject of quality is extensively covered in the literature and is beyond the scope of this book. The purpose of this section is to briefly discuss selected definitions and concepts of quality in a product development and commercialization process.

Quality products and services conform exactly to established customer requirements. The established customer requirements could be specified in a documented agreement between a supplier and a customer or they could be a customer's expectation of what the product or service entails and what value will be delivered. Customer expectations are established based on the supplier's representation and the customer's reference product/service such as competitors' alternative offering.

Quality management entails more than having zero defects in a design or manufacturing process. Quality management is enabling a customer's experience (in his/her operating environment) that satisfies the customer's needs and wants. Quality management is having a customer-focused culture in an organization and adopting a broad view of the customer that includes both internal and external customers.

Quality control, according to the Japan Industrial Standards (JIS), is "a system of means to economically produce goods and services which satisfy customer requirements."[11]

6.21.1 Quality Leverage in PDCP

The cost of fixing a product defect (the cost of poor quality) multiplies as it permeates throughout the value-added sequence of a PDCP (illustrated in Figure 6.7). During the engineering phase for generation and integration of knowledge and during manufacturing when material is formed and assembled into finished goods, a sequence of operations is performed in each "work area" and the output is passed on to the next work area. The "last stop" is at the

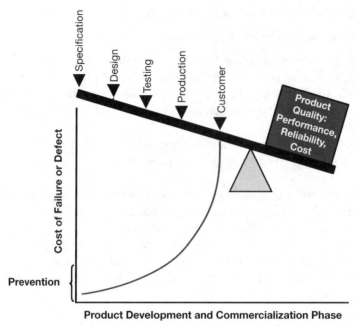

Figure 6.7. Product Quality Leverage by Phase of a PDCP.

customer's use environment. The cost of fixing a problem that occurs in a work area rises exponentially the further down the sequence the error is caught.

Experiencing a 100-times increase in the cost of fixing a design problem if it is caught by an end user versus finding the problem in the design "work area" is not uncommon. In the late 1990s, the seemingly minor, but undetected design problem with the Pentium chip cost Intel hundreds of millions of dollars when it was caught by the end users. Intel had to implement a global customer damage control program to reestablish consumer confidence.

6.21.2 Precision and Accuracy

The *Merriam-Webster's* dictionary gives the following definitions:

- *Precision*—"The degree of refinement with which an operation is performed or a measurement stated"
- *Accuracy*—"Conformity to truth or to a standard or model"

For a product or a process, *precision* is an indication of the reproducibility of the performance and *accuracy* is the distance of the performance from the "target." The concepts of precision and accuracy in product performance are illustrated in Figure 6.8.

In Figure 6.8 the consistent and predictable performance on the left side is preferable because the user can manage the situation. For example, with a small adjustment, performance of the product might be shifted on the target or the customer might be able to make adjustments to other parts of the operation. The performance on the right side of Figure 6.8, however, is unmanageable and undesirable.

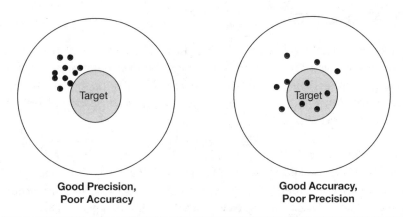

Figure 6.8. Precision and Accuracy in Product Performance.

Minimum variability in performance (i.e., high precision) must be the primary goal of product development. Product designers must achieve a design that can be produced and function consistently under all customer-use conditions. Taguchi and Clausing (1990) point out that "catastrophic stack-up is more likely from scattered deviation within specifications than from consistent deviation outside."[10]

REFERENCES

1. Iansiti, M., Stein, E. *Understanding User Needs.* Harvard Business School Case 9-695-051. Boston: Harvard Business School Publishing; 1995 January 30.
2. Baldwin, C., Clark, K.B. *Design Rules, Volume 1, The Power of Modularity.* Boston: The MIT Press; 2000.
3. Kroll, E., Hanft, T. Quantitative evaluation of product disassembly for recycling. *Research in Engineering Design* 1998; 10:1–14.
4. Klostermann, J., Ed. *Product Innovation and Eco-efficiency.* The Netherlands: Kluwer; 1998.
5. Manahan, S. *Industrial Ecology.* Boca Raton, FL: CRC Press; 1999.
6. Graedel, T.E., Allenby, B.R. *Design for Environment.* Upper Saddle Ridge, NJ: Prentice Hall; 1998.
7. Konaga, R. Basic concepts of product reliability. *Yaskawa Technical Review* 2000; 58(3).
8. Taguchi, G., Chowdhury, S., Wu, Y. *Taguchi's Quality Engineering Handbook.* New York: Wiley-Interscience; 2004.
9. Schrage, M. The culture of prototyping. *Design Management Journal* 1993 Winter; 4(1).
10. Taguchi, G., Clausing, D. *Robust Quality.* Harvard Business Review Article #90114. Boston: Harvard Business School Publishing; 1990 January 1.
11. Imai, M. *Kaizen, The Key to Japan's Competitive Success.* New York: McGraw-Hill; 1986.

ADDITIONAL READING

Internet Links: American Society for Quality, Reliability Division, www.asq-rd.org; IEEE Reliability Society, www.ewh.ieee.org/soc/rs/; ReliaSoft Corporation, www.weibull.com.

Abernethy, R.B. *The New Weibull Handbook: Reliability & Statistical Analysis for Predicting Life, Safety, Survivability, Risk, Cost and Warranty Claims, Fourth Edition.* North Palm Beach, FL: Dr. Robert Abernethy; 2000.

Boning, D.S., Mozumder, P.K. DOE/Opt: *A System for Design of Experiments, Response Surface Modeling, and Optimization Using Process and Device Simulation.* Dallas, TX: Semiconductor Process and Design Center/Texas Instruments; 1993 December.

Box, G.E.P., Hunter, W.G., Hunter, J.S. *Statistics for Experimenters, An Introduction to Design, Data Analysis, and Model Building.* New York: Wiley-Interscience; 1978.

Campbell, J., Iman, R., Londsine, D., Thompson, B. *A Tutorial on Reliability Modeling Using RAMP.* SETEC91-030. Albuqurque, NM: Sandia National Laboratories.

Dhudshia, V.H. Hi Tech Equipment *Reliability—A Practical Guide for Engineers and Engineering Managers.* Sunnyvale, CA: Lanchester Press; 1999 January.

Ireson, W.G., Moss, R.Y., Coombs, C.R., Jr., *Handbook of Reliability Engineering and Management.* New York: McGraw-Hill; 1995 December.

Murthy, P., Xie, M., Jiang, R. *Weibull Models.* New York: John Wiley & Sons; 2003 October.

Nelson, W. *Accelerated Testing: Statistical Models, Test Plans, and Data Analyses.* New York: Wiley-Interscience; 1990 November.

Pham, H. *Handbook of Reliability Engineering.* New York: Springer-Verlag; 2003 July.

Pyzdek, T. *Quality Engineering Handbook, Second Edition, Volume 60, Quality and Reliability Series.* Keller, P.A., Ed. New York: Marcel Dekker; 2003 April.

Roberts, N., Vesely, W., Haasl, D., Goldberg, F. *Fault Tree Handbook.* NUREG-0492. Washington DC: U.S. Nuclear Regulatory Commission; 1981 January.

7

FLAWLESS EXECUTION AND GLOBAL RESOURCES MANAGEMENT

You are what you repeatedly do. Excellence is not an event—it is a habit.
— Aristotle, 384–322 BC

No matter how much thought has been given to a firm's business strategy, no matter how imaginative its marketing plan is, and no matter how creative its technology is, without *excellence in execution*, success does not materialize and perceived opportunities will remain elusive. The requisites for operational excellence and flawless execution are a deep understanding of the multidimensional nature of the product development process, a systems-thinking approach in problem solving, and the practice of world-class management methodologies.

The dimensions of technology, the market, the business, and the people (organizational) in product development and their interdependence necessitate a "total" product development effort and an approach of "doing the *whole* job." Achieving a "total" product development effort and "doing the *whole* job" are possible through adherence to a PDCP and flawless execution in each of the following—core competency in the integration of diverse technologies; marketing savvy; profitability focus; customer-loyalty goals; and quality in every action.

"Systems thinking" considers the *whole* product/process and the interactions of its elements by applying systems analysis theory and adopting systems engineering and concurrent engineering practices. A firm that is engaged in the development of new high-tech products must practice world-class management methodologies and business processes in all operational aspects of the enterprise. These world-class practices are needed for efficient utilization of time, people, and financial resources; for effectiveness in producing results in congruence with objectives; for effectiveness in organizational-learning; for institutionalizing efficient business processes including the PDCP; and for taking advantage of the possibilities of information technology (IT) in all transactions (customer front end and back end, product development, manufacturing, supplier management, logistics management, inventory, and customer service). Furthermore, world-class project management practices must be commonplace in the firm.

Flawless execution is not possible without effective resource management because always fewer resources are available than the opportunities demand. Therefore, the firm must prioritize opportunities, determine resource requirements for timely execution, and have a good understanding of its core competency and how to leverage the resources of others.

In high-tech companies, at the project level and at the firm level, knowledge management must be ubiquitous—to create, retain, and integrate knowledge and to discern the core from the context in sourcing decisions (e.g., in the areas of technology, engineering, and manufacturing) and in intellectual property (IP) protection. The enterprise milieu and culture must also be conducive to innovation and entrepreneurship in product development and commercialization.

Today's high-tech work environment is rushed. Employees are overworked and projects often miss planned schedules. An orientation to "activity" is often rewarded over planning and thinking (because thinking is considered to be procrastination!). Chaos and "firing before the target is known" are pontificated as essential ingredients of success in fiercely competitive and turbulent high-tech markets. A high-level executive at a leading high-tech company once said, "It is OK to present an unrealistic schedule to top management because an aggressive schedule is what it takes to win their support for your plan!"

Frenzied practices result in wasteful trial-and-error activities and rework. Rework should be distinguished from experimentation. Rework is avoidable—rework is a mistake that results from a lack of planning and poor execution. Yet in the development of a high-tech product, rework that results from experimentation is often needed for knowledge generation.

Unfocused actions, irrespective of their intensity and/or having an appearance of being "hard work," result in a longer time to market, missed opportunities, and poor product quality. The answer to short time to market is not "don't think, just act" or "don't plan, just proceed!"

To achieve business success in the short term and to sustain it over the long term requires addressing both long-term and short-term needs. An organization must have a bias toward focused action and use short-term milestones to illuminate the way to reaching a long-term goal. Oftentimes visibility into the future is limited and the path is unclear, which requires managers to take risks and make timely tactical decisions to act (without adequate information and in spite of uncertain outcome) and to then use the knowledge gained from those actions to clear the path and correct the course in reaching the goal.

Effective execution in the product development process requires hands-on leadership. Only through proactive engagement can leaders motivate the team, set the direction and adjust it when necessary, maintain focus on the goal, and move the team forward when faced with challenge.

In a speech at Sorbonne, Paris in 1910, President Theodore Roosevelt said, "It is not the critic who counts; not the man who points out how the strong man stumbles, or where the doer of deeds could have done them better. The credit belongs to the man who is actually in the arena, whose face is marred by dust and sweat and blood; who strives valiantly; who errs; who comes short again and again, because there is no effort without error and shortcoming; but who does actually strive to do the deeds; who knows great enthusiasms, the great devotions; who spends himself in a worthy cause; who at the best knows in the end the triumph of high achievement, and who at the worst, if he fails, at least fails while daring greatly, so that his place shall never be with those cold and timid souls who neither know victory nor defeat."

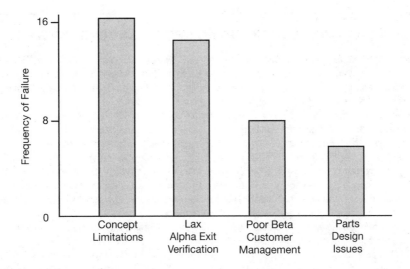

Figure 7.1. Root Causes of New Product Development Failure at a Leading High-Tech Company Over a Span of 8 Years—3 Product Lines, 3 Platforms, and Over 30 Derivative Products.

7.1 CHALLENGES IN THE DEVELOPMENT AND COMMERCIALIZATION OF HIGH-TECH PRODUCTS

Many product development projects fail or succeed only marginally because rigorous discipline in execution is lacking and good management practices are not followed. Figure 7.1 depicts the root causes of failure in the execution of 45 new product development projects in a high-tech company over a span of 8 years. As Figure 7.1 shows, by a factor of two to one, the causes of failure were rooted in deficiencies in project execution as opposed to shortcomings in the product or the technology concept. The execution deficiencies were broadly spread and included lax alpha exit verification, poor beta customer management, and poor product design. Even for projects that failed because of limitations in the product concept, one might wonder if some of these "poor concepts" could have been detected earlier (had the E&F phase been executed with more rigor) so that these projects could have been terminated at the right time.

The remainder of this section will discuss cases from the semiconductor equipment industry to further illustrate the challenges that high-tech companies encounter in product development. The cases demonstrate the criticality of practicing discipline and world-class management methods for flawless execution.

Cases 1 and 2 describe projects that fall behind a planned schedule and are therefore introduced too late into markets in which changing conditions will render the products "unnecessary" and result in lost market opportunity. Cases 3 and 4 are examples of poor execution of product development projects. Case 5 illustrates product challenges that arise from not following the product development process. Case 6 illustrates the product life cycle and portfolio problems that are caused by improper product/technology strategy and poor product quality. Case 7 concerns managing customer expectations and how signing up for a product that cannot be delivered results in customer dissatisfaction and loss of profitability.

CASE 1—A NOVEL INSTRUMENT FOR PROCESS CONTROL

Setting. In early 2000, the central research group at NATL Corporation had perceived a CTM (copper thickness mapping) instrument to enable integrated process control between copper deposition and planarization equipment in IC manufacturing. They envisioned a CTM instrument to map the copper thickness deposited on a wafer by electroplating and to transmit the information as a feedback signal to the deposition equipment and as a feed-forward signal to the planarization (CMP) equipment for process control. They believed that this methodology (known as integrated process control) would improve the quality of the process in both deposition and planarization equipment. The integrated process would reduce dispersion in the copper film thickness that was deposited by electroplating and improve the uniformity of post-CMP planarized copper film. The benefit to IC manufacturers was higher production yield.

By early 2000, copper technology was in its initial stage of market acceptance in the semiconductor fabrication industry, and the need for copper processing products was growing. A metrology capability such as CTM would be a technology enabler and in great demand.

NATL scientists, working with a professor from a leading university, had identified a technology that was ideal for measuring copper thickness at high speed. High speed in copper thickness mapping was crucial in CTM acceptance as a production-worthy instrument. The CTM development team conceived the product design concept and demonstrated its technical feasibility through an E&F phase. Because of shortages in available internal resources, the CTM project manager outsourced most of the Phase 3 development to a small local supplier which would design the sensor, develop the controller for it, and manufacture the alpha and beta phase prototypes.

The central research group that was developing the CTM was independent of the electroplating and CMP business units (BUs) at NATL. The two BUs were the internal customers of the central research group to whom their new product ideas such as CTM had to be "sold." The CTM development team planned to work with engineers from the two BUs to demonstrate the benefits of incorporating CTM into their products by mid-2000. The ultimate goal was to ship the CTM to two major beta customers of electroplating and CMP products by the end of 2000 and to win the IC manufacturers' endorsements for production.

Situation. By July 2002, the CTM product development effort was floundering. CTM had not been shipped to the beta customers and, worse yet, it had not even passed internal BU qualification testing! The prototypes made by the supplier had failed to perform to specification and subsequent design modifications did little to remedy the shortcomings. As it turned out, the root cause of the problem was the incompetence of the supplier in performing the job. The incompetence of the supplier had gone undetected for almost 2 years. Neither the engineers nor the supplier management organization at NATL had associated the prolonged failure of the CTM design with the supplier's incompetence.

Over the same time period between 2000 and 2002, numerous organizational changes at NATL caused the responsibility for the development of the CTM product to shift among several engineering teams. Ownership for CTM was transferred from the central research group to the electroplating BU in late 2000 and was then given back to them a year later! The turnover in personnel caused a loss in leadership direction and limited the continuity of knowledge retention in the development team. The lessons learned (in technology and the design issues with the supplier) were mostly lost in every turnover of organizational responsibility and change in project management.

By mid-2002, the CTM product was barely ready for alpha testing—1.5 years after it had been promised to beta customers! Market conditions in July 2002 were very different from early 2000 when the CTM project started. In 2002, NATL Corporation's copper electroplating product had only limited success in the market due to many first-order reliability problems. To the division general manager, the benefits of CTM appeared to be secondary in importance. On the other hand, by July 2002, the CMP division had developed their own *in situ* copper profile control module which included a real-time copper thickness measurement. They no longer needed the CTM product!

Outcome. The CTM product development project had missed the time-to-market schedule by 1.5 years! A significant investment had been wasted, the engineering team was frustrated, and the two beta customers were dissatisfied. In early August 2002, the company president called a meeting with the CTM team members to make a decision about whether (or not) to terminate the project.

CASE 2—FINETCH—A PRODUCT DEVELOPMENT PROCESS THAT LACKED FOCUS

Setting. The multibillion dollar dielectric etch market is one of the largest segments of the IC manufacturing equipment market. In May 1995, the president of Company X formed a team to develop the company's next-generation dielectric etch product to meet the needs of 180-nm technology devices and beyond (to be known as FinEtch). The product was planned for market introduction by December 1997.

The dielectric etch market was segmented by several applications. The etch technology requirements were vastly different in these application segments, as was the market size or served available market (SAM). The HAR (high-aspect-ratio) contact etch application was a technologically demanding segment and highly prized, but the size of its SAM was small. The back-end interconnect dielectric etch application was technologically less demanding and required low-cost high-throughput equipment. Because the backend equipment was used for etching multiple layers, its SAM size was very large (60% of the total market size). The SAM size for each of the remaining three etch segments was small (about 10% of the total).

Situation. The general manager (GM) of the product division of Company X wanted FinEtch to be able to serve all of the segments! He thought that if the new product met the toughest technology requirements, it would automatically take care of the other applications. He envisioned that developing a product that could serve all segments of the dielectric etch market was more efficient. In response, the marketing team prepared an MRS that contained the requirements for all of the etch applications, but did not provide a clear focus and prioritized direction for the product development team. In effect, they were to develop an "etch-all" product!

Over the next few years, the product concept changed several times and $20 million was invested in the product. The engineering team subsequently found that having an "etch-all" product design was impractical. The design that met the challenging HAR application needs was too complex to be low cost and high throughput in satisfying the needs of the back-end (and the other) applications.

In 1999, the president of Company X brought in a professor from a leading business school for a root cause analysis of the situation. She conducted a 3-month study and submitted a report that identified the root causes of the problem. The report concluded that the marketing strategy for the product development lacked clarity and focus and the execution of the product development process was grossly flawed. The report noted several shortcomings in project execution:

- The project's direction and its priority were changed several times during the course of the development project (which did not follow the company's established process for new product development).
- The project had no empowered (high-level) project manager with accountability.
- As the frustration of team members grew because of the lack of progress, so did infighting among engineering and marketing managers.
- Because the project schedule had slipped, in early 1998, the company president assigned several high-level executives and technologists to "help" the team. This "meddling" exacerbated the confusion, demoralized the team, and made the environment more political. As one team engineer noted, "The weekly design reviews with the assigned executive 'helpers' were a circus of political show-offs rather than a focused productive meeting."

Outcome. By August of 2000, the FinEtch product still had not been introduced to the market. The oxide etch market share of the company had eroded from a high of 30% in 1995 to 10%, as the company's older generation of products fell short of meeting the ever-increasing needs of customers. Some of the engineering managers argued that it was better to develop two different products, one for the "high-end" technology application (HAR) and one for "low-end" technologies. They also thought that it was best to develop the less-sexy "low-end" product first because the SAM size was very large.

CASE 3—FACTORY INTERFACE PRODUCT DEVELOPMENT

Setting. In 1998, SPEq Corporation, a supplier of IC manufacturing process equipment, was under pressure to accelerate the development of its 300-mm product lines. An important subsystem of all 300-mm process equipment at SPEq was the factory interface module (FIn).

The Systems and Automation Organization (SAO), the internal supplier of common platforms at SPEq, had the charter and the engineering resources to develop the FIn product quickly and to ship it to Intel, the largest customer and the forerunner in the "race" to 300-mm IC manufacturing. The approved commercialization plan called for product introduction by March 2000. FIn was not a stand-alone product. It was shipped as a module of the process equipment through various BUs in the company that had the overall system responsibility.

The major subsystems of the FIn product were two robots for moving the wafers within the FIn; two door openers to open the lid of a box (called FOUP) that was the carrier of up to 25 wafers and transported the wafers within the fab from one piece of equipment to another; and a controller, plus software.

After more than a year of architectural design considerations and intense deliberation among engineering gurus and high-level executives in the company, the "optimal" concept was selected for the product in January 1999. The first revision of the product was named FIn.0. The product architecture specified that the system controller (which controlled the functions of the entire process equipment and those of FIn) was to be housed within the FIn for packaging reasons.

Two local firms, E-Corp and Auto-Fab, were chosen as suppliers of the robots and the door openers, respectively.

The FIn development team hurried to complete the product design, to exit the alpha phase, and to ship to Intel according to plan. Alpha exit was successfully completed on schedule in December 1999 and the product was shipped to Intel (and a few other customers) soon after.

Situation. A few months later, performance results for FIn from the field were reported to the development team and company management. The performance results were disastrous, indicating that both the robots and door openers were extremely unreliable. The field data indicated that the MTBF for FIn was 10 hours—in gross disagreement with the alpha exit test results which had demonstrated the required MTBF of 300 hours. The validity of the alpha test methods, test results, and data analysis was seriously questioned. Furthermore, the manufacturing cost of FIn.0 was found to be $200,000 versus an MRS target of $100,000!

These serious FIn.0 reliability problems had to be resolved expeditiously. The ability of customers to ramp their 300-mm production was being impacted.

In the meantime, SPEq corporate management had created Fab-Pro, a new division, to expand the company's SAM space by capitalizing on opportunities in the white space of fab productivity improvement, which had been untapped by the company. An experienced vice president of the company was assigned to head the new group. She was a company old timer, influential and self-proclaimed to be a "best-product manager." The product management responsibilities for FIn were transferred to the new group as an important product line in the company's fab-productivity portfolio.

To incorporate the lessons learned from the initial revision of FIn.0, the new vice president "directed" the FIn engineering team to design a whole new FIn model (FIn.1), which was radically different from the FIn.0 design. The FIn.1 architecture and industrial design were different than FI.0 and incorporated a new door opener known as NDO, which was designed and fabricated by E-Corp (in spite of their poor performance on the robots!). Additionally, the engineering team had determined that the FIn.0 controller design was legacy-based and outdated and had to be replaced by a brand new compact control architecture (CCA) design.

The controller design approach turned out to be a significant execution challenge for the FIn development team. The new controller design, in concept, technology, and architecture, was a divisive issue in the engineering community at the company and a point of contention and infighting among the different "camps." To remedy the situation, to establish peace and to ensure that the new design approach was not only sound but adopted by all product groups, the company president formed an ad hoc corporate-wide committee of top engineers and engineering managers to choose the "best" control technology and architecture for the future.

This committee of peer members proved to be quite ineffective. The committee lacked an effective leader. Every member advocated only his/her own "superior" position. The committee could not even agree on a common procedure and set of metrics for selecting the "best solution."

In early 2000, company executives, SAO management, the new vice president of the Fab-Pro division, and the FIn engineering team were facing a dire situation. The disastrous field problems of FIn.0 had to be corrected urgently. The situation was impacting the company's profitability (as a result of excessive spare and customer support costs), its reputation, and the prospects for future business from very unhappy customers.

Nevertheless, the engineering team was distracted from solving the urgent FIn.0 reliability problems because most of the best engineering resources were working hard on the new FIn.1 design at the direction of the new vice president of Fab-Pro. She thought of the FIn.1 product as "hers" and was adamant that Fin.1 was the number one priority for the engineering team. She also argued that FIn.1 would solve the cost and the reliability problems of the existing FIn.0 revision—therefore there was no reason to "waste time and scarce resources" on the old version, which would "soon" become obsolete!

Outcome. The "strategy" of the vice president of Fab-Pro was flawed, however, because customers were demanding an immediate solution to the field problems—which meant fixing the problems with FIn.0. Even if the new revision was "better" than FIn.0, customers would not accept it because of their copy-exactly philosophy, their fabs were "filled" with FIn.0, and they had already qualified their products with the FIn.0 and did not want to re-qualify them.

The BUs of the SPEq who were selling FIn.0 as a subsystem of their products were siding with customers and putting additional pressure on the engineers to fix the reliability problems with FIn.0 and to reduce its cost. They did not care about FIn.1. Because of the lack of alignment between the strategies of the BUs and Fab-Pro, BU managers stopped communicating with the vice president of Fab-Pro and directly worked with the SAO engineers. In addition, the vice president of Fab-Pro did not take ownership of FIn.0 and essentially did not care about it. She pushed the SAO engineering team through daily meetings and weekly escalations to the company president to develop FIn.1 as quickly as possible. The president wanted SAO engineers to fix the FIn.0 problems and develop the FIn.1!

CASE 4—TOOL BUFFER STORAGE PRODUCT MARKETING—A STRATEGY IN DISARRAY

Setting. Case 4 is a continuation of Case 3. Case 4 concerns the development of another new product, in addition to the FIn, which would build the portfolio of products in the Fab-Pro division of SPEq Corporation. The new product was known as TBS (tool buffer storage) and was envisioned as an enabler to capitalize on fab productivity opportunities.

TBS was intended to radically change the traditional approach of customers in the management of work in process (WIP) storage in an IC manufacturing fab. TBS allowed fab operators to store wafers "locally" at each process tool, replacing the traditional practice of storing wafers at a central fab location or at an equipment bay. The compelling customer benefit of TBS would be the reduction of manufacturing cycle time in a fab.

The vice president of Fab-Pro had modeled many scenarios of wafer flow in a fab and had shown that the TBS approach reduced cycle time by as much as 30%, which was a very significant benefit that fab managers could not overlook. The main benefit of TBS to SPEq was not the added revenue that it generated (because its price was less than 10% of process equipment products), but rather the compelling competitive advantage that it offered when integrated onto process equipment at SPEq.

Situation. The vice president of Fab-Pro prepared a strategy to develop the new product with SAO engineers and to market and sell it directly to IC manufacturers, which was approved by the company president. Marketing TBS directly to customers ran the risk of TBS being purchased for integration on competitors' equipment in the fab. It was essential that TBS remained an integral subsystem of the SPEq process equipment and not be available as a stand-alone product. This meant that the process equipment BUs would market TBS with their product.

The BUs, however, were not "sold" on the TBS idea. They thought of TBS as a high-risk distraction to their main business. Because of this lukewarm reception, the company president encouraged the vice president of Fab-Pro to market TBS independently of the equipment BUs and to make the Fab-Pro version a reality as soon as possible. And so she did! She aggressively pushed the assigned design engineering team for speedy TBS development and left no stone unturned in her quest for early-adoption customers.

To ensure that customers did not buy TBS for integration on the equipment of competitors, the sales force at SPEq insisted that interested customers should not place purchase orders for a stand-alone TBS, but instead should place orders for TBS as a subsystem of their process equipment. This strategy created significant confusion and disruption for the BUs. The product configuration, cost, price, and gross margin of the BUs were impacted by inclusion of the TBS that was being developed, configured, promoted, and sold independently by the vice president of Fab-Pro, without their consent or knowledge!

Several customers bought the product, thanks to the effective selling techniques of the vice president of Fab-Pro. However, according to early data from the few participating fabs, the cycle time reduction benefit of TBS remained elusive. In the meantime, confusion was great among engineering, marketing, and management personnel in the BUs that considered TBS to be an undesirable aberration in their product marketing programs. The BUs actually lost a few points of gross profit margin because TBS was sold at a very low price to achieve market penetration! Also, the process equipment BUs had to take responsibility for early product problems of the immature TBS because customers considered TBS to be an integral part of the product that the BUs had delivered to them. TBS had numerous delivery and reliability problems that impacted the performance of the entire system for which the BUs were responsible.

Outcome. The corporate strategy, of forming an independent team and assigning an experienced and influential product line vice president as its leader, was very effective in the rapid development and market penetration of a new product in white space. However, no cross-division discussion was held to create a comprehensive and integrated technology, market, and business strategy for the TBS product, mostly out of fear that this process would take too long and market opportunity would be lost.

CASE 5—TBS PRODUCT DEVELOPMENT PROCESS

Setting. Case 5 is an extension of Case 4 and focuses on the TBS design development process. Case 5 discusses the product development issues that were caused by accelerating the time to market of a new product by bypassing the beta customer qualification phase and introducing the product straight into the pilot production of customers immaturely.

Situation. The TBS development project was officially kicked off in April 2003. By December 2003, the alpha phase was barely completed when ten TBS units were shipped to a major customer in Taiwan and installed in a brand new 300-mm production fab. The customer fab was touted as a showcase of efficiency in installation and start-up and a model foundry in competition with other Taiwanese foundries.

When shipped to the first customer, the development process (PDCP) for TBS had not successfully exited the alpha phase and the product had numerous engineering issues. Furthermore, the beta qualification phase of PDCP was skipped as well. The new product was installed directly into the customer's production—which was not a suitable environment for beta evaluation. The customer's main focus in production was to qualify the entire brand new fab and the manufacturing process flow of the initial product (a memory chip). TBS was expected to work flawlessly and to not hinder the production ramp process.

By February 2004, 25 additional units of the TBS had been shipped to 2 other major customers in the United States and Japan.

In the meantime, the TBS development team was frantically working to complete the alpha phase and to urgently resolve numerous field problems that customers were encountering in the installation and start-up of TBS. For example, the TBS software for communicating with the host computer in the fab was still in the engineering development stage. The software had many shortcomings when the product was shipped, which severely limited the ability of customers to start up their fabs and intensified their dissatisfaction with TBS. The TBS team had to dispatch large contingents of high-level engineers to three customer sites for real-time troubleshooting and customer relationship management.

The project engineering team members and BU vice presidents were disappointed and frustrated with the chaotic implementation of the PDCP. The development team regarded the Fab-Pro vice president as having "commercialized" the product before it was "developed!" She had initially requested the engineering team to alpha exit the product by September 2003, 5 months after the project start, and to ship 10 units to the first customer by end of December 2003, a date that she had committed to with

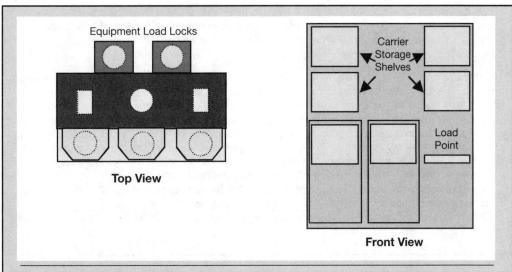

Figure 7.2. Product Layout—TBS.

the customer at the beginning of the project. The Fab-Pro vice president had argued that this date was critical to commercial success of TBS and the entire Fab-Pro marketing strategy.

The alpha exit date slipped several times. The engineering team had made, as their manager stated in a postmortem discussion, a "soft" commitment to a September date in their best effort to be responsive to "marketing demand." By September, the engineering project manager revised the alpha exit date to December 31, 2003, the commitment date for shipping the product to the first customer. Ten units were shipped to Taiwan a week late (by January 7, 2004), but without exiting the alpha phase of the PDCP. The actual date for the "formal alpha exit" was the end of January 2004.

The company had a strict policy against shipping any product to a customer before successful completion of the alpha phase. This policy had "teeth" and was backed by an accounting rule that revenue from shipping a new product could not be recognized without a formal alpha exit.

The justification for bending the "rule" for TBS was that it would take a month for the units to arrive in Taiwan and be installed in the fab. By then, the alpha exit would be completed. This deadline was met, but not without some "creative relaxation" of the alpha exit criteria and with approval of the Fab-Pro vice president! The relaxed criteria did not meet the customers' expectations. Hence, the alpha exit was a mere formality to comply with a company rule so that the revenues from the TBS shipments could be recognized by the accountants.

In spite of these many execution problems, TBS project execution was quite fast considering the complexity of the TBS design (illustrated in Figure 7.2). From the start of the project to the completion of the alpha phase took 10 months, including the schedule slips. The short project schedule was in part enabled by concurrent development of design and manufacturing with a key supplier. The design of two major subsystems of TBS (the drive mechanism and controls) was outsourced to a supplier that the Fab-Pro vice president knew of, without going through the company's standard "multiple-bid purchasing" process. This action was justified for the sake of the project schedule. Manufacturing of the engineering prototypes and the units shipped to the initial three customers were also outsourced to the same supplier.

Although the product development and commercialization process was fast, the profitability of TBS was quite poor. Manufacturing costs for TBS were $75,000—2.5 times higher than the MRS target and roughly equal to the average selling price for the first 35 units!

The concurrent design efforts for the TBS drive mechanism and controls with the supplier also did not go smoothly. During the initial engineering prototype testing, many reliability problems were encountered with the supplier-designed controller and drive system. The controller and drive system had to be redesigned by SPEq engineers. Three months after TBS was shipped to Taiwan, customer support engineers discovered several safety, reliability, and software problems with the product. SPEq had to extensively retrofit all field units at a very high cost, further driving the profit margin down into negative territory.

In spite of the engineering havoc and the customer dissatisfaction caused by the developmental process for the product, the very short time-to-market introduction of TBS created a unique market opportunity that would have been missed otherwise.

Outcome. By early 2003, transition to the 300-mm wafer had gained momentum in IC manufacturing markets. The opportunity for acceptance of a new product such as TBS, which promised to change customer "behavior" in fab wafer management (storage), was at the onset of the 300-mm transition. This was the time when fab managers were solidifying ideas for the layout and wafer flow of 300-mm fabs. Missing this crucial market timing would have made acceptance of the local wafer storage strategy (enabled by TBS) nearly impossible. The Fab-Pro vice president was quite aggressive (and successful) in selling TBS idea to early adopting customers. These customers bought the product based on the modeling results which claimed a 30% reduction in fab cycle time and the pictures of a very rough engineering prototype of an earlier TBS concept. However, the promised cycle time reduction did not materialize in the production environment and the product lost momentum.

TBS did not attain "traction" past the first few early customers. By late 2004, SPEq had discontinued the TBS product line!

CASE 6—SECOND GENERATION PRODUCT DEVELOPMENT AT ZYLEX CORPORATION—CONTINUOUS VERSUS DISCONTINUOUS INNOVATION IN A RAPIDLY CHANGING HIGH-TECH ENVIRONMENT

Setting. Zylex Corporation developed its highly successful FutureEtch product in 1987 when Zylex was a relatively small company with annual revenue of $20 million. FutureEtch was targeted for the thin-film etch segment of the semiconductor process equipment market. (See the Appendix for a brief description of the semiconductor manufacturing process.) The software real-time operating system (OS) and the graphical user interface (GUI) for the equipment were developed internally (homegrown), which was a common practice at the time due to the lack of a mature commercial solution.

Situation. By 1992, FutureEtch (Figure 7.3) had penetrated the market worldwide and could be found in most IC production fabs. Zylex had also successfully developed and commercialized its second generation product past the start-up stage and had grown its annual revenue to $175 million by 1992. By that time, software technology in the industry had advanced significantly since the inception of FutureEtch. Software engineering managers at Zylex sensed that their product had become archaic, which was reaffirmed by competitive pressure and input from the company's sales force. The sales force was relaying the concerns of customers about the limitations of FutureEtch software. Zylex software managers were not pleased to see the superior appearance of competitors' new products at various industry trade shows.

The legacy software design (or Classic, as it was later called) was limiting the life cycle evolution of the capabilities of FutureEtch. Its GUI was not user friendly and did not look appealing. The legacy code was not designed in object oriented (OO) structure. Most of it was written in assembly language. CIP projects to add new features and capabilities or to fix bugs were very difficult and time-consuming to implement. Partitioning work and doing simultaneous development by several developers for rapid execution was difficult. Furthermore, the engineering pool with the right skills to maintain the legacy software was becoming increasingly small. By 1992 most of the original designers and developers of the Classic product were no longer with the company and hiring anyone who knew the legacy methods or was willing to learn antiquated technologies was difficult—it was not good for their résumés! It was time to overhaul the FutureEtch software.

In 1991, Zylex hired Mike Hsu as a new software engineering director. He was a graduate of Carnegie Mellon University and was trained in modern software technologies and development methods. He immediately initiated a major project to replace the FutureEtch legacy operating system with a new OO design and to write the code in C-language. Mike alerted the electrical engineering department that the system controls had to be upgraded as well to be able to take advantage of the new software capabilities. The best software engineers in the department were assigned to the new project, which was named Enable. Hardware engineers, in turn, initiated their own parallel project.

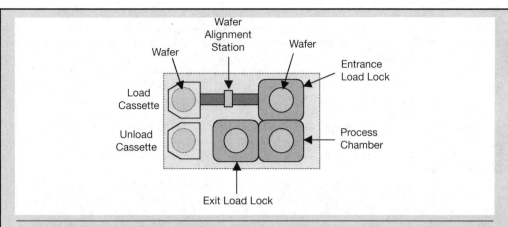

Figure 7.3. System Layout—FutureEtch.

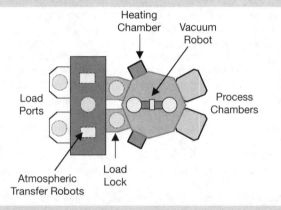

Figure 7.4. System Layout—Symphony.

The Enable project plan called for beta testing of the product by autumn of 1992, 6 months after the start of the project, and product release by January 1993. The Enable software design was also planned to be used in the company's new Symphony product line, which was based on a new multichamber cluster platform (Figure 7.4). Symphony was also in development in 1992 and planned for market introduction by early 1994.

 Following intensive research, the product development team selected NeXT Corporation as the supplier of several major components of the Enable software, including the operating system, the GUI framework, and a few utilities. In 1992, NeXT was shifting its product strategy from a hardware computer company (that competed with Apple Corporation) to a software product company. The Zylex Enable project was a great opportunity for NeXT, which would enable NeXT to penetrate the real-time OS market. NeXT had been founded by Silicon Valley icon Steve Jobs. Zylex engineers were excited to work with his company and to integrate leading-edge innovative technologies into their second generation products.

Mike and his team promoted their new strategy heavily inside the company and won the support of top management. The Zylex president was impressed by the sleek GUI demo that Mike and his team were able to put together after only a couple of weeks of effort. Mike was off to a great start at Zylex.

Because the Zylex team was so impressed with the GUI capabilities of the NeXT products, they did not adequately assess the suitability of the NeXT OS for real-time control applications. Also, as the team found out later, the initial commitment of NeXT to real-time OS technology diminished over time as the product strategy at NeXT shifted to other markets.

While the Enable software was being developed, Zylex continued to sell their legacy Classic products and grew the installed base. Meanwhile, Zylex customers, to keep up with their product needs, demanded continuous improvement of the legacy software (in their fabs) with new features and capabilities and improved reliability and usability. Although the software department's engineering pool to staff Classic software projects had diminished to a critical few in 1992, CIPs for Classic continued.

Products with Enable software were introduced to the market as planned. By 1995, its installed base had grown to more than 200 machines. The Classic product, with its continuously improved capability, was still shipping concurrently. Customers who had an installed base of Classic and wanted to increase fab capacity were reluctant to change their process tool—in order to maintain operational efficiency and to ensure quality in manufacturing process. Yet when they built a new fab to manufacture the next generation IC design, customers preferred to use the latest technology process tool and many switched to Enable. Most customers owned both Enable and Classic products and could compare their performances side by side.

In spite of its great initial promise and potential, the Enable software proved to be unreliable. Even by 1995 its features and capabilities remained below the Classic level. Because Classic capabilities and features were continuously enhanced, Enable could not catch up, particularly because most of the Enable engineering resources were tied up in resolving numerous critical reliability problems in the NeXT OS.

The problems with Enable were twofold—first, the problem that is inherent in the development of any new product that competes with a (continuously improving) legacy product; and second, the poor quality of the NeXT software and its shortcomings as a real-time OS.

The first problem, a new product in competition with a legacy product that is being continuously improved, is illustrated in Figure 7.5, which shows the growth paths of features and capabilities for the Enable and Classic products. Classic software development followed a typical new product profile—it started slowly, was followed by a steady rise, and finally leveled off as Classic's old software technology became a limiting factor in keeping up with market demand for more capabilities. In contrast, the growth of Enable started very rapidly for several reasons, including:

- Many capabilities of Classic could be directly ported to the new Enable platform.
- High priority was given to the Enable project.
- The developmental environment for the new technology for Enable was efficient.
- The system performance requirements for FutureEtch were well understood when the Enable project started.
- FutureEtch hardware (except for the new controller) was mature.

Having mature hardware was an important factor because when hardware and software for a new product are designed concurrently, software development is often hindered by hardware problems (as was the case in Classic development).

Despite the positive characteristics that lead to the rapid growth of Enable, by 1995 the capabilities of Enable were at best only on a par with Classic, except for the GUI look and feel, in which Enable was clearly superior. Reliability problems with Enable were also disappointing to customers. Yet the software engineering director, the FutureEtch product manager, and company sales personnel had told customers that Enable would be "a lot better" than Classic, which to customers meant more capabilities from the day that Enable was first shipped in early 1994!

In 1995, the future prospects of Enable were in jeopardy because of two major challenges. First, the patience of customers and Zylex management was running thin because of the numerous reliability problems. Customers were so unhappy with Enable that they were threatening to convert the software in their machines to Classic. Sales did not want to sell Enable. Second, NeXT, the supplier of the OS and GUI software, was showing signs that it was not committed to fixing the OS shortcomings and in fact might discontinue the OS product in the not so distant future.

Discontinuing the OS product was a huge problem for Zylex because the new Symphony platform also used the NeXT OS and had the same reliability problems. The situation with Symphony had not yet reached an acute state because Symphony's installed base in 1995 was still less than 50 tools, which were mostly in the R&D lines of customers and not yet in production when product reliability would be a major requirement. Symphony's situation, however, was a "time bomb," with a potentially more severe problem than Enable—Symphony was the "product of the future" for Zylex

Management at Zylex faced a major decision in 1995. Conversion of all or a large number of the Enable tools in the field to Classic was a very unattractive option for Zylex. Enable had been sold by Zylex at a premium price compared to Classic. Zylex would have to make refunds to customers!

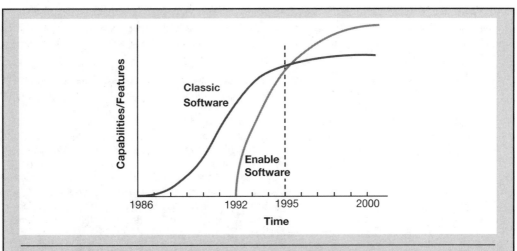

Figure 7.5. Capability/Feature Growths—Classic versus Enable Software.

Additionally, Enable software was accompanied by a new control system hardware module that would have to be replaced in any Enable-to-Classic conversion and it was estimated to have at least a 10-year life, extending to 2005. Accounting for the incidental costs of market share loss and customer dissatisfaction in addition to the hardware and software retrofitting costs and the refund, the total conversion cost was estimated to exceed $50 million. Furthermore, all converted equipment in customer fabs would have to be re-qualified for production—at huge downtime disruptions, production risks, and costs to customers.

The decision to be made had become a make-or-break-scale situation for Zylex and its business, which had grown to $750 million in 1995, thanks to successful development and commercialization of several FutureEtch derivative and CIP products. Contemplating the course of action to recommend at an upcoming strategy session with the president of Zylex, Mike Hsu summarized several issues with NeXT and its OS software:

- The future business viability of NeXT and its ability to support Zylex
- The technical and reliability limitations of the NeXT OS and the NeXT commitment to the OS and to fixing its problems
- The Symphony software and controls architecture and the GUI framework, which were based on NeXT
- The strategic importance of Zylex to NeXT (Zylex was a small customer of NeXT, with very little leverage, and therefore had little strategic importance to NeXT.)
- Contractual issues (Contractually, Zylex managers had done a poor job in negotiating an agreement that committed NeXT to tight performance specifications and provisions for default. Hence, NeXT was unwilling to license their software source code to Zylex so that the problems could be fixed!)

In evaluating the options, Mike and the product managers considered switching the OS from NeXT to Microsoft NT for both the Enable and Symphony product lines. In 1995, Microsoft NT was rapidly gaining market acceptance as an OS for many professional PC applications, but limited data about its appropriateness as a real-time OS was available. As Mike pointed out to team members, Zylex managers had learned from experience with Enable that replacing the software of an existing product was not so easy. Nevertheless, engineers and managers at Zylex spent many months exploring the NT option. The team considered writing entirely new software based on the NT OS for Symphony. However, during such a developmental endeavor, Zylex would have no choice but to sell Symphony with the NeXT OS—otherwise Zylex would lose market share and encounter irreparable damage to its market position.

Switching to the NT OS was also unattractive for the Enable product line because yet a third FutureEtch vintage product would be available (Classic, Enable-NeXT, and Enable-NT). Having three product versions that essentially performed the same function for customers would create many problems in product marketing, CIP development, and support and confuse customers! Furthermore, starting a new product project would consume significant company resources, not only in software engineering, but also in marketing, service/support, manufacturing, and elsewhere.

Outcome. By late 1995, the management team at Zylex concluded that the only reasonable solution was to fix the Enable NeXT problems. As a result, the company "limped along" with the situation for many years, gradually "patching" the many problems of Enable NeXT software to a bearable level.

Because of the rapid advances in software and controls technologies and because of the long life of capital equipment in IC manufacturing fabs, the situation and some of the problems discussed in Case 6 would perhaps have been hard to avoid. At issue, however, are the shortcomings at Zylex Corporation in managing technology and product development in the turbulent high-tech environment of the semiconductor industry. A senior executive at Zylex summarized the lessons learned from the Enable experience:

- The Enable software technology strategy and the supplier selection process were poor.
- The legacy OS, coding language, and system controller could have been changed through an incremental innovation scheme, without the radical switch to NExT. (This approach had been successfully implemented by a competitor of Zylex.)
- Product managers did not fully understand that the life of the Classic product would be long and that product capabilities would evolve.
- The Enable software development project was poorly executed.
- The copy-exactly customers were poorly managed.

CASE 7—MANAGING CUSTOMER EXPECTATIONS—SIGNING UP FOR WHAT YOU CAN DELIVER

Setting. In 2002, the CMP process (chemical mechanical planarization) was widely accepted in the semiconductor IC manufacturing industry. The CMP market share of NATL Corporation was on the rise. Although NATL was a late entrant in the market and its CMP product was still in its infancy, customers were intrigued by the product's architectural versatility. NATL also had a good reputation for product reliability that most other CMP suppliers lacked.

Also in 2002, the NATL sales force in Europe was determined to place the relatively immature NATL CMP tool at a new fab of a major customer. To that end, the sales force sought help from NATL corporate executives, who subsequently decided to offer an attractive "package deal" to the customer that would encompass all NATL products, including CMP. The package deal was formulated primarily between the European sales force and corporate executives, with minimal consultation with the CMP BU. The customer decided to purchase three CMP systems for a total price of $7.5 million.

Situation. Two years later in 2002, the CMP equipment at the European fab still did not meet the customer's original specification and the CMP division was struggling to make the product reach the customer's expectation level. The customer was very unhappy and would not sign off on the product acceptance. The customer was also withholding the final 25% payment for the three tools that they had purchased and received 2 years earlier. The tools were in production, but had many technical problems that limited the customer's ability to make their products and achieve planned output capability of the factory.

The situation for NATL was quite serious because of the customer's dissatisfaction; the inability of NATL to collect the 25% receivables; and the threat of having to reverse corporate revenue figures to comply with GAAP rules (generally accepted accounting principles). According to GAAP, NATL could not recognize revenue unless the product met the customer's specification and had a sign-off for acceptance.

Outcome. The root cause of the problem at NATL occurred at the time of sale. As the vice president of engineering at NATL put it, "Two years earlier nobody checked the customer spec against the actual tool performance. Even the design capability of the tool, according to the MRS, was below the performance level that was committed to the European customer!" In the corporate "package deal" with the customer for all NATL products, the customer's performance specification had been accepted at face value by sales executives to maximize the numbers of equipment sold!

7.2 STRATEGIES FOR FLAWLESS EXECUTION

Having a culture of flawless execution that is ubiquitous in the organization—for "doing the right thing, right and fast, the first time"—is essential.

The "right thing" is having a deep understanding of the customer's wants and needs in the target market segment. "Doing the right thing" is formulating market and business requirements in the form of an MRS, vigilantly monitoring external and internal changes, and redefining the requirements. Redefining "the right thing" may encompass the inclusion of new product capabilities and the reprioritization of the old capabilities and/or changing the product cost or market timing targets based on new competitive realities. Prioritizing new and existing projects in the firm's product development portfolio, including redirection of projects and even cancellation of a few, are important ingredients of "doing the right thing." A firm's scarce resources must only be spent, *efficiently*, on the right things.

"Doing the right thing" is to focus only on value-added product capabilities and value-added tasks and activities in the development process. A development team must define value-added product features and capabilities from the customer's viewpoint. Every task of the project must be critically examined for its contribution to accomplishing the objectives and whether (or not) the task is a value-added activity. A value-added activity creates a distinctive competitive advantage in the target market, is important to delivering benefits to customers and investors, and enables the desired market position for the product vis-à-vis other players in the value chain. Often, project teams become "defocused" and engage in tasks that are tangential or at best secondary to the MRS objectives. Project reviews must include an examination of the importance of every task. At each review, routinely ask *why is this task being performed*?

"Doing the right thing the first time" is eliminating rework through flawless execution that uses best practices in project management, systems analysis, decision making, and deployment of resources. Resources must be skilled in the assigned task, be equipped with efficient tools, and adhere to quality principles in performing tasks. Rework is different from iterative experimentation to gain new knowledge. Rework is caused when the necessary knowledge is available, but a task is carried out in such a way that the result is poor quality.

An ability to do things fast (in order to be the first to market) is often the only competitive advantage in high-tech markets. However, accelerating the time to market must be achieved through efficiency in project execution and knowledge generation/integration—not through shortcuts that bypass key stages of the PDCP (as companies are so often tempted to do). PDCP comprises successive steps of knowledge generation and integration as illustrated in Figure 7.6 (also see Figure 5.7 in Chapter 5). The *nominal process* is depicted by the solid curved line although the commercialization process may begin in the latter part of the beta phase. Accelerating the time to market should be achieved by *pulling* the curve forward to the position of the dashed curve and by *shortening* the time to completion of the PDCP phases—not by eliminating (or bypassing) or partially completing (with poor quality) any of the phases.

Intel's approach for accelerating the process of product development and manufacturing qualification is to improve the efficiency of knowledge generation and reuse. People from manufacturing go to engineering during product design and alpha testing and then go back to manufacturing during pilot production (first article) and the volume manufacturing ramp. The same team of engineering and manufacturing people also goes from one product development project to another to share learning from past lessons and best-known methods (BKMs).

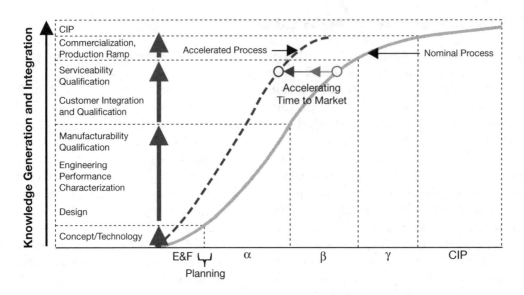

Figure 7.6. Accelerating Time to Market through Speed of Execution.

Controlling the content and scope of the alpha, beta, and gamma phases is important—so that neither expediency nor the intent of the phase and quality of its output is compromised. In other words, foregoing the essential intent and content of any phase for the sake of accelerating the time to market is unacceptable. Yet reducing the number of requirements of a phase (i.e., the scope), provided that associated risks are understood, quantified, and approved by management and are in compliance with those requirements, and deferring them to later phase is acceptable. Also acceptable is to pull the scope (from the MRS requirements) from a later phase to an earlier phase (e.g., from beta to alpha) in order to accelerate a process. Yet "assuming" that alpha testing of the product (done in-house) is an adequate substitute for beta qualification testing of the product in the actual operating environment of the customer is not acceptable. In most cases, "simulating" the customer's operating environment in-house is almost impossible!

Because of the urgency in development and market introduction of most high-tech products (in consumer as well as in industrial markets), concurrent development of myriad new products in the entire supply chain is often necessary. In such a case, however, the supplier must carefully manage customer expectations—to understand the state of development of the product and the need to take a joint and measured risk in exchange for the benefits of a short time to market. A joint and concurrent product development endeavor requires that both supplier and customer execute rapid cycles of experimentation and learning, share data, and appropriate higher investment budgets for their respective developmental projects.

Important considerations arise in a concurrent product development endeavor that involves a customer and a supplier when the supplier's product is a subsystem of the customer's product. In this situation, the question facing the supplier and the customer is how the PDCP should be applied. For example, the supplier of the subsystem must go through alpha phase characterization testing of its product internally and then ship "beta" units to the customer in time for qualification testing in the alpha phase of the whole system at the customer's location. Feedback from the customer's test results should subsequently be incorporated in the supplier's product. During subsequent system beta testing by the end user, new shortcomings with the supplier's subsystem might be identified, which the supplier must correct concurrently with its customer. Therefore, the supplier should go through the full PDCP process. The supplier should follow the PDCP even if the PDCP is internal to the company, as is the case in many large companies that establish an internal central organization to supply subsystems that are common to multiple product lines of the company.

7.3 PROCESS ORIENTATION

Management of a product development process must have "teeth" to ensure that the PDCP process is followed and that the exit criteria of each phase are obeyed by team members. Having "teeth" means that deviating from the established process has serious consequences. A management approval process with "teeth" is one that will not allow shipping of a new product to a customer, even for beta customer evaluation, until the alpha phase is successfully exited. This requirement does not mean that management cannot relax the exit criteria and take a calculated risk as a trade off for other commercialization imperatives such as time to market, customer relationship, or product positioning.

What is important is having clear success criteria for each phase of the PDCP, a list of measurable metrics in satisfying the criteria, and a rigorous methodology for process implementation that includes exceptions and provisions for deviating from the baseline process. The following guidelines are recommended when setting success metrics for exiting from each phase of a PDCP:

- Alpha phase metrics should include functional and reliability parameters. The success threshold for alpha parameters should not be below the MRS level; however, only a subset of MRS parameters can be included in the alpha criteria if compliance to the remaining MRS parameters is deferred to a subsequent phase.
- Beta phase metrics should include such parameters as manufacturing cycle time and labor cost; a "hit rate" in winning DTOR (design tool of record) and PTOR (production tool of record) positions with industrial customers; and the number of product performance defects reported and resolved.
- Gamma phase metrics should include sales volume and gross margin n months after product launch, installation and warranty (I&W) costs, and time to install and qualify the product in a customer's production ramp (time to money) for industrial customers.

7.4 KAIZEN IN PDCP

The PDCP process must be continuously improved to ensure that the process remains efficient as the enterprise context and external environment change over time. An organization must have efficient and flexible mechanisms, structures, management tools, and decision-making processes that are fact based, timely, and continuously renewed.

"Doing things right the first time" requires a concerted effort to improve the PDCP process through a series of small steps based on past learning and forward-looking needs. The Japanese refer to this approach as *kaizen*, which means "improvement."[1] Continuous improvement of a product development process should encompass all endeavors—from marketing and customer relationship management to product design, prototyping, and testing to launch and commercialization.

Successful organizations do not ask their people for heroism or miracles. Successful organizations seek and reward innovation, risk taking, commitment, and quality results from steady and focused efforts. Successful organizations practice the habit of conducting constructive self-examination for learning to avoid making the same mistakes and to achieve a high degree of environmental awareness about customers and competitors to continuously improve their responsiveness.

A well-managed company follows a business process that insists on accountability and ensures timely results. An effective project management process clearly defines the responsibilities and accountability of the resources within the company and in the supply chain; focuses on objectives for effective execution; monitors progress and measures success through a set of quantifiable and actionable indicators; and regularly reviews performance against a target for management decision making. Applying kaizen in all business processes in an organization must be an integral part of operational strategy and must include a reward system that promotes, recognizes, and rewards kaizen initiatives by everyone in the company.

7.5 MANAGING CRITICAL INTERFACES

Adhering to world-class project management practices is essential in "doing things right the first time" in product development. Above all, project management is about managing *interfaces* between *people*, *tasks*, and *product subsystems*. *People interfaces* shape the dependencies and influences and encompass the interactions among team members, the relationships with customers, the transactions with suppliers, and the interactions with company executives. Project *task interfaces* and team member (people) interfaces are interrelated. They are established by the project organization, how the tasks (and their input/output) are defined, and to whom the tasks are assigned (i.e., who does what and by when). *Product subsystem interfaces* define the subsystems and components of a product and their interactions.

The dynamics of any system, whether it is comprised of people, project tasks, or product subsystems, is determined by where the interfaces are drawn and how the elements of the system interact. In product development, the performances of the three "systems" must be simultaneously optimized—the "systems" of people, the development project, and the product.

The customer interface is established *formally* by contract, specification, and SOW (statement of work) and *informally* through marketing efforts in setting customer expectations. The customer interface is managed through customer relations management (CRM), expectations management, information management, and surprise avoidance.

The supplier interface is also established formally and informally. The supplier interface is best managed through a crisp definition of input/output, performance expectations, and the timing of deliverables.

Executive relationship management (ERM) is another important element of interface management in product development. The product development team must proactively engage in ERM, including information flow to management, understanding the changing priorities of company executives, being visible to company management (because "out of sight" is "out of mind"), and seeking management support for resources and assistance in removing obstacles.

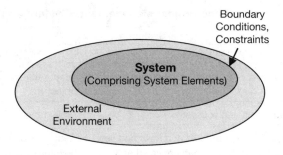

Figure 7.7. Schematic—The System Concept.

Efficient project management includes a continuous monitoring and feedback system through frequent design and project reviews in which closed-loop corrective actions and cycles of learning for knowledge creation are decided and enforced.

7.6 SYSTEMS ANALYSIS, SYSTEMS ENGINEERING, AND LIFE CYCYLE THINKING

In product design and in managing projects in product development, systematic thinking is essential for doing the *whole* job. Development projects are often comprised of multidiscipline tasks, involve technical risks, are driven by external factors such as customer requirements, and are constrained by resources and company priorities. Most high-tech products are also complex systems that must match the technology to a market context by integrating multiple technologies and must take into consideration many conflicting requirements and heed many constraints. System engineers must "flow down" the MRS requirements to the product elements (subsystems and components) in the ERS, integrate the elements, and verify system performance. All this can be done by applying systems analysis principles:

- Systems analysis is a systematic examination of a problem in which the system is designed for optimal performance by considering the behavior of all elements of the system, their interdependencies, and effects of boundary conditions (the environment), system constraints, and resources.
- Systems analysis methodology leads to established objectives by examining alternate approaches, applying a system model, and selecting the optimal approach based on a set of criteria.

A schematic representation of a generic system concept is illustrated in Figure 7.7.

Remembering that a complex product as well as a multitasked program is a system whose analysis and optimization can deploy systems analysis methodology, the terminology for both a product and a development project (as the system) in systems analysis is presented to clarify subsequent discussions (Table 7.1).

Product development from a systems point of view requires life cycle thinking (LCT). LCT considers the product in the context of the entire value chain throughout the product's life cycle. To design for manufacturability, safety, serviceability, and environmental sustainability, LCT requires diligent assessment of the interactions of the product with the external

Table 7.1. Product Development and Project Management—System Analysis Terminology

System		
Attribute	**As Product**	**As Development Project**
Function, Behavior	Output that satisfies MRS requirements	Output that satisfies project objectives
Elements	Components and subsystems	Project tasks
Structure	Architecture of a product and how modules and subsystems are interconnected and what portion of the total system behavior (or function) are carried out by each	Sequence of tasks of a project and how they are interrelated and what portion of the total system behavior (or function) is carried out in each task
Interfaces and Interconnects	The boundaries between the subsystems and between the system and the external environment	Organizational relationship, work flow, roles and responsibilities of the team members, and the sequence and input-output relationships of the tasks; the boundary between the project team and external stakeholders (management, suppliers, and customers)
Context	System dynamics established by the interactions between the system elements, the governing physical laws, and the boundary conditions as the driving force (System dynamics can be modeled heuristically or based on physical laws.)	System dynamics established by the firm's organizational hierarchy, culture, norms, value systems, business processes, and the structure of a project organization, including the authority and responsibilities of the team members and project manager
External Environment	Conditions within which a product is intended to perform and be evaluated for quality, including the MRS, system constraints, and customer operating environment establishing the product boundary conditions and customer's expectations (The external environment also includes the supply chain and other stakeholders who impact the product life cycle performance through their input or requirements for the product output.)	Expectations of stakeholders (customers, investors, management, competing projects, functional managers, peers); constraints and behaviors defining the boundary conditions on the project (system)

environment that encompasses manufacturing, the natural environment, and the consumer's operating environment.

This section is an overview of basic concepts in systems analysis. Numerous sources may be consulted for a comprehensive treatment of systems analysis and systems engineering for product development.[2–9] The section begins with a case study in systems engineering for thin-film deposition equipment used in an IC fabrication process.

CASE STUDY—SYSTEMS ENGINEERING FOR ROBUST DESIGN

Context. This case illustrates the importance of systems engineering in designing a complex product and in understanding its behavior. The case reviews thin film deposition equipment designed and manufactured by NATL Corporation. The system schematic in Figure 7.8 is comprised of a complex set of interrelated subsystems and components.

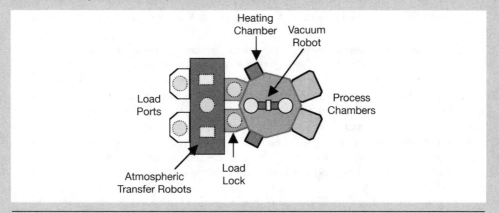

Figure 7.8. Schematic—Process Equipment System.

Situation. Ten systems were shipped to a major 300-mm wafer fab in 2001. Shortly after production ramp, the systems exhibited a major failure. Customer product and non-product wafers alike broke at the heating chambers of the systems in all ten of the tools in the fab. The frequency of breakage was 1 in 1000 wafers, 50 times higher than the customer specification, which caused a significant disruption in the fab operation. At the system process step, 300-mm product wafers were worth tens of thousands of dollars each, making the failures very costly indeed.

Action. A senior executive at NATL assembled a high-level team of engineers and personally led the effort to troubleshoot and resolve the problem as quickly as possible. The team installed several cameras on various tools in the fab and collected data for every possible variable that they could think of over several days. The team also reviewed the product design and assembly drawings to identify documentation changes or manufacturing discrepancies that could have contributed to the problem. After a week, the team summarized their observations:

- The vacuum robot transfer plane was 3 mm below the design specification. This discrepancy varied from one machine to another.
- Wafer lifter travel inside the heating chamber was 3 mm shorter than specification.
- To increase system throughput, the vacuum robot had been set by the customer's operators to travel at a higher speed than recommended.
- Most of the broken wafers were non-product, old, and recycled. Recycled wafers were thinner than standard and were usually warped out of specification. The edges of the recycled wafers were also damaged or had some amount of deposit on them from prior processing.

Based on the above findings and analysis of the camera photos, the following probable causes were identified:

1. The shorter-than-specification pin travel in the heating chamber and misalignment of the wafer plane created inadequate clearance between the wafer and the incoming robot, causing the robot to hit the wafer and break it.
2. The electrostatic wafer holder in the process chamber occasionally malfunctioned, causing a wafer to break.

3. Wafers were sticking to the vacuum robot end-effector pocket. They broke when pushed up by the lifter pins in the heating chamber. The thinner recycled wafers were weaker and broke more easily. The design parameters that contributed to the wafer sticking problem were:
   - The end-effector pocket was designed such that the wafer was held by the edge to minimize back-contact scratching and particle generation. Since the temperature of the wafer and the end-effector cycled during the operation, the clearance between the wafer and the end-effector pocket varied exacerbating the problem.
   - Variability in the end-effector flatness and material could also have contributed to the wafer sticking.

Outcome. This case clearly demonstrates the strong interdependency among numerous elements of the system and its boundary and environmental conditions. Interactions of subsystems (the vacuum robot, wafer lifter assembly, chamber wafer holder, heating chamber assembly, and wafer transport chamber assembly), buildup of tolerances (in design, manufacturing, and installation), variation in system operating conditions (wafer and end-effector temperature cycling), variability in input parameters (condition of the incoming wafers), and variability in the system (customer) operating environment (running the robot faster than specification) all played a role in how the system behaved and caused wafers to break.

Using a systems engineering approach, the team was able to diagnose and correct the wafer breakage problem in 3 weeks. However, those 3 weeks were very long and nerve-wrecking for the team!

7.7 PRODUCT DEVELOPMENT—SYSTEMS ANALYSIS METHODOLOGY

Figure 7.9 illustrates a systems analysis flowchart that can be used in all stages of product development and problem solving. In the discussion that follows in this section, system *refers* to a product and its modules or a project and its subproject task.

The systems analysis process begins with the objectives that must be accomplished. In product development, objectives are established by the MRS (market requirements specification). In managing projects for implementing the various phases of PDCP, objectives are specified in the project statement of work. The MRS and project statement of work also delineate system *constraints* that could be financial, timing or policy related, or that specify boundaries and additional requirements that the system solution must address.

The next step is *translation*, which is a restatement of the *objectives* and constraints in terms that are suitable for analysis. In product development, translation of the MRS and system constraints are developed in the engineering requirements specification (ERS) that engineers use in analyzing alternate design concepts for the system.

The third step is *analysis* to develop possible approaches for attaining the objectives. The analysis process takes into consideration the availability of resources and capabilities and takes advantage of (the firm's) retained knowledge, new technologies, and new approaches.

Trade-off studies follow the analysis step. Trade-off studies apply (predefined) selection *criteria* to choose optimal (design) approaches and tasks for implementation.

The next step in systems analysis is *synthesis* in which the selected (design) approaches or tasks are integrated into the *whole* system (i.e., the product or development project). Often it is necessary to *iterate* between the synthesis and the trade-off studies to improve the selected system, to characterize it (i.e., to evaluate the response surface and sensitivity of the solution to environmental factors, input parameters and assumptions), and to identify risk-mitigation backup approaches.

A system *model* is often used in trade-off studies and in characterizing the selected optimal system performance. The system model accounts for the interdependence of system performance

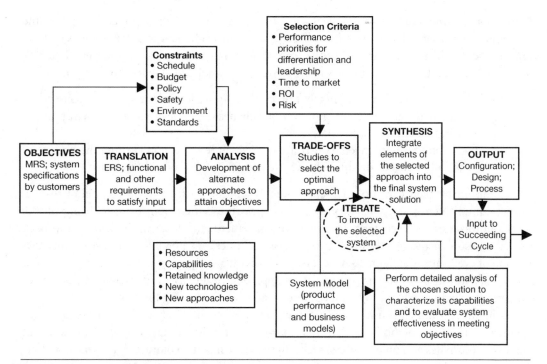

Figure 7.9. Product Development—Systems Analysis Methodology.

(vis-à-vis objectives), system attributes (see Table 7.1), and system resources. In product development, both a product performance model and business model are required in selecting the optimal product design for commercial success. Product performance models could be physical (based on governing equations of physics) or experimental (based on data collected through DOE methodology).

As a last step, the selected system solution must be *evaluated* for its effectiveness in meeting the objectives. In product development, the *output* of system analysis is an optimal product design, configuration, and manufacturing process. If systems analysis is done for a module of a product, the output will be an *input* to a subsequent cycle of systems analysis for the *whole* product.

Remember that systems analysis methodology applies not only to product design development, but also to problem solving, project management, and in fact to any set of integrated business activities (that constitute a system.)

Managers and engineers often focus on local *optimization* of the task at hand or a subsystem module, without regarding its impact on the overall program or system. The same applies to managing an enterprise, in which managers of organizational units are frequently preoccupied with maximizing the performance of their own unit, irrespective of whether (or not) doing so leads to optimal performance of the global enterprise. This local optimization approach results in misdirected deployment and wasteful utilization of resources and missed overall objectives. Systems analysis methodology via cycles of analysis and synthesis of system elements is necessary for *global* performance optimization.

Eliyahu Goldratt points out that the practice of local optimization in manufacturing results in missed production targets and excessive costs because it maximizes output at every production cell, builds a large WIP inventory to buffer variations in the input and output of the unit, and adopts a large-batch manufacturing method.[10] Instead, managers should focus on local improvements which have a strong positive impact on achieving the global objectives. Goldratt's theory of constraints advocates the following steps to link local and global optimization:[11]

1. Identify the "real" constraints that preclude achievement of the system objectives.
2. Eliminate the artificial constraints (typically because of legacy management policies and business processes).
3. Focus on the "bottleneck" constraints, direct all resources on keeping the bottleneck fully utilized, and build buffer inventory (safety) to feed the constraint.

Common problems in project management, including lack of resources, being rushed, unmet commitments, and unclear projects/task priorities, often stem from focusing on the local optimization of each task. In project management, the local optimization approach strives to resource and to execute all project tasks as quickly as possible and to maximize utilization of everyone by assigning several tasks to individuals. A project manager pressures every task owner to finish as early as possible. This approach results in an unreliable estimation of the overall schedule (i.e., mostly padded) and in all tasks competing for priority.

Goldratt recommends using the CCS method (critical chain scheduling) in project management.[11] The CCS method moves from a "hard" commitment to task deadlines to "soft" but aggressive estimates and only "buffers" tasks on the critical path. Goldratt argues that completing each task on time is not important, yet completing the entire *project* on time is essential. Hence, the project manager should move schedule "floats" at individual tasks to a project completion buffer and provide a *safety buffer* in front of each feeder task of the *critical chain*. Multitasking should be minimized and resource priorities should be set according to the buffer situation. Goldratt also recommends "percent of critical chain completed" and "percent of project completion buffer consumed" as primary indicators of progress for the project.

The behavior of a supply chain as a business system also reveals the need for overall system optimization to achieve efficient working of the chain. For example, the "beer game" demonstrates how a beer supply chain, from consumers to brewing factory, became unstable as a result of local optimization at every step unlinked to the overall system response.[12]

A strong interdependency also exists between the elements of the chain in the supply chain of the semiconductor industry. For example, mild cycling in the consumer electronic business is successively magnified in every step of the chain—from IC chip manufacturing to process equipment supply to components and material supply (see Chapter 11 for related industry data). Successively larger production capacity (or inventory) is built into the chain at every point of supply because of the lead time required to communicate needs at an upstream step. Rise in consumer market demand causes chip suppliers to build excessive channel (retail) inventory to keep up with the demand and to build additional capacity in anticipation of the up-cycle continuing. Wafer fab equipment suppliers, sensing a larger rate of change in their business (than IC manufacturers), ramp up their production capacity significantly. The response from subsuppliers (suppliers of the components and subsystems for wafer fab equipment) becomes even further amplified.

If lead time at every link is short, however, the supply chain becomes agile and can quickly adjust to business cycles, eliminating the downstream amplification effect. To shorten lead time and to minimize inventory at every link, suppliers must have a fast product development process, a short manufacturing cycle time, and a real-time communication process.

7.8 PRODUCT DEVELOPMENT—A GLOBAL PERSPECTIVE

The importance of having a global perspective to capitalize on global market opportunities and to safeguard against threats from global competition has been discussed in detail in Chapter 3. However, in implementing its global market strategy, a firm must adopt localized tactics, listen to local customers, understand the needs and wants that are shaped by local language, culture, and value system, and understand what entices customers to buy. Local competency in customer knowledge, customer support, product engineering, and manufacturing know-how is a strategic advantage.

Cultural diversity and global presence are imperatives of today's workforce strategy—which is to garner critical resources from across the globe (including people, technology, material and manufacturing capability). For example, in the design phase of a new product, the development team may be comprised of engineers from different divisions of the company and from different countries. A portion of the design might be outsourced to a contract engineering supplier with unique capabilities. Nowadays, outsourcing software development to engineers in India and Russia is commonplace among high-tech firms in the United States.

Global suppliers can be a great resource, not only for design, but also for rapid prototyping and manufacturing of the product. Taking advantage of the global supply base creates an opportunity for cost reduction in development and in product manufacturing, improved development speed, and access to product and materials technology. For example, in IC manufacturing equipment design, specialized ceramics or a coating material from a Japanese supplier can be an enabler in developing unique process capabilities. Use of low-cost and high-quality manufacturing in China has become a common practice in United States and Japanese firms.

Yet deployment of global resources in product development and manufacturing also creates unique constraints and challenges in project management. Managing a virtual team from across a global enterprise and a global value chain requires the right skills, infrastructure, and business processes. Real-time global communication, ensuring a win-win strategy for all participants, IP ownership/protection, and product documentation are a few of these challenges. For example, in product design, CAD tools used by team members in different locations must be compatible. U.S. firms which are still designing in English units must change to designing in metric units because the rest of the world uses metric units.

Product development with a virtual team also requires a certain degree of formality in the management of concurrent designs by disperse engineering groups. Definition of the interfaces of subsystems and the scope of the work and deliverables from different groups must be well documented and updated frequently to reflect changes in project direction and priority.

7.9 MANAGING CONSTRAINTS

Most high-tech product development endeavors are constrained by resource limitations, tight schedules, and myriad design and manufacturing constraints. Product development teams often feel that they do not have a sufficient number of engineers to do the job and that the project budget is too tight to build the right number of prototypes and buy the necessary equipment and materials for testing. The development schedule also appears to be too rushed for the team to do their job thoroughly. Constraints on product design are another source of frustration. Examples of design constraints include backward compatibility in design, the use of existing or commercially available parts, packaging in a limited space, design to target cost, and designing around a competitor's patented concepts.

Although most of the constraints imposed on a product development team seem stifling, they in fact stimulate innovation in many cases. If the constraints of time, resources, space, and interface compatibility are removed, the product development effort will be wasteful, which results in an inefficient and inelegant design that misses the market opportunity and will never be used by anyone.

Many large companies have found that having a "fat budget" is often a pitfall in a new innovative product development. In the development of breakthrough technology products, start-up companies with limited resources can win out over rival corporations with deep pockets. The low-budget constraint in a start-up company forces the team to focus on what is important to the market, to stay close to customers, and to not spend too much time on a wrong strategy or design approach. Teams at large companies often spend too much time and resources on selecting the optimal path, developing backup plans, and developing non-value-added features and capabilities for their products. Start-up companies are often nimble, have a sense of urgency, and are more resourceful in inventing solutions, in doing more with less, and in doing things in a clever and efficient manner. In start-up companies, prototypes are often built with used equipment and commercial parts at a fraction of the cost that large companies spend. In start-up companies, offices are not fancy, the facilities are inexpensive, and management does not spend much capital in developing the operational infrastructure, hiring non-critical staff, and increasing corporate assets and the cost base.

Some large companies try to overcome the inefficiencies caused by an "abundance of resources" and bureaucratic procedures by creating a "mini-environment" or an *incubator* within the firm to emulate the efficient team environment of a small start-up. These mini-environment teams are sometimes physically isolated from the rest of the company to maintain focus and to establish a strong sense of belonging to the team. However, the effectiveness of mini-environments and incubators is often limited because the large company's bureaucracy does not "let go" of all the operational strings such as purchasing or accounting rules and management approval procedures. Within a large company, the reward system for the innovators and entrepreneurs is another source of limitation in creating the resourceful environment of a start-up.

7.10 FOSTERING INNOVATION AND ENTREPRENEURSHIP

Innovation and entrepreneurship are the underpinnings of success in new product development in high-tech markets. Innovative ideas that are developed into revolutionary, quality products and are commercialized quickly are the engine of business success. Innovation is "thinking out of the box" and creating new ways of doing things and solving problems that captures the imagination of customers. Innovation is anticipating the market opportunities that will be enabled by disrupting the status quo and by substituting competition, even if that "competition" is a solution that is offered by one of the firm's own products.

The challenge facing management is to promote innovation while also following the PDCP with the discipline that is required for flawless execution. Organizations create procedures and routines such as quality management systems (QMS) to perform predictable and quality work. However, procedures and routines stifle the innovation that is crucial in market creation and product differentiation. Corporate leaders must proactively manage this tension—insist on having discipline and following best practices *and* also encourage creativity and reward innovation and imaginative thinking that will circumvent inefficiencies. Managers must discourage "we cannot do it" tendencies and encourage "what does it take to do it" thinking—a climate in which "why not?" and "how else?" are the norms of discourse.

Innovation is "uncomfortable" because it requires abandoning the familiar for the unfamiliar. Therefore innovation must be nurtured through development, recognition, reward, and role modeling. Successful innovation is characterized by skill, serendipity, motivation, concentrated and coordinated work, awareness of the work of others, and awareness of market needs (to make innovations relevant). Managers must create a work environment in which people can develop these necessary characteristics and in which measured risk taking and an absence of judgmental thinking are prevalent so that new ideas can flourish and be built upon.

7.11 COMMON INNOVATION PROBLEMS IN LARGE COMPANIES

Past successes and institutionalized norms and procedures often make large organizations "risk averse." Large companies feel that if they fall behind, they can always be a fast follower and catch up because of an abundance of resources and "deep pockets." Because past practices have led to success, large companies often tend to not anticipate market opportunities that can be created and threats that can be preempted by disruptive innovation that substitutes for existing solutions (including their own products).

Employees in many large companies have limited freedom to explore out-of-the-box ideas because of inadequate enticement (and insufficient funding) for "under-the-table" activities. Ironically, because of an abundance of resources, employees often lack the resourcefulness for doing *low-cost* pre-E&F experimentation. Instead they rely on budget allocations through the maze of approval procedures. Too much energy is consumed on variations of existing products compared to new technologies and disruptive products. Some large corporations adopt remedies to the above tendencies and shortcoming with varying degrees of success. Actions that can be taken in larger corporations to promote innovation include:

- Have executive management sponsorship of pre-E&F activities, which includes funds, attention, encouragement, and participation.
- Establish business incubators to facilitate disruptive innovation, whereby any employee may propose a plan for a new business initiative and receive funding if approved.
- Create a mini-environment with business processes that allow the mini-environment to function like a start-up company, including the authority for quick action, freedom in decision making, physical isolation, and an opportunity to receive rewards that are commensurate with results. An internal "board of directors" should be set up as the sole body to approve the strategies and business plans of the mini-environment and to authorize its funding.
- Require company BUs to include a *balance* in their budgets to allow for innovative product development in addition to CIPs. (See Chapter 10 for a detailed discussion of managing a balanced product development portfolio.)
- Have metrics for measuring the performance of a BU that includes an innovation metric such as "the percent of revenue from new products developed within the past 2 years." This metric will measure the appropriateness of innovation and the

BU's ability to anticipate market opportunities. For this metric, a number over 50% is an appropriate threshold in high-tech markets.

- Ensure that the team responsible for new product development has the "right" makeup.

Makeup of the team is a major factor in infusing innovative thinking and entrepreneurship in a new product development process. Managers and lead engineers who have a strong record of success in the company's past products may not be the best choice for development of next generation, breakthrough technology and disruptive products. In Tracy Kidder's Pulitzer Prize-winning nonfiction book, Seymour Cray, inventor of Cray supercomputer, is quoted as saying that "he liked to hire inexperienced engineers right out of school because they do not know what's supposed to be impossible."[13]

In early 1990, a study at GCA Corporation noted that the team that had developed a successful first-generation product for the company had failed to develop a successful second-generation product. The main reason for the failure was that the team wanted to repeat what they had done so successfully in the development of the first-generation product.[14] Yet at Lam Research Corporation, a completely new team (with many members who were new to the industry) was assigned to develop the company's second-generation product in 1985. By 1985 most of the engineers who had worked on the first-generation product were gone. They were members of the Lam start-up team that were no longer at Lam. However, the new team developed a highly successful second-generation product that gained market leadership in only 1 year after introduction. In many cases, even a new sales force or a different distribution channel will be required for a new disruptive product.[15]

An experienced team tends to repeat past practices and use the initial success formula, but the new realities of the market and technology often require a new formula and fresh thinking. The assumption that old rules can be extrapolated to new realities is often wrong. Christensen's research shows that when the functionality of technology surpasses customer needs, cheaper and simpler products, even if they have less functionality, can create a new disruptive market and be a substitute for older products.[16] In other words, the old rule of "more functionality is better" cannot be extrapolated past the time when it exceeds customer needs.

Innovation in product development is not the sole act of a lone genius in inspired isolation. Innovation in product development is a process of uninhibited and focused creation that is inspired by learning, integrating, and building on other ideas. To make an innovation process efficient and effective, the organization and the product development team must:

- Innovate in the space and dimensions that are important to the customer's success and create economic value.
- Traverse organizational boundaries for learning and take advantage of the team and the company's collective capability and knowledge.
- Form constellations or networks of linked capabilities and collaborate with other groups or individuals from other divisions, suppliers, and customers.
- Use best engineering practices and existing best solutions where applicable.
- Use adaptable and opportunity-based organizational designs to seize opportunities and execute swiftly.
- Focus on what the company does best (the *core competency*) and outsource the functions that are not critical to competitive differentiation (the *context*) to network alliance members.

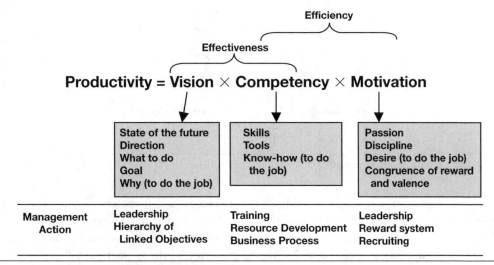

Figure 7.10. Model for Individual and Organizational Productivity.

7.12 ENGINEERING EXCELLENCE AND TEAM PRODUCTIVITY

To attain product leadership, the new product development team of technologists, engineers, marketers, manufacturing engineers, product support engineers, and others must be agile and flexible and have a high degree of productivity in the execution of the PDCP. The team must strive for excellence in every undertaking in the development process. As Aristotle said, "Excellence is not an act, but a *habit*."

Engineering excellence is achieved by doing the *whole* job, ensuring quality and timeliness of the output, pursuing perfection through kaizen, having discipline, and insisting on simplicity and elegance in design. Engineering excellence is an imperative of market leadership.

Individual and team productivity is attained through *efficiency* and *effectiveness*. *Efficiency* is achieving results with minimal consumption of resources, including time. *Effectiveness* is accomplishing the intended objective. To be productive, the expectations of what is to be done must be known and the individuals involved must have the necessary skills and resources and motivation to perform the job.

A model for individual and organizational productivity is shown in Figure 7.10. In this model, productivity is the product of three factors—*vision, competency*, and *motivation. Vision* is a statement of the future state—the direction, what is to be done, and why attaining the future state is important. The vision sets the goal and the basis of effectiveness. *Competency* is the skill, know-how, and tools that are necessary to perform the tasks for accomplishing the goal and for making the vision a reality. Competency refers to the individual team members' skills as well their collective ability to execute the tasks and to reach the goal. *Motivation* stems from a desire to perform the tasks and to accomplish the objectives. Motivation is related to the perceived importance of the goal to an individual or the team and the importance of the benefits derived from reaching the goal. Effectiveness is proportional to the product of vision and competency, and efficiency is proportional to the product of competency and motivation.

To maximize productivity, managerial actions are required for each of the three factors. Envisioning and articulating a clear and worthwhile goal requires strong leadership. Leadership action sets the direction and strategy and identifies the success indicators and criteria.

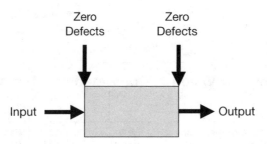

Figure 7.11. Defect-Free Development.

Management action for ensuring individual and organizational competency includes providing the resources and tools for performing the job and for training and development and establishing efficient business processes that facilitate performance. Motivation is maximized through leadership in creating a shared vision and conveying the importance of the goal. To motivate, managers must establish a reward system that is congruent to the employee's objectives and preferences. Great accomplishments are made by people who are passionate about a goal. Jack Welch, the celebrated CEO of General Electric Corporation, said, "You want the people who have passion, not those who know a lot of things, as the latter are curious and do not produce."

7.13 MANUFACTURING METAPHORS FOR LEAN PRODUCT DEVELOPMENT

Management of new product development can benefit from many quality tools that have been developed and successfully used in manufacturing in Japan, the United States, and other countries. Manufacturing concepts such as Just in Time (JIT), short cycle time, lean production, and zero defects are readily applicable in product development. This can be elucidated by adopting the manufacturing metaphor as observed by Patterson.[17] In manufacturing, value is added to material at every step of the process; in the product development process, value is added to information (or knowledge). The product development process can be envisioned as a "knowledge job shop" and as such many of the concepts and practices of manufacturing for increasing productivity, eliminating bottlenecks and waste (rework), improving quality, and reducing cycle time apply to product development.

For example, "defect-free" marketing is producing a complete specification that accurately captures the market requirements. Defect-free engineering is zero defects in design documentation, the software code, and experimentation. A PDCP is defect free when the inputs and outputs of all tasks are defect free (as shown in Figure 7.11). In adding value to information, input from one task (or discipline) to another is the output of that task or discipline. A project task is akin to a manufacturing work cell. For example, MRS is the input to engineering from marketing, and system architecture is an input to the mechanical design engineers from systems engineering. In product development, the task (work cell) owner's responsibility is to demand zero-defect input (and verify it upon receipt) and to produce zero-defect output.

According to Christensen, the "magic" of Japanese car manufacturing is the elimination of quality "randomness" by using a closed-loop control methodology.[18] Applying the manufacturing metaphor, defects in product development can be minimized by reducing quality "randomness" (or unpredictable quality) in specification, design, experimentation, and the output of other tasks in the process. Reducing quality randomness can be accomplished by early customer involvement, reducing time to market, and a systems approach that enhances the understanding of the interactions between different subsystems of the product and between the tasks of the project.

JIT in engineering is the availability of quality input information for an engineer to perform his/her task when he/she needs the quality input information. JIT in engineering minimizes wait, setup, load, and unload times, as is the case of a software engineer who receives the product "I/O map" from system control engineers at the right time (i.e., when the I/O map was needed).

Cycle time improvement in PDCP is eliminating queuing and waiting time. For example, in the development of semiconductor process equipment, often because of limited resources, the tasks of hardware, software, and reliability testing queue up at the only available prototype tool because this tool is being used by a process engineer who refuses to give access to other engineers who might change the tool configuration and impact process results.

The theory of constraints by Goldratt offers methodologies to improve manufacturing throughput by eliminating process bottlenecks.[11] Goldratt's methodology applies to both the project management and the systems design aspects of a product development process (PDCP). In a product development project, bottlenecks are the tasks on the critical path. The project schedule can be accelerated by focusing on these tasks and dedicating resources to them. In product design, system productivity, for example, can be improved by eliminating throughput bottlenecks because they determine the overall throughput of the system.

The concept of total quality management (TQM) includes doing the right thing, doing it right and fast, and doing so the first time. In PDCP, the "right thing" is an accurate MRS. "Right the first time" is eliminating rework in design. (See Chapter 6 for a discussion of these and other quality methodologies in product development.)

Kaizen, a manufacturing concept (continuous improvement of a process) which originated in Japan, also applies to PDCP. Organizational learning, knowledge retention, and reuse underpin kaizen in a product development process. An effective way of improving a development process is postmortem analysis of the methodologies deployed in design, testing, risk taking, decision making, market and competitive strategy, and other tasks of the PDCP. In a postmortem analysis, the team identifies what went wrong or what could have been done better. The improvements identified from such an analysis should be incorporated into the business processes and institutionalized to take effect. Important to note is that kaizen must be inspired by effectiveness and efficiency in achieving business results, i.e., the process should be changed only if the change reduces time to market, enhances the differentiating qualities of the product, and improves the product's ROI.

7.14 VIRTUAL TEAMS THROUGH STRATEGIC ALLIANCES AND SOURCING TO EXTERNAL AND INTERNAL SUPPLIERS

In product development, seldom does a firm have all of the necessary resources to execute the program and to commercialize and deliver the product to end users. Outsourcing design and manufacturing; acquiring existing materials, components, and subsystems from suppliers;

raising capital and sharing risk; acquiring complementary technology (IP) from partners and competitors; and acquiring market and enterprise operational assets from alliance members are necessary and desirable. Suppliers, alliance members, and partners in the value chain, together with the firm's internal resources, form a virtual cross-functional team for execution of the PDCP.

7.15 CORE COMPETENCY, CORE ACTIVITIES, AND LEVERAGING RESOURCES

In the formation of a virtual product development team, a firm must determine what capabilities are required for execution of its strategy and where the resources come from. The decision about whether the firm supplies the necessary resources internally or acquires them externally depends on the firm's business, technology, market, and operational strategies.

Should a firm own the required technology, should it hire people with expertise and know-how, or should an activity be performed internally or outsourced? The answers depend on the nature of the competency (technology or capability) and if the activity is "core" or "context."

Core competencies and activities are those that are imperative for creating sustainable competitive advantage and are enablers of achieving business and market strategy objectives. Core competencies enable a firm to do the "right-thing" better than other firms and core activities are activities that a firm must focus on in "doing things right." Core competencies and activities are essential to:

- Creating a unique value and developing a distinctive product differentiation
- Producing or delivering products and services to customers in a way that cannot be easily copied or substituted by the competition
- Strengthening the firm's market position for profitability and market share

Core activities should be "in-sourced" unless the company can maintain total control when the core activities are outsourced. Building and retaining core competencies within the company is important. However, time-to-market exigency, the cost and risk of acquiring core capabilities, and a firm's financial limitations might necessitate acquiring core competencies through partnerships and performing core activities through alliances.

Non-core activities and competencies that are often referred to as "context" should be outsourced. For example, many functions of a company's infrastructure could be considered to be a non-core activity, e.g., facilities management. Even engineering activities could be non-core when they are not contributing to a product differentiator. For example, the design of user-interface software for an electronic consumer product might fall into this category. (Later in this chapter, the framework for outsourcing and a methodology for supplier selection in product development will be discussed.)

7.16 STRATEGIC ALLIANCES

As mentioned earlier, the short-time-to-market requirements, risks associated with rapidly changing technology, dynamic high-tech markets, and large investments that are often required to create IP and manufacturing capacity, make acquiring core resources through strategic alliances and not pursuing a vertical integration strategy imperatives—true for both entrepreneurial start-ups with limited resources and larger companies.

Several criteria can be used in determining when the time is right to search for strategic alliances:

- The market is risky.
- Competition is too powerful.
- Developing the *whole* product (including the complementary and ancillary products and services) takes too long or costs too much.
- The company does not have the technology (IP) or necessary skills to develop the product.
- The company does not have the financial and technical resources and building the manufacturing capacity is too risky.
- Developing market assets (distribution channel and support infrastructure in the served geographic location) takes too long or costs too much.
- The company does not have knowledge of the segment or the customer relationship.

Strategic alliances and partnerships can be formed with all players in the value chain and with players that have complementary assets in other industries. A firm can partner with customers, suppliers, industry peers, and competitors to serve a strategic or tactical objective.

Partnerships with key customers for the development and definition of the *whole* product are important to ensure a deep understanding and timely compliance to customer requirements. In partnerships with customers, the development team must safeguard against the risks of too much customization for the partner (and hence missing the broader market opportunity that compliance with the MRS entails). Smaller companies or start-ups can capture the imagination of key customers and attract them as partners with an innovative, unique, and enabling technology. Occasionally, a partner/customer becomes interested in investing in a start-up company for development of their product in return for early access to the critical technology and competitive insulation. Customers might also be interested in partnering with a smaller company to create competition for their larger and more powerful suppliers and to level the playing field and strengthen their negotiating position.

Suppliers, as partners, can offer critical technology, know-how, production capacity, market access, and other enabling capabilities. Forming a strategic alliance with key suppliers is important not only to access their critical assets, but to also deprive the competition. Partnering suppliers can participate in the product design process, develop software or hardware modules, and manufacture components or subsystems of the product. Active participation of key suppliers in the PDCP accelerates the development of new technological capabilities and ensures that the product is designed to meet manufacturability and cost targets from the outset.

Peers that complement a firm's capabilities in *whole* product content, ancillary products assembly, delivery and support, including system integrators, distributors, and value-added resellers (VARs), are essential to commercialization success of the product. Formation of strategic alliances with these companies could provide critical customer access and market assets that the firm may lack.

Joining forces with competitors can also result in a win-win situation. Competitors can form alliances to create and penetrate a new segment in which they complement each other, share product development and production risks, and develop mutually beneficial industry standards and precompetitive technologies.

Strategic alliance with industry outsiders that are seeking diversification and that can provide critical resources in manufacturing, synergistic technological know-how, or geographic presence could be very beneficial. Strategic alliances can occur in companies of all sizes.

For example, in the semiconductor industry, instances of competitors sharing development risks abound. IBM, Toshiba, and Siemens formed a triad alliance in the late 1980s to share the risks of developing the state-of-the-art 256-Mb memory chip. More recently, Philips, ST Microelectronics (STM), and TSMC formed a vertical supply alliance to develop (STM), manufacture (TSMC), and market (Philips) IC chips for Philips' consumer electronic products.

Small pharmaceutical companies partner with large (and potentially competing) drug companies for the commercialization of their new products—as Scios Corporation did with Dupont, Merck, and Wyeth-Ayerst.

SanDisk, a leading supplier of flash memory cards to consumer electronics and computer markets, partnered with Toshiba in 2004 to build a new 300-mm fab to manufacture their jointly designed memory chip. Although Toshiba and SanDisk are competitors in certain market segments, both benefited from the alliance. They shared the risk and cost of building a $2 billion fab and gained time-to-market advantage by accelerating the joint chip design process (based on the design expertise of SanDisk and the manufacturing know-how of Toshiba). Samsung, the largest memory manufacturing firm in the world and an archrival of SanDisk, provided memory production buffer capacity to SanDisk.

Partnering with complementary outsiders wanting to get into the process equipment market helped Lam Research and Applied Materials in early 1990s. Lam partnered with Sumitomo Metal Inc. (SMI) to manufacture, market, and sell etchers in Japan. SMI, a large multibillion dollar corporation, had the manufacturing resources and large customer relationships in Japan that Lam lacked. SMI, on the other hand, needed the product and technology at Lam to enter into the semiconductor equipment market.

Applied Materials and Komatsu Corporation of Japan had a similar association. Applied Material formed a joint venture with Komatsu to manufacture and market process equipment for flat panel display (FPD) manufacturing worldwide.

Lam Research and Novellus, industry peers in the semiconductor process equipment market and potential competitors in the future, joined forces to compete with Applied Materials, a much larger and common competitor. Applied Materials, with a large portfolio of equipment, was capable of offering an integrated deposition, planarization, and etch solution to IC manufacturers. Neither Lam nor Novellus alone could offer such an integrated solution and effectively compete with Applied Materials, but with their alliance they could.

Partnership with suppliers is commonplace. Lam Research formed a partnership with Advanced Energy in 1994 to develop RF-power generation technology that was customized to the Lam plasma reactor design. Lam also contracted Brooks Automation to develop proprietary wafer handling equipment to accelerate time-to-market introduction of their new products.

Many consumer electronic companies outsource the design of their products, including software to Wipro Corporation of India. Fab-less IC houses, such as mobile phone companies, partner with and invest in their foundry IC suppliers for manufacturing of their chips.

Outsourcing of the engineering or manufacturing activities of a critical portion of a product is most successful if it is done in partnership with the supplier rather than on an arms-length contractual basis (Figure 7.12). Suppliers of core technology, critical know-how, or manufacturing capability should be an extension of an organization and actively participate in defining requirements, developing products, manufacturing prototypes, and supporting customers.

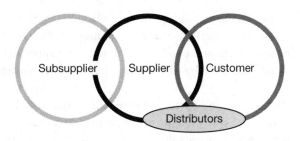

Figure 7.12. A Supply Chain Partnership.

A tendency within engineering organizations is to be vertically integrated and to do everything in-house. Purchasing organizations, on the other hand, prefer to have multiple suppliers to minimize dependencies and to ensure adequate supply and lowest price. Neither of these approaches works well in rapidly changing high-tech markets. Partnerships with key suppliers, combined with an open architecture and modular design, enable the development of a supplier capability for a timely product commercialization without creating an expensive and risky dependency on a sole bottleneck supplier—an approach that also encourages small entrepreneurial suppliers and complementors to participate and help the rapid growth of market assets.

7.16.1 Criteria for Choosing Strategic Partners

Choosing strategic partners carefully—to ensure a shared vision, compatible strategy, compatible chemistry, and a win-win outcome—is important. Strategic partners must have critical complementary capabilities so that the alliance gains combined strength. The partners must be able to trust each other, in commitment, in a win-win approach, and in top management's strategy and support.

Mutual understanding of the objectives, value contribution, and expectations of gain of partners helps to structure the alliance for a win-win outcome. For example, larger companies may be interested in a small company's new product for the opportunity to participate in a potentially lucrative emerging market, for replacing a costly in-house product development, for taking advantage of the small company's protected IP, and for leveling the playing field in the supply base of a critical capability. The small company, in turn, might be interested in the financial resources, production capacity, customer access, and/or market assets of the larger company.

Strategic alliances for developing and commercializing new products will last if win-win safeguards are built-in at the outset and the relationship is properly managed during the development process and the product life cycle. The central issue in a lasting strategic alliance is whether the perception of win-win interdependence extends past the initial celebratory enthusiasm of the parties in forming the partnership. How the relative power (for control) and the gain by a particular partner evolves over time, vis-à-vis its perceived value contribution to the alliance, determines the strength of the relationship.

Power is held by the company that controls a value chain choke point, the customer relationship (including access and the product interface with the customer), and the IP (protected IP and know-how). The customer relationship base of power changes as the product and the technology evolve over the market adoption life cycle. For innovators and early adopters, the partner that has the technology and system integration capability controls the customer relationship. In the early majority phase of technology adoption life cycle, the company that provides the *whole* product to customers and makes a commitment to service and support the *whole* product is in control. When the product becomes a commodity, the interface to late majority customers will be controlled by distributors that become the main point of contact with customers.

When Lam Research Corporation partnered with TEL in the early 1980s, and with SMI a decade later, to manufacture and distribute its products to IC manufacturers in Japan, the initial power arrangement in controlling the joint enterprise was stipulated as being equal by contract. Over time, however, the power position shifted significantly against Lam, resulting in breakup of the partnership in both cases. In the partnership of Lam and TEL, TEL controlled the customer relationship from the beginning, with Lam providing the key technological know-how. After a few years, when TEL developed its technological know-how on par with Lam, Lam no longer added any value to the partnership. The partnership broke up and TEL became Lam's number one competitor in the market worldwide. The alliance of SMI with Lam followed a similar path a decade later. Although SMI also broke off the alliance with Lam, SMI was not successful in becoming a formidable player in the market.

To remain relevant, maintain power, and sustain a win-win outcome in an alliance, a firm must ensure that it continues to add value to the alliance, e.g., through technological innovation, continuous improvement of the product's price/performance, support of partners to maintain constructive interdependence, protection of IP, development and maintenance of the customer relationship, and control of the interface to customers.

7.16.2 Strategic Alliances and Investors

Investors assign value to a company based on the actual and the potential served-market size, the share of the market that the company commands (or can capture), and business profitability. The question then becomes whether (or not) the strategic alliance erodes the firm's revenue, profit, and market position upon formation of the alliance and in future. For example, investors might discount a company's valuation in certain scenarios:

- Giving distribution rights in a large geographic segment to a partner for a long period and receiving a minimal royalty for the technology
- Entering into a low-margin pricing contract with a distributor who expects the firm to do significant product customization and to invest significantly in R&D for meeting future market needs
- Lacking IP protection and enabling partners (who might become competitors) to copy the product

7.17 SOURCING STRATEGY AND SUPPLIER SELECTION—IN-SOURCING AND OUTSOURCING

This section will first review cases in supplier selection. The cases will be followed by a discussion of issues in formulating an outsourcing strategy.

Suppliers are often independent corporations that provide needed products and services. The nature of the relationship between a firm and its suppliers is situational. For example,

Japanese automobile manufacturers classify the suppliers in product development into four categories—partnership, system supplier, "child," and contract manufacturer:[19]

- The *partnership* relationship is between equals. In this relationship the supplier has the technology, size, and global reach and the customer is interested in integrating the technology of the supplier into its products. The supplier assumes responsibility for an entire subsystem during product development and collaborates with the customer from the E&F stage onward.
- In the *system supplier* relationship, the supplier takes on a major responsibility with close customer guidance. The customer provides the specification for a complex assembly and the supplier develops the assembly on its own and suggests alternative design concepts (as necessary) to the customer.
- In a *child* relationship, the child supplier responds to the customer—the customer "calls the shots." The supplier develops assemblies according to the detailed specification of the customer.
- *Contract manufacturers* provide standard parts that are ordered from a catalog or make parts from the detailed design drawings of a customer.

In order to leverage economy of scale and improve efficiency, larger firms often centralize the functions of developing and delivering common products and services in other divisions of the company. These centralized organizations become de facto (internal) suppliers for other "customer" divisions in the company.

In the discussion of outsourcing and supplier selection, a broad view of the supply chain is taken and internal suppliers are included. A somewhat lengthy section is dedicated to the subject of internal suppliers because many large corporations attempt to centralize common products and services. These corporations often fail to make the internal supplier arrangement work effectively.

7.18 STRUCTURE AND MANAGEMENT OF INTERNAL SUPPLIERS

As already discussed, many mid- to large-size organizations centralize functions that are of common utility to multiple parts of the company to minimize duplication of efforts and to increase efficiency. For example, a company that is comprised of multiple product BUs centralizes finance, legal, and human resources management and delivers service to various BUs in a matrix-management fashion through the allocation of needed resources to each BU. Companies also centralize research, design, and development of technology, subsystems, and components that are common to the products of more than one BU. Although non-product central functions generally work well, internal suppliers of product subsystems and components are often problem-ridden.

This section examines the characteristics of product-related central organizations, and why so many companies struggle to make them work effectively, and discusses a framework that addresses the common problems. To clarify the discussion, a hypothetical case of a CPL division (**c**ommon **pl**atform) at SPEq Corporation (**S**emiconductor **P**rocess **Eq**uipment) is used as the setting for the discussion. Nonetheless, the concepts and the frameworks in this section are generic and apply to most firms and centralized providers of products and services.

The CPL division is an internal supplier of automation platforms, components, and subsystems that are common among product lines of several BUs at SPEq. Upon formation of the

CASE STUDY—THE HIGH PRICE OF NOT DOING THINGS RIGHT IN THE SUPPLIER SELECTION AND MANAGEMENT PROCESS

Setting. Manfred Casey (MC), chief engineer, and Jon Wang (JW), product manager, at Zylex were impressed by the two principals of ECo Corporation, whom they first met in 1986. The two principals were impressive communicators, astute engineers, and accomplished builders of precision electro-mechanical equipment. They were quintessential engineers with impressive credentials (Ph.D. degrees from Stanford University) and were very innovative and hands-on. Although these men ran a multimillion-dollar company, they spent half of each day in the testing lab, behind their CAD tool, designing products or operating machine tools and making precision parts. ECo was a local, small, private company that was founded just a few years earlier. The owners had grown it to a $5 million revenue level, primarily from the sales of custom products to R&D labs. ECo also engineered and manufactured all of their own products.

Situation. In 1986, semiconductor manufacturers were transitioning to a 200-mm wafer size to enhance fab productivity and to lower the cost of IC chips. Zylex engineers were designing a new 200-mm platform for the company's product lines and they needed to select key component suppliers.

To Manfred and Jon, the 200-mm robots at ECo seemed perfectly suited for integration into the new product family at Zylex. Manfred, who "promoted" himself as being extremely harsh on engineers and suppliers by demanding excellence in design, was recognized within Zylex as the "best engineer." He critically reviewed the brand new 200-mm ECo robot and sanctioned it in mid 1986. ECo robots were subsequently designed into the 200-mm platform at Zylex. The robots passed the alpha success criteria by late 1986.

The principals at ECo were "riding high" when Purchasing at Zylex notified them that the ECo product had been designed-in. They were assured of stable revenue for many years to come—that is, as long as 200-mm equipment was in IC production. Their egos were further inflated when executives at Zylex notified them of the company's intention to acquire ECo. Executives at Zylex were interested in acquiring ECo—not only for access to the seemingly innovative robot technology, but more importantly because Zylex wanted the ECo principals, who were regarded as model engineers, in the Zylex company. The ECo principals were touted as "geniuses" and they knew it!

The principals of ECo developed an ostentatious view of their capabilities and market price. At every opportunity, the ECo principals offered advice to the Zylex executives about how to design excellent products and manage an engineering organization.

Supplier contract negotiations between Zylex and ECo began in 1986. The standard Zylex contract was comprised of stipulations for IP ownership, production pricing, warranty, capacity planning, and other business matters. By early 1988, long after Zylex had informed ECo of the Zylex decision to design the robots into a future product line, still no written or even verbal agreement was in place. This situation existed in spite of Zylex having a supplier management organization consisting of 50 professionals who boasted that they could negotiate ironclad contracts with suppliers in the best interest of Zylex, ensuring that the selected suppliers were qualified according to tough set of criteria.

The Zylex executives, Manfred and Jon, did not want to upset the Eco principals and therefore side-stepped standard operating practices of Zylex and moved the robot qualification and the ECo acquisition negotiations forward—without a supplier contract. The Zylex executives argued that the decision was justified because they were sure that they would acquire ECo and the whole issue would become moot.

The negotiations for acquiring ECo and merging ECo with Zylex were conducted separately from the purchase contract negotiations and had the active participation of Zylex's top executives.

In spite of their "all-engineer" pretentiousness, the ECo principals were savvy business people and took full advantage of the situation. They were not in rush, so they took their time in negotiating the supplier contract of early 1986. Time was on their side for getting favorable terms, the Eco principals reasoned, because Zylex was more committed to the robots and started shipping them out in 1988.

In late 1987, Zylex offered to purchase ECo for $10 million. By May 1988, the price had climbed to $60 million. The ECo principals kept saying "no" to any price that was offered, without hinting at their asking price.

By late 1988, more than 50 of the 200-mm systems had been shipped to customers around the world and put into pilot production. However, in the field, ECo robots were failing at an alarming and unprecedented rate. At some customer fabs, the robot failure rate exceeded 50%! Customers were irate. Zylex was forced to order new robots at $15K each to replace the failed units in the field. ECo persistently denied there was anything wrong with the robots, blaming the system design or the operators for the failures. Because no contract was in place, the robots were not covered by a warranty even when ECo occasionally admitted that there was something wrong with a robot. The situation, ironically, was benefiting ECo because their sales volume increased every time a robot had to be replaced in the field. ECo refused to send any service engineers into the field because they had no one to send and the two principals were the only people at ECo who knew how to troubleshoot the failed units.

The robot failure issue at one Japanese customer site was so acute that the customer threatened to return all Zylex products! The Japanese customer summoned the product division general managers and met with the Zylex president in early 1989 to demand that all robots be immediately replaced by a Japanese robot.

By mid-1989, Zylex executives were so unhappy with the ECo robots and the behavior of the ECo principals that they abandoned discussions for ECo acquisition. They even considered bringing legal action against ECo for failed robots purchased by Zylex and for consequential damages in the amount of $4 million, but did not pursue the litigation option. ECo, however, took advantage of their boosted revenue (to a level of $20 million yearly), thanks to the Zylex order to replace failing robots, and secretly negotiated a $75-million merger agreement with another company in 1989!

By early 1989, the vice president of platform products at Zylex was convinced that ECo had to be replaced by alternative suppliers. She knew that it would take at least 9 months to develop alternative sources. In the meantime, she had to live with the ECo robots, fix the field problems, manage the customers, and buy more robots (although this would proliferate the problem!).

Outcome. A year later, ECo, under pressure and with a lot of help from Zylex engineers, resolved most of the problems (which happened to be manufacturing and product change control related). By then, Zylex had qualified robots from a reputable Japanese company and was ready to ship them to the field.

In 1989, Manfred and Jon characterized the ECo experience as "engineering enthusiasm, fueled by two excellent salesmen, overtaking doing things right." They admitted that they should have realized that ECo was a job-shop custom equipment supplier; had no experience in volume manufacturing; had poor document control and change management; and had very limited resources for customer support. The supplier management process was poorly managed at Zylex, putting the company at risk and in a very unfavorable negotiating position.

CPL division, the SPEq president assigned a senior executive who had been with the company more than 10 years as the CPL general manager.

The organizational structure of the CPL division could be characterized as central, internal, and fully controlled. The benefits of centralization to the company would be commonality in products and methods and synergy in innovation and knowledge generation across the company product lines. The benefit of keeping the common products and the methods internal and controlled versus purchasing them from external suppliers would be the protection of the IP and strategic technologies, which are competitive differentiators.

Table 7.2. Alternatives for Acquiring a Platform Solution at SPEq Corporation

Alternative	Make (Develop in BU)	Buy Externally	Buy from CPL
Advantages	• "Knows" problem • Controls priorities • Has good visibility of progress • Keeps staff deployed	• "Low" and predictable • Contractual control • Responsiveness • Core competency	• No IP jeopardy • Access and visibility to supplier engineers • Core competency • Proliferate innovation to other product divisions of company
Disadvantages	• Not enough resources • Platform not core competency of BU	• Leak of strategic know-how to competitors • Contractual delays	• Does not treat BU as a real customer in responsiveness and priority • Limited price control

The desire to have commonality of platforms, components, and methods across various BUs at CPL would be for enhanced efficiency through lower cost of R&D, manufacturing, and product support; faster time to market in development of new products; a common look and feel across product lines; and strengthened corporate brand recognition.

In order for the benefits of efficiency in time and cost to materialize, the CPL division must demonstrate that it can design, produce, deliver, and support products at a lower cost than competitors, including external suppliers and internal solutions by the BUs. The CPL division must also have significantly lower operating costs (R&D, general, and administration) than external suppliers.

The mission statement of the CPL division is to be the platform supplier of choice to SPEq product divisions by being more competitive than outside suppliers and by providing higher value (performance, delivery, support) at a substantially lower cost, as well as being more efficient than the make option of the product divisions.

When the SPEq BUs, which are internal customers of the CPL division, look for a platform solution for their products, they assess advantages and disadvantages of three alternatives:

- Develop the platform themselves (the make option).
- Buy from an external supplier.
- Buy from the CPL division.

The make-or-buy analysis of the BUs is summarized in Table 7.2.

7.18.1 Internal Suppliers—Framework for Competitiveness

Market context, the supplier's value proposition, and the supply chain structure form the bases for the competitive strength of a supplier. This framework holds true for an internal supplier as well. Market context is characterized by such factors as customer value systems and perception, the competitive landscape, and the state of maturity of technology in its life cycle.

The role of a supplier's value proposition in competitive insulation is determined by the strength of its product differentiators and supplier's power position in the value chain. For an

Table 7.3. Value Contribution and Power Position of CPL as an Internal Supplier at SPEq Corporation

	Value		CPL Contribution (%) Percent of Full Ownership of the Function	Switching Cost to BUs
1	Marketing (perceiving need and opportunity and end-user relationship)		30	Low
2	Product Development and Life Cycle Ownership	Components	70	Moderate
		System Integration	30	Low
3	Manufacturing and Subsupplier Management		10	Low
4	Sales (Distribution) and Logistics		0	Very low
5	After-Sales Support		5	Very low

internal supplier, the firm's organizational structure and business processes also impact the supplier's ability to effectively compete against customers' alternative sources of supply.

A qualitative analysis of the competitive strength of the CPL division at SPEq Corporation as an internal supplier of platform and automation products to the company's product business units (BU) is illustrated in Table 7.3. The table assesses the value contribution of the CPL division to the BUs in terms of performing the four fundamental functions of marketing, product development, manufacturing, and sales and support of a product. The value contribution of the CPL division is scored by answering the following questions:

- Does the CPL division perform the marketing function of perceiving opportunity and formulating product strategy in fulfilling the end users' automation needs?
- Does the CPL division spend R&D funds to develop and support products throughout their life cycle?
- What is the role of the CPL division in the manufacturing, distribution, sales, and support of automation and platform products? (*Note*: The CPL division is primarily an engineering organization. Its products are integrated as subsystems of process equipment that BUs sell to IC manufacturers in the semiconductor industry. Furthermore, SPEq manufactures all its products by a central manufacturing operation independent of the BUs and the CPL division. Sales and customer support are also done by the company's independent regional operations.)

Table 7.3 assesses the degree of dependence of the BUs on the CPL division as a supplier of platform and automation products in terms of the "switching cost" to alternative sources of supply (to make or to buy externally). The analysis in Table 7.3 is based on the assumptions that at SPEq, the equipment BUs have *competent engineering resources* to design and develop their own platforms and that they also have the *freedom* to buy platforms from external suppliers.

To protect the company's IP, the business process at SPEq barred the CPL division from marketing its products externally to either IC manufacturing customers or to competitors of its BUs. Furthermore, because the CPL division was an internal organization, it could not "protect" its IP (patented technology or unpatented know-how) from the BUs, i.e., when developing automation products using their own engineers, the BUs had unlimited access to all of the technology in the CPL division. Such unrestricted access to a supplier's technology and know-how is unique to internal suppliers and is a distinguishing factor of competitive strength from external suppliers.

As shown in Table 7.3, the market position and competitive strength of the CPL division as a contender to supply platforms and automation products for IC fab equipment are quite weak. Consequently, the CPL division struggled to remain a viable internal supplier. Only corporate executives and the centralized manufacturing organization at SPEq (not the internal customers of the CPL division, i.e., the BUs), cared about survival of the CPL division—the primary beneficiaries of the CPL division were the corporate executives and central manufacturing, which valued corporate synergy and product commonality.

The financial model for the CPL division was that of a central corporate engineering organization whose R&D budget was funded by the BUs through an allocation process. This model made the CPL survive not because of the merit of its contribution to the success of BU product divisions, but because of corporate support. The benefit of commonality that the corporate executives perceived as being justification to fund the CPL division was of minimal importance to the BUs. The BUs perceived the allocated cost of the CPL division as a "tax" on their R&D budget. Hence, resentment of the CPL division in the product divisions was high!

The situation of the CPL division is quite common in most corporations that fund a central R&D or manufacturing organization to develop and build common components and subsystems for use across several company product lines, e.g., Hewlett-Packard (HP) and General Motors (GM).

Hewlett-Packard. At HP, as the company grew and built a large portfolio of high-tech products in industrial and consumer markets, David Packard observed that most products used similar components. IC chips, power supplies, and microwave generators were among the most commonly used components across the HP product lines. Many components such as printed circuit boards (PCBs) could also be made in a central manufacturing operation.

Recognizing the benefits of efficiency in commonality and economy of scale, David Packard formed several central product and manufacturing divisions to serve as internal suppliers at HP. However, because these internal suppliers did not have to *compete* externally (or internally) to fund their operation based on the merit of their offerings to customers, none of the internal suppliers were successful. The products of the internal suppliers were "purchased" by a decree from corporate management in a captive internal market. Neither product performance nor the prices of the internal suppliers was tested in the open market for competitiveness. The internal suppliers "sold" their products to the business divisions of HP at cost, which was presumed to be lower than alternative external equivalents.

Centralization of common products, David Packard thought, had another benefit, which became known as "bench syndrome" at HP. Bench syndrome was a way of starting a new business operation for HP by developing a product that first served the internal market. If successful, an independent business division would be formed and the product would be marketed externally. A few internal supplier operations at HP over the years had limited success:

- IC business—a captive supplier, by management decree, that manufactured customized high-performance chips that were competitive differentiators for HP products—"HP product divisions always complained about the cost of chips manufactured by the internal supplier, but had no choice in switching to an external, more cost-competitive supplier," noted a senior executive at HP. After several years, the high cost of building new fabs to manufacture successive generations of IC technology eventually could not be justified by the production demand from HP products alone. The chip manufacturing division was allowed to sell externally, but it did not succeed because it did not have the necessary organizational infrastructure and marketing experience to compete with fierce Asian competitors.

- Universal power supply (UPS) for all product divisions—a successful power supply division of HP that sold its products externally, chartered by corporate mandate, developed a UPS for "all" HP products—The UPS was rejected by the product divisions (the internal customers) because of its undesirable form and cost factors. Because the UPS was designed to serve the requirements of a variety of vastly different applications, it became overdesigned for most products.

- Common microwave mainframe (MF)—the MF could be used by several product divisions that would add their own oscillator or other unique components as needed—The common MF became too large to be useful for most divisions and was rejected by all divisions.

- HP Common Manufacturing Division—a centralized internal supplier for making "strategic" parts, including PCBs, sheet-metal cabinets, and plastics—Establishment of this central manufacturing division was "forced" on HP by David Packard against the will of all the product divisions. Most of the operational units of the central manufacturing division were unsuccessful; the rest had partial success.

General Motors. GM also experienced similar results with common manufacturing. In 2000, an executive noted, "Common manufacturing has been a sour point at GM because product divisions don't have control or visibility over their product cost." GM's experience with Delphi Automotive Systems (GM's huge parts manufacturing business), however, was positive. While still an internal supplier, Delphi sold its unique fuel efficiency technology to Chrysler (and got the attention of other GM divisions!).

The root cause of failure of internal suppliers is the absence of free-market competitive forces. Having no competitor, internal suppliers are not obliged to be efficient or to deliver world-class performance and cost results. Hence, internal suppliers hinder the competitiveness of the product divisions—their internal customers.

7.18.2 An Internal Free Market Economy Model

The difficulties faced by internal suppliers at SPEq, HP, and GM can be overcome through the use of a business model that emulates the competitive forces of an open market—a model in which an internal supplier succeeds on the merit of its products and services having a compelling advantage over internal and external global competitors. One such model is proposed by Ackoff (1994, 1999)[20,21] and Halal, Geranmayeh, and Pourdehnad (1993).[22]

The Acroff model advocates an *internal market economy model* in which virtually all organizational units within a firm operate as profit and loss (P&L) centers within the company. The units can buy or sell products or services internally or externally, subject to an executive override. When an external transaction is not in the best interests of the corporation, the corporation pays the buyer or the seller the difference in lost opportunity.

Internal management consulting organizations at GM Corporation and Dupont Corporation have tried the internal market economy model with satisfactory results. The Strategy Support Center at GM, an internal management consulting organization, increased its share of business from GM divisions that sought management services. In competition with McKinsey & Co., Dupont Corporation had a similar corporate management consulting group that thrived in competition with external suppliers. They issued an American Express credit card account to their internal customers. These internal customers were charged when they used the services of the group.

7.18.3 The Internal Market Economy Framework—Applied to the CPL Division at SPEq Corporation

The president of SPEq approved adapting the internal market economy model to the CPL division after a year of trials and tribulations using the old cost allocation model. The adaptation was not "pure" because it applied to only one division (the Ackoff model is for all divisions and functions of a company) and had to heed several corporate constraints (noted below).

In setting the new strategy, the CPL division general manager argued that the internal market economy model would create efficient behavior by the stakeholders (including the BUs and the CPL division), resulting in the delivery of optimal value to internal and end-user customers. A financial model subsequently was established for the CPL division to promote conditions of a market economy inside the company and to make the CPL division a competitive supplier of platform products. Competitiveness of the CPL division depended on several factors:

1. Core competency in automation technology, performance in developing new products, and operational excellence
2. Rivalry through the presence of viable competitors
3. Demand conditions for its services (which was impacted by the resource availability and capability of the BUs in doing the job themselves)
4. The power position of the CPL division in the supply chain, including its relationship with end-user customers and subsuppliers of critical components such as robots and controllers

To be effective, the new business model for CPL had to be responsive to the above factors.

Within the new model, commonality and the benefits of synergy of the CPL division to the corporation could only be realized through delivery of value to the individual BUs as internal customers of the CPL division. The CPL division had to establish a supplier/customer relationship with the BUs and demonstrate sensitivity to their market needs with urgency, performance, and product cost. As such, CPL had to seek proactive collaboration with the BUs in understanding their market needs and in developing new products. Reward and loss consequences for the CPL division, based on its ability to satisfy market needs, also had to be in place.

However, the new model also had to allow the CPL division to run as an independent entity; to set its own priorities based on market conditions (rather than being micromanaged by the BUs or corporate management on a project-by-project basis); to set prices for its products; to generate revenue and fund its R&D and operation; and to ensure availability of resources to meet demand.

Because the finances of the CPL division were open to the BUs, the BUs drove the prices of the CPL division down to the cost floor. Preventing such a practice was challenging—it could only be met through an open-market bidding process in the market economy model. The BUs had a choice to make their own products or to buy them from alternative external suppliers. This environment created the necessary rivalry that drove the CPL division to "measure up" against world-class external suppliers and to become a responsive value-added supplier rather than merely a "corporate function" and "tax."

Management of the CPL division believed that they could operate effectively at a much lower gross profit margin than the external competitors because the CPL division had significant advantages—being an internal supplier and having very low marketing, sales, and operational costs. Platform and automation suppliers in the open market generally had a gross margin of 30 to 40% of revenue. The CPL business model, however, was structured for 8 to 10% gross margin, which made the CPL division a cost-competitive supplier, but it still provided sufficient funding for R&D and new product development.

To improve demand conditions for the CPL division, company management consolidated resources and competency for platform and automation engineering in the CPL organization—away from the BUs. This action was necessary to create momentum for the CPL division at the onset of establishing the new business model. Over time, however, the forces of an open market were allowed to play out, with the BUs being allowed to build up their own competency in platform engineering if they found the CPL division to be unresponsive to their needs.

Accounting for the prices paid for CPL products was "clean" at the BU level—prices paid were treated as cost of sales on their P&L, similar to an external supplier. At the corporate level, however, because CPL was an internal function, accounting had to be done differently. The indirect cost (of labor) for the CPL division was considered to be a "below-the-line" operating cost item on the corporate P&L.

The winning strategy for the CPL division was to gain (internal) market share by having a competitive advantage; leading customers in delivering differentiated solutions; and by collaborating with the BUs and winning their respect and intimacy. The CPL division discouraged the corporation from subsidizing its operation and strived to protect its market share by increasing the switching cost for its customers. Management of the CPL division believed that through responsiveness and strong subsupplier relationships that they could make the BUs dependent on the CPL and enhance their own competitive insulation.

The market economy model for CPL worked well. After a year, the BU customers considered the CPL division to be a responsive supplier of choice.

The next step for the CPL division was to move up the value chain—to become a system integrator of products for the BUs and to get closer to IC manufacturers (end-user customers of the company). The general manager of the CPL division thought this strategy would position the division as a world-class supplier of innovative platforms and automation products.

Management of the CPL division and corporate executives briefly considered a more ambitious model in which the CPL division was permitted to sell its products externally, inside and outside of the semiconductor industry. This meant that the CPL could sell its products to end-user customers and to competitors of SPEq. The idea of selling to competitors was rejected because the automation platform was still underperforming customer requirements and was deemed to be a source of competitive advantage in the process equipment market. Selling in non-semiconductor markets was also not pursued—out of a fear of "defocusing" the CPL division from serving the corporate mission of excelling in the semiconductor equipment market.

7.19 OUTSOURCING STRATEGY

The outsourcing strategy of a firm must enhance the competitive advantage of the firm and strengthen its position in the value chain. An outsourcing strategy must include provisions to protect core technologies of the firm; to enable exclusive access to critical technologies of suppliers in the target application; and to safeguard control of interdependent interfaces of product subsystems. The objectives of outsourcing in product development and commercialization are to:

- Accelerate product development projects and shorten time to market by leveraging the resources of suppliers
- Lower the costs of production
- Leverage suppliers' technology and manufacturing capabilities

When a design task and the manufacturing of a subsystem or component are outsourced, they should not contain a core differentiating technology, unless controlled. Furthermore, the interfaces of the outsourced subsystem/component to the overall system should be defined such that the outsourced function can be independently verified against specifications. If the performance of an outsourced subsystem/component cannot be readily defined and independently verified, the suppliers' switching costs would be high.

To the extent possible, buy "commodity components" and add value with the firm's own proprietary technology in integrating the component into the overall system.

Furthermore, to strengthen the firm's position in the supply chain and to maximize the share of value, do not lose control of the customer interface as a result of outsourcing. Providing a "total solution" to the customer with a differentiated and protected offering should be the basis of the firm's outsourcing strategy.

The outsourcing strategy should be regularly reviewed and updated to reflect realities of the marketplace, including changes in the bases of competitive advantage, technological maturity, competitive landscape, and evolution of the firm's core and context. Some companies form a *strategic outsourcing council* that regularly reviews the firm's core and context and updates the outsourcing strategy and decision process. The council membership should include key company executives from product engineering, manufacturing, marketing, supplier management, product business groups, finance, and enterprise operation.

7.19.1 Product Development—Implications for Design and Supplier Management

The above guidelines for outsourcing should be implemented from the onset in a product development process through application of the criteria and associated rules in Table 7.4.

7.19.2 The Outsourcing Decision Process and Dual-Source Strategy

Figure 7.13 depicts a flowchart for deciding if the design or the manufacturing of a component or subsystem should be outsourced and if a second source should be developed. Note that in addition to the design and technological criteria discussed above, Figure 7.13 safeguards against a supplier becoming a competitor of the firm and marketing the subsystem/component to end-user customers or competitors.

Table 7.4. Product Design and Supplier Management—Outsourcing Criteria and Tactics

	Decision Criteria	Implication for Product Design and Outsourcing	Implications for Supplier Management in Product Development
1	Is subsystem underperforming and a source of competitive advantage?	If answer is yes, consider not outsourcing, provided that the company has required competency and resources.	1. Integrate supplier's product-development project into the company's product development project. Have regular design and project reviews.
2	• Can function of subsystem be precisely specified and independently verified? or Can function of subsystem only be verified through overall performance of system? • Can interfaces to subsystem be precisely specified and controlled?	Redefine subsystem as a functional or structural module and specify its interfaces such that answer to these criteria is yes. Commodify subsystem!	2. Prepare ERS, roadmap, and verification testing criteria for subsystem as a part of the contract. 3. Have supplier commit to production cost target at onset. 4. Define company's strategy for customer support, spares, and CIP of subsystem. If any one of these is outsourced, ensure that supplier contracts with company and not customer.
3	Is subsystem comprised of technology and design that are not well understood, developmental, or proprietary of supplier?	If answer is yes, form a partnership with supplier for exclusivity or acquire technology.	

Note: ERS, engineering requirements specification; CIP, continuous improvement projects.

Developing a second source for the design or manufacturing of a core component or subsystem, or even a commodity/non-core component, requires significant investment and an extensive qualification process by the company and its customers. The firm's partnership obligations to the primary supplier may also constrain the second-source development and selection process.

A second source for design or manufacturing should be developed based on the framework in Figure 7.13. Furthermore, a second source should be developed if the primary (partner) supplier does not meet the company's performance, production capacity, or timing requirements because of poor execution (after having had an adequate opportunity to do so) or a change in the supplier's business conditions or a shift in strategy.

7.19.3 Supplier Qualification

Suppliers must be *qualified* in financial and organizational strength, technical and operational capabilities, quality of products and services, IP protection, and business contract for price and delivery. In developing high-tech products, a company often has to form partnerships with key suppliers for the development and manufacturing of core technologies, which necessitates that the partner supplier becomes an extension of the firm's engineering and manufacturing operations. The partnership arrangement must ensure that a supplier:

- Has adequate competent resources for timely product development, meeting production demand, and worldwide service
- Guarantees an acceptable price for production, including license fees

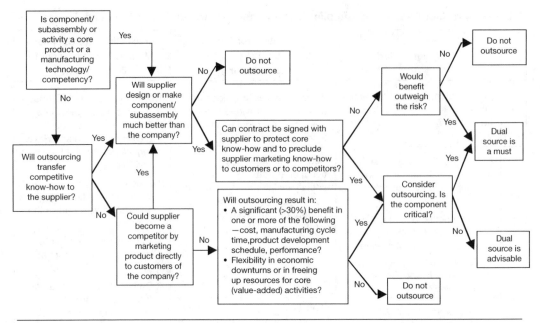

Figure 7.13. Outsourcing the Decision Process.

- Executes continuous improvement programs throughout the product life cycle
- Protects the company's IP and systems' know-how that will be inevitably shared with the supplier during product development

Supplier selection and partnership agreements must be executed carefully. Multiple sources of supply should be evaluated diligently before making a commitment. Alternate suppliers should be evaluated in the E&F phase of product development and screened for an enduring and winning partnership.

7.19.4 Make-or-Buy Analysis and the Sourcing Map of a Product

Starting in Phase 2 of the PDCP, product project planning, a make-or-buy analysis should be done for all development activities and for manufacturing of components, subsystems, and the entire system. Suppliers for commodity commercial components as well as key partner suppliers should be identified. If a make-or-buy decision and determination of the final supplier list are not possible in Phase 2, a list of leading candidates should be identified with an action plan and criteria for the final selection.

Figure 7.14 depicts an example of a make-or-buy tree (or sourcing map) of a process chamber module in semiconductor process equipment. The map is in the form of an assembly tree of all the major subsystems and components of process modules, with shading indicating (coding) the sourcing approach for each. The contract-manufacturer designation indicates that the part is designed in-house and made by a contractor. Outsource indicates that both design and fabrication of the component are done by suppliers. The T box (test point) indicates the point in the assembly sequence at which a subassembly will be tested to verify the manufacturing quality.

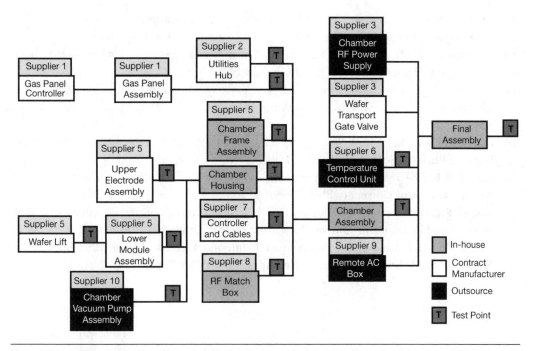

Figure 7.14. Make-or-Buy Tree (Sourcing Map)—Process Chamber Module of IC Manufacturing Equipment (see Figure 7.8 for layout of entire system). AC, alternating current; RF, radio frequency.

REFERENCES

1. Imai, M. *Kaizen, The Key to Japan's Competitive Success.* New York: McGraw-Hill; 1986.
2. Optner, S.L., Ed. *Systems Analysis.* London: Penguin Books; 1973.
3. Blanchard, B.S., Fabrycky, W.J. *Systems Engineering and Analysis, Third Edition.* Boston: Pearson Education; 1998.
4. Sage, A.P., Rouse, W.B., Eds. *Handbook of Systems Engineering and Management.* New York: John Wiley & Sons; 1999.
5. Kossiakoff, A., Sweet, W.N., *Systems Engineering Principles and Practice.* New York: John Wiley & Sons; 2002.
6. Blanchard, B.S. *Systems Engineering Management, Third Edition.* New York: John Wiley & Sons; 2003.
7. Faulconbridge, R.I., Ryan, M.J. *Managing Complex Technical Projects: A Systems Engineering Approach.* Norwood, MA: Artech House; 2002.
8. Oliver, D. W., Kelliber, T.P., Keegan, J.G., Jr. *Engineering Complex Systems, with Models and Objects.* New York: McGraw-Hill; 1997.
9. De Neufville, R. *Applied Systems Analysis: Engineering Planning and Technology Management.* New York: McGraw-Hill; 1999.
10. Goldratt, E.M. *Critical Chain.* Great Barrington, MA: North River Press; 1997.
11. Goldratt, E.M. *Theory of Constraints.* Great Barrington, MA: North River Press; 1990.
12. Heineke, J.N., Meile, L. C., Eds. The beer distribution game. In *Games and Exercises for Operations Management.* Upper Saddle Ridge, NJ: Prentice Hall; 1995, p. 101.
13. Kidder, T. *The Soul of a New Machine.* Boston: Little, Brown; 1981.

14. GCA Corporation, Bedford, MA: 1990, personal communication.
15. Lam Research Corporation, Fremont, CA: 1985, personal communication.
16. Christensen, C. *The Innovator's Dilemma: When New Technologies Cause Great Firms to Fail.* Boston: Harvard Business School Press; 1997.
17. Patterson, M.L. *Accelerating Innovation.* New York: Van Nostrand Reinhold; 1998.
18. Christensen, C. *Japanese Car Manufacturing Quality.* Cambridge, MA: Harvard Business School.
19. Kamath, R.R., Liker, J.K. *A Second Look at Japanese Product Development.* Reprint 94605. Harvard Business School Publishing; 1994 November/December.
20. Ackoff, R.L. *Re-Creating the Corporation: A Design of Organizations for the 21st Century.* New York: Oxford University Press; 1999.
21. Ackoff, R.L. *The Democratic Corporation: A Radical Prescription for Recreating Corporate America and Rediscovering Success.* New York: Oxford University Press; 1994.
22. Halal, W.E., Geranmayeh, A., Pourdehnad, P. *Internal Markets: Bringing the Power of Free Enterprise Inside Your Organization.* New York: John Wiley & Sons; 1993.

PROJECT MANAGEMENT IN PRODUCT DEVELOPMENT

The process of product development and commercialization (PDCP) is implemented through the execution of one or several interrelated *projects* or *programs*. A *project* is an integrated set of activities that has clear start and end dates and that achieves a goal within certain specifications and a funding limit. In *product* development, the overarching *program* goal is development and commercialization of a product that meets the objectives of the MRS (market requirements specification). For every phase and the tasks within it, one or more projects are executed to advance the PDCP to completion. Often an organization must choose among multiple product options in the investment of valued resources.

Effectiveness in project management (i.e., timely accomplishment of objectives) is not only dependent on the project manager, team members, and the methodologies that they apply, but also on the encompassing organization as a *whole*—its structure, business processes, and culture. The conditions for success that managers must create within their organization include:

- Everyone "pulls in the same direction." Team members serve the common objectives of the project that are aligned with global business objectives through a linked hierarchy.
- The *whole* job is done. Interrelationships and interfaces between product subsystems and various functions (marketing, engineering, packaging, suppliers, manufacturing, sales, and support) are understood. Interfaces are defined and inputs/outputs are served.
- Technologies and resources are integrated. Managers prioritize, track progress, perform trade-offs, hold meetings (following a hierarchy of objectives), and integrate the technology and tasks of the project into a *whole*. Subordinates, on the other hand, receive timely direction from managers and optimize their work.

- Accountability is built-in at all levels of the project. Accountability is not only essential for performance assessment, but also, more importantly, for empowering and motivating team members. People like to have clarity in responsibility and authority.
- Having an ubiquitous understanding of the essence of the project's purpose and why teamwork is essential for success is primary. Forms, reports, and methods are secondary.
- Have a dynamic structure, an agile decision-making process, and a real-time feedback system. The structure should serve all dimensions of the organization (including the technology, product, market, and business) and clarify reporting authority up the path of linked objectives.
- Plan by a discovery method. Ask: What does it take to meet the objectives—not what is the best I can do with what I have?
- Manage risk. Risk taking is accepted as necessary, but its impact is understood at all levels and risk mitigation actions serve the objectives.

Chapter 8 focuses on project management methodologies that enable the above conditions. Methodologies for managing a multiproject environment will also be discussed. (*Note:* The process of selecting a project through the prioritization of opportunities among a competing set and methodologies for aggregate product portfolio planning are discussed in Chapter 10.)

8.1 PROJECT MANAGEMENT TASKS AND A PROJECT MANAGER'S RESPONSIBILITES

The first step in project management is defining the project—its objective, scope, deliverables, and schedule. Subsequently, a project manager must be assigned to assume ownership of the project and to manage its tasks.

In different organizations, a *project* is referred to differently, including program, task force, tiger team, and others. In Chapter 8, *program* refers to "a large *project* that is comprised of several subprojects;" however, the terms *program* and *project* are used interchangeably. Although a *task force* or *tiger team* is often formed to respond to an urgent customer or organizational problem, and connotes urgency and elitism in membership, nevertheless, the rules of project management apply to these teams as well.

A project manager is also referred to by many designations, including team leader, champion, "honcho," owner, and task force manager. Projects for product development usually consist of many subprojects that carry out the tasks of the PDCP phases. These subprojects are referred to as tasks. Each task is similar to a project; therefore project management methodologies also apply to them. A task manager also has similar responsibilities to the project manager, albeit at the smaller scale of the task. The responsibilities of a project manager include:

- Prepare the *project plan* based on the MRS and the guidelines given in previous sections of this chapter (and also in Section 5.8.3, Phase 2—Product and Project Planning, in Chapter 5).
- If the project is funded externally through a contract, provisions of its SOW (statement of work) must also be included in the project plan.

- Although the project manager "owns" the project plan, he/she must prepare the plan in conjunction with resource managers (i.e., line or functional managers) and project team members. The proactive participation of functional managers and team members in the planning process ensures buy-in and internalization of the project objectives, strategy, and implementation approach by all stakeholders.
- Prepare the product's ERS (engineering requirements specification). The project manager must ensure that the ERS is prepared with the active participation of technical and marketing members of the team.
- Achieve project objectives on schedule and within budget. Produce the deliverables of the project, most importantly a released product, according to the PDCP guidelines and the project plan, within the project constraints of available resources, schedule, and approved budget.
- Meet external contractual obligations according to the SOW and the JDA (joint development agreements) with customers, partners, and suppliers.
- Be the communication focal point for the project and regularly report the project status and risk assessment to team members, company management, and customers.
- Manage the tasks of project management:
  - Maintain a sharp focus on project objectives.
  - Ensure effective deployment of resources, including people, material, plant, and equipment.
  - Clarify the project plan, its objectives, strategy, and assumptions. Update the plans and assumptions regularly as learning grows.
  - Manage internal and external dependencies.
  - Prioritize tasks, clarify decision criteria, and manage the tension between time to market, product performance quality, product cost, project cost (investment), and operational readiness.
  - Manage interfaces and integrate at all levels, from working level to management, fostering internal integration and integration of stakeholder needs into the product design.
  - Manage knowledge creation, retention, and integration within the project. Plan and implement cycles of learning for knowledge generation.
  - Manage risks. At all times, identify the top three project risks and the direct resources required to mitigate these risks. On a timely basis, communicate with management and customers about any risk that could jeopardize meeting a commitment. Communicate the corrective action plan for mitigating that risk.
  - Motivate team members for efficient and effective implementation of project tasks.
  - Monitor technical progress toward objectives, initiate corrective action plans, and follow up to completion until performance gaps are filled and risks are mitigated.
  - Hold regular project meetings to inform stakeholders, integrate dependencies, align objectives and priorities, and solve problems.

A successful project manager sees the "big" strategic picture, does the *whole* job, and aligns project objectives to corporate business goals. She/he is goal oriented and has a genuine interest in the project's success. A successful project manager has the attributes of a good leader—

one who motivates the team to have buy-in of the project's goals; stimulates and nurtures teamwork and the assumption of ownership and hard work; is an effective communicator, a skillful organizer, and an effective integrator in linking with critical suppliers and customers; and challenges internal and external obstacles.

An effective project manager follows the product development process and is familiar with the company's standard practices and processes, including BKMs (best-known methods) in project management. Management of a multidisciplinary project requires a *generalist* project manager more than a *specialist* project manager—i.e., someone who has a broad understanding of the technologies involved in the product and applications.

8.2 SOURCES OF A PROJECT MANAGER'S AUTHORITY AND INFLUENCE

Because most projects for the development of high-tech products are multidisciplinary, project teams are often cross-functional and managed in a matrix-type organization. This means that much of the resources necessary for the execution of a project do not functionally report to the project manager. In a matrix organization, many project managers find themselves in conflict with the functional managers (at the peer level or above) to whom the project's resources report. Furthermore, project team members have two "bosses." Therefore from whom they should take their direction concerning the priority of a task and how it should be done are unclear.

Without a clear arrangement and understanding of the project manager's authority by all stakeholders (including functional managers, BU general manager, corporate executives, and project team members), the project manager will not feel empowered in doing the *whole* job. Project managers may attain authority for directing resources and for setting priorities in managing project tasks in several ways:

- Organizational authority—Organizational authority is established when an organization has a project structure and project managers have hire/fire authority. Organizational authority is the most efficient source of authority. Project managers in this type of environment are sometimes referred to as "heavy" project managers.
- Delegated authority—Common in matrix organizations, delegated authority is attained when a general manager or an executive (who owns all of the functional resources of the project) bestows authority on the project manager, explicitly and implicitly. Delegated authority erodes over time. It must be sustained through continuous reinforcement and reaffirmation by the delegating executive.
- Implied authority—Implied authority is derived from an organizational title (e.g., director or vice president) or by an association that infers power (or access to power) for the project manager.
- Past successes and reputation—Having a reputation of being a leader who gets things done or as being a technical guru can be a source of authority.
- Leadership ability—Perhaps the most effective source of authority, leadership ability is attained over time and is a result of the project manager's actions in supporting the team "to win." Team members, in response to the actions of the project manager as a leader, follow the project manager enthusiastically if he/she has provided a clear vision and direction; has furnished the necessary resources; has

helped the team to solve problems; has made them "look good;" and has been a leader the team could "count on."

8.3 RESPONSIBILITIES OF A FUNCTIONAL MANAGER

Functional managers, including the managers of marketing, technology R&D, engineering, manufacturing, material procurement, supplier management, customer support, sales, finance, and quality, play a critical role in the success of a development project. Their active participation and support of projects from the beginning to the end is crucial.

Although project managers have primary responsibility for the "what, why, when, and how much" of a project, functional managers are primarily responsible for the "who, how, and where" of doing a job. Project managers establish project objectives, set priorities, define schedules, and control the budget. Functional managers assign the resources (who will perform the tasks), decide where the resources will come from (globally), and have the functional expertise about how the job is done. Functional managers are sometimes referred to as line managers, resource managers, or department managers. Project managers must work closely with functional resource managers and ensure that their project has the unwavering support of the functional managers over its entire duration. The most important responsibilities of functional managers are to:

1. *Ensure* that the department is staffed with an *adequate number of individuals* to meet the aggregate demand of all projects and that the department staff has the *right competencies* to perform project tasks.
2. *Train* the staff and provide the necessary tools for doing the job efficiently.
3. *Deploy* people to projects according to the requests of project managers.
4. *Motivate* and *guide* the staff to be "successful."
5. *Review* the work of staff members and ensure the *highest quality output*.
6. *Ensure* that the work area and conditions are *safe, equipped, and maintained*.

8.4 MIDCOURSE CHANGE IN PROJECT MANAGER

In a large multiphase project for a new product development, the leader or the project manager may change when moving from one phase of the PDCP to another. A change in leadership or change in the project manager might be made for a number of reasons, including alignment of the project manager's competency and the predominant content of a particular phase of the project. For example, in developing a high-tech product, Phase 1 (E&F) might be headed by a technologist, who is followed by a program manager who leads Phases 2 and 3. Phase 3, in turn, might be divided into three subprojects which are headed by three project managers who are savvy in various aspects of the product technology (e.g., hardware and packaging, software and firmware, and process technology, respectively). Phase 4 (customer and manufacturing qualification) might be headed by yet a different project manager who excels in CRM (customer relationship management) and customer support.

For example, the vision of CEO Ralph Stayer (Johnsonville Sausage Corporation) was for his company to have an organization that resembled "a flock of geese on the wing." For geese in flight, one goose leads the "V formation." When the lead goose becomes "tired," it moves to

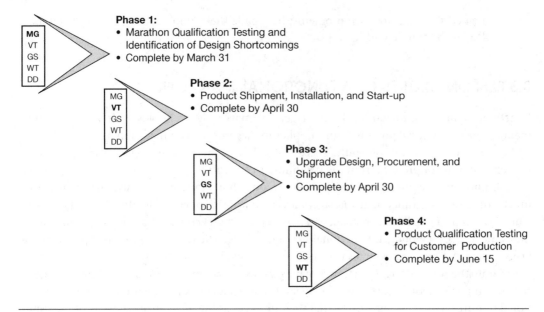

Figure 8.1. Geese-in-Flight Style of Project Management.

the rear of the formation and another goose takes over as leader. Stayer envisioned that instead of a traditional organizational chart with lines and boxes, his organization would resemble a "V" of individuals with a common goal.[1] Different individuals would "take turns" in leading, the structure would adjust to the task at hand, and each individual would be responsible for his/her own performance.

Product development projects can be managed by this geese-in-migratory-flight style as well—by changing the project manager at different phases of the project. An example of this style for the management of a wafer fab equipment development project at NATL Corporation is depicted in Figure 8.1. The project objective was to qualify an existing product for IC production at a new customer's fab. The team understood that the product design and process had to be changed to meet the customer's specification, but they first had to run some tests to "scope out" the required change. Final qualification testing of the product with modifications had to be done at the customer's site. Because the process of shipping and installing the product at the customer's site was quite lengthy and the schedule was very tight, the team decided to ship the equipment without any changes. They would upgrade it in the field after the design changes were identified. In other words, the phases of the project were overlapped as much as possible to accelerate the schedule. The scope of the project was divided into four phases:

- In-house "marathon" qualification testing of the product against the customer's specification to identify design/process shortcomings
- Shipment, installation, and start-up of the equipment at the customer's site
- Design development of an upgrade package, incorporating the marathon lessons to resolve performance shortcomings, and shipment to the customer
- Support of the customer's qualification testing of the product for production

The geese-in-flight metaphor applies to this project—because the organization was one in which the team membership remained the *same* over the entire duration of the project, but the project leadership *rotated* among the team members as the project moved from one phase to another. In Figure 8.1 the initials of the team members are shown in each phase, with the leader's initials underlined. The project had an overall program manager to oversee a smooth transition between phases and changes of leadership. Because of the criticality of the project, the overall program manager was the division's general manager.

8.5 THE PLANNING PROCESS

Planning development of a new high-tech product and planning projects and tasks of the PDCP are essential for success, but often they are either done haphazardly or improperly, partly because envisioning the path in a new situation is difficult and partly because planning is considered procrastination in an action-oriented world. Yet improper planning charts a course that is based on past experiences and the limitations of perceived constraints without challenging them.

For example, in Phase 1 of a PDPC which is an R&D project, scientists and technologists may refrain from planning the project, arguing that the path is unclear and that knowing how long it would take to solve an unprecedented technical problem cannot be ascertained with any certainty. Likewise, marketers may argue that the size of an emerging market and the market share of the new product cannot be forecasted and that planning the business is difficult.

In planning Phase 3 and 4 projects, managers start from the current state and formulate a sequence of actions that are necessary to reach the goal of satisfying product performance requirements. Additionally, they estimate the project schedule based on their past experiences with similar projects and the resources that are available to them. These plans are often nonresponsive to market timing needs and, hence, managers opt to proceed without a plan!

In today's world of high technology and rapidly changing markets, project planning (for product development and commercialization) must be discovery driven and iterative.[2] Project planning should start with the goal (market timing and business opportunity requirements) and identify a sequence of actions, timing, and assumptions to reach the goal. The process might need a few cycles of iteration to account for all task dependencies. For example, the planning assumptions could be about the state of the market, access to certain technology, or the availability of certain resources.

A discovery-driven planning approach asks "how" and "what does it take" to meet the MRS opportunities and refrains from enumerating the reasons why the objectives cannot be achieved (e.g., because of constraints.) The discovery-driven planning process challenges the constraints and inefficiencies of past experiences and identifies specific actions to remove obstacles and enact the plan. For example, a discovery-driven plan might require that software development be done in 3 months, although software development has taken 9 months for a similar product in the past. The challenge for the team is to identify the new software development tools, engineering expertise, and design practices that are needed to develop the software in 3 months.

It is important to make the list of planning assumptions explicit, to assess the associated risks of the assumptions, and to direct resources to mitigate the risks. Assumptions should be updated frequently and the project path should be changed as often as necessary. The development team often faces technology, schedule, business, and budget challenges as company management and customer support wavers from shifting priorities; when competitors act "irrationally;" and when the playing field and market assumptions become invalid. The team must remain vigilant of changes in the internal and external environment, update planning assumptions, and respond with agility.

In many new business and new product planning situations, the team, energized by the excitement of the future promise, may make many assumptions, but fail to document them. (This team will be surprised later on when things do not go the right way.) Project reviews are a good forum for appraising and updating the assumptions as the team's learning grows while marching down the development path. Project reviews at key milestones help to apply event learning to the assumptions and to revise the program accordingly.

8.6 THE PROJECT PLAN OUTLINE

The baseline project plan, which was prepared at the onset of the project, must be updated at completion of each phase of the product development process. An outline of a project plan is presented below (the content and format of each section is explored in more detail in subsequent sections):

1. SOW (statement of work), including the project mission statement, objectives, scope, constraints, assumptions, and risk areas
2. Product specifications, including the MRS, ERS, product concept, and manufacturing plan
3. Project budget and financial requirements
4. WBS (work breakdown structure) and DSM (design structure matrix), indicating task dependencies as sequential, parallel, and coupled tasks
5. Milestone schedule, including key events
6. Project organization, including the PM (project manager) and TMs (task managers) and their responsibilities and authorities; the reporting structure of team members by project tasks; the WBS responsibilities
7. Resource plan, including an estimate of the required person-weeks by task; the required development tools; and testing materials (including prototypes)
8. Work packages, including a definition of the work to be done by the various parties and identification of their *interfaces*, including in-house work and work done by suppliers, contractors, and consultants
9. Project cost breakdown and task budgets
10. Project procedures and management tools, including the authority and procedures for approvals; the project file (contract book); forms and tools for planning and tracking progress; a project performance measurement plan and incentives

8.7 THE STATEMENT OF WORK

A statement of work (SOW) is a narrative description of the project. A SOW is similar to an executive summary because it presents an overview of the work to be accomplished. A SOW begins with the mission statement and project objectives and lists the project deliverables and expected output. A SOW gives a brief description of the scope of the work, the overall schedule (start and end dates), major milestones, and a technical specification summary of the product. A SOW also lists the project constraints, assumptions, and risk areas.

8.8 THE WORK BREAKDOWN STRUCTURE

The work breakdown structure (WBS) is an important element of a project plan. A WBS is a list of all of the activities (tasks) that must be undertaken to accomplish the objectives of the project. The WBS is an effective tool for the project manager (and task managers) to ensure that all tasks are properly integrated; that nothing "falls through the cracks;" that adequate levels and the right types of resources are available to the project at the right time; and that out-of-scope work is easily identified during the project execution.

The WBS should divide project work into small tasks that are manageable with specific authority and responsibility; are independent or have well-defined interfaces; can be integrated into the *whole*, including the work by suppliers and external partners; and are measurable (for monitoring progress against success criteria).

The WBS can have several levels that signify different integration points of the product or project activities. For example, the design task of a product can be broken into smaller tasks for designing independent subsystems that are in turn divided into several tasks for component design. However, making WBS tasks too small or tasks that are shorter than 1 week in duration is not advisable.

WBS tasks should be accompanied by a task description, the expected output, and an output success criterion (include this information in Point 8 of the project plan outline in Section 8.6). All schedules and manpower estimates for the project should follow the WBS tasks. The WBS should also identify the major events of the projects, including phase review meetings, customer deliverables, and production release of the product.

8.9 THE PROJECT SCHEDULE

Because of unstable high-tech market conditions and technological uncertainties in the R&D and engineering of new products, scheduling of development projects with a high degree of confidence is often difficult. Nevertheless, applying the discovery planning method and planning a schedule that meets the market opportunity are crucial.

Perhaps the following adaptation of an ancient story by Levitt is relevant: "God told Noah to build an ark to save all species from the flood that he was letting occur in two weeks. Noah said, 'Two weeks? God, do you know how long it takes to build an ark?' God replied, 'Noah, how long can you tread water?' The ark was built in two weeks."[3]

Several scheduling formats with different content and degrees of complexity are used in product development projects. Some project managers use a simple table containing the WBS tasks. The table identifies the start and end dates of each task. Another format is the Gantt chart (or bar chart), which is the most common format because of its simplicity, A Gantt chart identifies the start and end dates of every WBS task and often highlights intermediate milestones. A disadvantage of a Gantt chart is its inability to show the interdependencies between the events and the project tasks. PERT (program evaluation and review technique) or DSM (design structure matrix) methodology also may be used. (See Chapter 6 and Figure 6.1 for discussion and an application of DSM in creating a map of project task dependencies.)

PERT (developed by the U.S. Navy in 1958) follows the WBS; sequences a network of events and activities according to their dependencies; makes expected time estimates for each activity; and identifies the critical path tasks and slack times for noncritical path tasks. The project's

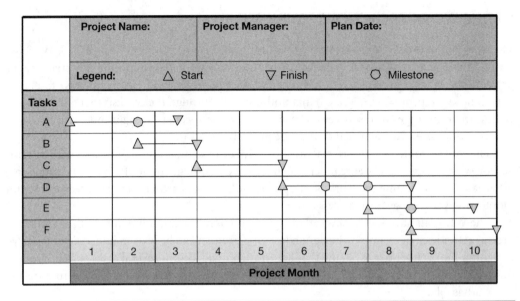

Figure 8.2. Gantt Chart.

critical path (or chain) is the sequence of activities whose accomplishments will require the greatest expected amount of time. PERT is event-oriented. It is suitable for R&D projects in which defining percent completion is difficult. A disadvantage of PERT is the complexity of the chart and the difficulty in using it as an overview chart in management reviews.

Popular project application software (e.g., Microsoft Project) allows the practitioner to create both Gantt and PERT formats and to link subprojects for interactive Web-based updates. Figure 8.2 and Figure 8.3 are generic illustrations of simple Gantt and PERT charts.

8.9.1 The Project Task Time Estimate

A time estimate for the performance of a task is usually based on past experiences with a similar task. The estimated time to reach a WBS milestone should be compared to the desired schedule (based on the MRS). A discrepancy requires a gap analysis to reexamine the assumptions, scope, and the execution approach of each task in order to resolve the discrepancy. For example, an assumption about available resources might have been too restrictive (and could be remedied by management action) or the scope of a critical-path task might have been over-interpreted (and could be reduced).

Kernzer suggests the following estimating technique for the expected duration of a task, t_e, assuming a normal distribution for the probability of completing a task:[4-6]

$$t_e = (t_o + 4t_m + t_p)/6$$

where,

t_o = **o**ptimistic time (if everything goes right)

t_m = **m**ost likely time (past experience for similar tasks)

t_p = **p**essimistic time (if many things go wrong for a high-risk task)

The total project schedule standard deviation is:

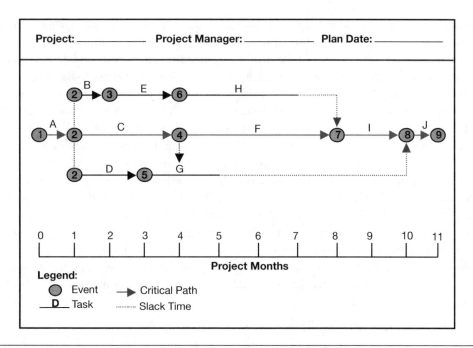

Figure 8.3. PERT Chart.

$$\sigma = \Sigma_i \sigma_i^2$$

where the summation is made over all critical-path activities i with a standard deviation of $\sigma_i = (t_p - t_o)/6$.

8.10 COST ESTIMATING

In new product development projects, the project manager must be concerned with both *product* and *project* costs. Product cost is comprised of the costs of manufacturing, delivery, installation, and warranty (or the cost of goods sold) and the costs of owning the product and paying for consumables and spare parts to operate the product.

The product "cost target" for profitability is specified in the MRS and budgeted to subsystems in the ERS. During the PDCP, product cost should be estimated at conceptual, preliminary, and detailed design milestones to ensure that the product design and manufacturing process stay "in line" with the target cost.

Product "estimated cost" is based on (in-progress) product/process design and uses engineering estimates, verbal and written quotations from suppliers, and catalog prices. Uncertainty in the product cost estimate is a function of the degree of completion of the design and process and the fraction of new versus existing components in the design.

The development team should also make a "should cost" estimate of the product. The "should costing" method estimates the cost of building a product if world-class manufacturing practices and benchmarks from other industries are employed. The gap between the "should cost" and "estimated cost" is indicative of shortcomings in product manufacturability and the efficiency of the planned manufacturing process. The should cost/estimated cost gap must be eliminated through design improvements, fabrication sourcing strategy, and driving corrective actions at culprit suppliers. Therefore, the development team must routinely track the "estimated cost" and the "should cost" of the product against the "target cost" and drive corrective actions in design, sourcing, and manufacturing to ensure alignment between the three.

In high-tech product development, project cost tracking is frequently deemphasized or even ignored because successful new products in high-tech markets often enjoy an excellent ROI (return on investment). Accelerating the time to market at the expense of higher project cost (investment) can therefore be justified. However, complacency in tracking the cost of development projects has serious consequences when a company grows and the number of new product projects multiplies. Without reasonably accurate knowledge of the estimated and the actual costs of development projects, making the right management priority decisions among the multiple product development opportunities is difficult for a firm. Without appropriate scrutiny, directing scarce resources in a wrong direction and investing significant amounts of money in unsuccessful products are not uncommon in large firms.

Project cost for the development of a new product is the total investment required for delivery of the *whole* product to the market to a point of turning a profit from sales of the product. Project cost is comprised of:

- The costs of developing the product and the process design, including the costs of:
  - Cross-functional team labor, fringe benefits, and overhead (regular, part-time, and contract labor)
  - Consultants and subcontractors
  - Prototype and testing material
  - Tools for engineering and qualification testing
  - Depreciation of capital equipment
  - Allocations for corporate functions and infrastructure services

- Customer joint-development costs, including evaluation prototypes
- Product introduction costs, including beta units
- The costs of developing market infrastructure, including sales staff, distributors, reps, partners, and suppliers
- Marketing and management costs
- Sales support collateral and customer demonstration units and facilities
- Promotion and marketing communication (MARCOM) costs
- The costs of the manufacturing infrastructure, including facilities, tooling, and inventory
- Service and support costs, including the people and facilities near customers, training courses, product and tools for training, and spares inventory
- Contingency costs as a percent of estimated costs based on uncertainty and risk

The total cost should be estimated with an uncertainty band at different stages of the PDCP—20 to 30% accuracy in the early stages is reasonable. Figure 8.4 provides a template for calculating uncertainty in estimating the cost of product prototype material. Cost uncertainty is estimated based on the type of quote and the state of development of the design.

Project Name: _____					Prepared by: _____							Date: ____	
Subsystem/ Component	Item Description	Part Number Drawing Number	Quantity	Unit Cost ($K)	Total Cost ($K)	Lead Time (Weeks)	Supplier Name	Quote Type*	Cost Uncertainty		Date of Quote	Comment
									%	$K		
Total												

Figure 8.4. Calculating Uncertainty in a Product Material Cost Estimate. * CP, catalog price; EE, engineering estimate; VQ, verbal quote; WQ, written quote.

8.11 PROJECT ORGANIZATION AND RESOURCE MANAGEMENT

Projects for product development must be organized differently from departmental (or unit) organizations that have been discussed so far in this chapter. Projects have three distinct characteristics that distinguish them from departmental organizations:

- Projects are comprised of a set of interrelated (WBS) tasks with clear scope, objectives, and interfaces.
- Projects must integrate resources from a variety of disciplines for the performance of tasks (most of the tasks).
- Projects are transitory, having a finite life and terminating after the objectives have been attained.

Project organizations should be job or task based and should identify the managers that are assigned to take ownership of the various tasks. In this organizational structure, the responsibility, authority, and accountability for doing the *whole* job of each task are clear. Nothing "falls through the cracks." Additional benefits of this approach include effective integration of WBS tasks into the *whole;* effective monitoring of progress in reaching different milestones along the way; effective risk identification and management and follow-through with assigned action items; and effective priority decision making (of what, when, who).

Project teams might be called integrated development teams (IDT), concurrent engineering teams, cross-functional teams, tiger teams, task forces, or other designations in different companies. Nevertheless, the organizational structure of a project must correspond to the WBS tasks and must identify all necessary resources from the entire value chain, whether they are assigned from within the firm or from joint-development suppliers, partners, and customers. A project organizational chart identifies the project manager, task managers, and key team members. An example of project organization for the development of an IC wafer processing

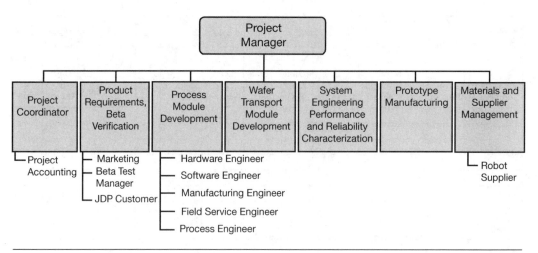

Figure 8.5. Project Organization for Development of Wafer Process Equipment.

equipment is shown in Figure 8.5. The tasks at the first level of the WBS are shown. For illustration, key resources are listed for some of the tasks.

As discussed earlier, successful product development projects have a strong leader (project manager), who establishes broad-based organizational objectives; gets team members to buy-in to the goals of the project; gives conceptual directions; stimulates and nurtures teamwork and proactive empowerment; integrates at all levels (from working level to management of the firm); fosters internal integration and integrates stakeholders needs into the detail design; links with critical suppliers and customers; is the agent of knowledge generation, retention, and integration; maintains a sharp focus on the project's objectives; and follows the product development process. Sobek, Liker, and Ward (1998) and Katzenbach and Smith (1993) provide additional information about organizing projects for effectiveness.[7,8]

8.12 PRODUCT DEVELOPMENT—AN INTEGRATED TEAM FROM ENGINEERING AND MANUFACTURING

Having collaborative partnerships among the development team members from engineering and manufacturing *throughout* the PDCP is crucial. Traditionally, however, R&D and design engineers have carried out product development through Phases 1, 2, and 3 of the PDCP and have then delivered the design documentation to manufacturing engineers for value engineering and pilot production in Phase 4. Subsequently, pilot manufacturing engineers have prepared documentation (at the completion of Phase 4) for volume production in Phase 5. This archaic hand-off approach (shown in Figure 8.6a) is slow, inefficient, and unfit for the imperative of short time to market in today's high-tech environment.

In an integrated team approach (shown in Figure 8.6b), the product is designed for manufacturability from the onset—the integrated team builds the engineering prototypes (in Phase 3) and the preproduction (pilot) prototypes (in Phase 4). This approach eliminates hand-offs and enables the team to release the product directly to production, significantly shortening the development cycle time and time to market.

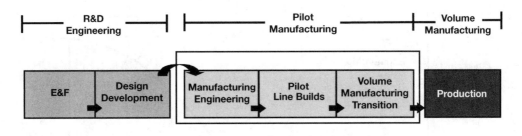

Figure 8.6a. Traditional Hand-Off Approach from Engineering to Manufacturing.

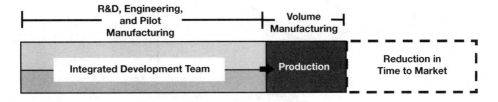

Figure 8.6b. Integrated Engineering and Manufacturing Team Approach.

Another important element of integrated team collaboration between engineering and manufacturing is how product prototypes are built during the PDCP. In the early phases, product design is immature and its documentation is scarce. The product cannot be built by manufacturing without the heavy participation of design engineers. As product development progresses through Phases 3 and 4, product design matures and detailed documentation becomes available to a level which is suitable for manufacturing. In the later stages, however, design engineers must still participate in the building of prototypes so that they can learn manufacturability issues firsthand and take rapid corrective action.

In short, in an integrated collaborative approach, an integrated team consisting of members from manufacturing and engineering collaboratively builds product prototypes in *all* phases of the PDCP. The level of effort of design engineers is high in the early phases and gradually decreases as product development progresses. For manufacturing, the trend is the opposite.

An example of the level of effort by an integrated team from engineering and manufacturing in building various prototypes collaboratively over the phases of the PDCP is illustrated in Figure 8.7. In the integrated team approach, manufacturing and supplier-management organizations assume ownership of a number of critical tasks of PDCP (as discussed in Chapter 5). The following sample task list is provided for reference. It is neither exhaustive nor does every listed task apply to all types of products:

- Proactively participate in product design development to ensure manufacturability. Assess product design modularity, poka-yoke, the materials of construction, tolerances, ergonomics, and safety. Offer ideas for parts reduction, standardization (reuse), and variability reduction.
- Develop the product manufacturing process for a lean manufacturing line design, production layout, and test strategy.

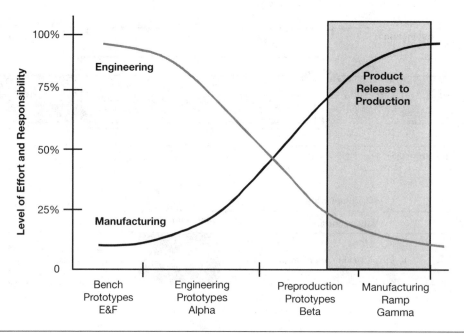

Figure 8.7. Integrated Team Collaboration in Building Prototypes.

- Achieve ERS goals for product manufacturing cost, quality, and cycle time. Demonstrate and verify the goals through a "controlled build" cycle prior to beta release.
- Perform *should-cost* analysis and value engineering.
- Develop supply chain assets. Prepare a sourcing map depicting the make/buy and outsourcing strategies for all components/subsystems; lead the supplier capability assessments and contract negotiations; sponsor the participation of suppliers in design; and ensure proper development of suppliers' manufacturing processes.
- Build engineering prototypes and first-article units per project plan and commercialization requirements. Manufacturing team members must be prepared to build prototypes from *inadequate* documentation and *immature* product designs during product development.
- Review product design drawings and specifications, prepare manufacturing assembly documentation, including operational method sheets (OMS), sequence of events (SOE), and system-ship packing design.
- Develop and verify manufacturing tooling and fixtures.
- Participate in installation and start-up of beta units in the field to identify manufacturing quality problems and take necessary corrective actions to incorporate the learning.

8.12.1 New Product Development and Release to Manufacturing—The Transition Team Concept

At some high-tech companies, the transition of new concepts from corporate R&D organization to engineering (in Phase 1 E&F) and the transition of product design to manufacturing

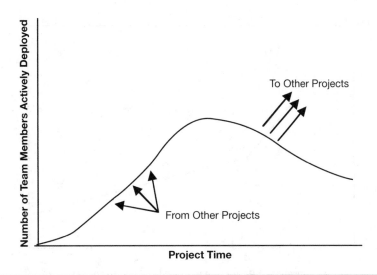

Figure 8.8. Typical Project Staffing Profile.

(in Phases 4 and 5) occur by transferring a few project team members from one organization to the next. For example, at a leading IC manufacturing company, when product development is completed, half of the engineering team (called the transition team) moves to manufacturing and reports to the manufacturing manager. The other half stays in engineering to develop the next generation product. Similarly, when ideas for new product technologies come from corporate research labs, one lab technologist (or more) transfers to engineering and joins the product development team for continuity and knowledge transfer.

At another semiconductor manufacturing company, process development engineers stagger IC technology nodes to maximize organizational learning and knowledge transfer. For example, in the succession of 0.25 μm, 0.18 μm, 0.13 μm, 0.10 μm technology nodes, the team that developed manufacturing processes at 0.25 μm would be assigned to develop the 0.13 μm technology; and the 0.18 μm team, when finished, would be moved to the 0.10 μm project. This technique not only maximizes organizational learning, but it is also motivating for the engineers because they will always have a chance to work on the "latest" technology.

8.13 STAFF DEPLOYMENT

A key responsibility of project managers is resource planning and deployment. The project manager must ensure that an adequate number of people with the right competencies is assigned to project tasks when needed and that these people are off of the project's budget when they have fulfilled their assignments.

The overall staffing profile of a typical project is illustrated in Figure 8.8. Initially, as the scope of the project increases, new people are assigned to the project, perhaps from other projects that are wrapping up. Toward the end of the project, as the number of active tasks lessens, people are moved off the project.

Project execution efficiency is adversely impacted when people are not dedicated to the project. Often, projects are staffed with part-time people who are assigned to multiple projects to the detriment of all. Because resources in most high-tech organizations are stretched thin,

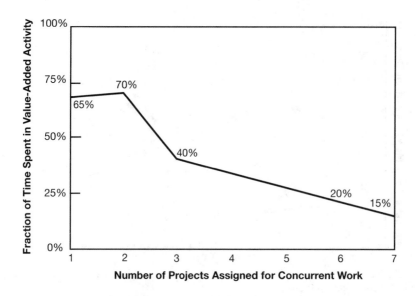

Figure 8.9. Impact of Multiple Concurrent Project Assignment on the Productivity of Development Personnel at IBM. (Source: Adapted from IBM research data in Christensen, C. *Field Case (Materials Technology Corporation): Teaching Note.* HBS Case 5-698-083. Boston: Harvard Business School; 1998, March 3.)

functional managers tend to assign each individual to several projects to enable the organization to carry out multiple projects in parallel. The result of this common staff deployment strategy is loss of overall efficiency (and even quality) in the execution of all projects that are staffed with part-time employees.

The profile of the work efficiency of an individual as a function of number of projects that the person concurrently performs is depicted in Figure 8.9. As described by Christensen,[9] "IBM asked over a thousand of its engineers to keep track over the course of one month of how they spent their time. At the end of each day they were asked to record the time they had spent in one of two buckets: value-added and non-value-added time. Value-added time consisted of time spent in productive individual engineering work and in meetings in which productive decisions were made and adhered to. Non-value-added time consisted of having to rework things that were done incorrectly or to rework things in which new requirements were imposed by subsequent decisions. Time spent in meetings revisiting decisions that previously had been made, or bringing members up to speed who had missed earlier meetings, and time spent traveling to meetings were also classified as non-value-added time. At the end of the month, the IBM engineers were also asked how many projects they had been assigned to work on simultaneously during that month." (*Note:* The author's experience with many projects also substantiates this reported efficiency profile.)

As Figure 8.9 shows, a worker's efficiency in carrying out a task is substantially reduced when that worker's attention is divided among three or more projects. Conversely, the worker is more efficient when working on two tasks rather than one. The contributing factors to shaping the efficiency profile are setup time, wait time, and freshness of thought. Working on two projects is more efficient than working on one project because the wait time for input for one of project is spent on working on the second project. Furthermore, the boredom that is associated with working on the same task for too long is minimized. Yet, when a person works on three or more projects concurrently, he/she must spend some amount of nonproductive time in gracefully closing an active task and restarting the next. Restart time is usually spent on preparing tools, rearranging the work area, accessing the right information, and coming up to speed about where work on the task left off. The total setup time to stop and restart multiple tasks becomes excessive and overall efficiency drops.

Another important factor, often ignored in planning resource requirements, is recognizing that 100% of each person's time is *not* spent on assigned projects. Employees spend time attending staff meetings and performing other administrative duties. Allowing 10% for such overhead activities is a reasonable practice.

Project managers should use task-assignment "contracts" in assigning project tasks and acquiring commitment for performance. This approach, if done using a task assignment sheet (see section 8.14), adds clarity of expectations and a certain degree of formality (without bureaucracy) to project execution and helps in receiving dedicated resource assignments from functional mangers.

8.14 THE TASK ASSIGNMENT SHEET

A task assignment sheet is a document, preferably limited to one page, that describes a task that is assigned to a team member or a functional group manager. It is a mini-SOW assigned by the project manager to an individual. A task assignment sheet identifies the expected output of the assigned task, the completion due date, and the names of the requestor and task owner. The task owner commits to the work by her/his signature on the document. A template recommended for use as a task assignment sheet is illustrated in Figure 8.10. Although simple, the form is quite helpful in clarifying responsibilities and commitments in a team.

8.15 PLANNING RESOURCE DEMAND AND DEPLOYMENT

Project managers and team members alike are often frustrated with the lack and misappropriation of resources in the rushed environment of high-tech product development. Resource allocation conflicts between project managers and functional managers are also a source of tension in managing projects. These conflicts arise from assigning part-time staff members to projects and then changing their assignment before they have met their expected commitment. Resource conflicts create confusion and loss of focus in the project staff and lead to customer dissatisfaction.

The root cause of resource allocation conflicts is the lack of a business process that governs resource requests by project managers and the response of functional managers with staff time commitments to create alignment. Too many organizations generate unnecessary negative energy and create unhealthy conflict among various project and functional managers because they do not implement a staff deployment process that is transparent and inclusive of all project and functional stakeholders. For multiproduct/-project organizations, a three-step staff deployment process is recommended:

- Project managers estimate their project staff requirements over the plan period, usually a year, identifying which key competencies or individuals in the organization are needed by the project. This is the *demand creation* step.

Task Assignment Sheet

Requester: _____   Date: _____

Assigned to: _____

Task Description/Scope: _____

_____

_____

Objectives/Requirements/Constraints: _____

_____

_____

Expected Output/Success Criteria/
Deliverables: _____

_____

Due Date: _____

Committed by: _____

Figure 8.10. Task Assignment Sheet.

- Functional managers together with project managers and the BU general manager then prioritize all projects in the unit.
- Project and functional managers negotiate and agree on staff deployment for all projects.

Figure 8.11 illustrates a simple template that project and task managers should use to estimate people requirements for a project.

Figure 8.12 provides a template for functional managers to plan staff deployment for approved projects. Functional managers should start with demand, combining requested staff by all projects and negotiating with project managers, to fill the table with committed staff for their projects. Negotiations should create an alignment between demand and the available resources in the department.

Commonly, however, requested resources add up to significantly higher numbers than the total people in a functional department. This discrepancy is resolved in the second step in the resource planning process, project prioritization, in order to enable selective staff deployment. The discrepancy between the requested and the available resources could also point to a resource capability gap in a department which must be filled urgently when high-priority projects cannot be staffed. (*Note:* The methodology for aggregate project prioritization is discussed in a later section in this chapter.)

Project Name:_____ Project Year:_____ Project Manager:_____ Date of Request:_____												
Staff (Name, Grade, Department, or Competency	Jan	Feb	Mar	Apr	May	June	July	Aug	Sep	Oct	Nov	Dec
CB (Marketing Manager)	1	1	1	0.5	0.5	0.5	0.5	0.5	1	1	1	1
JC (Senior Software Engineer)		1.5	2	1			1	1			0.5	
Controls Design Engineer	1	2	1.5	1	0.5						0.5	
Automation Mechanical Designer	1	3	4	2	1	0.5					0.5	
Test Engineer				1	2	2	2	2	1	1	1	1

Figure 8.11. Project Demand—Staff Requirements by Month. Numerical entries represent number of persons per month.

Department: _____ Department Manager: _____ Plan Month: _____ Date: _____						
Staff ⟋ Project/Task	Person A	Person B	Person C	Person D	Person E	Total
						Requested	Assigned
Project U							
Project V							
Project X							
Project Y							
Project Z							

Figure 8.12. Planning Tool for Functional Managers—Staff Deployment by Month. Numerical entries are number of hours or percent time of a person assigned to a project or task in the planned month.

Important to note is that in addition to the projects for product development and life cycle support, usually functional managers must staff several other activities such as business process improvement tasks, organizational development and training, and other internally driven activities. However, allocation of resources to such activities must be carefully monitored and routinely justified (on the basis of the ROI and benefit to customers) to preclude internally centered tendencies that grow in companies when they become large.

8.16 DRIVING PROGRESS AND PROJECT MEETINGS

Project managers must drive progress by maintaining focus on objectives, tracking status, and driving corrective actions to stay on course and produce results. Most of the actions of project managers take place in project meetings and include project working meetings, management review meetings, and design reviews, each serving a different purpose. Depending on the size of the project, a hierarchy of subprojects or tasks which would have their own set of project (or task force) meetings might exist. Common types of project meetings are reviewed and best-known methods are presented to maximize productivity in the paragraphs that follow. (*Note*: Methodology for conducting a meeting is presented in Chapter 9.)

8.16.1 The Project Team Meeting

A project team meeting is a working management meeting of task managers with the project manager to whom they report (according to project organizational chart). The purpose of a project meeting is to communicate status across project tasks; adjust and align priorities as needed by changes internal and external to the project; identify and resolve interface issues; identify performance gaps and risks that impact the whole project and decide on corrective action; and create a sense of direction and ownership among the team members. Project meetings should be held on a weekly basis. When the team members are not co-situated physically, it is necessary to conduct project meetings via videoconferencing or e-meetings through the Internet.

A template for recording and tracking action items at a project meeting is illustrated in Figure 8.13. A database of action items should be maintained and made accessible to all team members so they can update the status of their actions before the project meeting.

8.16.2 The Project Partner Meeting

A project partner meeting is a meeting with key suppliers or partners. It has the same purpose as a project team meeting. Project partner meetings should be held on a monthly basis. Occasionally, having a critical partner attend the weekly project meetings and be closely integrated in the team is necessary.

8.16.3 The Customer Review Meeting

The purpose of a customer review meeting is to communicate progress and risks; to receive customer's input for change in requirements and priorities; to attain alignment in introduction timing; and to seek support. Customer review meetings should be held regularly (monthly or quarterly) whether the customer is a joint development partner or a sponsor of product development.

Managing customer expectations properly at customer review meetings is important so the meetings do not result in unnecessary and frequent changes in priorities or in the scope of the project. Frequent changes in the project scope and the objective can result in delayed execution, poor ROI, and missed market opportunity. However, a midstream change in requirements and an adjustment to the course of the project might be inevitable in high-tech markets. In the development of new technologies in which customers and suppliers develop their products simultaneously and the knowledge of requirements grows during product development,

AI Number	Action Description	Date Assigned	Owner Name and Phone Number	Recipient of AI Output (Internal or External Customer)	Due Date	Deliverables	AI Status Indicator (Green/ Yellow/ Red) as of 10/9/02	Status Detail	Actual/ Forecasted Completion Date
1	Develop Installation Plan at Customer A	10/1/02	RJ	DJ Customer A Site Manager	10/21/02	Plan for Resources and Timing, Including Training	Red	Plan Review Scheduled on 10/10/02	11/1/02
2									
3									
4									
5									
6									

Figure 8.13. Project Action Item Tracking Template. AI, action item.

requirement changes and crisper definitions are likely. Nevertheless, midcourse adjustments must be made deliberately and with a careful assessment of the consequences on achievement of planned market timing and business objectives.

8.16.4 The Management Review Meeting

A management review meeting is an in-depth review of the project by the company president or the BU general manager and management staff. The purpose of a management review meeting is for the project manager to communicate project progress and risks to management; to seek management's support (including resources) to alleviate risks; and to align project objectives with corporate/BU market and business strategy.

Management review meetings should be held monthly. A time-stamped monthly review helps to create a regular pace and urgency for projects and to keep them focused on objectives. Monthly reviews enable business managers to assess risks and planning assumptions, monitor progress, identify performance gaps, and make timely decisions for corrective action.

The project manager should personally make the presentation at management review meetings, with help from key project staff, and cover critical issues of the project using several guidelines:

- *Project objectives* and their link to *customer benefits* should be explicitly articulated. A measurable set of KPIs (key performance indicators) should also be presented. KPIs constitute the success criteria. KPIs should be used to determine if project objectives are met and the project is completed.
- Project deliverables must be clearly identified. Project deliverables could include such things as design documentation, software release notes, hardware or software prototypes to the internal and external customers, and product and process characterization reports.
- The project schedule, linked with the time-to-market requirements of the MRS, should be presented, including critical milestones. Defining the project *end date* as

the time when the *whole* job is done, i.e., the solution is made available to customers and has met their expectation, is important.

- If the project is for the development of a derivative product and it implements a major redesign to an existing product hardware, software, or process, *backward compatibility* of changes to the installed base must be addressed as a design constraint. At the management review meeting, the product marketing manager should present his/her program to smoothly transition the product from the existing design to the new design in the marketplace, for both forward builds and the installed base.

- The project planning and execution report at the meeting must cover business aspects and engineering implementation. Ask: Are we delivering the right *solution* to our customers in a *timely* manner and is the *investment* in time and resources for the proposed customer benefits *justified*?

- The project manager is responsible for ensuring that all of the above are accomplished for the project and addressed at the review. Project management review meetings are a great opportunity for project managers to seek additional resources (if necessary) and other help from management.

Figure 8.14 provides a single-page template that is recommended for use at project management review meetings. Project or task managers who use this template should attempt to adhere to a "single-page" format. When the presenter is constrained to the space of a single page, he/she is more likely to address the most important project issues, e.g., the top three risks. Presenters must refrain from a lengthy status or activities report. In a management review meeting, enumerating the activities that the team engaged in during the reporting period is unimportant. Focus must be on the objectives, the gaps in KPIs, and an action plan to fill the gaps and to mitigate the top three risks of the project. As an example, in Figure 8.15, the template has been completed for a hypothetical "Super Robot" project for semiconductor process equipment.

Executive project status report. Product development projects are often of great importance to many executives in the firm within and beyond the BU in which the product is being developed. Project managers and the general manager of a BU periodically report the status of key product development and life cycle support projects to the CEO and other senior executives, including vice presidents of finance, manufacturing, and marketing; regional general managers; and peer BU general managers. The executive status report for a project must be concise, mostly visual, and comprised of the salient business and marketing issues of the development project. Figure 8.16 provides a sample template that project managers can customize to their specific circumstances and use for reporting the status of a project to company executives.

8.16.5 The Design Review Meeting

The purpose of a design review is to:

- Evaluate and critique the design for technical quality and excellence (DFx)
- Receive expert and peer input
- Ensure compliance with the ERS
- Identify and resolve interface issues with design of other subsystems/components
- Prevent surprises

Project Title: _____ **Project Manager:** _____ **Todays Date:** _____
Project Completion Date: _____

Project Objectives:

Product Benefits to Customers/Compelling Competitive Advantage:

Target Products/Applications and Customers:

Scope/Constraints/Deliverables:

Status of Compliance to Specifications:

KPI	MRS/ERS	Current Performance	Performance at Completion	Actions to Comply (Attach Plan and Data)
____	_____	_____	_____	_____
____	_____	_____	_____	_____
____	_____	_____	_____	_____

Key Milestones and Schedule (Provide Gantt Chart as Backup):

Milestone	Owner	Committed Schedule of Completion	
		Planned Date	Forecasted Date
_____	_____	_____	_____
_____	_____	_____	_____
_____	_____	_____	_____

Top Three Risks:

	Risk/Problems	Proposed Solutions/Decisions	Who	When
1	_____	_____	_____	_____
2	_____	_____	_____	_____
3	_____	_____	_____	_____

Project Cost Status:

Budget	Cost to Date	Commitment to Date	Cost to Complete	Cost at Completion	Variance/ Action
_____	_____	_____	_____	_____	_____
_____	_____	_____	_____	_____	_____
_____	_____	_____	_____	_____	_____

Figure 8.14. Project Review Template.

Design reviews aid knowledge generation, retention, and integration in product development and assist the design owner(s) to improve the quality of the design.

Often engineers prefer to be left alone to do their design, until they have completed the design, built and tested the prototypes, and corrected the shortcomings of the design. This is a high-risk approach that often results in a nonoptimal design, poor compliance to the ERS, and surprises during system integration.

Project Title: Super Robot

Project Manager: LC

Todays Date: 1/29/05

Project Completion Date: 10/31/05

Project Objectives/Product Features and Benefits to Customers:
Achieve 30% higher system throughput than any existing wafer transport system in the semiconductor process equipment market to improve customer productivity. Robot-limited throughput (for zero process time) = 120 wafers/hr for a 4-chamber system configuration, with chamber lift and slit valve open/close times = 1 sec each. Beta unit shipment by 6/30/05. Can be retrofitted on wafer transport platform of existing product line. Reliability: <1 fault per 250K wafer passes. New robot cost increase: <10% of the current generation robot cost.

Target Products/Applications and Customers:
The target product line is 200-mm and 300-mm dielectric etch, followed by the CVD system. The target beta customer is CICM in China, where throughput improvement would win us PTOR status.

Scope/Constraints/Deliverables:
- Design for both 200- and 300-mm etch and CVD platforms.
- Must be able to handle 400°C chamber wafer temperatures. Achieve high-speed motion and wafer centering with a simple two-axis robot without costly optical wafer sensing sensors and electronics.
- Deliver two test units to Etch and CVD Labs, deliver one 200-mm beta unit to CICM, and build three 300-mm beta units for TBD customers.

Status of Compliance to Specifications:
Initial lab test of robot on etch platform failed due to calibration and orienter firmware problems. Post-testing review found problem in clamp geometry and concerns about ±0.075 in. capture window and variation in leaf springs.
- Redesigned pushers and blade to eliminate the geometry issue. Increased capture window to ±0.125 in., the initial design target.
- System inspection, installation, and calibration procedures being created and reviewed.
- Etch software sequencer being reviewed to identify opportunities for throughput optimization.

Key Milestones and Schedule:

		Committed Schedule of Completion	
Milestone	Owner	Planned Date	Forecasted Date
1. Parts in-house	MY	11/15/04	Complete
2. Engineering Lab—200-mm system running	DM	12/1/04	Complete
3. Reliability cycling begins	IS	3/1/05	3/15/05
4. 200-mm units to Etch and CVD Labs	GC	3/15/05	3/21/05
5. Alpha exit of 200-mm system	LC	6/21/05	6/30/05
6. Ship beta 200-mm system to CICM	GC	6/30/05	6/30/05
7. 300-mm units to Etch and CVD Labs	GC	4/30/05	5/1/05
8. Alpha exit of 300-mm unit	LC	7/15/05	7/31/05
9. Ship beta 300-mm units to TBD customers	GC	7/15/05	7/31/05
10. Release 200-mm and 300-mm units to Production	LC	10/31/05	10/31/05

Top Three Risks/Problems and Proposed Solutions/Decisions:
1. BU internal customers have lost confidence in super robot due to long development cycle. Mitigation—Present benefits to the BU GM and execute with dielectric etch on schedule.
2. Clamp scratches backside of wafer. Mitigation—Quantify scratch by testing and take corrective action to meet specification.
3. Cost of manufacturing robot is too high. Mitigation—Identify cost reduction opportunities.

Project Cost Status:

Budget	Cost to Date	Commitment to Date	Cost to Complete	Cost at Completion	Variance/ Action
$275K	$147K	$180K	$135K	$315K	$40K

Figure 8.15. Project Review—Super Robot. BU, business unit; CVD, chemical vapor deposition; PTOR, production tool of record; TBD, to be determined.

| Project Title: _____ | BU/Product Line: _____ |

Project Manager Name: _____   **Report Date:** _____

| Project Objectives and Executive Summary: | Status Indicators: |

Customer Satisfaction

Technical

Schedule

Resources

Financial

Legend:
Dark Gray: At or better than plan
Light Gray: >5% and <10%
variance from plan
Black: >10% variance from plan

• **External Customer:**

• **Internal Customer:**

Start Date: _____   Planned Completion Date: _____

Budget ($K): _____   Forecasted Completion Date: _____

	Status	Customer Notified	Customer Approved
Schedule Variance (Behind/Ahead)	Number of Weeks	Yes/No	Yes/No
Scope Change	Yes/No	Yes/No	Yes/No
Compliance with MRS	Yes/No	Yes/No	Yes/No

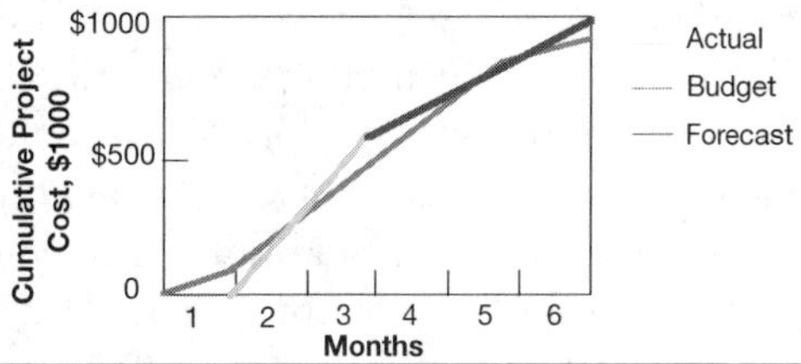

Cumulative Project Cost, $1000

$1000

$500

0

1 2 3 4 5 6
Months

Actual
Budget
Forecast

Reporting Period Accomplishments:

Issues/Risks and Mitigation Strategies:

Figure 8.16. Executive Project Reporting Template. BU, business unit.

Design reviews should be held upon completion of several key PDCP milestones for the entire system and for subsystems and components:

- The E&F phase
- The conceptual design
- The architecture/modular structure design
- ERS preparation
- The preliminary design
- The detailed design
- Phase 3 alpha exit

A design review should also be held when a task encounters a technical difficulty or reaches a technical decision point that impacts the performance/cost/schedule of the product or requires a change to an existing interface control document (ICD). "*Too many*" design reviews are preferred over "*too few*" reviews.

Participants in a design review should include:

- Subject matter experts/gurus (internal and external) and peers

- Systems engineering experts
- Project manager and design task manager
- Other engineers whose modules, subsystems, and products are impacted by and have an interface with the design in review
- PDCP stakeholders from manufacturing engineering, supplier management, product marketing, and product management

Participation of reviewers from outside of the department and division (BU) in which the design is being done should be encouraged.

The design team, including the engineers and technologists responsible for the design as well as the lead designers, should make presentations at a design review meeting. The team leader should send a notice to the reviewers a few days prior to the meeting, stating the objective of the design per ERS and MRS and providing adequate documentation to the reviewers to prepare for the meeting. Reviewers who are well prepared are the most effective in helping a design team excel.

At a design review meeting, presenters should highlight areas of concern with the design; the potential shortcomings in compliance to the ERS; and the problems in function, reliability, extendibility, maintainability, size, cost, and other pertinent design parameters. Design analysis, modeling approaches, and results of trade-off studies should also be reviewed. The leader of the design team and other presenters should not try to keep the meeting short or to "sell" their design. *Remember*: Reviewers are "free resources" who are attending the meeting to help improve the design. Design owners should take advantage of the participation of reviewers and stimulate discussion. The design task manager should take note of the ideas and suggestions of reviewers, even if the design team does not agree with them.

After the review meeting, the design team should recap the review notes and decide which design changes and ideas to adopt and what suggestions to forego. An action plan must be established and implemented.

8.17 A COST/SCHEDULE/PERFORMANCE TRADE-OFF MATRIX

Project managers must strive to meet all project objectives on schedule and within budget, but when faced with an execution problem, project managers often have to make a trade-off decision between the project scope, schedule, and investment of resources. Figure 8.17 illustrates a framework for the trade-off between project budget, schedule, and product performance to clarify a decision and the strategy going forward.

In Figure 8.17, project schedule or time to market is considered to be of the most importance (as is usually the case for high-tech products) and is "constrained" as the the *least* flexible factor in PDCP. Project budget or investment in product development is considered to be the *most* flexible factor; therefore a reasonable variance from the budgeted amount is "accepted" by adding resources. The third factor, product performance, is "optimized" by reducing the project scope without sacrificing the quality. For example, the scope optimization strategy could be selective introduction of the product features and capabilities to the market, starting with the highest priority set of features and deferring the introduction of low-priority features to a later date.

Parameter (Desired Result)	Constraint (Least Flexible)	Optimize (Minimum/Maximum)	Accept (Most Flexible)
Cost (Minimum Investment)			Allow Reasonable Budget Variance with Addition of Resources
Schedule (First to Market)	Meet Time-to-Market Objective		
Performance (Best)		Reduce Scope and Prioritize	

Figure 8.17. Example of a Project Cost/Schedule/Performance Trade-Off Matrix. MRS, market requirements specification.

8.18 PROJECT COST AND SCHEDULE VARIANCE ANALYSIS

Project managers must regularly track project costs and the project budget to identify variances from the plan. Based on the variance analysis, project managers must implement corrective actions to reduce variances and forecast a revised cost and schedule at completion.

The following methodology has been proposed for estimating schedule and cost variances:[10]

Cost Variance (as percent cost increase) = 100 (ACWP − BCWP)/BCWP
Schedule Variance (as percent schedule increase) = 100 (BCWS − BCWP)/BCWP

where,
ACWP = Actual Cost of Work Performed to Date
BCWP = Budgeted Cost of Work Performed to Date
BCWS = Budged Cost of Work Scheduled to Date

According to this definition, positive variances are favorable and negative variances are unfavorable.

A graphic representation of the actual and planned costs in Figure 8.18 illustrates the revised cost and schedule at the completion of a project. The methodology for estimating the cost and schedule at completion is based on the assumption that current project trends continue and hence extrapolate actual values into the future.[11] The preferred approach is to estimate the revised *Time to Complete* and *Cost to Complete* by replanning the balance of the project based on the remaining scope.

8.18.1 Project Cost Tracking

The peculiarities of most cost accounting systems necessitate tracking three types of reported costs—cost commitments, accruals, and cash flow (as shown in Figure 8.19). When a purchased part or service is placed on order, the organization is committed to pay the agreed-upon price (on the purchase order) to the supplier. However, the company is only invoiced when the

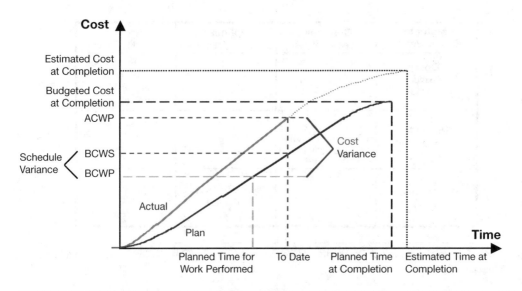

Figure 8.18. Project—Actual and Planned Costs and Variances. ACWP, actual cost of work performed to date; BCWP, budgeted cost of work performed to date; BCWS, budged cost of work scheduled to date.

part is delivered or when the service is rendered. Upon the receipt of an invoice, accountants "accrue" the cost of the expenditure and report it as a project cost. However, most companies do not pay their suppliers until 30 to 45 days (or longer) after receipt of an invoice. Therefore, the cash flow, accrued cost, and committed cost of a given expenditure are spread apart over time. Figure 8.19 illustrates common profiles of the three types of costs.

A project manager who only tracks the accrued cost might overspend the budget by not taking into account outstanding commitments. Furthermore, the project books cannot be closed at the end of the project until the delayed accounts payable (cash flow) are paid and reconciled.

8.19 PROJECT CLOSURE

Managers must identify clear success or completion criteria for projects. A project should not be allowed to "drag on to perfection." If implementing product improvements or adding next generation features is necessary, starting a new project is preferable to extending the schedule of an original product development project. Furthermore, technical and market risks, product viability, and ROI must be continuously assessed during a development project. The team should not be caught up in the "success is just around the corner" syndrome—a situation that is often an indicator that the project should be terminated or, better yet, redirected.

Projects must be closed when the objectives have been met or when it is determined that the objectives cannot be met for technical, market, or ROI reasons. In the case of failure to meet ROI objectives, a project must be formally discontinued and terminated with appropriate approval signatures.

Whether projects are successfully completed or terminated for cause, they should be closed gracefully and the project manager should hold a close-out postmortem review. This review should identify the highlights of what went right and the lowlights of what went wrong, the les-

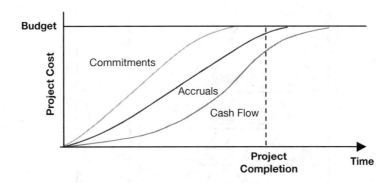

Figure 8.19. Tracking Different Categories of Project Costs.

	Corporate Objectives						
	Profitability Improvement			Market Share Growth		Shareholder Value Growth	
Project Type	Cost Reduction Projects	Packaging Improvement	Derivative Projects	Next Generation	Emerging Market/New Business		
Project Name	CR1	CR2	PI	D1	D2	NG	NB1	NB2

Figure 8.20. Development Projects Serving Business Objectives. CR, cost reduction; D, derivative projects; NB, new business; NG, next generation projects; P, packaging improvement.

sons learned, and recommendations for change. The project file and related documents should be closed and catalogued for future reference. For additional information about management of engineering projects, the reader should consult Balderstone et al. (1984), Dumbleton (1986), and Bergen (1990).[10,12,13]

8.20 AGGREGATE PROJECT PLANNING AND MANAGEMENT

This section focuses on key issues that a general manager of a *multiproject unit* must address to ensure that all projects in the unit are aligned with corporate and BU objectives; that projects are prioritized; and that resources are allotted according to established project priorities. (*Note:* Chapter 10 will discuss methodologies for developing and managing a *portfolio* of products and development projects that meets the firm's market and business objectives. A balanced portfolio, as discussed in Chapter 10, is a set of projects that meets all business objectives and is commensurate with company resources.) Figure 8.20 illustrates a portfolio of projects serving the corporate objectives of profitability, market share, and shareholder value growth. Creating an explicit linkage between project and business objectives is imperative not only for balancing the portfolio, but also for focusing and prioritizing projects.

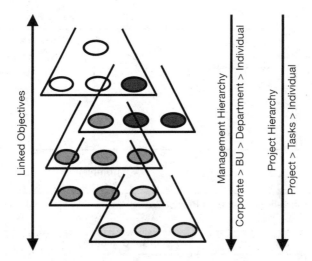

Figure 8.21. Hierarchies of Linked Objectives in Organizations and Projects. Ovals at base of each triangle report to oval at top of triangle and are linked up the organization. BU, business unit.

8.20.1 A Framework for a Hierarchy of Linked Objectives

The concept in Figure 8.20 of linking project objectives to business objectives can be broadly extended to apply to objectives of organizational units and project tasks. For example, the objectives of individuals in a department should serve the department manager's objectives. The objectives of department managers should serve the objectives of the general manager of the BU, which in turn should serve the objectives of the COO and corporate goals. For a project, the hierarchy of linked objectives goes from team members to task force managers to the project manager and, finally, to the business objectives.

Managers must create and explicitly articulate the hierarchy of linked objectives. At every level, how local objectives serve the hierarchy of objectives above that level should be clearly delineated. A framework for linking the hierarchy of objectives is illustrated in Figure 8.21. In Figure 8.21, an organizational unit (or a task of a project) is depicted as a triangle, with the objectives of that organizational unit shown as ovals within the triangle. Note how the lower-level objectives (at bottom of figure) are linked up the organization (or project).

8.21 PRIORITIZATION OF PROJECTS

The criteria to prioritize product development projects must be aligned with the technology and product portfolio strategies of the firm (see Chapter 10). A project prioritization process should be managed by the BU general manager and should involve all internal stakeholders, including product marketing managers, engineering functional managers, and project managers.

Figure 8.22 illustrates a template for documenting and presenting project priorities within a BU. Projects are grouped in high-, medium-, and low-priority categories. (*Note*: Some managers prefer to list projects by a numeric priority ranking, e.g., 1, 2, 3, etc. The experience of the author shows that this approach is impractical because of the high degree of granularity that is required in discerning small differences in project ranks.)

Priority	Product Line A Projects	Product Line B Projects	Product Line C Projects	Common Projects
High	Customer Specification Compliance New Products Upgrades for Competitive Advantage			
Medium	Manufacturing CIP Cost Reduction			
Low	Customer Low Priority Nice to Do			
Inactive Projects	End-of-Life Products			

Figure 8.22. Project Priority Table for a Multiproduct/Multiproject Organization. Common projects include platform, subsystems, components, and software that serve multiproduct families and BUs. BU, business unit; CIP, continuous improvement project.

#	Product Line	Project	Objective	Completion Date	Project Manager	Priority (H,M,L)	Product Type	Assigned Resources
	A							
	B							
	Common							

Figure 8.23. Multiproject Organization Staffing and Prioritization Aggregate Resource Planning. Product type: breakthrough exploration and feasibility (E&F), platform/next generation, derivative, continuous improvement projects/support.

In Figure 8.22, projects associated with different product lines are listed in the columns. In many "multiproduct family" firms, some components, subsystems, or platforms are used across several product lines. These common subsystems are usually developed in a common engineering or product organization that serves (as an internal supplier) more than one product line or BU. In Figure 8.22, one column is dedicated to common product development projects. Prioritization of these common projects must heed the diverse requirements of stakeholders in all pertinent product lines and BUs. Figure 8.22 also contains a category for inactive projects—to explicitly clarify the organization's assumptions about what is unimportant and not being worked on. Such clear statement of what "not to work on" in addition to what is important and "should be worked on" is valuable in keeping organizational resources focused and in precluding the initiation of unauthorized (pet) projects.

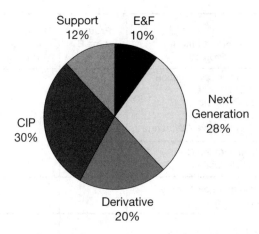

Figure 8.24. Investment of Resources by Product Type. CIP, continuous improvement projects; E&F, exploration and feasibility.

Figure 8.23 presents another useful tool in managing resource assignment in multiproject organizational units. In addition to the priority of projects for each product line, the project manager and key resources are identified in the spreadsheet. BU managers can also categorize projects by type to analyze distribution of resource investment and to manage the product portfolio. Figure 8.24 depicts a sample distribution of resource investment by project type in a high-tech firm.

8.22 THE AGGREGATE PROJECT PLAN—A SEVEN-STEP PROCESS

Based on discussions in this chapter, the aggregate project planning process can be summarized in a seven-step process:[14]

1. Define project types as breakthrough, platform, derivative, or R&D.
2. Identify existing projects and classify by project type.
3. Estimate the average time and resources needed for each project type based on past experience.
4. Identify the existing resource capacity.
5. Determine the desired mix of projects.
6. Estimate the number of projects that existing resources can support.
7. Decide which specific projects to undertake.

See Chapter 10 for an in-depth discussion of aggregate project planning.

REFERENCES

1. Stayer, R. *How I Learned to Let My Workers Lead.* HBR Reprint 90610. Boston: Harvard Business School Publishing; 1990 November 1.
2. McGrath, R.G., MacMillan, I.C. *Discovery-Driven Planning.* HBR Reprint 95406. Boston: Harvard Business School Publishing; 1995 July.

3. Levitt, T. *Thinking About Management*. New York: Free Press; 1993.
4. Kerzner, H. *Project Management: A Systems Approach to Planning, Scheduling, and Controlling, Eighth Edition*. New York: John Wiley & Sons; 2003.
5. Kerzner, H. *Applied Project Management*. New York: John Wiley & Sons; 2000.
6. Kerzner, H. *Project Management, Third Edition*. New York: Van Nostrand Reinhold; 1989.
7. Sobek, D.K., II, Liker, J.K., Ward, A.C. *Another Look at How Toyota Integrates Product Development*. HBR Reprint 98409. Boston: Harvard Business School Publishing; 1998 July.
8. Katzenbach, J.R., Smith, D.K. *The Discipline of Teams*. Boston: HBR Reprint R0507P. Boston: Harvard Business School Publishing; 1993 March/April.
9. Christensen, C. *Field Case (Materials Technology Corporation): Teaching Note*. HBS Case 5-698-083. Boston: Harvard Business School Publishing; 1998 March 3.
10. Balderstone, J., Birnbaum, P., Goodman, R., Stahl, M. *Modern Management Techniques in Engineering and R&D*. New York: Van Nostrand Reinhold; 1984.
11. Hammond, J.S., Keeney, R.L., Raiffa, H. *The Hidden Traps in Decision Making*. HBR Reprint R0601K. Boston: Harvard Business School Publishing; 1998 September.
12. Dumbleton, J.H. *Management of High-Technology Research and Development*. New York: Elsevier; 1986.
13. Bergen, S.A. *R&D Management. Managing Projects & New Products*. Oxford: Basil Blackwell; 1990.
14. Wheelwright, S.C., Clark, K.B. *Creating Project Plans to Focus Product Development*. HBR Reprint 92210. Harvard Business School Publishing; 1992 March/April.

BEST PRACTICES FOR PRODUCT DEVELOPMENT MANAGERS

Chapter 9 discusses selected management issues that are frequently encountered by managers in a product development environment. Also presented are applicable best-known practices from the high-tech industry.

Using simple tools in all management actions, including communication, aggregate project and resource planning, risk assessment, and decision making, is advisable. When automating integration across all dimensions of a business (technology, product, business, people, and market), refrain from complex (and often complicated) tools. Tools must enable managers to see relationships and to make timely decisions.

9.1 BUSINESS PROCESSES

Business processes that are appropriately *unstructured* in a small start-up company environment must change as the company grows in size and its product portfolio becomes larger and more complex. As the firm grows it must employ more rigorous and *structured* techniques, design world-class business processes, and practice them in product development.

Conversely, developing new high-tech products requires an environment that promotes innovation and out-of-the-box thinking. This apparent dichotomy is underscored when the innovators on a development team of a large company begin to express dissatisfaction with following established business processes, labeling them as "bureaucracy." Having bureaucracy, or a system of management processes, is useful and desirable because this type of bureaucracy can eliminate the repetition of old mistakes. Bureaucracy is only undesirable if it prevents or discourages experimentation and risk taking out of a fear of making a mistake.

In designing a business process, adopt global best practices. Do not merely rely on "good ideas." Best-known practices should be embellished with "good ideas" for improvement and

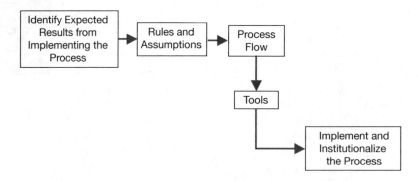

Figure 9.1. Developing and Adopting a New Business Process.

adaptation to the particulars of an environment. Designing a business process should start with establishing the *expected results* from the process if it is implemented, which is followed by the *rules of doing business*; the assumptions; the flow of tasks (*process flow*); and finally by identifying the *tools for* practicing the process and performing its tasks (Figure 9.1).

Adopting and institutionalizing a new business process after it has been designed is often challenging for managers because change management is involved in "selling" the new process to stakeholders and discipline is required to demand its practice until the process is institutionalized. Change management is usually a lengthy process that implements an initial pilot trial run on the way to ubiquitous adaptation.

9.2 DECISION MAKING

Managers are not rewarded by what and how much they know, but by the effectiveness of the decisions they make. Effective (or good) decisions result in appropriate actions that produce the desired outcome at the right time. Good decisions are not the impromptu creation of an inspired mind, but the result of a process involving deliberation and the use of intuition. Deliberation is the use of information, data, experience, and reason. Intuition connects us to our creative essence.

Although following a good decision-making process is necessary, it is not sufficient for attaining effectiveness (i.e., a *good* outcome). Decision making in new situations (i.e., in high-tech products and markets) is risk prone and the outcome is precarious. Even if a good decision-making process is followed, the result(s) might be less than desired because of the risks associated with making assumptions and having a lack of sufficient data and analytical models.

Figure 9.2 classifies decisions into three types—right, wrong, and bad—according to their outcomes and according to whether (or not) a good analytical process was followed in making the decision. Wrong decisions are made with deliberation and by using intuition (as are good decisions), but wrong decisions result in inappropriate action because of the risk taking associated with inadequate data. Bad decisions result in inappropriate action and an undesirable outcome that could have been avoided. Bad decisions are made arbitrarily, without deliberation, and by not trusting intuition.

Figure 9.2 underscores the importance of following a good decision-making process and recommends using a kaizen process to learn when a wrong decision is made or when an outcome

Type of Decision	Process Used in Decision Making	Outcome of the Decision (Results)	Required Kaizen Action
1. *Right* Decision	Good	Good	Reinforce
2. *Wrong* Decision	Good	Bad	Critique and Correct
3. *Bad* Decision	Bad	Bad	Eliminate

Figure 9.2. Decision Types.

is undesirable (*bad*). Not making a decision (when one is needed) or making a late decision has the same undesirable outcome as a bad decision. Most often the biggest problem with a bad or a late decision is lost opportunity, in addition to the investment that has been wasted in implementing the decision.

9.2.1 A Nine-Step Decision-Making Process

1. Clearly define the objective, the KPIs (key performance indicators), and the problem.
2. Define the decision to be made.
3. Identify the decision maker (the person who has the authority and who is accountable for the decision).
4. Select the critical issues and options relating to the decision. Avoid discussing irrelevant issues.
5. Thoroughly research the critical issues and options. Consult with those affected by the decision.
6. Analyze the information and use hypotheses to test the findings and options.
7. Make a decision. Operate with limited information based on experience (i.e., take an informed risk).
8. Perform a sensitivity analysis of the decision to changing conditions.
9. Implement the decision.

9.2.2 Pitfalls in Decision Making

In the decision-making process, cognitive biases, risk averseness, personal agendas, and undue haste to make a decision may derail an objective and creative outcome. These biases and "hidden traps" must be watched for and circumvented in a decision-making process.[1] Biases and hidden traps include:

- Anchoring—Initial impressions, estimates, or data that anchors subsequent thoughts or judgments
- Perpetuating the status quo—Choosing an option that creates the least change and risk
- Sunk-cost justification—To prolong the actions of past (bad) decisions

- Bias toward a preconceived outcome—Seeking out confirming evidence and information that supports inclinations
- Framing—Stating the problem that establishes anchoring or status quo biases
- Overconfidence—Thinking that information is not necessary
- Overcautious prudence—Seeking too much information and becoming paralyzed by analysis
- Recallability—Bias from past events and memories that might not be well calibrated

9.3 RISK MANAGEMENT

Development of new high-tech products involves a knowledge-generation process that advances current capabilities and opportunities and strives to achieve something that has not yet been accomplished. A development team is often faced with making a decision that involves choosing among several alternate market opportunities, technology paths, design approaches, and commercialization strategies. A trade-off study for selection of the optimal solution or strategy is often challenged by inadequate information and the lack of a model for analysis. For example, the outcome of a candidate strategic direction might be uncertain because of turbulent market conditions. Alternatively, system performance with alternate technology paths might not be predictable because of the lack of experimental data and theoretical modeling capability. Nevertheless, taking a risk and making a decision or choosing a strategy and adopting a technology or design concept are crucial. Product development and commercialization must proceed. Otherwise market opportunity will be missed altogether.

Risk taking involves making decisions and acting without all the *necessary knowledge* required to assess the outcome with certainty. Risk, according to dictionaries, is the "possibility of loss" or what risk taking actually entails. Any risk-taking decision must be informed, calculated, and based on the probability of the future outcome and its impact.

A calculated risk process has two characteristics—understanding existing knowledge versus necessary knowledge and assessing the impact and benefits of taking the risk versus the consequences of not taking the risk. Calculated risk taking in an organization must be rules based. The boundaries of operation should be known at every level in the organization, delineating the authority and process of empowered risk taking. Use of a common communication language is also important in making the process efficient. Postmortem analysis of taking a risk and the impact is also important to increase organizational learning and to improve the risk-taking process in the future. High-tech organizations must promote a culture of "calculated" risk taking. Managers should empower individuals to take and manage risks, allow failure, encourage open communication, and encourage the free flow of information between all project levels.

Effective risk management in product development and project management is a continuous process that is comprised of several steps:

1. Identify risks and state the conditions that lead to the risks and potential consequences. The three categories of risk are:
   - Business and market risks, including economic/business cycles, loss of market attractiveness, market acceptance of the new product, competition, customer/partner strategy shift, price erosion, market assets, and supply chain

capability (*Note*: A framework for assessment of emerging markets and new businesses is discussed in Chapter 10.)
- Technology and product risks, including immature technology, product performance, commercialization timing, market adoption resistance, and threat of obsolescence and substitution
- Project risks, including schedule, resources, performance of suppliers, and cost
2. Assess impact—What are the consequences of taking or not taking the risk? What are the probabilities of these consequences occurring?
3. Prioritize risks based on impact—Identify the top three risks at all times during the project.
4. Develop a mitigation strategy and action plan, including resource impact.
5. Track the status of the mitigation plan.

The paragraphs that follow discuss methodologies for risk impact assessment and decision making. The reader may also consult the resources in the *Additional Reading* section at the end of this chapter for more in-depth discussions of risk management.

High-tech *product development* risks can be mitigated by using a flexible development process (also see Chapter 5) that allows rapid adjustment in product development decisions through continuous and real-time knowledge learning and feedback. Project *schedule risks* are usually associated with tasks that are on a critical path, have several predecessors, are reliant on external groups, or have optimistic planning assumptions. *Resource risks* are associated with tasks which need scarce resources (including people and tools), lack adequate competent individuals, and have many part-time team members. Project *scope risks* are associated with tasks that have new (to the company) or breakthrough technologies and that have aggressive performance requirements.

Project managers must rank project risk factors and generate a contingency plan and mitigation actions for high-risk areas. Table 9.1 presents a framework for quantifying and ranking project risks. Project risks are scored according to:

- Impact on KPIs (key performance indicators)
- Seriousness to resolve
- Likelihood of occurrence

The example shown in Table 9.1 is for the Super Robot project described in Chapter 8 (see Figure 8.15). The table shows individual and overall scores of each risk factor. The overall score is calculated as the product of individual scores. The project manager might assign a *weight* to various parameters in the table before tallying up the total score. For example, the score of the impact on the schedule may be weighted three times more than the score of the impact on the project budget.

9.4 THE DECISION TREE IN RISK MANAGEMENT

Managers often ask—How much risk is there if we go this way or another? How much is the cost? How and when will we know that we are on the right path? If not, will we still have time to revert to an alternate approach and still meet the time-to-market and market-opportunity targets?

Table 9.1 Qualification of Risk Factors for the Super Robot Project

Risk Factor	Impact on KPIs				Seriousness to Resolve	Likelihood of Occurrence	Overall Risk Score
	Schedule	Project Budget	Product Cost	Product Performance			
Clamp scratches back of wafers	3	1	1	3	3	5	135
No wafer sensing sensors and electronics	5	1	3	1	3	3	135
Reliability qualification by customers	5	3	1	1	5	3	225
Wafer sliding in chambers due to increased capture window	1	1	1	3	3	5	45
Indexer calibration robustness	1	1	1	5	3	5	75

Note: Risk factor scores are from 1 to 5 according to the severity of impact on KPIs and other parameters, with 5 being the highest risk. KPIs, key performance indicators.

A decision tree is useful to answer some of these questions. A decision tree charts the course among alternative paths that a development process might take based on the trade-off of technology, time to market, and financial risks. For example, a risky product concept might be selected for an E&F design, prototype, and testing. At the completion of this task (the *event*), two outcomes are envisioned—either the concept meets the E&F requirements or it does not. A decision tree identifies each decision and the action plan that ensues as a result of each possible outcome. For the E&F example, if the design meets E&F requirements, then the next task might be the alpha phase, but if the design does not meet requirements, the decision might be to repeat the task with an alternate concept or to abandon the path altogether. The tree will then be extended from the *event* juncture along both paths to subsequent *events* for a decision until the end of all paths. (*Note*: Figure 10.24 in Chapter 10 contains a decision tree that represents this example.)

Decision trees can also be used to estimate the probability and financial commitment associated with alternate paths over time. This is done by estimating the probabilities of alternate outcomes at an event, and the costs of getting there, and calculating cumulative probability and cost by the end of each path on the tree.

To illustrate the decision tree methodology, two examples of wafer fabrication equipment development are depicted in Figure 9.3 and Figure 9.4.

9.4.1 Example 1—Zylex Corporation

In the late 1990s, Zylex Corporation was faced with a major challenge—the timely development and commercialization of a broad portfolio of 300-mm wafer fabrication equipment. Major IC manufacturing customers were planning to build new 300-mm fabs by the end of

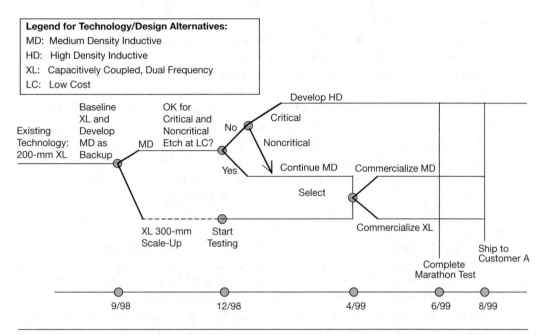

Figure 9.3. Decision Tree for 300-mm Dielectric Etch Development Strategy.

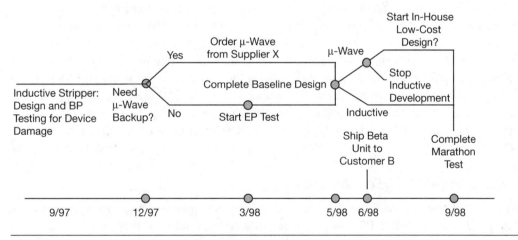

Figure 9.4. Decision Tree for 300-mm Photoresist Stripper Development Strategy.

the millennium to improve productivity, to lower cost, and to move down the path of Moore's law of the semiconductor industry.

At that time, dielectric etch equipment was one of the largest segments of the market. This market had been a traditional stronghold of Zylex. However, the ever-shrinking IC design rule had created a serious challenge to the traditional dielectric etch technology that Zylex had been successfully marketing up until that time. Technologists at Zylex thought that a new technological capability would be needed for the next generation IC design at and below the 0.25-μm node, which was the target of emerging 300-mm manufacturing.

Another challenge in the dielectric etch technology segment was the diversity of applications, which fragmented the market into multiple subsegments with differing technologies and cost-per-wafer requirements. For example, the largest subsegment was an interconnect etch technology that required very low costs and had the least technologically demanding requirements. This market was labeled "noncritical." On the other hand, the front-end applications were technologically demanding (critical etch), but small in market size. Although important, cost was not the primary concern of customers in the critical etch segment.

In September 1998, after many days of intensive (and at times heated) discussions among technologists, marketers, design engineers, and managers at Zylex, a decision tree was created (Figure 9.3). The legend box in Figure 9.3 illustrates the alternative technologies that the dielectric etch team considered. The team thought that a scale-up of the existing XL technology from 200 mm to 300 mm should be considered as baseline because it had the best chance of meeting the MRS for both critical and noncritical applications. Because they were not sure of that decision and were not ready to forego the potential of a new medium-density (MD) technology yet, the team decided to evaluate the competing MD option.

A minimum of 3 months was needed to design and build a bench prototype, test the MD technology, and generate sufficient data for the next decision point by December 1998. In the meantime, because all available resources had to work on MD, the XL baseline technology had to remain dormant until December 1998. This situation was not acceptable to the marketing team, who wanted to ship a beta tool to customers no later than August 1999. However, engineers assured marketing that a float of 3 months would not seriously jeopardize the end date.

At the December 1998 milestone (or event), if MD was found to have potential as a candidate for both critical and low-cost noncritical applications, it would be further developed in parallel with XL technology until April 1999, when a final showdown decision would be made between the two technologies. The team also decided that even if MD was found to only be a good solution for noncritical applications, MD would still be developed in parallel with XL technology until April 1999 as "insurance" against the potential risk of scaling up XL technology from 200 mm to 300 mm. If by the December 1998 event, MD was found to not be a contender for critical applications, the team thought that they should pursue another technology (HD) as a backup for XL technology. The various development paths and decision points are shown in Figure 9.3 (which became the dielectric etch product development strategy at Zylex).

9.4.2 Example 2—SPEq Corporation

In 1997, SPEq was considering the development of a new photoresist (PR) stripper product. SPEq had been marketing PR strippers successfully for a number of years. PR on wafers was removed by exposing it to oxygen plasma that was generated by an inductive source. As the IC design rule shrunk below 0.25 μm, manufacturers were expressing concern that radiation from the plasma would damage IC devices.

Scientists at SPEq had to either prove that their plasma stripper could operate under conditions that would not damage IC devices or they had to look for alternate technologies. An alternate technology that used microwave technology was known to cause less damage than the inductive plasma technology of SPEq, but the alternate technology could only be purchased at very high cost from Company X, which held a patent to the technology. If inductive plasma damaged IC devices, it could not be used. Therefore SPEq would have no choice but to purchase the microwave technology from Company X and reduce its cost at a later time in the development cycle.

Figure 9.4 shows the decision tree that SPEq process engineers presented to management as their strategy for developing the next generation PR stripper product. The development team had planned to assess the radiation damage of the inductive plasma by December 1997 and to decide if they had to switch to the microwave solution. As the decision tree in Figure 9.4 shows, the team had until May 1998 to complete the baseline product design (with either technology). The schedule for shipping a beta system to the first customer was June 1998, and an in-house marathon test was planned for completion by September 1998 (before product production release and commercialization).

9.5 PROBLEM SOLVING

During a new product development and commercialization process, a project team is usually faced with myriad problems relating to technology, design, product performance, manufacturing production, and enterprise operation as well as management. Some of these problems are unavoidable consequences of knowledge generation and learning in a new technology and market situation. Others are the result of poor execution and a lack of discipline. Nevertheless, to solve a problem effectively and in the shortest possible time, the problem owner must apply the best practices of project management and follow a disciplined *problem-solving process.*

This section continues with a discussion of applying project management methodology to solving a customer problem. Then a problem-solving process and several best practices for problem formulation/framing, root cause identification, and brainstorming in the problem-solving process are presented.

9.5.1 Applying Project Management Methodology to Solving Customer Problems

The discipline of effective problem solving is best manifested in winning customer satisfaction through after-sales support. Not uncommon is that a new high-tech product will fail to meet customer specifications and fall short of the customers' expectations during the beta phase of the PDCP or even after the product has been commercially launched and sold to a customer. The supplier's response in resolving issues is a major determinant of customer's trust and loyalty. To resolve the customer's problem effectively, a task force should be formed (treating the resolution of a problem as a *project*) and a project management methodology should be adopted:

1. Clearly frame the problem with the concurrence of the customer.
2. Establish the project guidelines and prepare a project plan, including the end objective, roles and responsibilities of all stakeholders (the team members, the customer, sales personnel, and others), milestone time line, status reporting frequency and format, and escalation path.
3. Ensure that a proper team structure is in place, including a project manager who owns the issue(s) and drives the activities, a motivated working team whose members meet their commitments, and an executive champion who oversees and supports the project. If he/she is an executive, the project manager should be a hands-on individual who manages details on a daily basis.

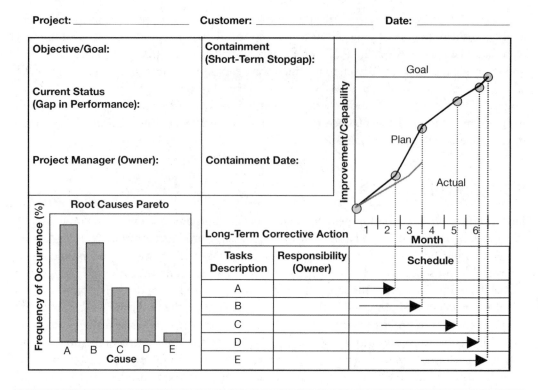

Figure 9.5. Objective/Gap/Action (OGA) Template for Managing Problem-Solving Projects.

4. Establish success metrics (indicators) and criteria that are measurable and agreed upon by the customer and understood by the team members.
5. Use the problem-solving template in Figure 9.5 to track progress; hold weekly working group meetings that focus on action items affecting the success metric; and hold monthly 'Executive' and customer meetings.

See Section 9.5.2 for a rephrasing of this approach in a generic problem-solving process.

An effective template in managing and reporting a problem-solving project is the objective/gap/action (OGA) chart shown in Figure 9.5. This template is useful in managing progress and in presenting project status at customer and management reviews. Note that *by design* the OGA template encapsulates salient information for problem solving on a single page. This single-page constraint forces a project manager and team members to maintain focus on the essence of the challenge. Figure 9.6 contains an example of an OGA chart applied to solving a wafer process equipment reliability problem at an IC manufacturing fab.

9.5.2 A Ten-Step Problem-Solving Process

The following is a generic problem-solving process that applies to solving a variety of problems that are encountered in managing product development organizations and PDCP projects. Note how this problem-solving process utilizes the systems analysis methodology of Chapter 7.

1. Define the problem.
2. Clarify the current situation.
3. Stopgap (containment) to continue operation.

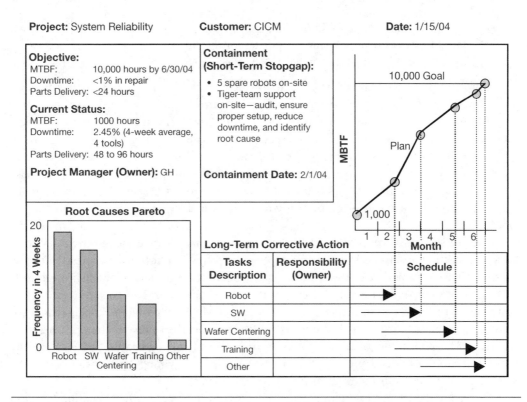

Figure 9.6. System Reliability Project at the CICM Factory. MBTF, mean time between failures.

4. Identify and analyze root causes.
5. Develop alternate solutions.
6. Prioritize and select the "winning" solution, based on selection criteria.
7. Implement, evaluate effectiveness, and validate the solution.
8. Iterate if problem is not solved (go back to step 4).
9. Embed solution and learning in the system to prevent recurrence.
10. Determine future direction (including the problem-solving kaizen process).

9.5.3 Problem Definition and Framing

The scope and urgency of a problem are best understood when a complete description of the conditions of the problem is expressed based on troubleshooting data and input from all who feel the pain. Sorting out facts from inference and feelings and ensuring a common understanding and interpretation of the situation among all the players are critical.

Framing a problem is one of the most important steps of the solution process. Examples of poor problem definitions are statements such as: "The part broke. It does not work. The sales order was wrong, communication was poor, and resources were inadequate." A well-defined problem statement has several characteristics:

- States the effects, not the symptoms or causes
- Is specific and includes measurable key performance indicators
- States the gap between "what is" and "what should be"

- Is positively stated and does not place blame
- States the consequences, "pain," or impact for the customer
- States "what happened" and "what was happening"

A problem statement should have the following *format—During* (date) (main contributor) *accounted for* (X) of (key performance indicator, metric) *which was* (gap) from (goal) *and resulted in* (pain). For example, for the system reliability problem in Figure 9.6, the problem statement might read: "During the last 4 weeks, system failures accounted for 1000 hours of MTBF which was 10 times lower than the goal and resulted in a significant loss of the customer's factory output capability." The corrective action plan to solve the problem should also be specific. State the improvements in the KPIs toward the goal by a specific date and state the name of the problem owner—the person who is accountable for solving the problem (see Figure 9.6).

Problem-solving success criteria state the conditions that must be present to achieve customer satisfaction and to declare that the problem is solved. Success criteria must be clearly stated and have concurrence of the customer at the onset of the problem-solving project. Note that success criteria may have to include more than just meeting the KPI goals. For example, a customer might expect an immediate stopgap solution while the problem is being diagnosed or might demand a change in the supplier's business process to prevent the problem from recurring. The stopgap or containment step of the problem-solving process is the immediate action taken to deal with the problem (before thoroughly investigating the root cause) in order to continue the operation and minimize additional damage.

As listed in the 10-step problem-solving process in Section 9.5.2, after a solution has been found, the solution must be embedded in the product and in the business system of the firm to prevent recurrence of the same problem. A plan must also be devised to take advantage of the lessons learned and to improve the efficiency of problem solving in the future.

9.6 ROOT CAUSE ANALYSIS

Root cause analysis is a systematic investigation that identifies the most basic causes for a problem and the factors that, if eliminated or corrected, would have prevented the problem from existing or occurring. For root cause analysis of problems in a complex system (such as a high-tech product or manufacturing process), a project manager should assign a dedicated team to the root cause analysis task. The makeup of the team should include system, testing, and quality engineers in addition to functional design and process experts. The team should have adequate troubleshooting resources, including access to the failed system(s).

The team should first define their objectives and schedule. Then, to discover the root causes of a problem, the investigating team should identify the systems or processes that allowed the problem to occur or to escape detection and identify what changed, when, and why. Common errors in root cause analysis include:

- Confusing correlation with causation
- Flawed assumptions
- Stopping too soon
- Being time driven versus results driven
- Lacking necessary team competency

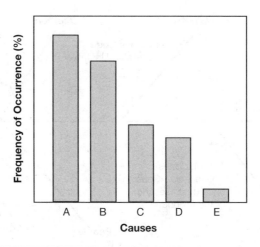

Figure 9.7. Pareto Chart.

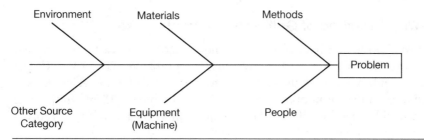

Figure 9.8. Cause-and-Effect (Fishbone) Diagram.

- Confirmation bias; trying to justify preconceived opinions
- Personal agendas

9.6.1 The Tools of Root Cause Analysis

In the product reliability discussion in Chapter 6, a few tools used in root cause analysis were reviewed, including fault tree analysis, failure mode and effects analysis (FMEA), and factor analysis in an experimental design. Additional common troubleshooting and analysis tools include the pareto chart (Figure 9.7) and the cause-and-effect diagram (Figure 9.8). The cause-and-effect diagram is also known as a fishbone diagram.

A pareto chart classifies root causes or failure modes according to their *frequency of occurrence.* If all root cause categories have the same impact on system performance, then problem-solving resources can be prioritized according to the pareto chart severity. A cause-and-effect diagram (or fishbone) attributes root causes of the problem to *several generic sources*, including material, method, equipment, people, and environment. For each category, root causes and effects are identified on the chart and a corrective action plan is developed and implemented. Figure 9.9 shows an example of a cause-and-effect diagram and classifies software reliability problems that SPEq wafer fabrication equipment had in an IC fab.

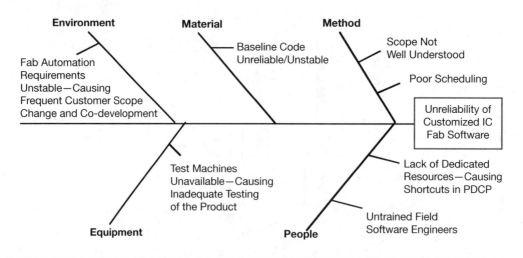

Figure 9.9. Cause-and-Effect Diagram for Software Reliability Problems at SPEq Corporation.

9.6.2 The "Five-Whys" Method of Getting to the Root Cause

The "Five-Whys" (5-Whys) method is an effective technique that can be used to ensure that symptoms and effects are not mistaken for the root causes of a problem. The "5-Whys" start with asking "why" the problem occurred; then asking "why" again to the response; and repeating the "why" question five times or until responding to "why" becomes difficult. In this case the root cause has probably been identified. Adapting an example by Taiichi Ohno (Toyota Motors) will clarify the methodology:[2]

Problem: The machine stopped when the switch was turned on.

    Question 1:   Why did the machine stop?
        Answer: A fuse blew because of an overload.
    Question 2:   Why did the overload occur?
        Answer: The bearing did not have adequate lubrication.
    Question 3:   Why did the bearing not have adequate lubrication?
        Answer: The lubrication pump functioned incorrectly.
    Question 4.   Why did the lubrication pump function incorrectly?
        Answer: The pump axle was worn out.
    Question 5.   Why did the pump axle wear out?
        Answer: Sludge got into it.

Root Cause: Sludge can get into the pump.

Corrective Action: Attach a strainer to the lubrication pump by 11/30/07.

Embed the Solution (Preventative Action): Document the strainer as an integral part of the installation of a lubrication pump, effective 12/31/07.

9.6.3 Testing the Root Cause

An *identified* cause is a root cause if it passes one or more of the following tests:
    •   The problem would not have occurred had the cause not been present.

- The problem will not recur due to the same causal factor if the cause is corrected or eliminated.

9.7 CREATIVE BRAINSTORMING

According to dictionaries, brainstorming is "a group problem-solving technique that involves the spontaneous contribution of ideas from all members of the group." Brainstorming is an effective practice in all aspects of the problem-solving process—in framing the problem, identifying the root causes, identifying alternate solutions to the problem, and in prioritizing and selecting the "winning" solution.

In a high-tech product development environment, a high degree of creativity and out-of-the-box multidisciplinary thinking is often required to solve a problem. The problem-solving team should also be aware of existing knowledge to avoid "reinventing the wheel." Both of these objectives can be achieved by brainstorming. For a brainstorming session to be effective, however, participants must be carefully selected and have diversity in competencies. The brainstorming meeting must be properly managed. A brainstorming session should be conducted through a five-step "funnel" process:

- Start with a creative free flow of ideas that are recorded without judgment.
- Group the ideas into distinct classes.
- Assess the ideas within each class—to keep or to reject.
- Prioritize the selected ideas and classes based on objective criteria (e.g., the cost/benefit ratio).
- Prepare an action plan for the implementation of the selected ideas.

The initial phase of divergent thinking and idea generation is most productive when no judgments or evaluation are made and when as many ideas as possible are sought out. To do this, having participants seated at an oval-shaped table so that the facilitator can go around the room, always in the same direction, giving an opportunity to each of the participants, one by one, to express one idea at a time, is best. Clarifying questions should be allowed to expand and build upon an idea. The facilitator should keep humor alive, laugh at fears, and encourage risk taking. Furthermore, adequate time and effort must be allowed for a deep dive into the subject and immersion into the task.

To encourage creativity, a heuristic approach should be followed in which no clear path is offered or encouraged. Not focusing on the outcome (at the beginning) and not judging where the ideas may lead are important. Because of the fear of being judged by others, many good ideas do not even come into the conscious awareness of people at a brainstorming session. Do not allow group thinking or an atmosphere of collective judgment to take over a brainstorming meeting in which one person, particularly a person with influence or power, dominates the discussion or causes self-filtering of ideas by the participants.

Many new ideas are inspired by and built on the ideas of others. This type of collaborative creativity requires intense listening to others—without thinking about a response. Research information about the issue being considered should be shared freely. The ideas expressed in the session should be recorded on a board that is visible to everyone in the group. The facilitator should promote "seeing" the relationships, patterns, exceptions, and new opportunities.[3-5]

Remember: "Everyone had seen apples fall from trees; it was only Newton who paid attention to the relationship!"

9.8 CYCLES OF LEARNING

The phases of the PDCP for a new high-tech product represent cycles of learning and knowledge generation that lead to the product release and market offering. For example, in developing wafer process equipment for IC fabrication, after the components and subsystems are designed, the following learning cycles are implemented:

- *Integration* of the subsystems into the system in Phase 3
- *Characteristics* of the process in Phase 3
- *Integration* of equipment into IC manufacturing fab in Phase 4
- *Production-worthiness* learning in the IC fab in Phases 4 and 5

Within the phases of a PDCP, additional cycles of learning are also required to create the necessary knowledge for assessing a new technology, to optimize a new design, or to solve a new problem. In planning the implementation of a PDCP (Phase 2) and the tasks within each phase, recognize the required *cycles of learning* and allot a realistic schedule and budget for their implementation.

A graphic illustration of a learning cycle in the design of a product, showing the sequence of events, tasks, and decision points, is presented in Figure 9.10. In this example, the performance of the current design is assessed against the target specification, the problem represented by the gap is framed, and alternate solutions are identified to fill the gap by improving the design. The most promising design alternative (the "winning" solution), based on a set of criteria, is selected for implementation. The selected design alternative is built and tested to verify compliance to the target specification. If the selected design falls short of the target, the cycle is repeated. Note the similarity of the process in Figure 9.10 to the problem-solving process discussed in earlier sections of this chapter.

9.9 EFFECTIVE MEETING MANAGEMENT

A prevalent, time-consuming, and important task of managers is interaction with others, i.e., spending time in meetings. Meetings are important integrative events that must be executed as efficiently and as effectively as other management tasks. People in an organization often resent having to attend too many meetings that are not important to their jobs. The primary root cause of dissatisfaction with meetings is poor meeting management—of the planning/agenda selection, preparation, makeup of participants, conduct of the meeting, and follow-up.

In order to manage meetings effectively and efficiently, methodologies must be adopted that are suitable to the particular category of meeting that is to be held. Generally, four categories of meetings occur in a business environment:

- Management decision meeting (MDM)—The purpose of an MDM is to *make decisions* and to *create an action plan* for what, who, and when. Project meetings, project reviews, operations reviews, and staff meetings are examples of MDMs. *Note*:

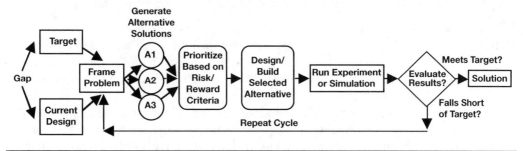

Figure 9.10. Design/Build/Test Cycle of Learning.

Staff meetings are often a combination of an MDM and an IEM (information exchange meeting).

- Problem-solving meeting (PSM)—A PSM is intended to analyze data and concepts, receive input from participants for improvement, brainstorm alternative solutions to a problem, and select the optimum solution. The optimal solution is decided in this meeting if there is no impact on resources or higher-level objectives. Otherwise, a recommendation is formulated and forwarded to relevant management. Design reviews, problem root-cause analysis, technical data or modeling analysis/synthesis, and meetings to solve a customer problem are examples of PSMs.

- Information exchange meeting (IEM)—The purpose of an IEM is the dissemination of information across functional lines to create synergy, learning, and organization-wide alignment of purpose and approach. "All hands" division or company meetings, awards ceremonies, and employee training and development classes are examples of IEMs.

- People relationship meeting (PRM)—A PRM is most often a one-on-one meeting between two people. Performance feedback and appraisals to employees, career development planning, mentoring and coaching of employees, interviewing, and conflict root-cause analysis and resolution are examples of PRMs.

The paragraphs that follow will discuss in detail a methodology for managing an MDM. Adaptation of the MDM methodology to the other types of meetings is straightforward and therefore will not be discussed.

In managing projects for product development, performance is achieved through teamwork and collaboration—in which the performance objectives of various individuals integrate to serve a team objective and the objectives of various tasks (subprojects) integrate to serve the overall project objective. Regular MDM meetings are necessary to review/resolve interface issues, make priority decisions, assign/redirect resources, and revise plans going forward. Participants in an MDM meeting also commit to assigned action items.

Participants in a project MDM are project task managers (or subproject managers); the meeting owner is the project manager. Task (subproject) managers must, in turn, hold their own task MDMs and drive actions to achieve their task objectives.

9.9.1 A Process for Managing a Management Decision Meeting

Effective and efficient management of an MDM should follow a process, with guidelines for each step of the process. The meeting owner and team members must follow several steps:

1. Identify the meeting owner/leader—An MDM meeting leader is the person who has the *authority* to make decisions in the meeting and the person who is *accountable* for the results of the decisions.

2. Prepare for the meeting—The team leader is responsible for updating objectives (if necessary). Participants are responsible for identifying issues which impact achievement of the objectives and for making action recommendations to fill in the gaps. A report of the issues and the recommended actions should be made available to everyone *before* the meeting. Have a database of issues, action items, owners, and due dates that is accessible to all team members.

3. Select the agenda—The team leader must prioritize the issues (from Step 2) and generate an agenda for the meeting. The prioritization criteria must be based on the team KPIs and the impact on accomplishing the objectives. Before finalizing the agenda, the meeting owner should "test" the items on the agenda against an "ownership criterion" by asking: should the team take on this item or should this item be delegated to a subordinating group?

4. Select and invite participants—MDM participants should include those who control the needed resources for implementation of the meeting decisions; must commit to the meeting decisions and to own the action items of the meeting; and have the expertise for input and consultation.[6,7] The leader of a regularly held MDM, such as a project meeting or a staff meeting, in addition to being the decision maker, is usually the meeting facilitator and integrator as well. In certain special types of MDMs, particularly large, controversial meetings (e.g., an organizational strategy meeting), having a facilitator/integrator other than the team leader, someone who has little to gain or lose from the meeting's decisions, is advisable. According to Ichak Adizes, the necessary functions in managing an MDM are integration, authority, power, and influence—and the participants who are chosen to cover these four functions.[8] Adizes argues that an MDM requires **CAPI**, in which **C** refers to the meeting facilitator/integrator who **c**oalesces; **A** refers to the participant with the **a**uthority to say "yes" to the decision and who will also be accountable for the outcome of the decision; **P** refers to the participants with the **p**ower to say "no" to the decision (i.e., to sabotage), such as people who have to implement the decision; and **I** refers to the participants with **i**nfluence who are knowledgeable about the agenda subjects.

5. Conduct the meeting:
   - Discuss the agenda items and review the OGA [objective/gap (root cause)/action plan] charts (see Figure 9.5), if necessary.
   - Decide on changes to priorities, plans, and resource deployment.
   - Decide on action items (AIs), including what to do, to whom an AI is assigned, and when an AI must be completed.
   - Document the decisions and the action plan in a database. The AI database should follow the format in Figure 8.13 in Chapter 8.

   A consultative style of conducting an MDM is most effective—in which the leader listens, seeks input, and encourages interaction among meeting participants.

When a decision is made by the leader, he/she should articulate the rationale (the why) behind the decision and enumerate the assumptions. If an MDM is a regularly held meeting (e.g., project or staff meetings), periodic assessment of the effectiveness of the meeting by the participants using kaizen is recommended.

6. Follow-up—All AI owners have a responsibility to follow up on the decisions of the MDM and to update the database with progress.

9.10 EFFECTIVE PRESENTATIONS

In business, an important method of communication and delivering a message is in an oral presentation. Engineers and managers alike are often required to present their strategies, plans, technical concepts, and results in various venues, including project meetings, project reviews, management reviews, and customer meetings.

The quality of a presentation could be the determinant factor of success or failure in achieving an end objective, whether the objective is selling a product to a customer, selling an idea to management, motivating an audience to support a strategy, or communicating the results of a technology investigation in a design review. Excellent strategies, which promise technological innovations and imaginative marketing plans, can only become a reality if they are communicated well and win the support of investors, customers, constituents (team members), and corporate-management. An excellent presenter has command of the language in which he/she is presenting, irrespective of whether (or not) the presenter (or the audience) is native to the language!

To make an effective oral presentation, a speaker should follow several guidelines:

1. To prepare the presentation:
   - Know the objective for making your presentation. For the presentation to be successful, what should happen as a result of your presentation?
   - Know the audience well, including their background, values, personalities, prioritized needs and preferences, decision-making authority, job titles, subject matter knowledge, and whether they are supportive or antagonistic about you and the subject. What is the purpose of the audience in attending the meeting? What do they expect from your presentation?
   - Know the allotted and the optimal presentation time. Familiarize yourself with the venue, presentation equipment, room lighting, seating arrangement, and support resources.
   - Design and tailor your presentation message and material to the audience:
     - Keep the verbal and visual formats simple.
     - When using PowerPoint slides or flipcharts, decide what the message of each slide is. Slides should be self-explanatory and include the subject, your analysis, and a clear take-home message. For example, if a slide is about problem solving, the slide should state the problem, how to solve the problem, a proof of the solution, and a benefit statement for the audience and include a conclusion with a take-home message.
     - Modularize the presentation for flexibility by ordering the content of the presentation according to the priorities and time constraints of the audience.

- When using the PowerPoint format, present items bullet by bullet (only one item at a time) to prevent the audience from reading ahead and not listening to what you are saying.
- Choose a font size and colors that are easy to see in the lighting environment of the presentation room.
- Bring impact-generating visual aids, such as models, parts, and posters.
- Anticipate questions from the audience and prepare your answers. Embed these answers in the presentation material or have backup material for responses.
- In executive business meetings, having your presentation in the following order might be advantageous:
    1. Your message, with conclusions about the issues and opportunities that are based on research and analysis of data or theory
    2. Recommendations that are results- and action-oriented, identifying what, who, and when
    3. Supporting information and data analysis
    4. A restatement of your message and the action you expect from the audience
- Practice your presentation. Do a "dry-run" presentation with co-workers; critically watch a video of your dry run.
- Bring backup people with you who can answer questions from the audience in detail and in real time. An alternative is to have backup people available on a cell phone.

2. To deliver the presentation:
- Keep it simple and focused.
- Excessive information does not help. Excessive information could hurt a presentation.
- Make sure that "take-home messages" are well understood.
- When you make a point, prove it.
- Use concise and relevant data with conclusions.
- Guide the audience from general information to details and then back to general information.
- Deliver with enthusiasm. Speak slowly and use hand gestures when/where natural to help explain a point.
- Stay connected with the audience:
    - Ensure that the audience is following you.
    - Ensure that the language or the speed of speaking is not a problem.
    - Scan the entire audience for eye contact.
    - Ask questions of the audience to confirm problems and needs.
    - Tailor topics to match the expressed interest.
- Expect and solicit questions:
    - Encourage questions and answer them directly.
    - Ensure that you clearly understand the question asked. Ask for clarification if necessary, before giving an answer.
    - Listen carefully, pause to think, and answer sincerely.
    - Ensure that the answer is satisfactory.

- Handle objections calmly. Pause, gather your thoughts, repeat the objection, and offer a response, including a list of compelling advantages.
- If you do not know the answer to a question that is relevant to the meeting objective, take action to get back to the person later with an answer.
- Think about and treat every question as a lead to the discovery of an audience (customer) problem and an important need.
- Control the audience so that your presentation is not derailed from the objective of the meeting.
- Conclude the presentation:
  - Summarize your message, conclusions, and recommendations.
  - Seek feedback.
  - Finish with action items and required follow-ups for closing the meeting.
- Be prepared and accept change:
  - Have supporting material for agenda changes.
  - If the time is cut short, make key points only.
  - If a top-level individual enters the room during the presentation, summarize the key points already presented and continue with presentation.
  - Where applicable or necessary, ensure enough handouts are on hand for everyone.

REFERENCES

1. Hammond, J.S., III, Keeney, R.L., Raiffa, H. *The Hidden Traps in Decision Making.* Harvard Business Review Article #R0601K. Boston: Harvard Business School Publishing; 2006 January 1; originally published as Hammond, J.S., III, Keeney, R.L., Raiffa, H. *The Hidden Traps in Decision* Making. Boston: Harvard Business School Press; 1998 (product #8575).
2. Imai, M. *Kaizen, The Key to Japan's Competitive Success.* New York: McGraw-Hill; 1986.
3. Rogers, C.R. *On Becoming a Person: A Therapist's View of Psychotherapy.* Chapter 13, *Personal Thoughts on Teaching and Learning;* Chapter 14, *Significant Learning: In Therapy and in Education;* Chapter 19, *Toward a Theory of Creativity.* Boston: Houghton Mifflin; 1961 /1995.
4. Ray, M., Myers, R. *Creativity in Business.* New York: Doubleday; 1986.
5. Adams, J.L. *The Care and Feeding of Ideas.* Stanford, CA: Stanford Alumni Association/The Portable Stanford; 1986.
6. Daniels, W.R., Mathers, J.G. *Change-ABLE Organization: Key Management Practices for Speed & Flexibility.* Mill Valley, CA: ACT Publishing; 1997.
7. Daniels, W.R. *Group Power II: A Manager's Guide to Conducting Regular Meetings.* San Diego: Pfeiffer; 1990.
8. Adizes, I. *Managing Corporate Lifecycles.* Upper Saddle Ridge, NJ: Prentice Hall; 1999.

ADDITONAL READING

Allgood, G.O. Assessing Risk of Innovation. Oak Ridge National Laboratory, Oak Ridge, TN. (Sensors Expo 2001, Philadelphia, PA). OSTI DE00788685. Oak Ridge, TN: Office of

Scientific and Technical Information; 2001. Available at: http://www.osti.gov/energycitations/servlets/purl/788685-LW9IxP/native/

Carnegie Mellon University/Software Engineering Institute. *Principles of Risk Management.* Pittsburgh: Carnegie Mellon University; 2006. Available at: http://www.sei.cum.edu/risk/principles.html.

Kendrick, T. *Identifying and Managing Project Risk: Essential Tools for Failure-Proofing Your Project.* New York: AMACOM/American Management Association; 2003

Maxwell, J.A. *Performance Based Specifications: An Investigation of Risk Management Options.* Army War College, Carlisle Barracks, PA. NTIS ADA366755. Springfield, VA: National Technical Information Service; 1999. Available at: www.ntis.gov.

Mulcahy, R. *Risk Management, Tricks of Trade for Project Managers.* Minneapolis, MN: RMC Publications; 2003.

Pisano, N.D. *Technical Performance Measurement, Earned Value, and Risk Management: An Integrated Diagnostic Tool for Program Management.* Anti-Submarine Warfare Systems Project Office, Washington, DC. NTIS ADA404646. Springfield, VA: National Technical Information Service; 2002. Available at: www.ntis.gov.

Roberts, B., Smith, C., Frost, D. *Risk-Based Decision Support Techniques for Programs and Projects.* Defense Acquisition University, Alexandria, VA. NTIS ADA423518. Springfield, VA: National Technical Information Service; 2003. Available at: www.ntis.gov.

Smith, P., Merritt, G. *Proactive Risk Management: Controlling Uncertainty in Product Development.* University Park, IL: Productivity Press; 2002.

Van Well-Stam, D., Lindenaar, F., van Kinderen, S., van den Bunt, B.P. *Project Risk Management: An Essential Tool for Managing and Controlling Projects.* London: Kogan Page; 2004.

Weiss, W.W. *Risk Reduction with a Fuzzy Expert Exploration Tool.* New Mexico Institute of Mining and Technology, Socorro, NM. OSTI DE00822119. Oak Ridge, TN: Office of Scientific and Technical Information; 2000. Available at: http://www.osti.gov/energycitations/servlets/purl/822119-OqbFrQ/native/.

MANAGING PRODUCT AND TECHNOLOGY PORTFOLIOS FOR SHAREHOLDER VALUE

Tools are no substitute for judgment.

Today's business environment is characterized by rapid development and commercialization of new technologies and the globalization of markets, products, and competition. This complex environment requires holistic and integrated R&D investments that are linked to corporate business strategy, serve business objectives, and result in an improved competitive position and a superior return on investment (ROI.)

The purpose of Chapter 10 is to discuss guidelines for aggregate planning and resource allocation in the creation and management of balanced technology and product portfolios. The chapter begins with a case study in R&D resource allocation. The case presents the common tension that exists between business opportunities that compete for a firm's scarce resources. Next is a section that briefly discusses the factors that affect long-term growth in shareholder value and form the basis of product portfolio management and ROI decisions.

The discussion then moves on to a strategic framework for the creation of a balanced portfolio and a R&D resource allocation that supports the firm's existing business (through customer satisfaction and market share improvement), helps launch new business, and enhances the company's market position and shareholder value. This framework is also applied for decision making and priority setting in product selection and project assessment to ensure both local (business unit) and global (firm) optimization of R&D investment. Lastly, a framework is presented to relate product development and commercialization decisions (including product features and pricing versus customer value tradeoffs) to profitability and ROI.

CASE STUDY—COMPETING DEMAND FOR SCARCE RESOURCES

Setting. In 2002, the semiconductor market was in a deep recession and Excel Corporation was experiencing severe financial challenges. Excel had seen other recessions in the past and was well aware of the cyclic nature of business in the semiconductor industry. However, this recession seemed different and particularly painful. Only 2 years earlier, Excel had reached a historical, peak level of revenue after 1.5 years of phenomenal growth that had doubled the size of the company, but now Excel was experiencing a downturn in business that was dramatic—the company's revenue had plummeted by a factor of three (from its peak run rate) in a span of 1 year! As a result, Excel had to resize its operating cost base, including the R&D investment, to stay profitable in 2002. The headcount had been reduced by 30% through three layoffs in 1 year.

Situation. Excel consisted of several semi-autonomous BUs that marketed different product lines and were accountable for delivering their planned CP (contributed profit) to the corporation. The company CFO set CP targets for all BUs and allocated R&D resources based on the projected BU revenue. As the total corporate R&D pool continued to shrink, competition for the remaining R&D resources intensified.

In 2002, BU general managers (GMs) who were feeling "squeezed" by their new CP targets started looking at their peer BUs, challenging the distribution of R&D funding in the company. The company's lack of a rigorous investment decision-making methodology (for choosing among various product lines and prioritizing product development projects) had resulted in bad investments in the past and had created an unhealthy, competitive work environment.

Outcome. In March of 2002, the company CEO called a meeting to discuss the need for a further reduction in force. She invited all BU GMs, the Corporate Strategy VP (SVP), and the CFO. The following discussion reflects typical discussions among BU GMs at Excel in 2002 and highlights the need for a methodology for making aggregate R&D investment decisions that is transparent and strategy based. (*Note:* After 4 hours, no action decision was made at this meeting!)

SVP: Instead of just cutting costs like the planned 20% headcount reduction, let's do things differently this time.

BU1: We're cutting costs just to meet commitments to the stock market. Why not report a loss so we don't jeopardize our future?

BU2: We haven't been given any reduction target yet so we can't judge the impact.

BU3: In our division, we've been reducing costs in every part of our operation all year long. Our division will be profitable, while our competitors are losing money. The company's problem is with corporate functions (like manufacturing) that haven't reduced their cost base. All they do is to transfer their costs to us (BUs). (Note: This BU was in worse shape than the others. In the last 2 years, the BU had lost market share and money and had many organizational difficulties.)

BU1: All my resources have been taken away. At the peak, we had twice as many people as we do now. Many of our engineers have transferred to other BUs. Our controllable (variable) R&D cost is much less than the fixed costs (including facilities, finance, HR, and IT) that are allocated to us by the corporation.

BU2: After the Product Roadmap Review a month and a half ago, we didn't prioritize our products and programs, although we had the chance.

BU4: In our BU, we've had three cuts over the last year, but the number of projects hasn't been reduced proportionately, in spite of a lot of analysis.

SVP: Why is it that Company Y (a competitor of BU5) that was bankrupt a few years ago has come back? They're beating us in the market with new products. Our infrastructure might be too large for the business.

BU3: What's the model for the corporate infrastructure? For example, how many buildings per $100 million in revenue should we have?

BU4: Company Y has leveraged their R&D budget through joint programs with European Union government R&D institutes.

BU5: We have too many internal reviews. We're not getting anything back from our central corporate R&D initiatives. Corporate tax by the central functions is too high.

CFO: This is the report card of some of our unsuccessful R&D investments in the last 3 years. They demonstrate that we have execution problems and that we must link our investment decisions to revenue:

- Product A—After a $200,000,000 investment, execution is nonexistent and product strategy seems flawed.
- Product B—It has a low market share and an almost negative gross margin after $180,000,000 in investment. Product development execution has been poor, which resulted in inferior technical performance and product reliability problems.
- Product C—It has lost position with a major customer and is struggling with another customer. This other customer is evaluating competitors' technologies. Investment to date is $80,000,000, while total revenue from this product is $60,000,000; execution has been problematic.
- Corporate R&D—This unit spent more than $50,000,000 last year.

SVP: R&D at Company Y is 6 to 7% of revenue. Our R&D is 18%. Maybe we have too much money in R&D.

BU1: Today, our BU GMs, compared to a few years ago, have more reviews, more complex lives, a less controllable R&D budget, and spend lots of energy on internal issues.

SVP: The cost of our projects isn't captured properly. We don't have a project accounting system, so it is easy to overspend.

BU5: The corporate R&D group didn't focus on new technologies. They spent their time marketing themselves—and the regional offices are very overstaffed.

SVP: People around this table should propose what to do—not just express problems.

BU2: We must flatten the corporate organization. The BUs get arbitrary financial targets. We only control 20% of the total R&D costs. The rest is allocated to us without our representation. The headcount in the Japan region is too high.

BU5: Application labs in Asia are inefficient and expensive. The practice of "uniformly allocating" the costs of facilities is out of control.

CEO: It's difficult for us to leverage R&D resources through joint development partnerships with our customers. Our major customers demand exclusivity and only small companies can afford this. We're a big company and have to do it differently.

SVP: Accountability is strong, but the space of control of the BUs is limited. Should the company restructure?

BU1: We just talk, but we take no action. My controllable is only $4,000,000. I don't know—what's the point of me saying anything? We, as a company, aren't like an army—we're fragmented—we have too many disagreements.

BU3: Create a model for corporate allocated costs (from manufacturing, facilities, IT, etc.) versus revenue.

SVP: Our problem is that we have a lot of cash, so we aren't forced to take the necessary actions.

CEO: There's a task force to reduce the number of buildings by a factor of 3, in 2 years. If all the BUs don't want the application lab in Japan, we should do something about it. The BUs should also act like the regions work for them.

BU4: We have too many layers of management. We focus on reporting and talking rather than executing. We reorganize too frequently and as a result lose continuity and learning.

SVP: This is a summary of what should be done:

- Our balance sheet is strong. We should leverage it to get ahead of competitors.
- We should review the company's structure.

- Put everything on the table and discuss it (variable and fixed costs of R&D, corporate allocations, etc.).
- We must seriously rethink further downsizing of the company before we proceed with the planned 20% headcount reduction.
- R&D projects must be prioritized.

CEO: In summary, we must address three issues:

- Structure, allocation, and reviews
- Execution in product development
- Leveraging our balance sheet through mergers and acquisitions

10.1 FACTORS AFFECTING LONG-TERM GROWTH OF SHAREHOLDER VALUE

Market leadership, customer loyalty, and operational excellence are the bases for continuous growth in shareholder value. Product innovation and commercialization lead to a commanding market share if the product and the technology are differentiated and an efficient marketing program is implemented to develop intimate customer relationships and loyalty. Possessing a commanding market share together with strong brand equity and a powerful position in the value chain enables a firm to secure attractive value for its offerings and to grow the business. Operational efficiency, through capable business processes, low cost base, leveraged infrastructure and assets, and a strong cash position, results in superior financial performance and an excellent return on shareholder equity. Key financial indicators of long-term business success are return on assets (ROA) and return on equity (ROE).

10.1.1 Return on Assets

ROA indicates how much income each dollar of assets produces on average. ROA is an indicator of efficiency in asset utilization, i.e., management's ability to return profits from utilizing company assets and generating revenue from existing and new products:

$$ROA = \text{Net Profit/Total Assets} = \text{Profitability} \times \text{Asset Turnover}$$

where,
Profitability = Net Profit/Revenue
Asset Turnover = Revenue/Total Assets

Some firms use the *operating assets* (inventory + receivables + buildings + equipment − cash) and calculate the return on operating assets. Some analysts define ROA as EBIT/Total Assets, where EBIT is earnings before interest and tax.

As the above equation shows, firms can achieve a high ROA either by boosting *profitability* or by generating more revenue and having a higher asset *turnover*. A high-volume (revenue) business results in a high asset turnover even if product gross margin is low. On the other hand, a high-margin product results in high profitability even if sales volume (revenue) and asset turnover are low. In other words, the strategic outlook of a business is an important consideration in the ROA analysis of a company or an investment.

The ROA performance of a firm should be assessed against a *hurdle rate* such as the money market interest rate and the cost of capital or the ROA performance of competitors and benchmark companies from other industries. An investment creates shareholder value if it can achieve an ROA that exceeds the cost of capital. In high-tech businesses, the ROA must be high enough to allow the firm to internally fund its growth in revenue and in the development of new technologies and products.

To achieve superior ROA performance, establishing world-class targets for key operational metrics that impact ROA, tracking their performance, and adopting strategic and tactical actions to achieve the targets are essential. Some key operational metrics include receivable terms from customers; revenue/employees; market share; product average selling prices; manufacturing fixed and variable costs; inventory turns; and efficiency in the use of buildings and facilities.

10.1.2 Return on Equity

ROE (return on equity) is a measure of sustainable growth and an indicator of how hard the investment of shareholders is working. ROE measures the average return on the firm's capital contributions from its common stockholders—or how many dollars of income are produced for each dollar invested by the common stockholders:

$$ROE = \text{Net Profit/Stockholders' Common Equity}$$

or

$$ROE = \text{Profitability} \times \text{Asset Turnover} \times \text{Leverage}$$
$$ROE = ROA \times \text{Leverage}$$

where,
Leverage (or Equity Multiplier) = Total Assets/Common Equity

10.2 RETURN-ON-INVESTMENT MODELS

Several methods may be used to assess return on investment (ROI) in product development. Two simple methodologies are presented in the section that follows which will prove to be sufficient for decision making in most product development situations, including the development of a product portfolio.

10.2.1 Valuation of a New Product

Using a present-value method, viability of investment in a new product can be assessed. This method is used by some venture capitalists to valuate (place a value on) start-up companies.[1,2] The present value of an investment in a new product can be calculated using the following equation:

$$V = R_n \cdot PAT \cdot PE/(1 + d)^n$$

where,
R_n = Revenue from the product in the year n after investment
n = Investment period (in years) or years to liquidity (by investors)

PAT = Expected profit after tax/revenue ratio, at year n

PE = Expected price/earning ratio at year n

d = Discount rate based on these factors—desired hurdle rate, investment stage (in the product or the start-up company), risk (in the technology, the market, and the product development team), and illiquidity

In the above equation, PAT and the discount rate are dependent on market characteristics, the nature of the technology, and the ability of the product team to execute the PDCP flawlessly.

Investors consider the presence (or absence) of several factors in assigning a discount rate and in deciding whether (or not) to invest in a start-up company. The presence of the same factors also applies when an established large company wants to assess the soundness of an investment in developing a new product:

1. The people and the management team who can "get the job done" and execute flawlessly
2. An innovative technology, with commercialization potential and nature (disruptive or next generation and the associated risk)
3. A large, attractive, and rapidly expanding market
4. A strategy for a "compelling competitive advantage"
5. An attractive price per share target

10.2.2 Return Map

A return map is a graphic representation of the investment, revenue (sales), and profit profiles during product development and commercialization phases.[3] The ratio of cumulative profit to cumulative investment is defined as the return factor (RF) and is used as a metric of ROI. In assessing the attractiveness of a product, investors can use a hurdle rate for the RF at a specified time after product introduction to the market (or after product development start date). The RF criterion can also be used to compare (potential) financial contributions of different products.

The return map in Figure 10.1 illustrates several key events in the PDCP. Some of the time periods marked on the return map can be used as KPIs (key performance indicators) of efficiency and effectiveness of execution in a product development project. For example, the breakeven time after release (BEAR or the time taken after product release to reach RF = 1) is a good success indicator for product commercialization. The essence of success in product development and commercialization is maximizing value of outputs from the innovation process divided by the cost of all inputs. The return map in Figure 10.1 presents a straightforward methodology for quantifying success.

Figure 10.2 provides a graphic summary of the key parameters that impact each term of the RF and the profit equations. The chart in Figure 10.2 is an important chart. The author recommends that BU executives and project managers review this chart with their staff members to ensure a deep understanding of its implications and why a holistic approach (doing the *whole* job) to product development is crucial. To maximize the product RF, the development team must be cognizant of the implications of their decisions and actions on a daily basis.

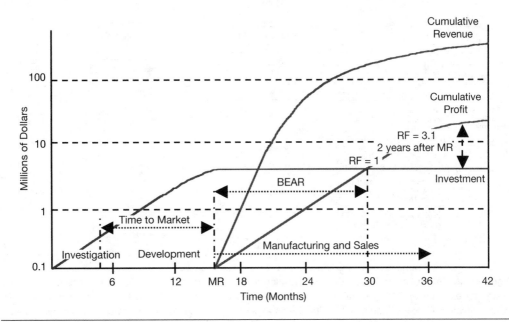

Figure 10.1. Return Map. BEAR, breakeven after release; MR, market release; RF, return factor.

10.3 PRODUCT AND TECHNOLOGY PORTFOLIO PLANNING

The objective of product portfolio planning (PPP) is to answer three key questions:

- Is the product portfolio representative of the firm's business strategy? The PPP must ensure that all business objectives are supported by new or existing products and must identify the projects that are "off strategy."
- Will the product portfolio strengthen the firm's market position and deliver superior and sustainable financial and business performance? This question must be addressed for all portfolio products collectively and individually. To sustain a superior performance, the product portfolio must be balanced in the product project categories, including breakthrough E&F, next generation, platform, derivative, and support projects.
- Are there adequate resources to execute the planned product projects? The PPP must identify the functions that present critical shortages (in capacity and competency) and plan corrective actions.

Portfolio planning may be performed at different levels of an organization, including a BU, a sector, or at the corporate level.

10.4 A FRAMEWORK FOR PRODUCT PORTFOLIO PLANNING

A PPP framework is used to analyze and select an optimal set of product development projects for individual BUs as well as the entire firm.[3–7] Figure 10.3 illustrates a PPP framework comprised of five steps:

1. Strategic objectives

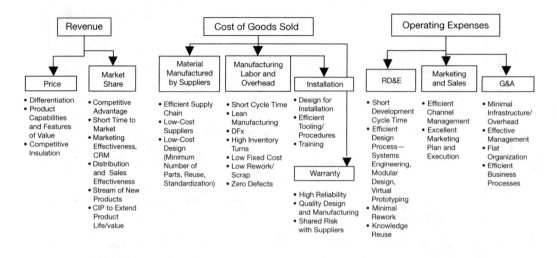

Figure 10.2. Return-Factor Driven Product Development. CRM, customer relationship management; DFx, design for excellence; G&A, general and administrative; Investment = RD&E cost + commercialization cost; Profit = revenue − cost of goods sold − operating expenses; RF = cumulative profit/cumulative investment.

2. Key thrusts (to achieve objectives)
3. Product project analysis (completed individually for each project)
4. Portfolio analysis (to compare different sets of projects, to prioritize and decide on the portfolio)
5. Portfolio management (to execute projects and provide feedback)

Note: Chapter 2 discusses Steps 1 and 2 in detail—Step 1: strategic objectives are derived from the business, market, and technology strategies (see Figure 2.13); and Step 2: key thrust areas are represented by product and technology roadmaps.

Figure 10.4 illustrates a template for summarizing the link between the firm's target markets, the product roadmap, and the business strategy and for identifying key strategic thrusts for research, development, and engineering (RD&E) of new technologies and products. To make the template useful, entries in the table must be quantifiable and actionable metrics.

The remainder of this section will focus on Steps 3 and 4 of the PPP framework. Step 5 is covered in Chapter 7.

10.5 PRODUCT PORTFOLIO PLANNING—STEP 3—PRODUCT PROJECT ANALYSIS

Step 3 of a PPP is the analysis of every product and project within the portfolio, whether the product is at proposal stage or it is an ongoing project. The ranking of projects for suitability within the portfolio and their attractiveness relative to other opportunities must be assessed using several complementary attributes:

1. Strategic alignment
2. Market impact

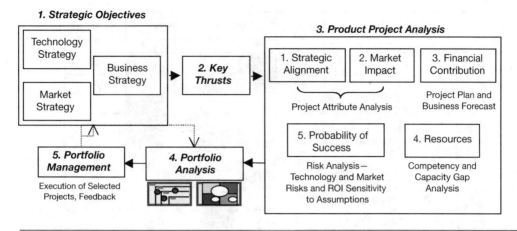

Figure 10.3. Framework for Product Portfolio Planning.

Market Segment	Product Lines Serving the Market	Annual Sales	Gross Profit Margin (%)	Bases of Competition, Market Drivers	Business Strategic Objectives	Key Thrusts in R&D and Development Projects
A	A1	150	45	Technical Performance, Brand	Improve Market Share, Positioning in New Segment	New Product Development
	A2	75	25	Cost, Productivity	Maintain Market Share, Improve Profitability	CIP Existing Products
B	B1 (New)	N/A	N/A	Technology	Leadership in Next-Generation Technology	Acquire new IP, New Platform Development
	B2	350	55	Reliability	Customer Satisfaction, Compliance to Specification	CIPs of Existing Products

Figure 10.4. Linking Business Strategy and Key RD&E Thrusts. CIP, continuous improvement projects.

3. Financial contribution
4. Resources analysis
5. Probability of success

10.5.1 Strategic Alignment

The strategic alignment of a product project is assessed with respect to its contribution to achieving the strategic goals of the BU and the firm as a *whole*. A strategic alignment analysis

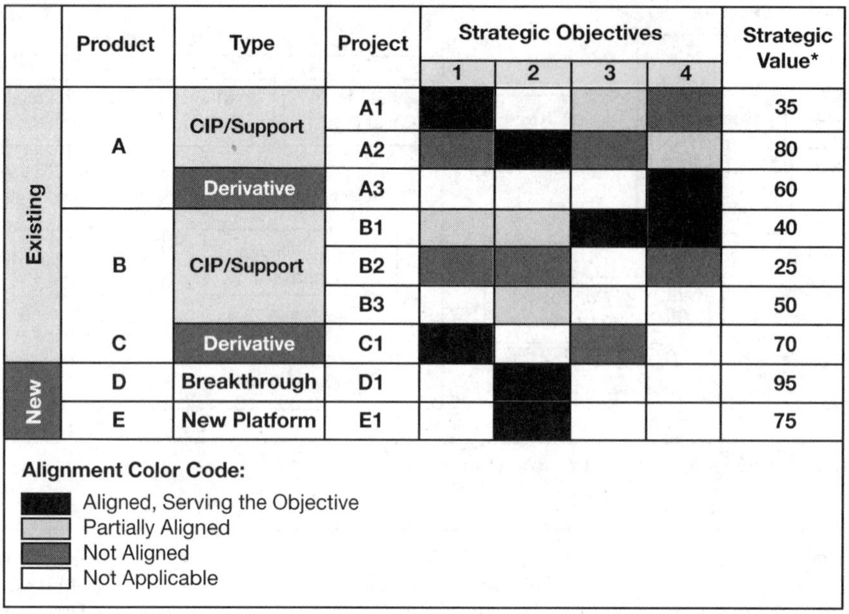

	Product	Type	Project	Strategic Objectives				Strategic Value*
				1	2	3	4	
Existing	A	CIP/Support	A1	■			■	35
			A2		■	■		80
		Derivative	A3				■	60
	B	CIP/Support	B1			■	■	40
			B2	■			■	25
			B3			■		50
	C	Derivative	C1	■		■		70
New	D	Breakthrough	D1		■			95
	E	New Platform	E1		■			75

Alignment Color Code:
- ■ Aligned, Serving the Objective
- ▢ Partially Aligned
- ▨ Not Aligned
- ☐ Not Applicable

Figure 10.5. Strategic Alignment Analysis. * Strategic value—high = 76–100; favorable = 51–75; moderate = 26–50; low = 0–25.

establishes the relationship between the product projects and the strategic objectives and assesses the overall strategic value of the projects.

Figure 10.5 illustrates a template that can be used for a strategic alignment analysis—by listing the firm's strategic objectives and then highlighting whether (or not) the objectives are served by existing or new projects. This analysis helps to identify gaps that must be filled with new projects as well as the projects that should have a lowered priority or be terminated.

10.5.2 Market Impact

Market impact analysis assesses key customer, competitive, and value chain factors in both existing and new markets. Attributes for a market impact analysis should include:

- Technological maturity and product life cycle
- Differentiation and competitive insulation
- Customer value
- Customer relationship and commercialization momentum
- Value chain positioning

Figure 10.6 illustrates a template for analyzing the market impact of projects.

10.5.3 Financial Contribution

Financial contribution analysis assesses the attractiveness of investment in products based on the rate of return from generated revenue and profitability. Financial factors include:

- Investment (cost of execution)
- Market size

Product	Project	Existing Market (Existing or New Segments)							New Market	Value Chain Position
		Technology Maturity and Product Life Cycle	Differentiation and Competitive Insulation	Customer Value	Customer Relationship and Commercialization Momentum	Improve or Maintain Market Share	Replace Current Products or Technologies	Penetrate New Customers	Impact	Create New Market

Scoring of Market Impact:

Enter values in chart as defined below:

- **Technology Maturity**: Breakthrough/E&F = 76–100, Growth = 51–75, Mature = 26–50, Aging = 0–25
- **Product Life Cycle**: E&F = 76–100, New Product Development = 51–75, CIP = 26–50, Aging = 0–25
- **Differentiation and Competitive Insulation**: High = 76–100, Moderate = 51–75, Low = 26–50, None = 0–25
- **Customer Value** (cumulative score based on weighted importance and impact on customer value parameters):
  New or Strong Benefit = 76–100, Significant = 51–75, Moderate = 26–50, Minimal = 0–25
- **Customer Relationship and Commercialization Momentum**: Strong = 76–100, Moderate = 51–75, Limited = 26–50, None = 0–25
- **Other Factors Including Value Chain Position**: Strong = 76–100, Moderate = 51–75, Limited = 26–50, None = 0–25

Total Score = Sum of Individual Scores with Desired Weight

Figure 10.6. Market Impact Analysis. CIP, continuous improvement projects.

- Market share
- Revenue
- Profitability (calculated as ratio of CP to revenue in the plan year)
- ROI (calculated as Net Present Value (PV) or the Return Factor (RF) = cumulative CP divided by cumulative investment from project start)

Figure 10.7 illustrates a template for financial contribution analysis and ranking projects accordingly.

10.5.4 Resource Analysis

In resource analysis, *required* resources to complete projects are compared with *available* and *committed* resources. Figure 10.8 illustrates a template for resource analysis. Resource gaps identified in the analysis are grouped into "capacity" and "core-competency" categories (creating a "resource gap matrix").

Capacity shortage can be addressed by outsourcing or prioritizing projects and resequencing project starts to match resource availability. A competency gap, however, must be addressed by hiring, training, or the formation of partnership/alliances that complement the firm's capabilities. As discussed in earlier chapters, IP protection and market positioning issues must be carefully considered in "outsourcing" as a strategy to fill core competency gaps.

Product	Projects	Investment	SAM	SOM	Revenue	Profitability (Contributed Profit (CP)/ Revenue)	ROI Indicator (NPV or RF = Cumulative CP/Investment)	Year 2 SAME Factors as Year 1		Year 3 SAME Factors as Year 1	

Figure 10.7. Financial Contribution of Products and Return on Investment. CP, contributed profit; NPV, net present value; RF, return factor (see return map in Figure 10.1); ROI, return on investment; SAM, served available market; SOM, share of market.

Product	Project	Labor Engineering Required	Committed	Other Labor (List) Required	Committed	Other Resources Material Required	Equipment Committed	Overall Availability*
A	A1							
A	A2							
B	B1							
B	B2							
C	C1							

Figure 10.8. Resource Analysis—Required versus Committed. Entries in chart are employee hours to finish the project. *Note:* Overall availability score = percent of required skills and knowledge that is available and committed.

10.5.5 Probability of Success

The attributes in the probability of success category account for technological, commercial, market, and execution risks in achieving project objectives. Figure 10.9 illustrates a template for assessing the probability of success. Several factors are listed. An overall probability of success is assigned to each project based on a weighted average of technological and commercial success probabilities. The "weight" of each risk factor is highly dependent on the business, market, and technology situation:

- Technology risk factors:
  - Technical development (because of resources gap or priority)
  - Technology newness
  - Threat of substitution

Product	Project	Technology			Probability of Technical Success	Market			Probability of Commercial Success	Overall Probability of Success
		Technical Development Risk (Technological and Execution Risks)	Technology Newness	Threat of Substitution		Market Opportunity Risks (Size, Channel, and Other Value Chain Assumptions)	Market Penetration Risk (Entry Barrier, Differentiation, Market Assets, Customer Commitment)	Market Newness to the Company		

Figure 10.9. Probability of Success. Entries in chart are probability of success (based on risk) in percent (%)—larger number indicates less risk and a higher probability of success.

- Commercial risk factors
  - Market opportunity
  - Market penetration
  - Market newness

An important aspect of risk analysis is to make planning assumptions explicit and to assess the sensitivity of the ROI to the assumptions. Later in this chapter, the decision tree framework of Chapter 9 for estimating the probability of success of a project and the financial exposure at different key events of the PDCP will be discussed.

10.6 PRODUCT PORTFOLIO PLANNING—STEP 4—PORTFOLIO ANALYSIS

Step 4 of a PPP is a portfolio analysis to determine if the portfolio is balanced and if it strengthens the firm's (or the BU's) competitive position (see Figure 10.3). Managers should be mindful of several cautionary notes when performing a portfolio analysis:

1. The analysis is time consuming and should be undertaken only if an organization is willing to take action based on the outcome of the analysis.
2. If the analysis is too complex, it will not be useful and will not provide a "clear" decision-making guide. Therefore, simplicity and conciseness are advised over comprehensiveness.
3. The analysis should not be viewed as a deterministic tool for decision because many input values are subjective, but rather it should be viewed as means of thoroughly examining the issues and making an informed portfolio decision.

Many managers consider portfolio analysis to be cumbersome. Its outcome is also imprecise and subjective and hence they shy away from it. The author's experience is that the portfolio analysis process provides a useful insight into the firm's R&D investment situation and, as a minimum, identifies the bottom 20% of projects.

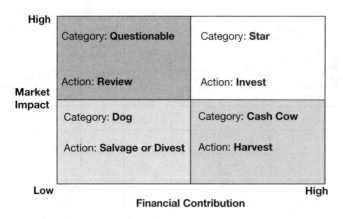

Figure 10.10. Market Impact versus Financial Contribution of Product Portfolio.

10.6.1 Frameworks for Using Product Project Analysis Information

Figures 10.10 through 10.19 illustrate various frameworks for using the information generated in Step 3—the product project analysis—to make investment priority decisions and to answer the PPP questions that were posed at the beginning of this section to fulfill the objectives of the portfolio planning. These frameworks assess the firm's product portfolio in pertinent business dimensions and help managers to choose the optimal portfolio.

Market impact. Figure 10.10 groups projects according to their market impact and financial contribution. Based on the category to which a project belongs, the recommended management action to align the portfolio with the firm's strategic objectives is noted in Figure 10.10.

Strategic and financial contributions. Figure 10.11 illustrates a framework for categorizing projects (within several product lines) according to their strategic and financial contributions. This figure also highlights the hurdle rate for R&D investment at the firm. In the example in Figure 10.11, project A1 seems to have weak justification for existence. Project A1 should be discontinued. The decisions for Projects B2 and B3 are more difficult. The firm appears to be investing in these low-ROI projects and products for their strategic value. Managers must therefore reexamine the soundness of the rating that they have assigned to the strategic value of these two projects. If projects B2 and B3 are confirmed to be of strategic value, action plans must be developed to improve their financial return by improving product differentiation or reducing the products' costs.

Use of Figure 10.11 will be valuable in making priority decisions among different projects if the resource level required for continuing all of the projects exceeds the firm's total available resource pool. The size of each project circle in Figure 10.11 is proportional to the required headcount level. The probability of success for each project is noted next to each project circle as an additional factor in the prioritization process. For example, project C4 is a good candidate to prioritize as being low in investment ranking because it has a low strategic value, questionable ROI, requires a significant amount of resources, has a low probability of success, and the product technology is aging (see figure legend), implying limited future

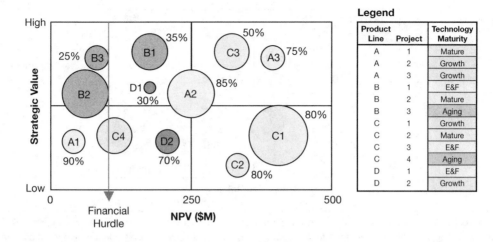

Figure 10.11. Strategic Value versus Financial Contribution with Probability of Success. Circle size is proportional to number of FTEs (full-time employees) required in first year; percentages are overall probability of success. NPV, net present value.

potential. Similar analyses and decisions should be made for every project and product line in Figure 10.11 in the portfolio planning process.

Profitability and revenue contributions. Figure 10.12 assesses the 1-year and the 3-year profitability and revenue contributions of projects in the portfolio. The information from this chart should be used in making the firm's 3-year investment plan. For example, Projects C2 and C3 are important to keep because of their long-term revenue and profitability potential. However, because both the 1- and 3-year potentials of Product line A are low, Product A should be discontinued or a corrective action plan must be put into place to remedy the situation.

Market considerations. Figures 10.13 and 10.14 assess the firm's product line portfolio in market position (share) and profitability against the market opportunity or the size of the served market (SAM). In the portfolio, Figure 10.13 identifies underperforming niche products and Figure 10.14 identifies the business distracters—both distracters should be terminated.

Competitive differentiation. Figure 10.15 evaluates the competitive differentiation (insulation) of products against their market position. This framework identifies winning products (with a high market share) that are in jeopardy because of eroded differentiation and highlights the need for a corrective action plan. The differentiated products that have a low market share must also be reviewed to assess why they are underperforming. The root cause might be poor positioning/customer communication or an erosion of customer value for the differentiated attributes of the product. The low-impact products that are undifferentiated and have a low market share must be discontinued to save the scarce resources for other projects or an action plan must be implemented to rapidly remedy the situation.

R&D strategy. Figure 10.16 is a framework for assessing R&D investment vis-à-vis the technology portfolio. The size of the circles in Figure 10.16 is proportional to the current-year project budget and displays the direction of the firm's investment. As technology matures, the

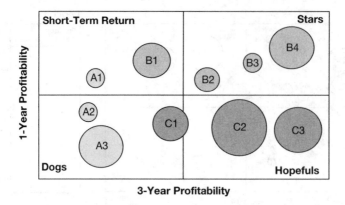

Figure 10.12. Short- and Long-Term Profitability Contributors. Product lines and projects are designated within each circle, e.g., A1 indicates Project 1 for Product Line A, etc.; circle size is proportional to expected cumulative revenue in next 3 years.

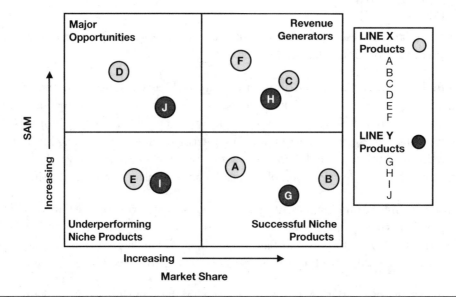

Figure 10.13. Product Line Market Position. SAM, served available market.

company's competitive advantage is likely to erode—either because competitors catch up or because customers migrate to newer generations of technological capability. Therefore, an R&D investment plan must ensure that there is a pipeline of new technological capability in order to sustain competitive advantage. A balanced R&D strategy invests in high-potential emerging technologies, develops products for growth, supports mature technologies, and minimizes investment in aging technologies with weak competitive insulation.

Customer value and competitive insulation. Figure 10.17 assesses the portfolio by ranking projects according to their customer value and competitive insulation. (*Note*: This analysis uses the format of Figure 4.8 in Chapter 4 to identify project types and to illustrate whether the

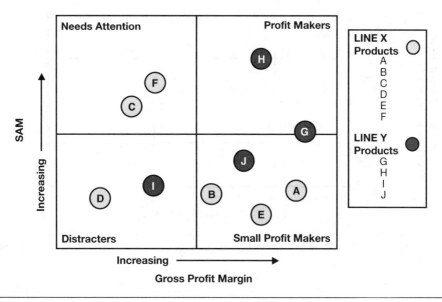

Figure 10.14. Product Line Profitability. SAM, served available market.

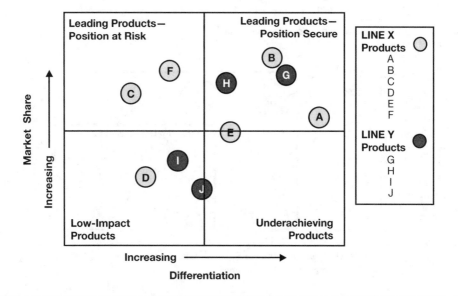

Figure 10.15. Product Line Differentiation.

portfolio is balanced in supporting current products as well as developing next-generation and breakthrough disruptive technologies.) Figure 10.17 reveals how customers and competitors will view the products in development. Competitive insulation is characterized by the number of months required for a competitor to catch up with an equivalent solution. Customer value is defined according to the importance of product attributes (function, features, and cost) to the customer, e.g., in improving a customer's competitive advantage and operational efficiency in business markets.

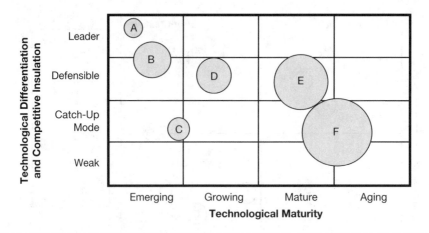

Figure 10.16. Project R&D Budget versus Technological Position. Circle size is proportional to current-year project budget.

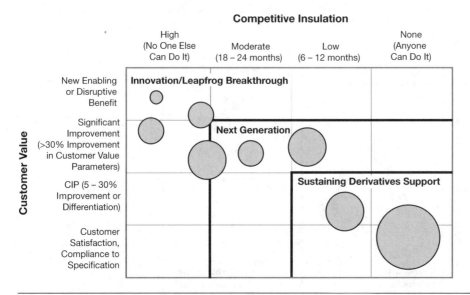

Figure 10.17. Project Portfolio vis-à-vis Competitive Strength and Customer Value. Size of circles is proportional to project resource required in current planning year.

In addition to breakthrough and next-generation products, Figure 10.17 includes projects that are currently in place to solve customer problems with existing products and to address the installed base performance gaps from the customer specifications or expectations. This category of projects is usually intended to gain customer satisfaction, achieve compliance to specifications, and receive a (business) customer's sign-off and payment for a product.

Project portfolio balance. Figure 10.18 is a framework for developing a balanced portfolio of projects that make continuous improvements to current products while investing in future technologies and market opportunities. This framework assesses the distribution of investment in projects compared to their market impact. The state of knowledge generation

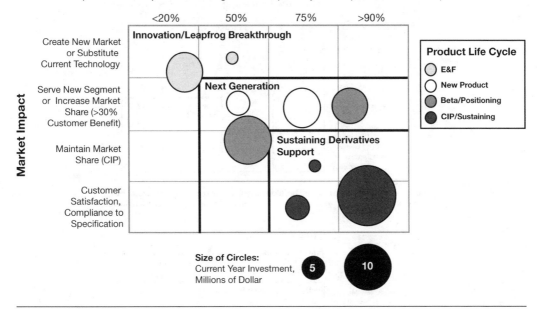

Figure 10.18. Market Impact of Projects by Product Type and Resource Commitment. CIP, continuous improvement projects; PDCP, process of product development and commercialization.

and integration in the PDCP reflects the newness of technology and the life cycle stage of development projects.

Alternative portfolio strategies. Figure 10.19 illustrates how alternate portfolio strategies, commensurate with the company's strategic objectives, can be planned for the direction of resources. In a *growth* strategy, typical of start-up and early stage companies, R&D resources are focused on disruptive or next generation product development. By contrast, a *harvest* strategy focuses R&D resources on existing product technologies to maximize profitability or to solve customer problems. The harvest strategy is a short-term strategy that is adopted either because the magnitude of the problems with the existing products overwhelms the company's resources or because the company plans to enhance profitability by reducing the R&D budget and manufacturing cost. A balanced portfolio strategy allots R&D resources to achieve both short- and long-term competitiveness and business growth.

10.7 RESOURCE DISTRIBUTION

To achieve short- and long-term business objectives, often important is that the project/product portfolio be balanced between E&F (breakthrough and disruptive), new product development, derivatives, and sustaining CIP and support projects. A balanced portfolio distributes resources of the organization accordingly.

For high-tech companies, a rule of thumb for R&D resource distribution is 10% for E&F, 60% for new generation products, and 30% for derivative and sustaining projects/products. This model should be tested and refined according to the specifics of a firm's business, market,

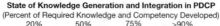

GROWTH PORTFOLIO

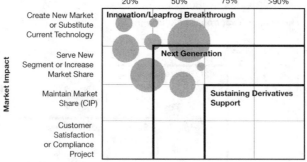

STRATEGY:
Focus exclusively on strategic breakthrough and next-generation projects—typically in early-stage companies or companies trying to remake themselves.

HARVEST PORTFOLIO

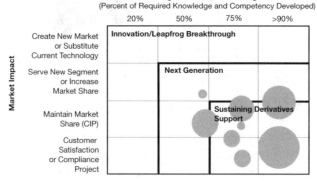

STRATEGY:
Focus on near-term projects for profitability or for reacting to pressures from customers concerning shortcomings of current products against committed specifications.

BALANCED PORTFOLIO

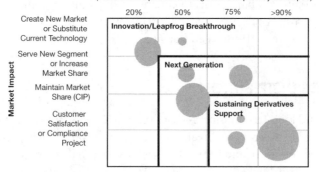

STRATEGY:
Focus on the right mix of projects that make continuous improvements to current products while investing in future technology and market opportunities.

Figure 10.19. Alternate Project Portfolio Strategies. CIP, continuous improvement projects; PDCP, process of product development and commercialization.

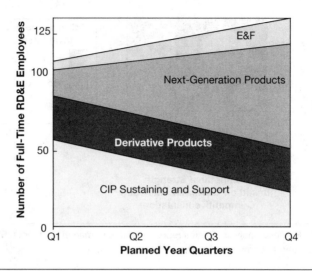

Figure 10.20. Distributions of Engineering Resources by Project Type at a High-Tech Company. CIP, continuous improvement projects.

and competitive situation. For example, in the 1990s, Hewlett-Packard (HP) Corporation reported that 70% of their revenue came from products developed over the prior 2 years. In high-tech industries, the experience at HP is not unusual and perhaps a good model to emulate. In order to do this, however, CIP products and sustaining old products should not consume a significant portion of R&D resources. In other words, the company must develop products that are reliable and meet customers' expectations and specifications and hence require minimal sustaining support.

Figure 10.20 illustrates an example of resource distribution in an engineering organization at a high-tech company. Note that the total engineering pool grew over the year and that the distribution changed from being heavily devoted to CIP sustaining and support projects to a more balanced portfolio.

10.8 ASSESSING MARKET AND BUSINESS OPPORTUNITIES

This section offers a methodology for assessing the attractiveness of alternate market and business opportunities. Larger companies that are serving multiple markets should routinely assess the attractiveness of served markets and their business viability. Additionally, when a new technology is developed, an organization might face a choice among alternate market segment opportunities for initial commercialization. This situation occurs when the new technology has application potential in different segments of the market or if it offers the firm an opportunity to grow into new markets.

The attractiveness of a market must be assessed with respect to its size (the opportunity); the competitive advantage and insulation of the proposed technology application; barriers to entry; and the resources required to develop the product and to reach the customers in that market. Figure 10.21 illustrates an example of a methodology for comparing various market segments based on market attractiveness (size and barrier to entry) versus the competitive

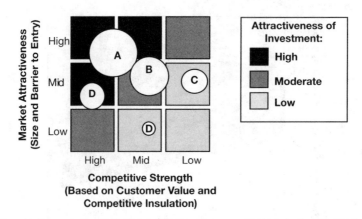

Figure 10.21. Business Portfolio Analysis. Circles represent different market segments. Size of circle is proportional to investment required to commercialize the technology.

strength of the proposed technology product. The size of each circle on Figure 10.21 represents the required investment for developing and commercializing the technology in the corresponding market segment. Attractive markets—markets in which competitive strength is high (the top left area of the box in Figure 10.21)—are most attractive for investment. However, resource limitations might drive the firm to choose a less-attractive market segment commensurate with available funds, e.g., market segment D might be selected over the more attractive segment A.

Figure 10.22 depicts a framework for evaluating alternate market opportunities for a new technology application. Alternative market segments are scored in key factors for attractiveness, business potential, and the probability of successful commercialization of the technology. The optimal market is selected based on an *overall score* that is calculated as the weighted sum of scores of key factors. Note key factor 8 in Figure 10.22. This factor is included to assess the alignment and synergy of the proposed technology/product with the firm's strategic business and technology objectives.

10.9 PROJECT VIABILITY ASSESSMENT

The aggregate portfolio planning illustrated in Figure 10.3 involves the evaluation of product development projects in serving the firm's strategic objectives and their rank in contribution to the firm's growth and profitability. In this section, the assessment process of individual projects will be recapped. The assessment process of individual projects is needed not only in the portfolio planning process, but also in Phase 0 of the PDCP when a new technology innovation and commercialization product is initially proposed. Furthermore, during development of a new product, the product must be continually assessed as knowledge of technology and the "match" to the application context accumulates. A product's pro forma return map and its technology and commercialization risks must be periodically updated at project reviews to reaffirm the product's business viability.

Product project analysis or viability assessment is a six-step process as shown in Figure 10.23. Projects are evaluated based on impact on strategic objectives and the firm's internal and

Product/Technology Application:								
Market/Industry	**Importance Weight**	**A**			**B**		**C**	**D**
Segment/Target Application:		I	II	III	I	II	I	II	I
Key Factors:								
1. Opportunity (SAM in $ Millions)								
2. Firms Positioning Strength in Market Segment • Product/Technology • Market • Company								
3. Compelling Competitive Advantage								
4. Barriers to Entry and Customer Acceptance								
5. Time to Introduction and Revenue								
6. Core Resource Availability and Control by the Firm • RD&E • Operations (Manufacturing)								
7. Market Assets (Customer Reach, Support)								
8. Strategic Alignment and Synergy (Technology Strategy, Business Objectives, Customers)								
Overall Score								

Figure 10.22. Framework for Assessing Market and Business Opportunities for a New Technology Application. In chart, enter a descriptive assessment and a 0 to 100 score (in which goodness scores high). Items in chart can be prioritized and weighted (before adding up overall score) according to market-specific situation and firm's preferences. SAM, served available market.

external driving factors. In Step 1, alignment of the proposed product with the firm's strategic objectives is appraised by measuring its contribution to enabling the objectives. Market opportunity, competitive factors, and value chain impact are quantified in Step 2. A project plan is prepared in Step 3 to determine the scope of the development project and the required investment to complete the project successfully. ROI analysis is also performed to establish the potential benefits of undertaking the project. Step 4 evaluates the required and available resources for executing the project, in both capacity and competency, and identifies the gaps. The probability of success is assessed in Step 5 based on technology and market risks as well as sensitivity of project ROI to the assumptions in the product business plan.

The outcome of the process is the determination that the project has an attractive risk/reward potential (i.e., it exceeds the corporate hurdle rate), with a manageable risk, and that it ranks

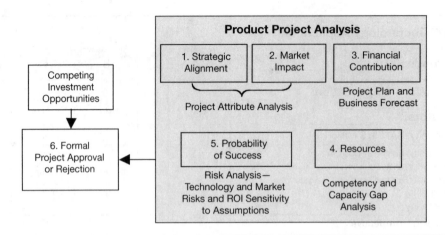

Figure 10.23. Product Project Viability Assessment Process. ROI, return on investment.

higher than other projects that are competing for the same resources. The project viability assessment process ends with a formal approval or rejection of the proposed project in Step 6.

10.10 ESTIMATING THE PROBABILITY OF SUCCESS AND FINANCIAL EXPOSURE IN PRODUCT DEVELOPMENT

Chapter 9 discussed the use of *decision tree* methodology as a tool of risk management in product development projects (see Figure 9.4). Decision tree methodology can be used in planning a project in which the probability of the occurrence of alternate decision paths following key events is estimated. The overall probability of reaching termination of all probable paths and the cost of getting there can also be estimated, as shown in Figure 10.24.

Figure 10.24 demonstrates the methodology for a generic product following the phases of the PDCP. At the conclusion of each PDCP phase, the probability of passing the phase success criteria is noted. If the criteria are met, the project continues to the next phase along the baseline branch. If the success criteria are not met, alternate paths that the project might follow are also shown (with the noted probability). Subsequent events and alternate project directions along the baseline and alternate paths are identified in a similar way until the end of each branch. The end of the baseline branch, for example, is the successful completion of PDCP for which the cumulative probability is calculated as the product of probabilities at each phase exit. As noted on the example of Figure 10.24, probabilities of success at the E&F, alpha, and beta phases are estimated to be 90%, 95%, and 90%, respectively. Therefore, the overall project success probability is 77%. The cost of reaching the end of the baseline branch can also be estimated by adding costs of executing all branch segments. The overall probabilities and costs of getting to the end of the branch are also calculated for alternate branches. This analysis provides critical information to managers for calculated risk taking in product development and to investors and corporate executives for incrementally funding the program and understanding the exposure.

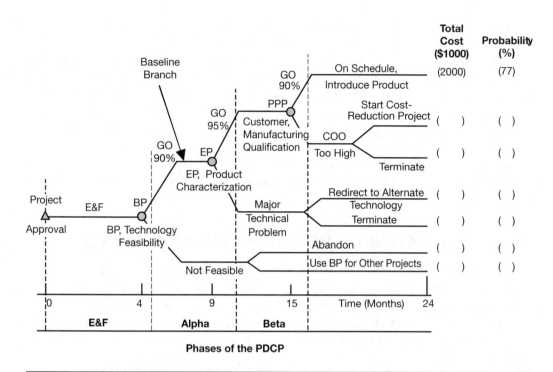

Figure 10.24. Estimating Probability of Success and Financial Exposure in Product Development Using a Decision Tree. Estimate probability of occurrence of every branch; estimate cost and schedule of completing each branch. BP, bench prototype; COO, cost of ownership; EP, engineering prototype; PPP, preproduction prototype.

10.11 INTELLECTUAL PROPERTY PORTFOLIO PLANNING AND PROTECTION

Intellectual property (IP) is a technology, a design, knowledge, know-how, a tool, a manufacturing process, or a management process that:

- Differentiates the firm and its products from competitors
- Improves competitive insulation, making "winning over" the firm's customers difficult for competitors
- Creates barriers for competitors to enter the segment
- Has potential to be developed into a new product and/or service
- Makes operation of the firm more efficient and lowers the cost structure, hence improving profitability and competitiveness by facilitating pricing latitude

Examples of IP include the designs of components and systems; software algorithms; controls methodologies; the formulation of a drug or a material; manufacturing processes (the sequence of steps, the variables and controls tolerances, etc.); scientific theories and the understanding of why and how things work; know-how, i.e., the knowledge and skills gained as a result of experiences in which theories were not well understood and processes could not be precisely quantified; tools used in product design, manufacturing, and testing (of equipment, material, and software); and information technology used in the business processes of the enterprise (including operations, sales, and marketing.)

The IP of a company is a major constituent of the company's valuable assets, underpinning its competitiveness and profitability, which must be protected. IP exists in tangible or intangible forms. IP can be documented or undocumented. Too often, engineers, marketing managers, and even corporate executives do not recognize or value the company's IP and inventions. Consequently, action is not taken to protect them. IP protection is particularly important for small start-up companies that are "short" in other resource areas and are in competition with the "deep pockets" of larger companies. A firm's technology strategy must include a portfolio of protected IP that enables implementation of the firm's product portfolio and market strategy.

10.12 PROTECTION OF INTELLECTUAL PROPERTY AND PATENTS

Invention identification, documentation, and the discipline to protect valuable IP require an appropriate business process within the firm and the education of those who are likely to generate new knowledge or to disclose it to others. Making presentations to customers, to suppliers, or at industry events and publishing scientific papers in journals are just a few examples of opportunities in which unpatented IP may be inadvertently disclosed to others outside the company.

In negotiating agreements with suppliers and customers for a joint development project (JDP), distinguishing between the existing and new IP categories and adopting appropriate language in the agreement to protect both are essential. Existing (background) IP should be identified and if necessary, provisions should be incorporated into the agreement to allow for the parties to use each others' IP. The new or development IP that will be developed during the course of the joint effort is either developed by the firm, developed jointly by the firm and the partner, or developed by the partner. In each case the methods of identifying and documenting the new IP during a co-development project should be agreed upon in writing.

IP protection can be achieved through copyrights, patents, trade secrets, confidential and proprietary information safeguards, and trademarks. In today's world, in which technology, products, and markets are ubiquitous and global, IP protection strategy must also be global. Laws and practices to document and enforce IP protection are different in different parts of the world, although recent GATT agreements (the General Agreement on Tariffs and Trade, Uruguay Round, effective since July 1995) have created a framework for improved international IP protection.

10.12.1 Safeguarding Trade Secrets and Know-How

Keeping information about the firm's engineering and manufacturing core technologies a secret is most important. In many cases, customers and suppliers do not need to be told how things work or how they are made. Unfortunately, people like to talk about company information because they want to boast about their knowledge and "smarts!"

Under certain circumstances keeping confidential technical information from business customers might be impractical, particularly in the early stages of a technology adoption cycle. If information must be divulged, marking everything as "confidential" is prudent to raise the sensitivity of employees and customers about the importance of confidentiality.

Copyrights. Copyrights provide an exclusive right to publish one's work, including scientific or technical information, literature, film, art work, music, and audio and video recordings. However, copyrights only protect the form (i.e., the format) in which an idea (or the data) is presented, not the idea itself. In copyrighting software, according to U.S. copyright law enacted in 1980, the source code algorithm must be divulged (i.e., give away the idea and teach the world!). Hence, copyrighting software might not be a good idea, particularly because enforcement is very difficult. In the United States, a copyright can be registered with the U.S. Copyright Office in Washington, D.C. for a fee (effective July 1, 2006, the U.S. Copyright Office increased basic registration fees to $45 per application; additional fees may also be required).

Trademarks. Trademarks protect the names or designs that distinguish a product or the source of goods and services from the products of others. A trademark can be established by commercial use, without any government involvement in granting rights. Trademarks can be registered with the U.S. Patent and Trademark Office in Washington, D.C. Trademarks must be renewed after 10 years. Generic use of a trademark name results in loss of the rights to the trademark, e.g., as occurred with aspirin, escalator, and nylon.

Patents. Patents exclude others from the commercial application of the patented invention for 20 years from the date of the patent application. The objectives of having a patent portfolio are:

- Freedom of action for engineers in designing products and not being barred or hindered by the patents of competitors (i.e., the firm has a large portfolio of patents and can trade some of them in exchange for access to the patents of the competitors).
- Exclusivity against competitors for product-differentiating functions and features (blocking patents)
- Receiving fees from licensing company patents

To be patentable, an invention must satisfy three major requirements:

- The invention must be new and useful.
- The invention must be reduced to practice (i.e., the invention "works"—it does what it is intended to do).
- The invention must be nonobvious (i.e., the invention must be sufficiently different from existing inventions so that a skilled person would not know how to solve the problem that the invention is directed at solving by using an existing invention or mechanism that is exactly the same).

Patents must be filed within 1 year of the public disclosure of the invention. International applications have another 1-year grace period from the date of the filing in the United States. Patent applications are filed for a new patent or filed as a "continuation in part" during the life of an existing patent to minimize the possibility of an "invent around" situation by competitors. U.S. patent applications are not made public until they are awarded, which usually requires 1 to 3 years. International patent practices are different. For example, in Japan up to 7 years may be required for a patent to be awarded. However, in Japan the application is made public as soon as it is filed. In the United States obtaining a patent may cost as much as $10K to $20K. Additional costs are required to maintain and defend the patent after it is issued.

Obtaining and maintaining international patents can be much more expensive. Using a good patent attorney is advisable. *Note*: If companies who violate patent rights are not put on notice or legal action is not taken against them, a patent may become invalid.

10.12.2 Patent Portfolio Management

To achieve the above-stated objectives in patenting inventions, a balanced portfolio must be developed. The firm must plan a patent portfolio that is valuable, provides adequate coverage, and contains an adequate number of patents. A typical process of acquiring a patent involves two steps:

- Engineers/scientists document and submit invention disclosures for review and for a management decision to file for a patent.
- The disclosure is submitted to a patent attorney (internal or external), who drafts and files for one or more patents, with or without a search for prior art.

Often important inventions are missed because engineers think that their inventions are trivial and not patentable or they are too busy or they are not interested in writing the documentation and disclosures. Yet other disclosures are written that are related to unimportant inventions that do not serve the company's objectives of freedom of action, exclusivity, and licensing fee potential. The root cause in either case is that many engineers and managers do not understand the relationship of disclosed ideas to product differentiators. Hence, the number of patents becomes a metric of success rather than the contribution of the portfolio to product differentiation and business objectives.

The value of a patent portfolio is in its potential to enable gaining market share, capturing higher value (price), and avoiding R&D investment. To assess the strength of a portfolio in protecting product differentiators, a marketing and engineering team should map the patents in the portfolio against the differentiating attributes of products. This matrix helps to identify gaps in the portfolio and to direct resources to develop or acquire the necessary technology and to fill the gap.

Product differentiators that are not patentable should be identified because they point to areas in which the firm's competitive advantage will be short lived. Engineering and marketing plans must be created to overcome this shortcoming.

The patent portfolio should also be evaluated for its competitive insulation. The R&D team should identify how competitors might "get around" existing patents or new inventions and cover those "get around" methods in the invention disclosure and patent application.

REFERENCES

1. Baird, M.L. *Engineering Your Start-Up, A Guide for the Hi-Tech Entrepreneur.* Belmont, CA: Professional Publications; 1997.
2. Stolze, W.J. *Start Up, An Entrepreneur's Guide to Launching and Managing a New Business, Fourth Edition.* Franklin Lakes, NJ: Career Press; 1996.
3. House, C.H., Price, R.L. *The Return Map: Tracking Product Teams.* Harvard Business Review Article #91106. Boston: Harvard Business School Publishing; 1991 January 1.

4. Roussel, P.A., Saad, K.N., Erickson, T.J. *Third Generation R&D: Managing the Link to Corporate Strategy.* New York: McGraw-Hill; 1991.

5. Wheelwright, C. *Revolutionizing Product Development.* New York: Free Press; 1992.

6. Bower, J. *Managing the Resource Allocation Process: A Study of Corporate Planning and Investment.* Boston: Harvard Business School Press; 1986.

7. Christensen, C. *Using Aggregate Project Planning to Link Strategy, Innovation, and Resource Allocation Process.* Harvard Business School Note #301041 (N9-301-041). Boston: Harvard Business School Publishing; 2000 September 15.

APPENDIX— SEMICONDUCTOR MANUFACTURING PROCESS EQUIPMENT

Throughout this book, examples and case studies from the semiconductor wafer fabrication industry are used to elucidate concepts in product development and commercialization. This appendix briefly describes semiconductor integrated circuit (IC) manufacturing technology and business trends as a reference material for the reader.

Over the past few decades, advances in the semiconductor industry have been rapid as a result of the ubiquitous application of electronic technology in consumer and industrial products worldwide. The application of IC chips is widespread—even in places that are neither visible nor suspected. For example, in 2001, 40% of the cost of building a car was in the electronics and software.

As shown in Figure A.1, in technology and production demand, end-user products in consumer and industrial markets drive the entire supply chain of the semiconductor business. The supply chain starts with consumer electronics products that create a demand for IC chips and drive their design. Chip design sets requirements for the fabrication process technology that in turn influences the design and manufacturing of the wafer process equipment. IC fabs are furnished with process equipment and they then produce a variety of semiconductor devices such as microprocessors and memory chips.

Figure A.2 illustrates the history of worldwide semiconductor sales over the last three decades of the twentieth century. Figure A.2 illustrates how the advent of personal computers, software, and communications technology and products has contributed to the growth of the semiconductor industry.

Figure A.3 illustrates the supply chain driving the semiconductor wafer process equipment industry and the market size at each stage. The market for consumer and industrial electronics products and services drives the demand for semiconductors that is fulfilled through building IC fabrication (fab) capacity. Note that most of the capital spending by IC manufacturers

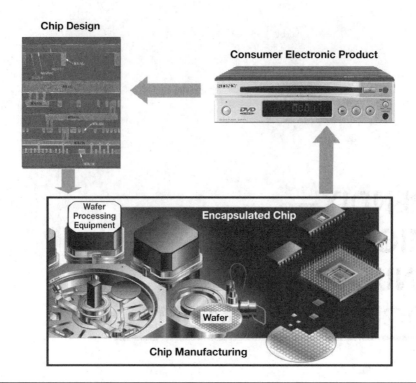

Figure A.1. Electronics Products and Semiconductor Manufacturing Supply Chain.

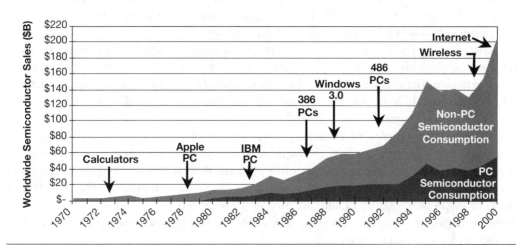

Figure A.2. Worldwide Semiconductor Sales History. (Source: Data from WSTS, Applied Materials, Dataquest, and IDC.)

goes into the acquisition of process equipment. The market sizes shown in Figure A.3 are for the year 2000, which was a peak revenue year for the entire industry (because of the Internet infrastructure that was beginning at that time).

Figure A.4 demonstrates that both the semiconductor and wafer fabrication equipment industries have grown by a compound rate of 15% over the time period of 1975 to 2000—a

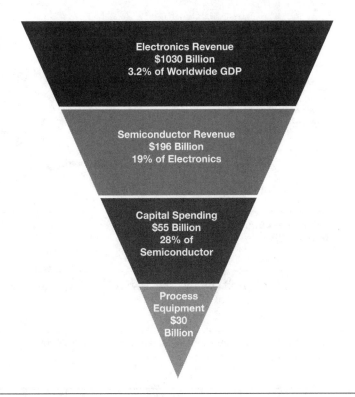

Figure A.3. The Worldwide Semiconductor Supply Chain in 2000.

rate which has been faster than the growth rate of the overall U.S. economy and that of other industries over the same time period. This impressive growth in the semiconductor industry has been enabled by achievements in technology (e.g., through Moore's law as illustrated in Figure 1.3 in Chapter 1) and by cost reduction. The relentless improvement in functionality per unit cost over three decades has been truly phenomenal and has made semiconductor devices so ubiquitous that life without them is hard to imagine.

Figure A.5 illustrates an example of the functional improvement of semiconductors following Moore's law. The functionality of Intel microprocessors (measured in MIPS or millions of instructions per second) has improved by 340 times over the 15 years from 1985 to 2000. Innovations in design and manufacturing process technologies at Intel made this achievement possible.

At the same time (as Figure A.6 illustrates), the cost of manufacturing IC chips has gone down logarithmically in spite of the ever increasing complexity of these devices. Contributors to the 25% to 30% per year reduction in cost per function of IC devices are also shown in Figure A.6. Moore's law has driven functionality improvements while innovations in every aspect of the supply chain in IC manufacturing have contributed to cost reductions. Steadily, and at a rapid pace, manufacturing yield has improved, wafer size has increased, and process equipment productivity per unit cost has been enhanced.

Throughout the history of the semiconductor industry, enabling or even keeping up with these impressive accomplishments has, as expected, presented tremendous challenges for players. Figure A.7 illustrates how the pace of the IC production ramp to the design yield has

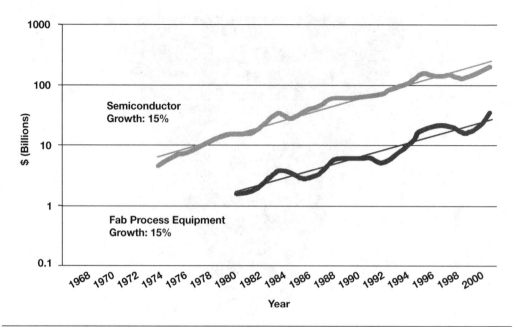

Figure A.4. Semiconductor and Fab Process Equipment Market Growth (1975–2000).

Microprocessor	Year	Design Rule (μm)	Clock Speed (MHz)	MIPS
386	1985	1.5	16	5
486	1989	1.0	25	20
Pentium II	1997	0.35	233	300
Pentium IV	2000	0.18	1500	1700

Figure A.5. Evolution of Intel Microprocessors. MIPS, millions of instructions per second.

increased over several generations of technology. For example, manufacturing 250-nm micro-processors on 200-mm wafers required seven quarters to go from equipment installation to full production. In 2002, 10 years later, the duration of an equivalent ramp for 90-nm microprocessors on 300-mm wafers required only four quarters. This improvement occurred in spite of the much increased complexity in manufacturing technology at a 90-nm versus a 250-nm device (demonstrated in Figure A.8).

Figure A.8 is a graph of a number of the process steps (indicators of process complexity) in IC fabrication as a function of the device design rule (i.e., transistor characteristic dimension). Figure A.8 also shows a plot of the corresponding number of process equipment (also known as WFE or wafer fabrication equipment) in production which is directly proportional to the cost of building the fab. The increasing complexity of the technology, the device design,

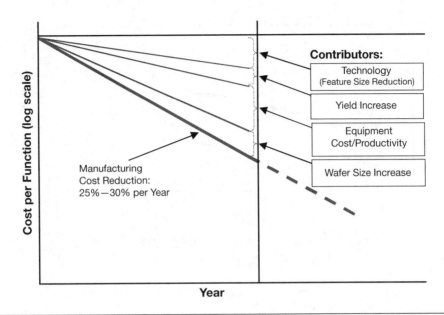

Figure A.6. Qualitative Representation of Trends—Semiconductor Fabrication Cost Reduction Over Three Decades. (Source: Adapted from Robertson, F., Allan, *A. Future Fab International* 1997. San Francisco: Montgomery Research, Inc.)

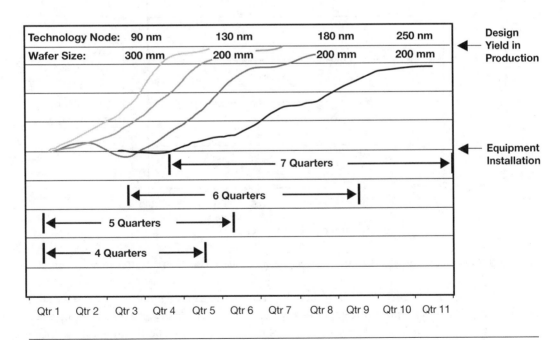

Figure A.7. The Increasing Pace of the Production Ramp in Semiconductor Chip Fabrication.

and the manufacturing process has progressively increased R&D costs at every design node. The combined cost of R&D and building a fab has made "technological leadership" in the semiconductor industry very expensive (Figure A.9).

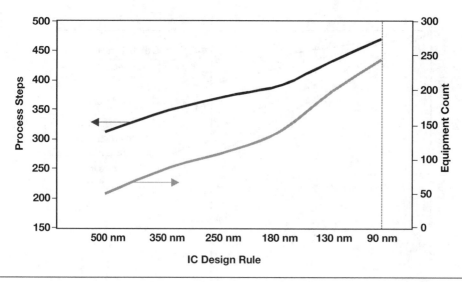

Figure A.8. Increasing IC Manufacturing Complexity and Cost. (Source: Data from SEMATECH International.)

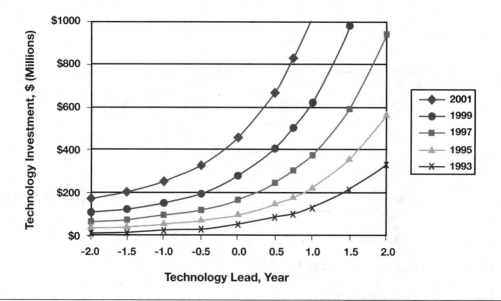

Figure A.9. The Increasing Cost of Technological Leadership. (Source: Data from SEMATECH International.)

Figure A.10 and Figure A.11 are schematic representations highlighting key steps and equipment in the process flow in IC manufacturing. Figure A.12 illustrates a typical equipment configuration for the automated handling of 300-mm wafers and for performing one or more process steps in IC fabrication.

For more detail on the fabrication of integrated devices, the reader may consult References 1, 2, and 3.

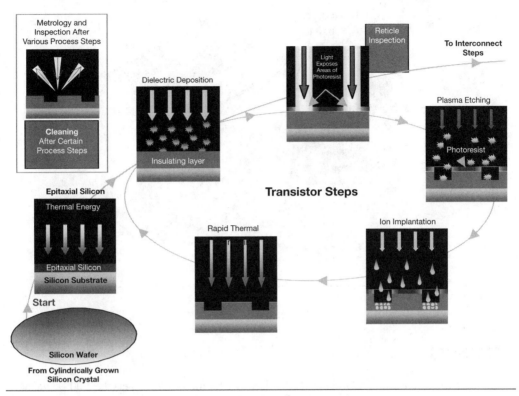

Figure A.10. Chip Manufacturing Process Flow—Transistor Steps.

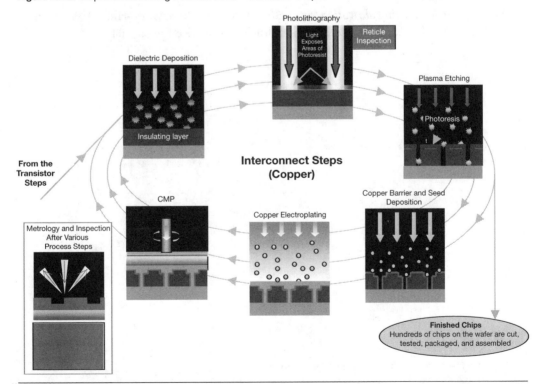

Figure A.11. Chip Manufacturing Process Flow—Copper Interconnect Steps. CMP, chemical mechanical polishing.

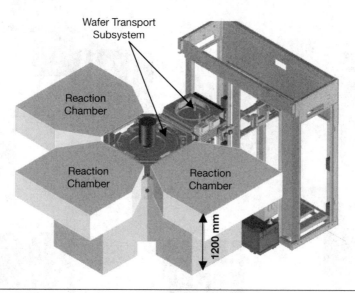

Figure A.12. Wafer Process Equipment.

REFERENCES

1. *Making the Microchip—At the Limits.* Updated by Semiconductor Service; 2003. Available at: www.semi.org.
2. Van Zant, P. *Microchip Fabrication, Fifth Edition.* New York: McGraw-Hill; 2000.
3. Wolf, S. *Microchip Manufacturing.* Sunset Beach, CA: Lattice Press; 2004.

INDEX

DATE DUE

November 28			